SOCIAL SCIENCE
AND NATURAL RESOURCE
RECREATION MANAGEMENT

SOCIAL BEHAVIOR AND
NATURAL RESOURCES SERIES
Donald R. Field, Series Editor

ABOUT THE SERIES

The *Social Behavior and Natural Resources Series* is about human adaptation to natural resources and the constraints these resources place upon institutions and work and play in everyday life. Natural resources, after all, are products of society. The very definition of natural resources arises from the interaction of population, culture, and the biophysical environment.

Biological and physical scientists are providing us with a clearer picture of the nature of species and habitats and the requirements of systems to function under varying management regimes dedicated to conservation and preservation. Social scientists are providing complementary information about the human species, our habitat, and how social systems respond to a wide range of resource management policies. The integration of social science with biological and physical science is the focus of this series.

Resource management issues are human problems that can only be solved with social science knowledge in combination with knowledge from the other sciences. The utilization of these different types of knowledge within the resource management arena depends upon the establishment of a partnership between scientists and managers. Sound management requires agreement on what information is pertinent, how information should be collected, and how information should be employed in decisionmaking.

Here the social sciences can help. Social scientists have a keen appreciation of the power, as well as the limitations, of science to resolve policy conflicts. This is important for understanding how managers filter the concerns of competing constituencies and their own professional cadre while managing the natural resources under their charge.

SOCIAL SCIENCE AND NATURAL RESOURCE RECREATION MANAGEMENT

EDITED BY
Joanne Vining

WESTVIEW PRESS
Boulder, San Francisco, & Oxford

Social Behavior and Natural Resources Series

Copyright © 1990 by Westview Press, Inc.

Published in 1990 in the United States of America by Westview Press, Inc., 5500 Central Avenue, Boulder, Colorado 80301, and in the United Kingdom by Westview Press, Inc., 36 Lonsdale Road, Summertown, Oxford OX2 7EW

Library of Congress Cataloging-in-Publication Data
Social science and natural resource recreation management/edited by
    Joanne Vining.
       p.   cm.—(Social behavior and natural resources series)
    Includes index.
    ISBN 0-8133-7814-1
    1. Outdoor recreation—Management. 2. Natural resources—
Management.   I. Vining, Joanne.   II. Series.
GV191.66.S63   1990
333.78—dc20   89-14747
                                                                                CIP

Printed and bound in the United States of America

The paper used in this publication meets the requirements
of the American National Standard for Permanence of Paper
for Printed Library Materials Z39.48-1984.

10   9   8   7   6   5   4   3   2   1

CONTENTS

PREFACE

Throughout history natural environments have been important sources of human inspiration, solace, and adventure. From the backyard garden to the Amazon expedition, recreational activities in outdoor settings are sought by millions of people. Moreover, human well-being has been linked with a range of interactions with nature, from simply being able to see trees from a hospital room to the therapeutic effects of outdoor challenge experiences. Whereas it is clear that people want outdoor recreation experiences, it is becoming evident that they also need them.

Natural environments afford such powerful positive experiences, in fact, that many are in danger of being "loved to death." The present recreational use of parks, public lands, and other natural areas is intensive, and is projected to increase in the future. Managing these natural resources to enhance recreation experiences, diminish conflict among users, and protect the environment is a complex and daunting task. Using social science research to understand the perceptions, attitudes, satisfaction, and behavior of the public, whether they are recreationists, local residents, or managers themselves, is critical to intelligent, effective management and planning.

Social scientists interested in the interaction between people and outdoor recreation environments were among the first to systematically study social and behavioral aspects of natural resource uses. Over the past three decades social scientific research on natural resource recreation issues has generated a body of knowledge which is now actively used in the management of recreation opportunities. Three intellectual threads or themes have emerged from this body of knowledge: the ecology of behavior and social interactions; the interrelationship between values, behavior, and culture; and the social composition and institutional structure of natural resource recreation participants and organizations.

Social scientists conducting outdoor recreation research soon recognized the complexity of the balance between behavior and setting. It became clear very quickly that one needed to understand the context of social interactions and behavior in order to manage a setting to optimize experiences and satisfaction as well as to protect the resource. This orientation can be seen in management formats such as the Recreational Opportunity Spectrum, which emphasizes finding a fit between human activities, expectations, and the nature of the space that they use. The ecology of behavior is also the foundation for studies of carrying capacity and to a lesser extent, studies of the relationship between characteristics of the recreation setting and satisfaction with outdoor experiences. Although much of the empirical work on the ecology of behavior has been driven by the need for management applications, this theme is also represented in recent theoretical work which seeks a basic understanding of the relationship between people and nature.

The second major theme of outdoor recreation research underscores the importance of human values and attitudes in the search for high quality outdoor recreation experiences. Each individual comes to the outdoor recreation experience with a set of attitudes and expectations which are determined by a complex variety of factors. These factors might include past experience with the setting or with similar areas, reports of the experiences of others in that setting, values associated with a particular activity or social group, cultural values, and the image of the setting that is projected by advertising, formal agency public relations, or information programs. Empirical and theoretical work in this area has focused on the relationship between attitudes and expectations, outcomes, and evaluations of outcomes. Applied empirical research has been designed to aid in devising communication, educational and management strategies which enable individuals to optimize the quality of their experiences and reactions while preserving or even enhancing the resource.

A third intellectual theme focuses on organizational and policy issues which affect natural resource recreation. Studies of this theme area have arisen from an increasing awareness of the role of organizational structure in determining both the public image that an agency projects and the policies which it enacts. All resource management agencies balance a host of competing uses of resources, among which recreation may or may not be the nucleus. An agency's orientation toward recreation versus other land use opportunities is defined by a sort of institutional personality or image. This agency image is in turn determined by a complex array of factors including the social organization, institutional structure and organizational climate, legal mandates, regulations, and the relationship with local and federal governments.

Over the past thirty years, social science studies of recreational uses of natural resources reinforced the realization that managing natural resources involved managing people as well as trees, land, or water. Social scientists now study many aspects of interactions among people and natural resources, including behavioral and emotional responses to pollution, public involvement in resource management decisions, and perception of environmental quality. The growing number of social scientists interested in resource management issues achieved a critical mass in 1986 when the First Symposium on Social Science in Resource Management at Oregon State University attracted more than 250 participants. More than a quarter of the papers at that meeting reported social scientific studies of outdoor recreation.

The chapters in this volume are based on papers presented at the Second Symposium on Social Science in Resource Management which was held at the University of Illinois at Urbana-Champaign in 1988. These chapters confirm that outdoor recreation continues to be a popular and active research topic among social scientists interested in natural resource issues. The eighteen chapters which appear here represent a subset of more than sixty that were presented at the Symposium. Each chapter was revised following Symposium discussions and peer review before being accepted for inclusion in this volume.

The three chapters in the first section provide conceptual frameworks reflecting the three dominant themes of social scientific studies of natural resource recreation. The chapter by Schroeder explores ecological concepts as they apply to recreation behavior in natural resource environments. He applies concepts such as competition for resources, niches, and natural selection to recreation activity and natural resource management concerns. The resulting model provides a view of recreational and biological processes as interrelated components of the ecosystem, and enables the use of a common set of theoretical constructs with which to conceptualize and manage both human behavior and ecology.

In Chapter 2, Schreyer examines the dynamics of conflicts among recreationists. He presents a typology of recreation conflicts developed from interactions with participants at training sessions for outdoor recreation managers and planners. His typology illustrates the diversity of conflicting recreational activities, and emphasizes the variety of demands for recreation opportunities.

Meis introduces the organizational perspective in a discussion of the role that social scientists can and should play in natural resource agencies. Using the Parks Canada as an example, he discusses the benefits of social science research in agency decisions and policy. He goes on to provide recommendations and a framework for developing social science functions in other agencies.

As recreational pressures on natural resources and natural environments rise, concerns for the quality of experiences will also grow. The second section of this volume presents research concerned with assessing the nature of recreation experiences. The quality of outdoor recreation experience was one of the first natural resource issues to be examined by social scientists. As a result, the literature on user preferences and satisfaction is quite large and fairly well-developed. The chapters in this section present some fresh thinking on, and approaches to one of the earliest and most pervasive outdoor recreation issues.

The recreation needs and preferences of diverse racial/ethnic groups are addressed in the chapter by Dwyer and Hutchison. They report the results of a study comparing the outdoor recreation participation and preferences of black and white Chicago residents. Their results indicate that cultural values help to shape attitudes and expectations about outdoor recreation.

The chapter by Moore, Shockey and Brickler incorporates the themes of behavioral ecology and human values. They address some of the conceptual issues surrounding conflict and competition which were introduced by Schroeder and by Schreyer in Section I. Their study demonstrates the use of log-linear analysis to determine the role of social encounters in perceptions of the quality of wilderness experiences.

In Chapter 6, Hollenhorst uses the construct of recreation specialization to explain satisfaction with outdoor recreation, specifically rockclimbing. The results of his study show that outdoor recreationists can be arranged on a continuum of specialization, and that distinctly different participants attributes, behaviors, expectations, and preferences characterize each level.

Rollins and Chambers examine another dimension of outdoor recreation experience in a study of camping satisfaction. Using the fulfillment theory of satisfaction, they examine the relationship between satisfaction with campground attributes and overall satisfaction. The results of their study are used to provide implications for management of campground facilities on public lands based on user values and attitudes.

Lichtkoppler and Clonts argue for a revision of Recreation Opportunity Spectrum criteria to accommodate the special recreational character of eastern U.S. forests. Using survey and travel cost methodologies, they apply a Limits of Acceptable Change approach to characterize the recreational resources in these forests. The result of their analysis is a revised classification system which is responsive to diverse and changing recreation resources and recreation behavior.

Outdoor recreation activities have impacts on those who live in and near natural areas as well as those who visit those areas. Conversely, the activities and cultural values of local residents may affect the quality of the outdoor recreation experience for visitors and alter the nature of the management task. The chapters in Section III describe some of the issues surrounding the interface among the values and attitudes of local populations, resource managers, and outdoor recreationists.

Graham and Payne argue that customary and traditional knowledge of indigenous peoples can be used to support the establishment or management of a park, and to educate visitors about cultural and natural heritage of the area. They present several case studies which emphasize the value of informal or traditional sources of knowledge about environments as input to parks management and decision processes. They conclude that information attained from formal scientific and rational (or normative) decision processes must be combined with informal traditional knowledge for optimal park siting and management.

Glass, Muth, and Flewelling examine the fine line between the recreational and subsistence nature hunting and fishing activities in indigenous communities which are developing modern economies. Using several conceptualizations of subsistence and recreation, they examine case study data from Yakutat, Alaska. They conclude that contemporary subsistence is a complicated entity which may have a strong psychological or sociocultural component often associated with purely recreational pursuits, while also providing a significant income.

Daniels and Krannich use a case study to illustrate conflicts which may arise in interactions between recreationists, other resource users, and land managers. Their analysis emphasizes the interpretation of the Recreation Opportunity Spectrum (ROS) classification system. They conclude that proper use of the ROS can help to diminish conflict by identifying the expectations of user groups and agency officials.

The chapter by Wright, Cordell, and Brown examines the interaction between outdoor recreationists and private landowners. Their survey of private landowners provides information about the nature and availability of private lands for public recreation, and constructs a profile of the policies, values, and perceptions of private landowners. They suggest that access to public lands for recreation may be critical in compensation for shortages of public land, particularly near urban environments.

As patterns and prices of natural resource use have changed, the emphasis on the marketing of outdoor recreation is increasing on both national and local levels. For example, tourism has become an important source of income for many local populations which historically relied on income resources such as timber or minerals. With the increased emphasis on the value of tourism new concerns for marketing outdoor recreation resources and publicizing attractions have arisen. Section IV presents two studies of tradeoffs between tourism and other resource uses.

The chapter by Price examines changing patterns of forest use. He traces the history of the interrelationship between uses of Swiss forests for timber harvest and for tourism. He suggests that forest management can increase attractiveness and marketability of the forest as well as timber yield, and concludes that tourism and forestry may be mutually advantageous rather than mutually exclusive activities.

Val examines the value of tourism for the economies of developing areas. After describing the relationship between tourism and aboriginal peoples in several worldwide locations, he examines social, economic, cultural, and geographic factors which influence parks policies in the

Northwest Territories in Canada. He emphasizes a model of tourism development which incorporates both economic interests and conservation values.

One of the fundamental concerns of social scientists interested in natural resource recreation is assessing the value or benefit associated with recreation experiences. Outdoor recreation values need to be included in decision apparatus with other resource assets such as range, timber, and minerals. As seen in the previous section, the significance of the economic contribution of outdoor recreation activities is increasingly recognized, but difficulties in assessing amenity values are also acknowledged. The fifth section of this volume presents several approaches to determining values for recreational experiences.

In a study of the travel cost methodology, Stynes and Peterson investigate the role of knowledge about recreation sites in travel cost estimates of outdoor recreation values. They present data to support their position that consumer information is an important mitigating variable in estimating demand for outdoor recreation opportunities. They suggest that incorporating consumer information into demand models will extend the usefulness of the travel cost method to marketing programs as well as increasing the accuracy of value estimates.

Donnelly, Swanson, Loomis, and Nelson report the results of an extensive study of the economic values for fishing and hunting in Idaho. Using the contingent valuation and travel cost methodologies they develop models describing the consumption values for hunting and fishing various species. They conclude with a discussion of value trade-offs and recommendations for the application of such values in resource management decisions.

The chapter by Brown, Richards, Daniel, and King presents a study of economic and psychological approaches to amenity values. They compare assessments of perceived scenic beauty and economic values for visits to forested campgrounds both on-site and from photographs of the campground areas. Their findings indicate that photo-based estimates of economic and scenic value are very comparable. However, on-site estimates of scenic value were higher than photo-based measures, indicating that participation in recreation may enhance the judgments of one's surroundings.

Clonts and Malone also depart somewhat from the traditional economic approach to examine the role played by environmental attitudes in resource valuation. Their survey of Alabama residents compares user and non-user estimates of the recreation, option, existence, and bequest values of free-flowing rivers, and also incorporates an analysis of attitudes toward the resource. Their results indicate that preservation of river systems is strongly preferred by both river users and non-users. The results of their study emphasize the importance of public attitudes in resource management decisions, and highlight some of the difficulties associated with hypothetical value assessments. They conclude that the intensity and character of public opinion is best indicated by assessments of both attitudes and value.

The conceptual frameworks, case studies, and experimental studies presented in this volume provide an excellent platform for future research on outdoor recreation specifically, and for human interactions with natural resources more generally. It is my hope that they will stimulate further thinking for both research and management applications.

Joanne Vining

ACKNOWLEDGEMENTS

Editing this volume has been both more rewarding and more arduous than I anticipated. The tasks of coordination and communication were facilitated by a wonderful secretary, by reviewers who were prompt and constructive, and by authors who provided careful revisions on time. I am also grateful to Don Field and Rabel Burdge for their enthusiasm and encouragement.

The efforts of individuals who provided peer reviews of the chapters in this volume are greatly appreciated. For each chapter, two, and sometimes three blind reviewers provided detailed constructive comments which enabled the authors to make significant substantive and stylistic improvements in their manuscripts. In many cases, gratitude is also due participants at the Second Symposium on Social Science in Resource Management who provided constructive suggestions during meeting sessions.

To the authors of the chapters in this book I am indebted for providing their interesting ideas and approaches to the topic of outdoor recreation. Their cheerful persistence in revising their chapters and respect for deadlines were very much appreciated.

Finally, I am very grateful to Linda Little, a thoughtful and skillful secretary. Linda not only handled the necessary typing and correspondence with aplomb, but also contributed to the editing and layout of the volume. Without her intelligence, patience, and excellent word processing skills this book would not have been possible.

Joanne Vining

SOCIAL SCIENCE AND NATURAL RESOURCE RECREATION MANAGEMENT

I

CONCEPTUAL FRAMEWORKS

CHAPTER 1

AN ECOLOGICAL APPROACH TO RECREATION IN NATURAL RESOURCE SETTINGS

Herbert W. Schroeder
USDA Forest Service
North Central Forest Experiment Station

The purpose of this chapter is to explore some applications of ecological concepts to recreation behavior in natural resource settings. Ecology is the branch of biology that studies the relationships of organisms to their environments and to each other. Over the last century or so ecologists have developed theoretical concepts and models to account for observed interactions among plants, animals, and their surroundings. The premise of this chapter is that some of these concepts and models may also be applied to the behavior of humans interacting with their surroundings and with each other while engaged in outdoor recreation.

The application of ecological concepts to humans is not new. Most ecology texts contain sections on human population growth, pollution, and resource depletion (e.g., McNaughton and Wolf 1973, Kormondy 1984). Human ecology is a well-established field, and has developed useful analyses of how human cultures and settlements function and interact with their physical and biological surroundings (e.g., Boyden, Millar, Newcombe and O'Neill 1981). In the field of recreation research, there is growing recognition that human recreation behavior must be understood in relation to the environment in which it takes place, and that the concepts and theories of ecology may contribute to that understanding (Machlis, Field and Campbell 1981, Hammitt 1983, Field, Lee and Martinson 1985).

This chapter is offered as a contribution to the ongoing discussion and development of these ideas. The first part of the chapter discusses some ecological concepts that seem relevant to recreation behavior. The second part suggests one approach for *ecologizing* models of recreation site choice.

ECOLOGICAL CONCEPTS

Activities

The approach taken here assumes that recreation behavior occurs in repeatable and identifiable patterns, which I will refer to as activities. Although this assumption is not always true, it seems like a reasonable starting point. That is, I assume that a recreationist can be classified according to the activity she or he is engaged in, and may be regarded as a member of the distinct population of individuals engaged in that activity. The unit of analysis is not the individual per se, but the individual engaged in a specific activity. If an individual switches from one activity to another, he or she thereby becomes a member of a different population.

Adaptation and Fitness

I further assume that recreation activities are adapted to their settings in much the same way that biological organisms and their behaviors are adapted to their environments. Individuals will engage in a recreation activity only as long as they obtain sufficient benefits from the activity. The *fitness* of an activity in a particular setting is a measure of how well that activity functions under the conditions of the setting. If an activity is unsuited to its setting (e.g., downhill skiing on flat terrain), benefits will be absent. The activity must then change, cease to exist, or be displaced to a more suitable setting. Thus a process akin to natural selection operates on recreation behavior, and over time activities should become adapted to the specific settings in which they take place.

Niches

The fitness of an activity in relation to its environment leads us to the ecological concept of niche. Perhaps the simplest definition of a recreation niche would be *the set of environmental conditions under which a particular activity is able to function successfully.* In some cases, activities have evolved specialized forms that are adapted to different niches. Downhill and cross-country skiing are good examples of this. Other activities (e.g., picnicking) are able to exist under a wide range of conditions.

Ecological niches have been conceptualized abstractly as volumes in a hyperspace whose dimensions are the environmental attributes that determine the fitness of the organism (Hutchinson 1965). Applying this notion to trail activities, for example, with trail surface and terrain as the dimensions of the hyperspace, we might hypothesize that bicyclists will obtain the most satisfaction by riding on a smooth paved trail over gentle terrain, while backpackers will enjoy rough unpaved trails in hilly terrain. This would produce a niche diagram something like Figure 1. The niche of each activity is the region in the diagram in which that activity functions successfully, that is the set of all combinations of terrain and trail surface to which that activity is adapted. Note that the hypothesized niches of the two activities overlap, implying that some combinations of terrain and trail surface are suitable for both activities. In these types of settings we might expect to observe competition or conflict between the two activities.

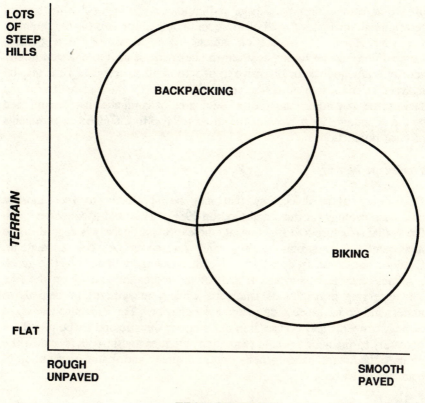

Figure 1. Niche diagram for two trail activities.

Population Dynamics

Growth and interaction of populations is a topic of major concern in ecology. The growth rates of wildlife populations are governed by biological processes of reproduction and mortality. For populations of people engaging in recreation activities, the main processes governing population dynamics are not biological but psychological, i.e., the number of people engaging in an activity at a specific site is the outcome of individual preferences and choices with regard to the characteristics of that site. Nevertheless, the population dynamics of recreation may have features in common with the dynamics of biological populations. Ecologists classify interactions among populations according to the effect that the presence of one population has on another. Some common types of interaction include predation, competition, parasitism, and mutualism. It is possible to think of recreational analogues for all of these, but competition is probably the most significant form of interaction among populations of recreationists. Competition may be direct, as when the behavior of people engaged in one activity is antagonistic or offensive to people in other activities, or it may be indirect, as when two otherwise compatible activities must compete for the same space and other resources. The degree of competition is conditioned by the abundance or scarcity of resources relative to the niche requirements of each population.

Landscape Ecology

Another area of ecology that may be applicable to recreation is landscape ecology (Forman and Godron 1986). This field is concerned with the spatial structure and function of landscapes, particularly in regard to the movement of organisms, energy, and substances between ecosystems. Outdoor recreation frequently involves movement, both as travel to reach a suitable recreation site and as part of the recreation activity on the site. The emerging principles of landscape ecology may therefore help us to understand some aspects of recreation behavior. For example, landscape ecology concepts may be useful in determining the size and shape of habitat necessary to maintain specific recreation activities and in understanding the effect of landscape heterogeneity on the diversity and spatial distribution of activities in an area.

SITE CHOICE MODELS

Recreation research has produced models for predicting how people will choose among recreation sites having various attributes. These predictions are often based on logit choice models (Peterson, Dwyer and Darragh 1983,

Stynes and Peterson 1984, Louviere, Schroeder, Louviere and Woodworth 1986, Schroeder and Louviere 1986). Logit models assume that the utility of a site for an individual is a weighted sum of the attributes of the site. The probability of choosing a site is calculated from the logit function:

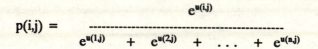

$$p(i,j) = \frac{e^{u(i,j)}}{e^{u(1,j)} + e^{u(2,j)} + \ldots + e^{u(n,j)}}$$

where $p(i,j)$ is the probability of individual j choosing site i, and $u(i,j)$ is the utility of site i for individual j. By summing the probabilities of choice for all prospective users, we obtain a prediction of the number of users who will select each site. Logit models as described above and as usually applied are static. That is, they describe the probability of choice at a single point in time, assuming that the attributes of the sites are given and fixed. Ecological population models, on the other hand, are dynamic (May 1974). They describe a population's rate of change, based on the attributes of the environment and other populations, and trace the growth and decline of interacting populations. Research on mathematical models of ecosystems suggests ways of *ecologizing* logit models to represent dynamic interactions among populations of recreationists engaging in different activities.

We can set up a utility equation for each different activity at a site, so that the utility of the site for one activity is determined by the number of people doing other activities at the same site. We then assume that the number of users doing a particular activity converges towards the number of people predicted to do that activity by the logit choice equation. Because the activities are changing at the same time, the utilities are in constant flux, and it is not necessarily easy to predict where the system will end up. Computer simulation is the easiest method for determining the ultimate fate of the interacting activities. The system reaches equilibrium when the numbers of people using the site are consistent with the predictions of the logit equations for all the activities.

The following example illustrates how such a dynamically linked set of logit models for interacting activities can behave. The example deals with two competing activities. That is, an increase in the number of people doing either one of the activities decreases the utility of the site for people doing the other activity. For this example I also assume that people engaging in either one of the activities like to be near other people doing the same activity. That is, an increase in the number of people doing either activity increases the utility of the site for other people doing the same activity. I will refer to activities with this property as cohesive. (An alternative assumption might involve *dispersive* activities, i.e., activities for which people dislike being close to other people doing the same activity.)

The model was set up and run on a microcomputer by first letting one activity reach equilibrium on the site by itself. Then the number of potential users for the other activity was gradually increased until it reached a maximum value, to simulate increasing demand for a competing activity. The output of the model shows how the numbers of users in both activities change over time. The model was run several times, with different values for the strength of cohesiveness within activities and for the strength of competition between activities. The examples shown here all have the same strength of competition but different degrees of cohesiveness.

Figure 2 shows what happens when there is no cohesiveness within activities. As the number of people doing the *invading* activity increases,

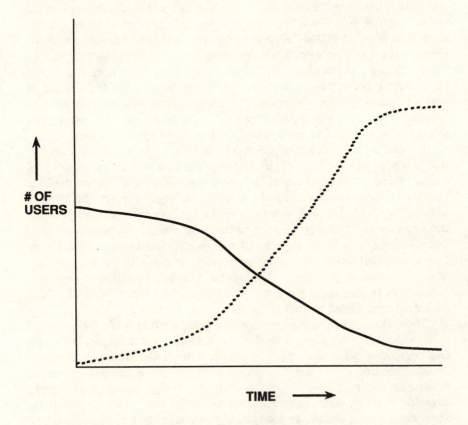

Figure 2. Change over time in number of users for two conflicting activities, when there is no cohesiveness within activities.

there is a steady decline in the number of people doing the original activity. In Figure 3 the degree of cohesiveness for both activities is equal to the degree of competition between activities. (That is, the increase in utility caused by one person doing the same activity equals the decrease in utility caused by one person doing a different activity.) Here the invading activity grows less rapidly at first, and the original activity remains almost constant up to a point. Then the invading activity increases while the original activity falls off very rapidly. The attraction within activities enables the original activity to *hang together* until the new activity becomes strong enough to overpower it, at which point the original activity suddenly collapses and the new activity dominates.

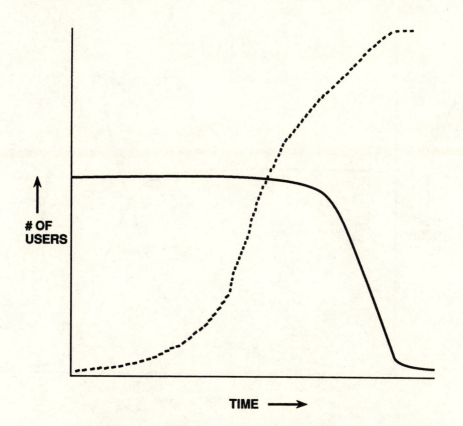

Figure 3.   Change over time in number of users for two conflicting activities, when cohesiveness within activities equals competition between activities.

In Figure 4, the within-activity cohesiveness is twice as strong as the competition between activities. Now the original activity is able to hang on even after the new activity has become well established, although it still collapses suddenly after the new activity achieves a high enough level. The general conclusion from these simulations is that a strongly cohesive activity will be able to maintain itself in the face of an invading competitor up to a point, but when that point is exceeded, its collapse will be quite sudden.

The assumptions adopted in these examples probably represent in very general terms what is happening in rapidly urbanizing areas, where established users of outdoor recreation sites are faced with increasing demands

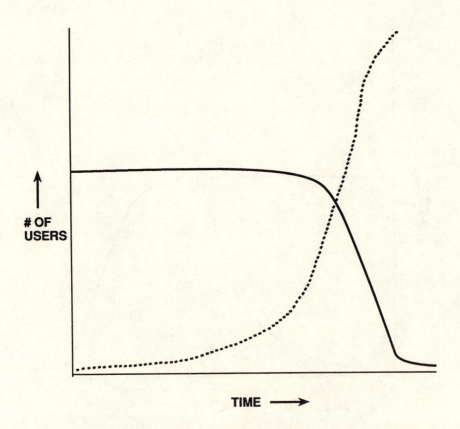

Figure 4.   Change over time in number of users for two conflicting activities, when cohesiveness within activities is greater than competition between activities.

by new kinds of users for nontraditional activities. The cohesiveness property is probably particularly strong where the original and the competing activities are engaged in by people with different ethnic or cultural backgrounds. Under these conditions, the general prediction of the models is that managers should expect to see abrupt changes in clientele and activities on their sites. Much more detail would be required to make exact predictions about changing use levels at particular sites. By altering the assumptions and parameters of the models, it may be possible to explore a variety of time-related phenomena in recreational settings. The general concept of ecological succession may be useful in understanding the changes that accompany urbanization of recreation sites.

CONCLUSIONS

Applying ecological concepts to recreation is more than an interesting intellectual pursuit. Ecology may provide a conceptual framework that can begin tying together disparate areas of recreation research. Research on recreation motivation and satisfaction, perception and choice, and economics may all fit together within an ecological framework. At the same time, we should not assume that all ecological principles that have been developed for biological systems necessarily apply to recreational systems. For example, one of the basic tenets of bioecology is the rule of competitive exclusion, which says that two species with identical niches cannot coexist; one or the other must eventually become extinct through competition. I am not convinced that this would necessarily occur for recreation activities occupying the same niche. Pursuing ecological parallels will undoubtedly reveal that some principles of bioecology simply don't apply to recreation, and that new ecological principles must be formed to account for some phenomena in recreation.

In addition to improving our understanding of the processes of outdoor recreation, an ecological viewpoint will promote the integration of recreation management with other resource uses. By casting models of recreation in conceptual terms similar to models of wildlife and other ecosystem components, it will be easier for recreation scientists to communicate with biologists and resource managers, and to link their research with models and data about biological aspects of natural resource recreation settings.

REFERENCES

Boyden, S., S. Millar, K. Newcombe and B. O'Neill. 1981. *The Ecology of a City and Its People: The Case of Hong Kong.* Canberra: Australian National University Press.

Field, D.R., M.E. Lee and K. Martinson. 1985. *Human Behavior and Recreation Habitats: Conceptual Issues.* Paper presented at First North American Riparian Conference, Tucson, AZ.

Forman, R.T.T. and M. Godron. 1986. *Landscape Ecology.* New York: Wiley.

Hammitt, W.E. 1983. Toward an ecological approach to perceived crowding in outdoor recreation. *Leisure Sciences* 5:309-320.

Hutchinson, G.E. 1965. *The Ecological Theater and the Evolutionary Play.* New Haven, CT: Yale University Press.

Kormondy, E.J. 1984. *Concepts of Ecology* (3rd Ed.). Englewood Cliffs, NJ: Prentice Hall.

Louviere, J.J., H.W. Schroeder, C.H. Louviere and G.G. Woodworth. 1986. *Do the Parameters of Choice Models Depend on Differences in Stimulus Presentation: Visual Versus Verbal Presentation?* In Proceedings of the Association for Consumer Research, October 1986, Toronto, 79-82.

Machlis, G.E., D.R. Field and F.L. Campbell. 1981. The human ecology of parks. *Leisure Sciences* 4:195-212.

May, R.M. 1974. *Stability and Complexity in Model Ecosystems.* Princeton, NJ: Princeton University Press.

McNaughton, S.J. and L.L. Wolf. 1973. *General Ecology.* New York: Holt, Rinehart and Winston.

Peterson, G.L., J.F. Dwyer and A.J. Darragh. 1983. A behavioral urban recreation site choice model. *Leisure Sciences* 6:61-81.

Schroeder, H.W. and J.J. Louviere. 1986. *A Model for Predicting Distribution of Recreational Use Over a System of Parks.* In proceedings of Forestry Microcomputer Software Symposium, Morgantown, WV, 623-631.

Stynes, D.J. and G.L. Peterson. 1984. A review of logit models with implications for modeling recreation choices. *Journal of Leisure Research* 16:295-310.

CHAPTER 2

CONFLICT IN OUTDOOR RECREATION: THE SCOPE OF THE CHALLENGE TO RESOURCE PLANNING AND MANAGEMENT

Richard Schreyer
Department of Forest Resources
Utah State University

What should be the appropriate domain of skills for a person qualified to practice recreation resource management? Traditional viewpoints would most likely center around facilities maintenance and demand projection. However, people actively involved in recreation resource management increasingly suggest that the most appropriate skills should be competence in conflict analysis and management. This chapter is intended to be an overview of the scope of conflict in recreation resource planning and management.

A focus on conflict seems to emphasize a pejorative view of recreation. Leisure and recreation center around notions of human well-being and fulfillment. Conflict appears to be the antithesis of these ideals, particularly in the context of identifying needs for professional training.

Nevertheless, well-being and fulfillment are best abetted by understanding things which can enhance their attainment, and those which hinder or constrain them. Understanding conflict becomes very important in the effort to provide quality recreation experiences. Outdoor recreation in natural settings primarily involves the use of public lands ostensibly open to everyone. An inevitable consequence is the interaction of persons from varying backgrounds who bring with them differing recreational agendas, and who may not particularly get along with one another.

Conflict and Diversity

The U.S. population is a very diverse collection of differing subcultures with a wide variety of values and preferred recreational activities. There may be a certain amount of pride in that *melting pot* diversity, but it may also result in the fact that not all people with differing values will be compatible. While that is not a particularly profound revelation, it has substantial implications for recreation resource management and planning.

The more diverse the subcultures that compose this nation, the greater the likelihood that people in public recreation settings will behave in ways that will result in conflict situations.

Diversity in values and preferences among people who use recreation resources is not a new phenomenon. However, there has been a dramatic increase in the range of diversity affecting public demand for outdoor recreation opportunities within the last generation (Johnson 1983). This diversification is occurring not only in the backgrounds of the persons who use such resources; it is also being seen in the types of uses being made of environments for recreational purposes. As public interest in recreation grows, as tastes change, as fads emerge, and as technologies evolve, the range of recreational activities and styles of participation appear to expand exponentially.

The proportion of recreationists in the outdoors representing the *traditional sportsman* (i.e., huntin', fishin', campin') is diminishing as people with demands for other activity opportunities increase. Outdoor recreation initially had its roots in rural America. However, just as the U.S. has become an urban nation, use of the outdoors has increasingly reflected urban values and lifestyles. Such trends will lead to increasing clashes of culture among diverse groups seeking their own distinctive opportunities.

The Growing Importance of Leisure and Conflict

Many forces are influencing conflict in leisure. There is an increasing tendency for people to use recreation as an elaboration and symbol of their lifestyles, as a vehicle for personal identification (Devall 1976, Kando 1980, Kelly 1987). In order to avoid being swallowed up in mass culture, people may prefer instead to seek lifestyle *images* that are more personalized and distinctive. While specific empirical research on this topic is limited, there is a growing literature that attempts to characterize and classify the diversification of lifestyles in American culture (Garreau 1981, Mitchell 1983). An underlying implication is that distinctiveness serves to emphasize the differences between groups, and emphasis on differences can fuel perceptions of incompatibility and conflict.

To the extent that people are increasingly willing to express their identities through recreation participation, such pursuits may have a greater potential role to play in their lives than what might otherwise be construed as being merely a pleasurable use of time (Haggard and Williams 1988). When something gains increasing importance in defining personal identification, it is not uncommon to give higher priority to that aspect of life. If this involves a recreational activity, then the activity itself may play a significant role in defining the individual's sense of personal well-being. Such priority may in the long run serve to enhance expectations, and a person may become more demanding of what the activity should provide, as there is more of a stake in the outcomes.

Increasing expectations for more detailed and specific conditions necessary to provide desired outcomes are a likely consequence of involvement in recreation as a vehicle for personal identification (Jacob and Schreyer 1980). When people have high expectations, particularly in public recreation settings, there will likely be a greater potential for such people to encounter situations in which those expectations are not met. In many cases this could be precipitated by the behavior of others. Assuming that diversity in American culture exists, and assuming that people increasingly seek to express individual lifestyle values through recreation, then the future of recreation resource management and planning will inevitably involve dealing with conflict among various groups.

Conflict in Perspective

There is the question of the extent to which conflict actually exists in outdoor recreation settings. Are a few graphic examples of conflict blown out of proportion, when people generally tend to get along and are basically happy with their recreational pursuits? Studies addressing this question suggest that the number of people experiencing conflict is often not large. However, how much conflict is necessary before it should become a concern of resource management and planning?

A recent study of visitors to the Whiskeytown Unit of the Whiskeytown-Shasta-Trinity National Recreation Area indicated that twenty percent of visitors experienced conflict with others (Lee, Field and Martinson 1988). Is twenty percent perceived conflict large or small? How many private businesses would be proud of the fact that every fifth person entering their establishment experienced conflict? A study of recreationists in Vermont recorded that forty percent of persons surveyed experienced some type of outdoor recreation conflict in the course of a season (Lindsay 1974). When surveys reveal that level of perceived conflict, recreation resource planners and managers should be paying attention.

There is the question of the extent to which perceived conflict will affect overall visitor satisfaction. People do adapt to circumstances and adjust their behavior to derive the benefits they desire. However, there is ultimately a limit to adaptation, and people may cease to participate in a certain activity or place because of the likelihood of conflict. Thus, an outcome of conflict may be that people choose not to utilize opportunities ostensibly available to them.

It does not take a majority of visitors to constitute a movement or make a complaint. A vocal and active minority can be very forceful in affecting policy. Recreation resource planners and managers are communicating that dealing with conflict is one of the most fundamental aspects of their duties. Moreover, they perceive their jobs as being increasingly occupied with situations involving recreational conflict. This is the theme of this chapter. It involves the perceptions of people who actually work in the field and have expressed what they encounter in their daily activities. It is also an attempt to describe the different ways in which conflict in recreation participation may be viewed, understood and dealt with.

Conflict is often treated as a simple product of the clash between a few basic cultural groups. Motorized recreationists don't get along with non-motorized recreationists, and that's all there is to it. Besides, if people just learned to get along, there wouldn't be these problems in the first place. Yet, recreation planners and managers need to take a much more serious view of the behavioral dynamics that result in conflict situations. Professional training in recreation resource management may require a much more sophisticated knowledge of conflict management and planning strategies to avoid such situations. The bottom line is the recognition that professional recreation resource management and planning is not as simple-minded as training people to make decisions about where to put the outhouse.

Understanding Conflict in Recreation

It is possible to analyze conflict from a variety of perspectives. There is a large literature on social conflict in human society (Jacob 1978b). As history in general has reflected a continuing succession of conflict, it is not surprising that outdoor recreation should also be subject to such social behavior. However, the literature specifically addressed to the study of conflict in recreation settings is not large.

Four topics related to conflict are useful in understanding its manifestation in outdoor recreation:

1. Topics dealing with the interaction of various social groups, and the extent to which they may or may not conflict.
2. Concepts of conflict as applied to outdoor recreation specifically.
3. Conflict management -- dealing with conflict when it occurs.
4. Offshoots of conflict; things that happen as the result of conflict that may be described in other terms, such as displacement, succession, carrying capacity, etc.

All of these topics are addressed in this book. The specific purpose of this chapter is to discuss the second issue, the dynamics of conflict as they relate to recreation, and particularly, how people in professional roles in recreation resource management and planning perceive the nature and diversity of conflict. The first issue is addressed in Section III. This section focuses on the interface between the various publics related to recreation, including recreationists themselves, people in communities affected by such participation, and private and public providers of recreational opportunities.

The third topic is addressed in Section II, dealing with public preferences and ways in which managers and planners respond or do not respond to those preferences. A key point is that identifying the sources of problems and developing strategies for dealing with them are not independent activities. The fourth topic is the indirect impacts of conflict, such as displacement and substitutability. The breadth of topics that relate to conflict serves as an indication that conflict is instrumentally related to the whole range of recreation planning and management. That is not intended to be a negative statement, so much as it is a suggestion for the need for research, dialogue, and education on the topic.

The remainder of this chapter will be devoted to exploring ideas about the social dynamics of recreational conflict. It will also describe perceptions of recreation professionals concerning their encounters with conflict situations.

THE NATURE OF CONFLICT IN RECREATION

Goal Interference

The presence of conflict in a recreation setting may be determined through the direct comments of visitors who experience conflict, or through more systematic means such as survey research. The basic questions are how conflict occurs and how can it be avoided? In regard to the first question, Jacob and Schreyer (1980) developed a conceptual framework for the analysis of the social psychological dynamics of conflict in outdoor recreation participation. Within this framework, conflict is defined as *goal interference attributed to another's behavior* (p. 369). The focus on goals is based on the belief that recreation is essentially goal-directed behavior (Driver and Tocher 1970). The frustration of one's goals in any situation would therefore likely result in feelings of conflict.

This notion has been reflected in research such as Driver and Bassett's (1975) study of conflicts among canoeists and trout fishermen on Michigan's Au Sable River. They concluded that the conflict was primarily due to the pursuit of different and incompatible goals by persons in these activities. The notion of goal interference was also used to study conflicts between water-skiers and fishermen at a midwestern reservoir (Gramann and Burdge 1981). The authors found support for this notion, though the degree of relationship was weak. In a study of conflict experienced by canoeists on the Delaware River, Todd and Graefe (1988) examined the extent to which goal interference was related to level of previous experience. Their results again showed only weak relationships. Interestingly, they found more intra-group conflicts than inter-group.

Much of the focus on goal incompatibility comes from research involving the assessment of the different motivations and/or expectations of recreationists. A large body of research addresses the desired psychological outcomes of various types of persons in recreational pursuits (Knopf 1983). Some of this research has compared the types of outcomes sought among groups who are in conflict, in order to make inferences about goal incompatibility. Jackson and Wong (1982) illustrated differences between cross-country skiers and snowmobilers. In the conflict-related area of crowding perceptions, Schreyer and Roggenbuck (1978) showed that crowding perceptions were related to differences in the relative intensities of certain desired outcomes, such as solitude.

The Dynamics of Conflict

Some of the difficulty in linking potential goal incompatibility to perceptions of conflict may be the fact that *goal* can represent a tremendously diverse range of desired outcomes from recreation participation. Further, many different underlying dynamics may be at work to influence perceptions of incompatibility. Four major dynamics may affect conflict perceptions (Jacob and Schreyer 1980).

The first is *activity style*, or the way in which the individual defines the meaning of an activity and behaviors appropriate to carrying it out. The underlying conception is that people who vary in notions of appropriate behaviors for a particular recreational activity will likely experience conflict. This has been one of the major elements in conflicts among different types of users of the same activity, such as river running (Schreyer, Roggenbuck, McCool, Royer and Miller 1976, Nielson and Shelby 1976, Heberlein and Vaske 1977). However, incompatibilities across different activities have also been a common source of attention (Gramann and Burdge 1981, Driver and Bassett 1975, Jackson and Wong 1982, Knopp and Tyger 1973).

Conflicts may arise not only from differing goals, but from differing previous experiences and commitment to the activity. Commitment has been commonly represented as specialization (Bryan 1977). The more involved an individual becomes with an activity, the more valuable it becomes. To the extent that it is important in representing an extension of an individual's personal identity, as discussed above, the more critical it becomes for that person to attain the desired experience. This would lead to more strongly defined expectations concerning the *appropriate behaviors* of others. In some cases this could also be associated with a greater need to derive status from identification with the activity (West 1977).

The amount and type of previous experience a person has had may affect his/her perception of the activity and the behavior of others. In a study of river recreationists, Schreyer, Lime and Williams (1984) showed that more experienced visitors tended to perceive more conflict. This finding was supported by Hammitt, McDonald and Noe's study of river floaters in the southeast (1984). In another river study, Schreyer (1982) also found that more experienced floaters tended to have more strongly defined expectations about what they wanted to encounter on the trip.

The second dimension is *environmental relation*. People develop attachments to places just as they do to other people or to recreational pursuits (Tuan 1974). Such attachments may be associated with a sense of possession (this is *my* place), which in turn may be linked to a stronger definition of appropriate behaviors for an area (Lee 1972), and a stronger feeling that one should be able to have input about how the area is to be managed (O'Leary 1976, Bryan 1979). Persons with intense feelings of identification with and attachment to a given recreation setting would likely be more sensitive to the behaviors of others in those environments.

Owens (1985) suggested that ongoing interactions with recreation environments result in *more or less enduring psychological structures...which in part pre-determine and guide behaviour (help to set its goals), and help to identify and differentiate individuals and/or groups by their disposition to react differently in different situations* (1985; 250). Schreyer and Knopf (1984) further suggest that persons with new and differing values may constitute a threat to experienced users' established relationship with and definition of a given recreation place.

The third dimension is *mode of experience*, which relates to the ways in which environments are perceived. For some persons, sensory interaction involves a very detailed, demanding focus on the setting. For others, the setting is merely a backdrop, a broad, undifferentiated place in which to carry out one's activities. Yi-Fu Tuan (1978) characterizes this as the distinction of *place vs. space*. The more focused and demanding a person is of the environmental interaction, the more likely that person may be disrupted by someone in a less focused mode. This would lead to perceptions of conflict. Differences in environmental perception may be significant factors contributing to the frequency of conflict situations between mechanized and non-mechanized recreationists, though other factors are also likely at work.

The fourth factor is *lifestyle diversity*. Many different subcultures with widely divergent lifestyles use public outdoor recreation places. The problem comes when one group perceives another's values, behaviors, or even presence as inappropriate. Perceived differences may be enhanced if other conflict factors, such as those described above, are present. This can heighten feelings that the *others* are different and exhibiting inappropriate behaviors.

Studies have documented differences in life values among conflicting recreation groups, such as cross-country skiers and snowmobilers (Knopp and Tyger 1973, Jacob 1978a). Bury, Holland and McEwan (1983) suggested conflict potential is dependent on the divergence of values of recreationists concerning dependence on technology and dominance over the environment. Differences in lifestyle values related to mechanized technology appear to be a significant force underlying the frequency of conflict between motorized and non-motorized recreationists (Martin and Berry 1974, Devall and Harry 1981).

Types of Conflict

Given the range and diversity of conflict situations, it helps to put some structure on the types of conflicts experienced by people in recreation. Differentiations may be made among conflict situations based on their underlying presumed dynamics, such as in the framework presented above. It is also possible to focus on conflict situations based upon the types of groups involved. Hammitt (1988), in a paper on conflict in recreation, cites a typology proposed by Little and Noe (1984) which proposes a nine-fold classification of all possible interactions between visitors, resource managers and associated communities.

This chapter will use a four-fold classification scheme based on different types of groups. There is nothing empirical about this classification. It is relatively simple, and it is the scheme around which the data reported here are organized. The four broad types of conflict are:

1. *Outdoor recreation vs. other resource uses.* This is obviously a broad Pandora's box that encompasses almost the entire domain of decision making concerning resource allocation and competition for access to resources. While it is generally not included in analyses of recreational conflict it is nevertheless the source of much conflict in outdoor recreation, as reflected in articles in the general media (e.g., U.S. News and World Report 1986). The growing use of wildlands for a variety of purposes can lead to a more bewildering diversity of conflicts, such as the recently reported one between fishermen on the Au Sable River and military maneuvers, complete with artillery barrages (Wall Street Journal 1988).

2. *Outdoor recreationists vs. resource managers.* Anything present in the recreation setting that does not satisfy visitors could conceivably be considered the fault of resource management. This underscores the

importance of managers' understanding visitors' needs, wants and preferences. Managers often assert that they know *what the public wants*. And yet, a number of studies on perceptions of visitors and managers have concluded that there are often significant differences in perceptions between resource managers and their clientele (Merriam, Wald and Ramsey 1972, Clark, Hendee and Campbell 1971, Bultena and Hendee 1972).

3. *Interactivity conflict.* This is the classical situation of identifying conflicts between users in different types of activities. Interactivity conflict has been the source of considerable research, such as between cross-country skiers and snowmobilers (Knopp and Tyger 1973, Jackson and Wong 1982), fishermen and canoeists (Driver and Bassett 1975), waterskiers and fishermen (Gramann and Burdge 1981), canoeists and motorboaters (Lucas 1964), wilderness users (Lucas and Stankey 1974), various types of trail users (McCay and Moeller 1976) and reservoir users (Lee *et al.* 1988).

4. *Intra-activity conflicts.* Persons who are ostensibly participating in the same *activity* may frequently come into conflict with one another. Differences in their behaviors and styles of participation within the activity may result in conflict situations. It is not unusual for these situations to be addressed in other ways, such as focusing on the topic of carrying capacity. The assumption is that too many people are engaging in the same activity in the same area. Much of this research has been carried out through studies of river recreationists (Schreyer and Roggenbuck 1978, Nielsen and Shelby 1977, Ditton, Fedler and Graefe 1982, Heberlein and Vaske 1977). However, there have also been examples where the focus has been on variations in the lifestyles and behaviors of different types of participants within the same activity (Devall 1973).

THE SCOPE OF CONFLICT

I want to present an illustration of the scope and diversity of conflict that comes from resource managers themselves. It is not the result of a systematic analysis designed to generate data generalizable to the world at large. Rather, it is the result of an informal exercise in which managers have talked about their own experiences in dealing with recreational conflict.

Utah State University and Clemson University have offered training sessions for outdoor recreation planners and managers for over ten years. These sessions have been sponsored by the USDA Forest Service. The goal of the courses has been to give persons in professional recreation management/planning positions training in the *state of the art* in knowledge about this discipline. The practical implication of this course is that each year managers and planners from all over the nation gather together to interact and learn. While the course is intended to impart knowledge, these people represent a tremendous resource themselves, in that they have a wealth of experience in recreation resource management under all possible environmental circumstances and situations.

Conflict is obviously one dimension of that topic. At various times shortcourse participants have been given an assignment requiring them to examine conflict in recreation. The goal of the assignment has been to encourage them to think through the forces which may precipitate conflict. The assignment asks each person to identify an outdoor recreation conflict he/she is familiar with as a consequence of his/her own particular job, and to analyze it using the theoretical framework developed by Jacob and Schreyer (1980). No other direction is given. They are not directed to choose the most important or most prevalent conflict. Rather, they are to select one that they have to deal with as a part of their real world responsibilities. While the assignment is intended to have the participants think through the dynamics of these situations and understand the underlying factors that may precipitate such situations (and consequently -- hopefully -- lead to insights concerning how such conflicts may be managed), there has emerged a tremendous range and breadth of conflict situations identified.

The information reported here is not so much the *state of conflict in outdoor recreation*, as it is an illustration of what recreation managers perceive as part of their regular responsibilities. They were not asked to come up with interesting, titillating or unusual examples. Yet from the 114 persons represented in the information presented here, there were 67 *different* conflict situations identified. This represents the reports of participants at the Utah State University shortcourse for the years 1981, 1982, 1984, and 1987.

The four categories of conflict identified in the previous section were used to organize the reporting of this information. Table 1 shows conflicts related to outdoor recreation vs. other types of uses and Table 2 lists conflicts between outdoor recreationists and managers. The frequency that each type of conflict was mentioned is shown, but this is only relevant to the population reported here. No one was instructed to come up with a specific type of conflict situation by category. These numbers are merely relative indicators of the types of situations on managers/planners' minds. If these people had been instructed to come up with examples of conflict situations with other resource users or with resource management, there would likely have been many others listed.

Table 1.   Outdoor Recreation vs. Other Resource Uses

N	
1	Commercial boaters vs. Recreational boaters (Lake Superior)
1	Irrigation water users vs. Recreational water users
1	Ranchers with N.F. access control vs. Recreationists

Table 2.   Outdoor Recreation vs. Resource Managers

N	
1	Non-Traditional users vs. the Forest Service
3	ORV recreationists vs. Resource managers
1	Charter fishermen vs. the Forest Service
1	Motorcyclists vs. Resource Managers
1	Concessionaires -- Private vs. University recreation department
1	Opposition to individual threaded hydrants in a recreation area

Table 3 shows examples of the more traditional conflicts that have to do with clashes between different types of activities. The ones that are more stereotypical examples of conflict tend to be the most frequently cited, such as backpackers vs. horseback riders and cross-country skiers vs. snowmobilers. However, there is a considerable diversity in the number and types of recreational activities represented. Consider the recreational challenges presented by interactions between gold dredgers, quail hunters, windsurfers, botanists, kayakers, llama trekkers, hang-gliders, survivalists and nude bathers! So whatever happened to all those *happy campers*?

Finally, Table 4 lists perceived conflicts between participants in what would ostensibly be considered the same activity. An important lesson to be gained from this listing is that a major weakness of recreation resource management and planning is to treat recreation participation primarily in terms of *activities*. Any given activity may be participated in by a variety of people from varying backgrounds with differing needs, relationships to the resource and relationships to other users. As a result, people within the same activity may vary considerably in the ways in which they choose to behave, and in the process, may foster negative responses from other participants.

Table 3.   Inter-activity Conflicts

<u>N</u>

N		vs.	
14	Backpackers	vs.	Horseback riders
4	Backpackers	vs.	Motorcyclists/Trailbikers
2	Backpackers	vs.	Three wheelers and ATV's
2	Backpackers	vs.	ORV's
1	Backpackers	vs.	Mountain bike riders
1	Backpackers	vs.	Botanists
1	ORV users	vs.	Quail hunters
1	ORV users	vs.	Beach non-motorized recreational users
1	ORV users	vs.	Horseback riders
1	ORV users	vs.	Play tubers vs. family tubers
8	X-C skiers	vs.	Snowmobilers
4	Anglers	vs.	Power-boaters/waterskiers
2	Anglers	vs.	Swimmers
2	Anglers	vs.	Canoeists
3	Anglers	vs.	Whitewater Floaters
1	Anglers	vs.	Windsurfers
1	Anglers-Locals	vs.	College-aged hikers and nude bathers
1	Fly Fishermen	vs.	Chicano bait-anglers vs. Duck hunters
1	River floaters	vs.	Jet boaters
1	River floaters	vs.	Kayakers
1	River floaters	vs.	Pilots vs. Subsistence users vs. the Feds
1	Horseback riders	vs.	Mountain bikes
2	Horseback riders	vs.	Llamas
1	Campers	vs.	Three wheelers
2	Summer home owners	vs.	Dispersed recreationists
1	Summer home owners	vs.	Swimmers
1	Recreational aircraft	vs.	Hang-gliders
1	Recreational aircraft	vs.	Boaters
1	Hunters	vs.	Survival training climbers
1	Sailboaters	vs.	Motorboaters
2	Motorcyclists	vs.	Non-motorcycling campers and landowners
1	Novice climbers and bikers	vs.	Experienced climbers and bikers vs. each other
1	Recreational gold dredgers	vs.	Tubers
1	Recreational gold dredgers	vs.	Campers
1	Recreational gold dredgers	vs.	Fishermen
1	Recreational gold dredgers	vs.	Sightseers

DEALING WITH CONFLICT

A part of this chapter has been devoted to describing the dynamics of conflict in recreation. These concepts may help in understanding the social psychological aspects of conflict, but they also contain implications for management. Treating conflict as *goal interference* makes it incumbent on planners and managers to understand more clearly the different goals pursued by people using public resources, and how the interactions of different types of users may impact the attainment of those goals.

Conflict is not merely a function of the fact that *some people just can't get along*. Working with it requires a recognition that the behaviors of certain persons can and do make it impossible for others to attain the outcomes or benefits that motivated them to engage in that activity in the first place.

The concept of *activity style* has much to say about variability *within* activities. It is not sufficient for recreation planning and management to deal with hikers and horseback riders as *activities* that may conflict. Rather, an understanding of the dynamics of recreation participation requires recognition of the diversity that occurs within activities, as illustrated in Table 4. Diversity is affected by factors such as the amount of previous experience a person has and his/her personal commitment to the activity (Virden and Schreyer 1988).

Resource relation is a concept that needs to be understood more clearly by resource managers in dealing with their *turf*. There is a tendency to view outdoor environments as *settings* that consist of a collection of *attributes* that may be more or less capable of providing opportunities for the enjoyment of various activities. However, this overlooks the fact that humans do develop affective bonds with *places*, and that their use of such environments ties into personal identification, a sense of continuity in connectedness with an environment that may represent a considerable amount of life history, and a variety of other symbolic and cultural meanings. The resource management rationale *Well, we won't let them do that activity here, but they can just as easily do it over there*, is a classic example of missing this point. Just as a home is much more than a house, a recreation place can be much more than a natural ecosystem with facilities.

Mode of perception serves to promote the recognition that some activities, by their very nature, are incompatible. While public sector recreation resource management has tended to be based on the philosophical assumption that people should have equal access to all resources, the concept provides a rationale for understanding that not all people can be accommodated in the same environment. This goes beyond issues of crowding, although such issues are obviously of growing concern for

Table 4.   Intra-activity Conflicts

N	
4	Campers -- Family vs. Youth celebrating/High school graduation
1	Campers -- Loud music lovers vs. No music
3	Campers -- Traditional vs. Non-traditional
1	Campers -- Tent vs. RV campers
1	Campers -- Horse vs. Non-horse campers
2	Hunters -- Local vs. Out of state
1	Hunters -- Hiking vs. 4 wheel drive
1	Hunters -- Bear vs. Grouse
1	Hunters -- Stand hunting vs. Dog hunting
1	Hot spring users -- Families vs. Power boat crews
1	Hot spring users -- Families vs. Counterculture
1	Hot spring users -- Families vs. Nude bathers
2	River floaters -- Commercial vs. Private
1	Canoeists -- Motorized vs. Non-motorized
1	Boaters -- Motorized vs. Non-Motorized
1	Houseboats -- Private vs. Rental
4	Picnickers -- Families vs. Large social groups
1	Hikers -- Dog haters vs. Dog lovers
1	Cross Country skiers -- With and without dogs
1	Skiers -- Downhill vs. Ski-bob skiers
1	Four-wheel drive recreationists -- Active vs. Passive
1	People at destination attractions crowding each other.

resource management. Rather, it provides a rationale for zoning and for planning systems that can consciously develop a range of settings managed for a variety of recreation experiences.

The concept of *lifestyle tolerance* affects all sectors of human activity. Within recreation, it may serve to help understand the nature of the intensity of conflicts between groups as being a function of the perception that the others are *different*. A potential management strategy for encouraging conflicting user groups to work out their differences is to create a greater awareness of the mutuality of interests they share. For instance, it is frequently a shock to cross-country skiers to learn that one of the most important reasons people say they engage in snowmobiling is to *experience nature* (Jacob 1978a, Haas, Driver and Brown 1980). Breaking down barriers of perception can be an important first step in developing communication among conflicting user groups.

Conflict may have many causes. It may not be just simply a case of one basic problem. Some causes may go beyond the recreation environment, resulting from social conflict in society in general. As such, they may represent forces over which recreation planners and managers have little control. A part of the humility of dealing with these situations may very well be the recognition that conflicts are inevitable, that they may not be problems to be solved so much as conditions to be lived with.

It is also worth observing that conflict is not inevitably bad (Jacob and Schreyer 1980). Rather, conflict can be a healthy expression of the interplay of differing values in culture. The airing of differences may serve in many cases as a forum for the recognition of diverse values that planners and managers need to respond to. If there were no conflict, it could only be the result of the fact that there was no diversity of thought, and that would be a tragedy for the nature of human perspective.

Future Directions

Just as this chapter did not report the results of an empirical study generalizable to the entire domain of resource management, there can be considerable argument concerning the nature and extent of conflict in outdoor recreation. However when recreation resource managers talk about what is on *their* minds, conflict is one of the things that invariably is mentioned. The listing of the different conflict situations reported in this chapter, from all over the nation and across a number of years, is intended as an illustration of that fact.

The information presented here represents theoretical concepts drawn from the existing literature on conflict in outdoor recreation, as well as the subjective perceptions of a small sample of resource managers. The few articles cited in this chapter are reflective of the limited amount of research on conflict in outdoor recreation. More information is needed concerning the general prevalence of conflict in recreation, and its intensity among those who experience it. Concepts presented in this chapter on the social dynamics of conflict in recreation are based primarily on speculation, drawing from literature on conflict in other disciplines. There is a need for more systematic inquiry into the means of explaining conflict in recreation settings.

A considerable need for resources to help planners and managers deal with conflict situations also exists. Some of this information may come from systematic research, but there is likely a wealth of knowledge that can be tapped through the experiences of planners and managers who have had to confront conflict situations.

Perhaps more significantly, the diversity of conflict identified in this chapter implies that the process of recreation resource management is becoming increasingly complex and demanding. Recreation can no longer be treated as a collection of *activities*. Rather, recreation resource managers and planners need to be able to understand the significance of the diversity of persons visiting their resource, the different needs and goals they are pursuing, the things they need from the resource in order to attain those goals, and the consequences of people interacting with others who have different agendas. That may seem like a lot to ask, but no one ever said that outdoor recreation management/planning was supposed to be fun and games.

REFERENCES

Bryan, H. 1977. Leisure value systems and recreational specialization: The case of trout fishermen. *Journal of Leisure Research* 9:174-187.

Bryan, H. 1979. *Conflict in the Great Outdoors: Toward Understanding and Managing for Diverse Sportsmen Preferences.* University, AL: University of Alabama, Bureau of Public Admin. Sociological Studies No. 4.

Bultena, G.L. and J.C. Hendee. 1972. Foresters' view of interest group positions on forest policy. *Journal of Forestry* 70:201-206.

Bury, R.L., S.M. Holland and D.N. McEwan. 1983. Analyzing recreational conflict: Understanding why conflict occurs is requisite to managing that conflict. *Journal of Soil and Water Conservation* 38:401-403.

Clark, R.N., J.C. Hendee and F.L. Campbell. 1971. Values, behavior and conflict in modern camping culture. *Journal of Leisure Research* 3:143-159.

DeVall, B. 1976. Social worlds of leisure. In N.R. Cheek, D.R. Field and R.J. Burdge (Eds.), *Leisure and Recreation Places.* Ann Arbor, MI: Ann Arbor Science, 131-142.

DeVall, B. 1973. The development of leisure social worlds. *Humboldt Journal of Social Relations* 1:53-59.

DeVall, B. and J. Harry. 1981. Who hates whom in the great outdoors: The impacts of recreational specialization and technologies of play. *Leisure Science* 4:399-418.

Ditton, R.B., A.J. Fedler and A.R. Graefe. 1982. Assessing recreational satisfaction among diverse participant groups. In *Forest and River Recreation: Research Update.* St. Paul, MN: University of Minnesota Agricultural Experiment Station Miscellaneous Publication 18, 134-139.

Driver, B.L. and J.R. Bassett. 1975. Defining conflicts among river users: A case study of Michigan's AuSable River. *Naturalist* 26:19-23.

Driver, B.L. and S.R. Tocher. 1970. Toward a behavioral interpretation of recreational engagements, with implications for planning. In B.L. Driver (Ed.), *Elements of Outdoor Recreation Planning*. Ann Arbor, MI: University of Michigan Press, 9-31.

Garreau, J. 1981. *The Nine Nations of North America*. N.Y.: Avon.

Gramann, J.H. and R.J. Burdge. 1981. The effects of recreation goals on conflict perception: The case of water skiers and fishermen. *Journal of Leisure Research* 31:15-27.

Haas, G.E., B.L. Driver and P.J. Brown. 1980. A study of ski touring experience on the White River National Forest. In *Proceedings, North American Symposium on Dispersed Winter Recreation*. St. Paul, MN: University of Minnesota Agricultural Extension Service, 25-30.

Haggard, L.M. and D.R. Williams. 1988. *Resource Recreation and Personal Identity*. Unpublished manuscript. Salt Lake City, UT: University of Utah, Department of Psychology.

Hammitt, W.E. 1988. *The Spectrum of Conflict in Outdoor Recreation*. Paper presented at Benchmark 1988: A National Outdoor Recreation and Wilderness Forum, Tampa, FL.

Hammitt, W.E., C.D. McDonald and F.P. Noe. 1984. Use level and encounters: Important variables of perceived crowding among non-specialized recreationists. *Journal of Leisure Research* 16:1-8.

Heberlein, T.A. and J.J. Vaske. 1977. *Crowding and Visitor Conflict on the Bois Brule River*. Madison, WI: University of Wisconsin Water Resources Center, Technical Report WIS WRC 77-04, 93 pp.

Jackson, E.L. and R.A.G. Wong. 1982. Perceived conflict between urban cross-country skiers and snowmobilers in Alberta. *Journal of Leisure Research* 14:47-62.

Jacob, G.R. 1978a. *Conflict in Outdoor Recreation*. Unpublished M.S. Thesis. Logan, UT: Utah State University.

Jacob, G.R. 1978b. *Conflict in Outdoor Recreation -- A Bibliography of Relevant Literature*. Logan, UT: Institute of Outdoor Recreation and Tourism.

Jacob, G.R. and R. Schreyer. 1980. Conflict in outdoor recreation: A theoretical perspective. *Journal of Leisure Research* 12:368-380.

Johnson, D. 1983. *The U.S. Workplace in a Time of Social and Demographic Change*. Insight -- Social Science for the Public Land Managers. Seattle, WA: NPS Co-op Park Studies Unit, University of Washington Paper No. 1., 13p.

Kando, T.M. 1980. *Leisure and Popular Culture in Transition*. St. Louis: The C.V. Mosby Co.

Kelly, J.R. 1987. *Freedom to be: A New Sociology of Leisure.* NY: MacMillan.

Knopf, R.C. 1983. Recreational needs and behavior in natural settings. In I. Altman and J. Wohlwill (Eds.), *Behavior and the Natural Environment.* New York: Plenum, 205-240.

Knopp, T.B. and J.D. Tyger. 1973. A study of conflict in recreational land use: Snowmobiling vs. ski-touring. *Journal of Leisure Research* 5:6-17.

Lee, M.E., D.R. Field and K.S. Martinson. 1988. *Visitor Conflict at Whiskeytown: A Carrying Capacity Approach.* Corvallis, OR: Cooperative Park Studies Unit, College of Forestry, Oregon State University, 55 pp.

Lee, R.G. 1972. The social definition of outdoor recreational places. In W.R. Burch, N.H. Cheek and L. Taylor (Eds.), *Social Behavior, Natural Resources and the Environment.* New York: Harper and Row, 68-84.

Lindsay, J.J. 1974. Outdoor recreation conflict in Vermont, 1973. Burlington, VT: University of Vermont, School of Natural Resources. Research Report SNR-RM2, 46p.

Little, W. and F.P. Noe. 1984. A highly condensed description of the thought process used in developing visitor research for southeast parks. Unpublished manuscript. Atlanta, GA: National Park Service, Southeast Regional Office, 40p.

Lucas, R.C. 1964. Wilderness perception and use. The example of the Boundary Waters Canoe Area. *Natural Resources Journal* 3:394-411.

Lucas, R.C. and G.H. Stankey. 1974. *Social Carrying Capacity for Backcountry Recreation.* St. Paul, MN: USDA Forest Service North Central Forest Experiment Station, General Technical Report NC-9, 63 pp.

Martin, T.W. and K.J. Berry. 1974. Competitive sports in post-industrial society: The case of the motocross racer. *Journal of Popular Culture* 8:107-121.

McCay, R.E. and G.H. Moeller. 1976. *Compatibility of Ohio Trail Users.* Upper Darby, PA: USDA Forest Service, Northeastern Forest Experiment Station, Research Note NE-225, 18 pp.

Merriam, L.C., K.D. Wald and C.E. Ramsey. 1972. Public and professional definitions of the state park: A Minnesota case. *Journal of Leisure Research* 4:259-272.

Mitchell, A. 1983. *The Nine American Lifestyles.* New York: Warner Books.

Nielsen, J.M. and B. Shelby. 1977. River-running in the Grand Canyon: How much and what kind of use. In *Proceedings: River Recreation and Management Symposium.* St. Paul, MN: USDA Forest Service, North Central Forest Experiment Station General Technical Report NC-28.

O'Leary, J.T. 1976. Land use redefinition and the rural community: Disruption of community leisure space. *Journal of Leisure Research* 8:263-274.

Owens, P.L. 1985. Conflict as a social interaction process in environment and behavior research: The example of leisure and recreation research. *Journal of Environmental Psychology* 5:243-259.

Schreyer, R. 1982. Experience level affects expectations for recreation participation. In *Forest and River Recreation: Research Update*. St. Paul, MN: University of Minnesota Agricultural Experiment Station Miscellaneous Publication 18, 154-159.

Schreyer, R. and R.C. Knopf. 1984. The dynamics of change in outdoor recreation environments -- some equity issues. *Journal of Park and Recreation Administration* 2:9-19.

Schreyer, R., D.W. Lime and D.R. Williams. 1984. Characterizing the influence of past experience on recreation behavior. *Journal of Leisure Research* 16:34-50.

Schreyer, R. and J.W. Roggenbuck. 1978. The influence of experience expectations on crowding perceptions and social-psychological carrying capacities. *Leisure Science* 1:373-394.

Schreyer, R., J.W. Roggenbuck, S.F. McCool, L.E. Royer and J. Miller. 1976. *The Dinosaur National Monument Whitewater River Recreation Study*. Logan, UT: Utah State University, Institute of Outdoor Recreation and Tourism, 186 pp.

Todd, S.L. and A.R. Graefe. 1988. *Sources of Conflict in the River Recreation Experience*. Paper presented at the Second Symposium on Social Science in Resource Management, Champaign, IL.

Tuan, Y. 1974. Topophilia: *A Study of Environmental Perception, Attitudes and Values*. Engelwood Cliffs, NJ: Prentice-Hall.

Tuan, Y. 1978. *Space and Place: The Perspective of Experience*. Minneapolis, MN: University of Minnesota Press.

U.S. News and World Report. 1986. The big grab for wildlands. Apr. 28, 68-69.

Virden, R. and R. Schreyer. 1988. Recreation specialization as an indicator of environmental preference. *Environment and Behavior* 20:721-739.

Wall Street Journal. 1988. The sound of war above a river has anglers up in arms. June 17, p. 1.

West, P.C. 1977. A status group dynamics approach to predicting participation rates in regional recreation demand studies. *Land Economics* 53:196-211.

CHAPTER 3

THE SOCIO-ECONOMIC FUNCTION OF THE CANADIAN PARKS SERVICE AS A MODEL FOR THE U.S. NATIONAL PARK SERVICE AND OTHER AGENCIES: AN ORGANIZATIONAL FRAMEWORK FOR MANAGING NATURAL RESOURCE RECREATION RESEARCH

Scott M. Meis
Socio-Economic Branch,
Canadian Parks Service, Environment Canada

The original focus of the material presented in this chapter was a contrast between the organizational features of the social science capabilities of the Canadian Parks Service and those of the U.S. National Park Service.[1] The discussion presented here was originally an advocacy argument calling management of the U.S National Park Service to action to strengthen the social sciences as management capabilities of that organization. Now, in response to the different requirements of the present publication, the discussion is generalized to apply to the question of appropriate organizational conditions for the all the social sciences in natural resource management agencies in general.

The kinds of background information drawn upon in this chapter are consistent with its genesis. Much of the information is based on the author's informal personal knowledge -- gained in the past decade spent as a social science research manager with the Canadian Parks Service -- concerning the organizational foundations of social science in various sister resource management agencies. Other information comes from unpublished internal memoranda and internal background documents of the various agencies. A third source was discussions with various colleagues inside and outside of government who were consulted to obtain current background information on the state of the USNPS social science initiative, the state of the draft report of the National Parks and Conservation Association Commission on Research on Resource Management Policy in the National Park System, and the state of social science and research management in general within other resource management agencies in the United States and Canada.[2]

The discussion begins by examining the mandate and need for social science as program focus in resource management agencies. I then examine a definition of what such a program focus might encompass: firstly, in terms of Canadian applied research management terminology; secondly, in terms of recent internal proposals for the U.S. national park system; and thirdly, in terms of a general view and specific examples of the direction the Canadian Parks Service has taken over the past 15 years in developing a strong social science function as an integral part of the staff and managerial capabilities of the organization. The discussion ends with the assertion that, based on the success of the Canadian experience in this area, adoption of the proposed measures to strengthen social sciences as a managerial capability is recommended strongly for all natural resource and recreation management agencies.

THE MANDATE FOR SOCIAL SCIENCE IN RESOURCE MANAGEMENT AGENCIES

Based on their respective founding legislation, the Canadian and United States national parks services have as fundamental responsibilities the goals of (1) conserving parks resources and (2) providing resource experiences that are enjoyable to current and future park users and other publics. Furthermore, although other additional goals may also be involved, I believe that these two fundamental goals, in one form or another underlay much, or part, of the philosophies of all North American public agencies dealing with natural or cultural resource management.

Like it or not, in my opinion, based on their founding legislation, *the Canadian and United States National Park Services and all similar natural resource management agencies can be considered as social service programs!* The designation of special natural resources for protection is a social objective of both societies. What resources do and don't get the benefit of national designation and protection is a societal decision. As such, all park lands or similar categories of protected resources are social institutions. The provision of public appreciation or enjoyment of such protected resources is also a social objective. And lastly, the concern for the welfare of future generations with respect to these and other societal resources is the ultimate social goal of any society.

In my opinion, *to address these fundamental objectives in a rational and responsible manner, such agencies must have a strong organizational capability in the social sciences.*

THE CURRENT SITUATION IN THE U.S. NATIONAL PARK SERVICE

To meet this challenge in 1987 a new social science focus was proposed for the United States National Park Service (USNPS) for financial year 1988 and beyond.[3] The proposal would establish what has been called a *Human Resources Management Program.*[4] The focus of this program, the *Human Resource System*, would consist of all the social resources relating to the Parks Services operations and interests including: current and future park visitors, park employees and their families, concessioners, inholders, neighboring residents, adjacent landowners and industries, gateway communities, and travel and tourism industry interests.

The stated objectives of the proposed new social sciences program are identified as (1) helping park management understand the human resource system of the parks and the socio-economic interactions of the various publics that make up that system, and (2) enabling park management to utilize this knowledge and understanding to better accomplish the mission of the individual park unit and the agency.[5] In the view of the recent internal proposal, to meet these objectives, *the Service needs accurate and comprehensive social information*, not only about park visitors but also about the various other publics with whom the Service interacts.[5]

At present, however, the Service is unable to adequately satisfy this requirement. In the view of the recent social science proposal, again, *the Service does not have the basis for assessing the adequacy of park facilities and services, for evaluating the effectiveness of park interpretive and educational programs, or for determining how the actions of park management affect visitor use and enjoyment of parks*. The new social sciences program of the National Park Service proposes to redress these weaknesses.

Interestingly, both the U.S. National Forest Service and the Bureau of Land Management have also recently reevaluated their mandates with respect to their fundamental agency objectives and their public responsibilities. In each case, they too have taken steps to redirect their strategic priorities. First, they have placed a greater emphasis on their mandate for public service and public recreation. Second, and correlated with that, they have emphasized their need for more and better scientific information on their clients and publics.

Basing my recommendation on the success of our Canadian experience in this area of the past 15 years, I strongly suggest that the directorate of the U.S. National Park Service, and senior management of other natural and cultural public resource management agencies, continue to support their recent initiatives to create strong social science capabilities within their organizations at this pivotal stage in their evolution. But what kinds of activities exactly are we referring to when we talk of the social science disciplines in a government agency context? And what is the Canadian experience?

THE DEFINITION OF GOVERNMENT SOCIAL SCIENCE ACTIVITY

Within the administrative vocabulary used to describe various Canadian government expenditures and activities the general category of science and technology (S&T) is divided into two general fields: natural sciences and engineering (NSE) and social sciences and humanities (SSH).[6]

The term social sciences in this context is regarded as being synonymous with social sciences and humanities, and embraces all disciplines involved in studying human actions and conditions and the social, economic and institutional mechanisms affecting humans. Included are such disciplines as anthropology, demography, economics, geography, history, languages, literature, linguistics, law, library science, philosophy, political science, psychology, religious studies, social work, sociology, and urban and regional studies.[7]

Within the category of social sciences in particular such activities are grouped into two main sub categories:

1. *Scientific research and experimental development (R&D)*, which is defined as creative work undertaken on a systematic basis in order to increase the stock of knowledge about man, his actions and his institutions, and the application of this knowledge in new ways.[6]

2. *Related scientific activities (RSA)*, are defined as those activities which complement and extend R&D by contributing to the generation, dissemination and application of scientific and technological knowledge. More specifically the kinds of related scientific activities that are included in this category for the social sciences:

   general purpose data collection;
   scientific information services;
   socio-economic feasibility studies;
   educational support (ie. awards intended primarily to support the education of the recipients);
   operations and policy studies.[6]

Distinctions are also made between terms describing the means used by a government agency to deliver these types of activity. Thus, within this area of activity a natural or cultural resource management agency may typically choose to perform social science S&T and RSA activities within its own organization using primarily government personnel. In such cases, these activities are classified as intramural expenditures. Such intramural performance typically includes:

scientific activities carried out by personnel of units assigned to the programs;

the acquisition of land, buildings, machinery and equipment for scientific activities;

the administration of scientific activities by program employees;

the purchase of support services such as EDP and travel.

Alternatively an agency may choose to perform these activities extramurally by selecting another non-government organization to perform   S&T and RSA requirements such as industry, universities, non-profit institutions, other levels of government, other national performers and foreign performers.[6,8]

The administration of social science activity in the Canadian government also distinguishes among these activities by the purpose or ends to which they are directed.   More specifically, distinctions are made between *basic research, applied research* and *experimental development* that also deserve definition in this context.

Basic research is experimental or theoretical work undertaken primarily to acquire new knowledge of the underlying foundation of phenomena and observable facts, without any particular application or use in view. Basic research formulates and tests hypotheses, theories or laws, thereby providing the basis for future applied research. The results of basic research are not generally marketable or directly applicable to policy or operational decisions. The Canadian Parks Service's theoretical work in the early 1970s on outdoor recreation demand is a good example of this type of activity.

Applied research on the other hand is also original investigation undertaken to acquire new knowledge. It, however, is directed primarily towards a specific practical aim or objective.   Applied research is undertaken either to determine uses for the findings of basic research, or to determine methods or ways of achieving some specific and predetermined objectives.   In parks agencies such as the CPS, background research relating to a park management plan (i.e., master plan) is the most frequent example of this type of activity.

Experimental development is systematic work, drawing on existing knowledge gained from research or practical experience, or both, that is directed to producing new material, products or devices, to installing new processes, systems and services, or to improving substantially those already produced or installed. Systematic testing that is done for the development of government regulations such as new fee policies or fine tuning research of operational public programs are also included in this category of S&T activity.[8,9] Also included would be the development activity in the CPS in the mid-1980s that was associated with the development of the Visitor Activity Management Process. More recently, the subprojects associated with the development of the Park Use Related Data System fall within this category.

These are the administrative descriptions of social science activities in a government administration. I will now describe in operational terms the organization of social science activities in the Canadian Parks Service.

THE SOCIO-ECONOMIC FUNCTION
IN THE CANADIAN PARKS SERVICE

The Socio-Economic function of the Canadian Parks Service refers to a distinct set of organizational units within the service that are responsible for the application of the professional disciplines of sociology, economics, and statistics to parks management. In addition, when occasions demand, these responsibilities are extended to include management applications involving aspects of demography, anthropology, political science, social and environmental psychology, recreational geography, and market research.

Work in these disciplines is undertaken by the Parks Service of Environment Canada in support of planning, developing and operating the five types of heritage units within the program portfolio: National Parks, National Historic Parks and Sites, Heritage Canals, Co-operative Heritage Areas, and National Heritage Rivers.

The Parks Service, by virtue of its policy mandate, is committed to undertaking and encouraging *applied* research for the identification, protection, understanding and use of these heritage resources. In carrying out this work the Service draws upon the expertise of human resources from within its own organization as well as from other federal, provincial or territorial agencies, the university community and the private sector.

ORGANIZATION OF THE FUNCTION

Social science activity emerged in the Canadian Service as a distinct functional unit some 15 years ago with the establishment of the Socio-Economic Branch (SEB) in Ottawa out of the old Park Use Research Division in headquarters. Since its emergence as a distinct managerial responsibility is still a relatively new functional focus within the Canadian Parks Service, its organizational structure is still evolving. Currently, the role and the associated responsibilities of the function exist at all three levels of the organization; that is, at the field or park level, at the regional office level and at headquarters. At present, however, the responsibility is not yet staffed at the field level. This is, in fact, under examination as an emerging future requirement. Currently, the field responsibilities are carried out by other field staff members with advice and functional direction from the professional staff in the regional offices. At the regional office level, there is now a small professional and technical support working group of three to six persons working in each of the five regional offices.

At headquarters the Socio-Economic Branch consists of 14 to 20 persons, depending on the developmental or applied research project workload in any given financial year. Internally, this group is organized into two working Divisions, the Evaluation and Analysis Division and the Socio-Economic Information Division. Each consists of from 7 to 10 persons at any given time.

Thus in total, as of this year, the Canadian Parks Service employs about 40 persons working within the socio-economic function as part of an overall labor force of a little over 5000 full time equivalent person-years. This is about one half of the overall labor force of the U.S. service.

In terms of financial resources, in the financial year 1985-86 the total combined budget allocation to the activities of the Canadian socio-economic function was approximately 2 million dollars.

In terms of reporting relationships, the Socio-Economic Branch and the function as a whole, as a distinct and significant area of senior management professional accountability, reports to a specialized director in the headquarters senior management team. This Director, Socio-Economics Branch, reports in turn to the Director General of Program Management. He or she, in turn, reports to the most senior manager of the service, the Assistant Deputy Minister, Canadian Parks Service.

While these organizational features indicate that the Canadian Parks Service has a relatively strong social science function, no similar U.S. service has yet developed an equivalent organized social science capability. Firstly, despite the fact that a similar social science program has recently been proposed for the U.S. National Park Service, to date, no such similar distinct organizational structure yet exists within that agency. Secondly, to my knowledge at present, in comparison to the   professional staff of approximately 30 to 40 persons in the CPS, the NPS has only two or maybe three active sociologists or economists in an overall labor force of about 9,000 full time equivalent positions. Thirdly, while I do not have current figures, one source (Hughes 1986) indicated that in the 1985 financial year, out of an overall research budget approximately $15 million, approximately $1,400,000 was allocated to social sciences research, with anthropology receiving $1,000,000, sociology receiving $400,000 and virtually no identified funds allocated to research in economic aspects of U.S. national parks. By comparison, the $400,000 dollars the U.S. service devoted to sociology in that year was about equal to what the Canadian service spent on socio-economic data collection alone in 1985-86.

Similarly, while staff and resource levels for the social sciences may be higher than the NPS in the other resource management agencies, nowhere else has there yet emerged the established recognition of a distinct organizational identity and separate senior management accountability for social science activity that are present in the Canadian Parks Service organization.

ROLES AND RESPONSIBILITIES OF THE SOCIO-ECONOMIC FUNCTION

What exactly then, do these specialized resource commitments do for the Canadian Parks Service? The general role and specific responsibilities of the function have been formally specified and approved in the mid 1980s. The official role is to provide analysis, information, and methodology to determine the social and economic factors influencing the operations of the Canadian Parks Service. The associated responsibilities include: 1) social science policy; 2) social science research methods and techniques; 3) information in support of planning processes; 4) technical and scientific advice and services; 5) collecting, analyzing, exchanging and providing socio-economic data; 6) associated data and records management;   7) research management, coordination and control; 8) representation and liaison; 9) skill requirements identification; and finally, 11) staff training (SEB 1987).

It would be impossible in the space available for this chapter to examine in detail all of the above mentioned areas of professional activity. In order to provide a more concrete sense of what the function does and how the agency benefits, I will present in detail some aspects of just one of the most visible activities and comment on its significance: the evaluation of social and economic aspects of park plans and development proposals.

PLAN AND PROJECT REVIEW IN TIMES OF ECONOMIC RESTRAINT

An important challenge facing parks systems in the 1980s and 1990s is the level of funding they receive. In Canada over the past 10 years the general trend in these figures, when controlled for inflation, has been downward. This decrease has been most prevalent within the capital component of the program which has undergone a reduction of 24 percent since 1983-84. This affects the Canadian service's activities in natural and cultural heritage protection, its ability to provide satisfactory park experiences to the public, and as well its ability to generate economic development (SEB 1987).

In recent years, the needs to measure the economic dimensions of the Service and the economic efficiency of its decisions have become particularly important because of the Canadian government's concern to reduce its expanding fiscal deficit, strengthen its national and regional economies and demonstrate effectiveness and efficiency in deploying government funds (SEB 1987).

As a result of these pressures, the Socio-Economic function has been called upon to act as an internal check and balancing force for the economic efficiency of management decisions. In response, the Evaluation and Analysis Division of Socio-Economic Branch, has developed a series of computer based models for quickly assessing the economic aspects of the Service's operations and development initiatives (SEB 1987).

Thus, in the face of increasing external fiscal pressures, the Canadian Parks Service has responded by developing the analytical capability to substantiate its proposed capital investment plans and defend the continuation of its current level of operational funding. As a consequence, in relative terms, despite difficult times we have fared better than many other social and environmental programs that have been more seriously and deeply cut than Parks. Several of these competing agencies are now beginning to imitate our economic models!

Aside from the use of these analytical tools to support external funding submissions, our economic analysis capability is also being used internally, (by non-social science staff) to control and optimize our internal discretionary resource allocation processes. Currently, the Evaluation and Analysis Division of the Socio-Economic Branch at program headquarters reviews all park management plans and major regional capital projects against established criteria (Whiting 1987) to identify those development projects which have a social or economic component and to determine the type of supporting analysis which is required for the project to receive funding approval(SER 1987). For example, in one recent case, the Evaluation and Analysis Division of headquarters reviewed a proposal of Prairie region to spend 2.7 million dollars in upgrading and building administration and visitor interpretation and reception facilities in Riding Mountain National Park. In that instance we recommended the region be given authority to spend $119.0 thousand for the project definition stage of the work, providing certain additional conditions were satisfied first, namely: demonstrated visitor demand; reliable estimates of peak user loadings and circulation patterns; an analysis of target market needs or abilities; more reliable cost estimates; and finally, life-cycle costs of remaining design or delivery options.[10]

In another case of a proposed park management plan, based on its review, we recommended the plan NOT be approved unless certain contentious aspects of the plan and its substantiation were resolved first.[11]

These examples are just a small sample of the products of the Socio-Economic function of the Canadian Parks Service. Elsewhere in this volume, other authors identify other examples. Graham and Payne (Chapter 10), for instance, identify some of the kinds of social science research activities that have typically been completed as background to the processes of identifying and acquiring prospective park areas. They then go on to further specify some of the limitations of existing social science information collection and analysis activities and propose one possible means of improvement.

In another case, Rollins and Chambers (Chapter 8) describe the Visitor Activity Management Process, a new decision framework developed by social scientists, line managers and other functional staff within CPS, to prestructure rational and informed decision making regarding services to identified publics and associated research and information assembly activities. They then go on to report on a new standardized survey that is being developed within the function to measure and monitor visitor satisfaction with campgrounds and associated services within Canadian National Parks.

Is the U.S. National Parks Service or any other U.S. natural resource agency in a position to inform, defend and critique comparable technical assessments relating to its decisions? Some might argue with me, but from what I have seen, they are not. At least, not yet, as broadly throughout all levels and regions of the organizations. Furthermore, it is not for a lack of available academic social science of potential relevance to the services. In fact, because of the relative differences in the size of the academic communities between the two countries, there is much more of that to draw from in the U.S. than in Canada. Instead, the problem is, in my opinion, that inside the USNPS decision makers are generally uninformed about what relevant knowledge exists outside in the social science community. Frequently, no one participates in the various internal decision making processes with the knowledge, experience and ability to synthesize and abstract the relevant social science information and argue its relevance to the problems of current concern.

The U.S. Service is now, however, taking the important first steps to correct this problem. The need has been identified and acknowledged. A member of the directorate has been assigned the responsibility of developing an organizational response. A representative of the Canadian service was invited to make a presentation to the directorate on the Canadian experience. A solution has been proposed, that is similar in many respects to the Canadian model. Responsibilities have been delegated to the regional directors. New social science positions have been identified and described. Human resources are in the process of being reallocated. An inventory of existing work has been developed. Standing authority to conduct park visitor surveys has been obtained from the Office of Management and the Budget. The standardized visitor mapping system of information collection has received official program wide support, as well. All this, in less than two years!

The directorate should be congratulated on its significant progress in initiating these organizational changes in a difficult bureaucratic context. Nevertheless, there is much more to do if it is to meet the challenge of the agency's founding social objectives and the social complexities of our times. I urge the Service directorate to continue the new initiative to develop the social sciences as a staff function within the Service, irrespective of whatever other changes in direction may emerge with its new administration. I also recommend strongly that all other natural and cultural resource management agencies continue their recent initiatives to rationalize and strengthen their similar responsibilities to their respective recreation clients and publics. Finally, I recommend that they base such decisions on a strong, organized and accountable internal staff capability to obtain and use appropriate social science information.

SUMMARY

In summary, we have seen that in the United States National Park Service a strong organizational capability in the social sciences is required to adequately address the fundamental objectives of the agency as outlined in its founding act. We have also seen that USNPS has only begun the process of developing this essential capability. By contrast, the Canadian Parks Service has developed strong social science function with an emphasis on sociology, economics and statistics that has become an integral part of the decision making structure of the organization. We have seen how this function is delineated and organized and what activities it performs in the Service. We have seen examples of specific products of the function such as planning analysis reviews and gained some insight as to how the agency benefits from these capabilities.

Lastly, we have seen that organizational changes similar to those instituted in the Canadian service have been proposed and, more recently, are beginning to be implemented to address the current limitations of the USNPS and other similar resource management agencies. Based on the success of the Canadian experience in this area, continued adoption and implementation of the proposed measures to strengthen social sciences as a managerial capability is recommended strongly for its sister service on the North American continent and other similar public agencies mandated with managing natural and cultural resources for the protection and enjoyment of the public.

NOTES:

1. Earlier versions of this chapter were presented successively to a senior management meeting of the United States National Park Service in Everglades National Park, February, 1988; the Second Symposium on Social Sciences in Resources Management, University of Illinois, and Urbana, Illinois, June, 1988; and finally the Workshop on NPCA Commission: Research and Resource Management Policy in the National Park System, The Fifth Triennial Conference on Research in the National Parks and Equivalent Reserves, Tucson, Arizona, November, 1988.

2. Those consulted included the following: E. Zube, University of Arizona; D. Galvin, USNPS; D. Briceland, USNPS; W. Burch, Yale University; D. Dottavio, USNPS; D. Field, University of Wisconsin; K. Hornbeck, USNPS; J. O'Leary, Purdue University; R. Graham, University of Waterloo; and J. Piene, USNPS. Where appropriate I have noted these sources of particular information obtained from this personal correspondence. Any errors, omissions or misinterpretations are, of course, my own responsibility.

3. Details of the USNPS proposal are drawn from personal communications with G. Patten, USNPS; and D. Briceland, USNPS and associated internal background documentation supplied by D. Briceland.

4. The choice of this particular concept to describe the subject matter of an intramural social science program is somewhat idiosyncratic to the agency. On the positive side, it appears to originate; on one hand, from the established social science tradition and theory of human ecology. It also sits nicely in apposition to the previously well established bureaucratic concepts of the Service: the Natural Resource System and the Natural Resource Management Program. On the negative side, however, the concept of human resource management already has a specific and well defined meaning in general public administration theory within the U.S. government that is different and much more restrictive. In that context the term is new administrative jargon for total personnel management.

5. Internal working document: U.S. National Park Service, FY89 Social Science Budget Initiative, May 6, 1987.

6. The source of these definitions is the annual publication of Statistics Canada on Canada's science effort, Federal Scientific Activities 1985-86, Minister of Supply and Services Canada, 1986 Catalogue 88-204E.

7. The definitions used in this discussion chapter and the Canadian government reporting of scientific activity in general are compatible with those put forward by the OECD in the Frascati Manual, *Organization for Economic Cooperation and Development, 1976: Research and experimental development* and by UNESCO in its *Manual for Statistics on Scientific and Technological Activities*.

8. Some of the significant differences between the scientific activities of the Canadian and American resource management agencies occur here in the delivery mechanisms being used. While no specific comparative figures are available, it appears to me that, in the social sciences in particular, a much larger proportion of Canadian scientific activity is done intramurally. This may in part be due to our relatively weak administrative arrangements with Canadian universities. In addition, when Canadian scientific work is done extramurally, the major part is performed by private industry consultants. In U.S. resource management agencies, on the other hand, it appears to me that the bulk of the work is performed by university personnel working either on cooperative study projects, university based experimental stations, or special temporary appointments.

9. Again, while I may be incorrect in my assessments of American resource agency social science programs, it is my impression that the *mix* is relatively heavily weighted towards fairly basic research that is driven primarily by theoretical concerns and academic interests. The Canadian Parks Service agency's social science program mix, on the other hand, is primarily weighted towards direct applied research targeted to immediate management requirements with some secondary but growing interest in experimental development. The weakness here is that little or no attention is given to basic research issues.

10. Internal Memorandum, J. Beaman, Director, Socio-Economic Branch, Canadian Parks Service, *Riding Mountain Management Plan Review*, August 29, 1986.

11. Internal Memorandum, W. Smith, Evaluation and Analysis Division, Socio-Economic Branch, Canadian Parks Service, *Riding Mountain Operations Improvement Program #67899*, August 20, 1987.

REFERENCES

Hughes, J. M. 1986. The role of the university in government science. *Proceedings of the Fourth Triennial Conference on Research in the National Parks and Equivalent Reserves*. Fort Collins, CO: Colorado State University.

Socio-Economic Branch (SEB), Evaluation and Analysis Division. 1987. *The Environment - Economy Relationship: A Perspective*. Ottawa: Canadian Parks Service, Environment Canada.

Socio-Economic Research, Ontario Regional Office. 1987. *Strategy for the Socio-Economic Analysis in the Capital Project Development Process*. Cornwall: Environment Canada, Parks.

Whiting, P.G. 1987. *Project Options Analysis*. Ottawa: Socio-Economic Branch, Environment Canada, Parks.

II

USER EXPERIENCES
AND
PREFERENCES

CHAPTER 4

OUTDOOR RECREATION PARTICIPATION AND PREFERENCES BY BLACK AND WHITE CHICAGO HOUSEHOLDS

John F. Dwyer
USDA Forest Service
North Central Forest Experiment Station

Ray Hutchison
University of Wisconsin-Green Bay

The President's Commission on Americans Outdoors (1987) reports that *our greatest recreation needs are in urban areas close to home* and that *many urban residents have special needs*. However, in many instances planners and managers have difficulty serving these special urban needs because they lack information about them. A review of the recreation literature suggests that little is known about the recreation preferences and patterns of the urban black population, which is the largest minority group in Chicago and in many other large cities (Wendling 1981). Consequently, planners and managers do not know what approaches should be taken to provide recreation opportunities for this group. As a step toward filling this void, this chapter reports on an effort to more precisely delineate the outdoor recreation patterns and preferences of black and white Chicago households, compare these patterns, and explore explanations for similarities and differences. It also discusses recommendations for recreation resource management and research.

Our research is based on a secondary analysis of data collected on recreation participation as part of the Illinois Statewide Comprehensive Outdoor Recreation Planning process. The Illinois effort, designed to forecast participation in recreation activities for the next several decades, included a telephone survey of 10,402 households selected by random digit dialing. Our analysis is based on responses by 269 black and 481 white non-Hispanic Chicago households. The data reflect several aspects of recreation behavior including participation (percent of households where at least one individual engaged in the activity), frequency of participation (days by the household in the previous year), and distance travelled to the most frequently used site. In addition, questions were asked about preferences for site development, social interaction, and the importance of *free time*.

Data were also gathered on household structure and social background characteristics of the household head. Not enough complete cases were received to examine variations within the black or white group, consequently the analysis is confined to comparisons between the two groups. This is done with recognition of the significant variation in outdoor recreation preferences and behavior within each group. The present study is to provide policy makers with general guides for meeting the needs of these groups and to suggest research that will provide more specific recommendations for recreation resource planning and management.

REVIEW OF THE LITERATURE

Previous studies show that urban blacks are more inclined to concentrate their recreation activities closer to home than are urban whites. Kornegay and Warren (1969) and Enosh, Christiansen, Staniforth and Cooper (1975) report vacation travel to be less frequent among black households, and even when vacations were taken, the distance was much shorter than for white households. O'Leary and Benjamin (1982) report that for a wide-ranging set of recreation activities, blacks were more likely than whites to use city/town resources than rural resources. They also found higher participation by blacks than by whites for activities ordinarily engaged in close to home. Greater use by blacks of local parks and less use of state and national parks is reported by Yancey and Snell (1971) and Craig (1972). Enosh *et al.* (1975) report a greater proportion of black households participating in picnicking and park activities. Washburne and Wall (1980) report that in activities ordinarily engaged in closer to home, black participation was most similar to that of whites. Hauser (1962) indicates that the greater the degree of urbanization, the greater the similarity between white and non-white participation in particular activities. A study of black and white fifth grade Chicago public school children indicates that black students who had visited forests were more likely to have done so close to home than were their white counterparts (Metro, Dwyer and Dreschler 1981).

Previous research suggests that blacks are more likely than whites to prefer *meeting people* over *getting away* as well as *developed sites* over *preserved sites*. Cheek, Field and Burdge (1976) report that blacks favor interaction with other groups when involved in outdoor recreation. Hutchison (1988) reports that in Chicago parks, blacks were more likely than whites to participate in group rather than individual activities. Black preferences for *developed* recreation sites are also reported by Peterson (1977), Washburne (1978), and Washburne and Wall (1980). Weak black preferences for *getting away* and *preserved sites* are suggested by somewhat negative attitudes toward experiences associated with nature, wildlife, and rural parks and preserves that are reported by Dorsey (1972), Kellert (1984), Meeker (1971) and Washburne (1978). Peterson (1977) reports that black teenagers, both male and female, are more likely to prefer urban rather than rural parks than are their white counterparts. Strong black preferences for *meeting people* and *developed sites* as well as substantial participation in organized camping may be attributed, in part, to higher black participation in voluntary organizations within the local community such as churches or clubs that sponsor retreats or other meetings at camps and other developed recreation sites (Babchuk and Booth 1969, Babchuk and Thompson 1962, Antunes and Gaitz 1975, Olsen 1970, Williams, Babchuk and Johnson 1973).

Washburne and Wall (1980) report significantly higher black preferences for spending federal recreation funds in urban areas and for more facilities. A study of users and nearby residents of neighborhood parks in Chicago indicates heavy use of these resources and strong support for their continued management and maintenance by both blacks and whites. However, blacks were much more concerned with the maintenance of these parks than whites (Joseph, 1980). This concern may have been heightened by greater use of these parks by families and other groups. Washburne and Wall (1980) report inadequate maintenance as a significant barrier to the use of urban parks by blacks.

Previous studies have shown that black preferences for specific outdoor recreation activities also differ from those of whites. Kornegay and Warren (1969), Washburne (1978), and Washburne and Wall (1980) report that if we look at preferences for activities rather than activities actually engaged in, black/white differences may increase rather than decrease.

The reasons behind black/white differences in recreation preferences and behavior continues to be debated. Two viewpoints predominate in the literature, each with a distinctly different implication for recreation resource management (Hutchison 1988, Hutchison and Fidel 1984, Wendling 1981, Washburne 1978). The *marginality* perspective holds that black/white differences are attributable to the generally lower socio-economic position of blacks in society. It calls for efforts to overcome the barriers to participation and enjoyment that are the result of that position, so that black/white differences will disappear. The *ethnicity* perspective attributes black/white differences to the preferences of a distinctive black subculture. It calls for efforts to provide the different opportunities sought by the black subculture. The empirical test generally applied to these perspectives is to control for socio-economic variables and attribute the associated reductions in black/white differences to marginality and the differences that remain to ethnicity. Even when the test is applied, the results are widely divergent in the different applications, offering support for both the marginality and ethnicity perspectives. However, the ethnicity approach as usually implemented is problematic in its underlying assumption of homogeneity within the black population and its assertion that blacks represent a distinct *ethnic* group (Hutchison 1988).

Based on the foregoing review of the literature, we propose the following hypotheses in the present study:

1. Participation by white households will exceed that of black households for activities that ordinarily take place substantial distances away from home.

2. Among households that participate in a given activity, white households are likely to travel greater distances to their most frequently used site than are black households.

3. Black households will be more likely than white households to select *visit or meet new people* over *getting away from a lot of other people* and will emphasize the need to *develop facilities and conveniences for people* over *preserve the area in its natural state*.

4. It is not clear whether differences between black and white participation patterns will persist after controlling for socio-economic variables. Consequently support for both the *marginality* and *ethnicity* perspectives will likely be found for explaining black/white differences.

RESULTS

Participation

Participation by white households exceeded that of black households for 19 of the 23 activities studied (Table 1). In 11 instances these differences were statistically significant (p < .05), spanning all six major activity categories. Black participation exceeded that of whites in four activities; but in no case was the difference statistically significant (p < .05). Although large differences were found for black and white participation in particular activities, a ranking of activities by percent of households participating was similar for the two groups. Predominantly urban-based activities top each list, particularly those activities that ordinarily take place close to home. O'Leary and Benjamin (1982) reported similar rankings of activities for urban blacks and whites in Indiana. The clusters of activities in which Chicago households tended to engage are similar for blacks and whites. A factor analysis of the 23 activities (not presented here) identified the following three distinct groups of activities for both blacks and whites: (1) urban activities, (2) camping and overnight hiking, and (3) boating and primitive camping.

Table 1. Participation of Black and White Chicago Households in 23 Selected Outdoor Recreation Activities

Activity	%Black Households	%White Households	Difference (1)-(2)
Swimming			
Pools	40	35	5
Lake Michigan	23	32	-9*
Other beaches	7	28	-21*
Biking and non-motorized riding			
Day hiking	13	31	-18*
Overnight hiking	4	6	-2
Bicycling	30	32	-2
Horseback riding	15	17	-2
Boating			
Large horsepower motorboating	3	14	-11*
Motorboating on Lake Michigan	5	7	-2
Small horsepower motorboating	2	8	-6*
Lake canoeing	3	5	-2
River canoeing	2	5	-3*
Lake Michigan sailing	4	6	-2
Sailing on other lakes	2	3	-1
Camping			
Developed	10	20	-10*
Organized	9	7	2
Primitive	2	5	-3*
Transient	2	5	-3*
Overnight Lodging			
Lodging without housekeeping facilities	6	14	-8*
Lodging with housekeeping facilities	8	11	-3
Off-road vehicles			
Motorcycles	4	4	<1
Snowmobiling	<1	4	-4*
4-wheel drive	2	1	1

*difference significant at 0.05 level

Days of Participation

For the set of activities studied, black households that participated in an activity tended to engage in fewer days of the activity than whites, averaging 78 percent of white participation for the total set of activities (Table 2). Although the percent of households participating in 23 activities points heavily toward higher participation for whites (Table 1), the black/white pattern in median days per participating household in each activity was more diverse. Because of the small number of responses for each activity (especially among blacks), we can investigate only 11 activities in greater detail, and black households reported more days of participation than whites for five of these activities (Table 2). However, as with participation, the general pattern in days of participation points toward a greater concentration of black recreation activity close to home.

Travel Distance

Comparisons of distances travelled by black and white households engaging in a particular activity are based on the median travel distance to the most frequently used site (Table 3). Black households tended to travel shorter distances than whites for a given activity. White households had longer median travel distances for eight activities, travel distances were the same for one activity, and black households travelled longer distances for only two activities. One of the two instances in which blacks had a longer median travel distance was a difference of four miles for bicycling on trails by blacks compared to three miles by whites; the other instance is more substantial and involves a median of 148 miles for organized camping by blacks compared to 100 miles by whites. Black participation in organized camping might be linked with a high rate of black participation in voluntary and church groups, some of which have organized camps.

Activities in which black households were as likely to participate as white households tended to be those with short travel distances such as swimming at pools and bicycling on trails (Tables 1 and 3). Black participation is similar to whites in seven of eight activities in which Chicago residents have a median travel distance of 40 miles or less but similar to whites in only five of 15 activities with median travel distances of greater than 40 miles.

Black households have higher median days of participation in five of eight activities for which the median travel distance is less than 100 miles but none of the three activities with a median travel distance of more than 100 miles. Days of participation for black households are especially high compared to whites for activities that generally take place close to home,

Table 2.   Median Days of Participation in 23 Selected Outdoor Recreation
Activities per Participating Chicago Household, per Year

Activity	Black Households	White Households	Difference (1)-(2)
Swimming			
Pools	20	14	+6
Lake Michigan	9	8	+1
Other beaches	10	7	+3
Biking and non-motorized riding			
Day hiking	5	6	-1
Overnight hiking	3	4	-1
Bicycling	30	16	+14
Horseback riding	5	3	+2
Boating			
Large horsepower motorboating	2	7	-5
Motorboating on Lake Michigan	4	8	-4
Small horsepower motorboating	3[a]	10	-7[b]
Lake canoeing	5[a]	6	-1[b]
River canoeing	10[a]	4	+6[b]
Lake Michigan sailing	4[a]	10	-6[b]
Sailing on other lakes	4[a]	7	-3[b]
Camping			
Developed	4	5	-1
Organized	5	6	-1
Primitive	9[a]	5	+4[b]
Transient	5[a]	4	+1[b]
Overnight lodging			
Lodging without housekeeping facilities	3	5	-2
Lodging with housekeeping facilities	4	7	-3
Off-road vehicles			
Motorcycles	5[a]	6	-1[b]
Snowmobiling	21[a]	5	+16[b]
4-wheel drive	7[a]	3	+4[b]

[a] median based on less than 10 observations and consequently suspect
[b] difference is suspect because one of the medians was based on less than 10 observations

Table 3.   Median Travel Distance to the Most Frequently Used Site, by Activity for Black and White Chicago Households

Activity	Chicago Households (1)	Black Households (2)	White Households (3)	Differences (2)-(3)
*Transient camping	302	700[a]	300	400[b]
Lodging with housekeeping	201	127	292	-165
*Primitive camping	199	90[a]	400	-310[b]
*Lodging without housekeeping	180	156	201	-45
Overnight hiking	151	119[a]	280	-161[b]
Organized camping	126	148	100	48
*Developed camping	121	120	125	-5
*Small horsepower motorboating	101	60[a]	111	-51[b]
*River canoeing	100	78	105	-27[b]
Lake canoeing	98	98[a]	99	-1[b]
*Snowmobiling	91	1[a]	99	-98[b]
Sailing other than Lake Michigan	91	100[a]	91	9[b]
*Swimming other than Lake Michigan	90	50	86	-35
*Large horsepower motorboating	85	250[a]	80	170[b]
*Day hiking	50	15	75	-60
Horseback riding	36	25	46	-21
4-wheel drive	33	30[a]	55	-25[b]
Off-road motorcycles	30	42[a]	20	22[b]
Lake Michigan sailing	10	3[a]	10	-7[b]
Motorboating on Lake Michigan	10	8	10	-2
*Swimming at Lake Michigan	5	5	5	0
Biking on trails	3	4	3	1
Swimming at pools	3	2	4	-2

*activity in which a significantly larger portion of white households than black households participated.
[a]median based on less than 10 observations and consequently suspect
[b]difference is suspect because one of the medians was based on less than 10 observations

such as bicycling and swimming at pools. O'Leary and Benjamin (1982) report a similar pattern of a greater number of days participating for blacks in primarily urban-based activities.

The only activity in which black households have higher participation and participation rates than whites is swimming at pools. This activity has the shortest median travel distance to the most frequently used site.

Preferences

Three general attitudinal measures permit a test of differences in perceptions between the black and white households. Respondents were asked whether (1) they viewed outdoor recreation as an opportunity to *visit or meet new people* or for *getting away from a lot of other people*; (2) in the development of new recreation areas it is more important to *preserve the area in its natural state* or to *develop facilities and conveniences for people*; and (3) when meeting new people, they preferred to talk mainly about their *work*, their *free-time activities*, or *both*. Blacks and whites gave significantly different ($p < .05$) responses to questions concerning their preferences for social interaction and for recreation area development. Blacks indicated a strong orientation toward *meeting people* rather than *getting away* whereas whites divided their responses evenly between the two categories (Table 4). With regard to site development, blacks strongly preferred *developed facilities and conveniences* rather than *preserved natural areas*, while whites strongly preferred *preserved natural areas* (Table 5). Cross-tabulating the responses to these two questions shows that *meet people* and *develop* are the predominant responses for blacks while *get away* and *preserve* are the most common for whites (Table 6). The responses tend to correspond to the concentration of black participation in activities that are ordinarily engaged

Table 4. Preferences for Social Interaction by Black and White Chicago Households

Preference	Percent of Black Households (N=263)	Percent of White Households (N=468)
To meet people	51	36
To get away	27	35
Both	15	18
Neither	8	12

X^2 = 17.24, p < .001

58

Table 5.   Preferences for Development of Recreation Areas by Black and
White Chicago Households

Preference	Percent of Black Households (N=257)	Percent of White Households (N=463)
Preserved	27	57
Developed	53	24
Both	20	19

$X^2 = 72.42, p < .001$

in close to home and are characterized by lots of facilities, site development, and a large number of users. When asked about their preferences for talking about *work* or *free-time* activities when meeting new people, both blacks and whites have a similar probability of mentioning free-time activities (Table 7). Therefore, free-time activities seem to have a similar significance for both groups.

Social Class and Ethnicity

A direct test of the effects of social class and ethnicity across the 23 activities would require a comparison of *race* (as a proxy variable for ethnicity) and *income* (as a proxy variable for marginality). Because of the limited number of cases for which we had income data, we could only make two tests of the marginality and ethnicity perspectives. In the first we used education as a surrogate measure to estimate the possible effects of marginality on participation in activities. In the second, where our analysis was not constrained to individual activities and the limited cases available, we used income as a surrogate measure for marginality in an analysis of recreation preferences.

The set of multiple linear regression models were estimated to predict participation in the eleven activities that had a significant difference in participation between blacks and whites. These models include race; household size; presence or absence of children; and gender, age, and education of the household head. In eight of the cases, the coefficient forrace was significant. And in five of those instances, race had the largest standardized coefficient, offering support for those who advocate the ethnicity perspective. In the other three instances race was not significant.

Table 6.   Cross Tabulation of Preferences for Social Interaction and
           Development of Recreation Areas for Black and White Chicago
           Households

| | Site Development | | | |
| | Black Households[a] | | White Households[b] | |
Preference for Social Interaction	Preserved	Developed	Preserved	Developed
To meet people	32	78	90	48
To get away	19	34	104	30
Total	51	112	194	78

[a] $X^2 = .48$, ns
[b] $X^2 = 4.52$, p $< .05$

However, the limited explanatory power of the equations and the limited
variables used precludes a strong endorsement of either perspective.

The stronger black preference for *meeting people* and *developed sites*
persisted even when accounting for income, which offers additional support
for the ethnicity perspective.

DISCUSSION

The results correspond closely to the expectations raised by previous
studies.   Each of the hypotheses outlined at the beginning of the chapter
are supported by the data presented here.

The most significant underlying dimension in the differences between the
recreation participation and preferences of black and white Chicago
households is the stronger urban orientation of black households.   It is
primarily urban-based activities in which black participation (percent of
households) and participation rates (days) approach or exceed those of
whites.   Lower participation and participation rates for blacks are most
common in activities for which Chicago residents ordinarily travel the longest
distances.   Black participants in particular activities also tended to travel
shorter distances than whites. Blacks were more likely than whites to prefer
meeting people and *developed sites*, both of which are more likely to
characterize experiences in or near urban areas.

Although this and other research tends to confirm the more highly urban
orientation of the recreation behavior of urban blacks in comparison to

Table 7. Preferences for Talking about Work, Free Time Activities, or Both when Meeting New People, Black and White Chicago Households

Preference	Black Households	White Households
Work	10	9
Free Time	57	62
Both	22	21
Neither	11	8

$X^2 = 1.99$, ns

urban whites, researchers disagree about the reasons for this difference. Like many of those before it, this study leaves unanswered questions in this area.

The persistence of black/white differences in participation after accounting for household characteristics adds support to the ethnicity argument. The existence of significant black/white differences in preferences for site development and social interaction after accounting for income also supports the ethnicity theory. However, these findings are far from overwhelming and other results should be considered as well.

The higher concentration of black outdoor recreation participation in activities engaged in closer to home, as well as lower median travel distances for blacks engaged in specific activities, cannot easily be attributed to either the marginality or ethnicity perspective. The shorter distances might be the result of limited resources available to black households (marginality), or blacks may choose activities and areas close to home where they may participate with other persons similar to themselves. Also fear of discrimination in areas more distant from home cannot be ruled out.

Although distance can be interpreted as a cost barrier (i.e., marginality), other costs are associated with particular activities such as equipment costs (i.e., off-road vehicles and boats) and daily expenses for fuel, supplies, rentals, and user fees. Washburne (1978) and Washburne and Wall (1980) report that blacks are more likely than whites to report cost and transportation as barriers to participation. All of the activities in the present study for which black and white participation are similar took place close to home, involved low costs, and were not necessarily associated with a natural environment. Many could be categorized as opportunities that occurred on developed sites and provided opportunities to meet people. At the same time many of the activities with low black participation could be characterized as occurring on preserved sites, providing opportunities for getting away from people, and requiring substantial supplies, equipment, etc.

It is not yet clear to what extent black/white differences are attributable to the socio-economic constraints placed on blacks (i.e., the marginality perspective), to a distinctive black subculture (i.e., the ethnicity perspective), or to other causes. This study offers some encouragement for each of these explanations and the associated policy implications. In other words, distinct black preferences should be recognized and efforts undertaken to meet them; but barriers to black participation should also be recognized in some kinds of outdoor recreation and efforts undertaken to break them down.

The foregoing discussion focused on two important population segments -- urban blacks and urban whites. Most of the attention has been given to differences between the two groups and not to similarities between the groups or variations within each group. This is because our purpose was to determine if different approaches should be taken to providing recreation opportunities for each group. However, it is important that similarities between groups as well as variations within each group be recognized in efforts to provide improved opportunities for recreation.

Similarities between urban blacks and whites include a strong urban orientation and attaching great importance to free-time activities. Efforts to enhance opportunities for recreation in and near urban areas are likely to benefit both groups.

In interpreting the results, it is important to avoid stereotyping any group in terms of the typical or average behavior. Behaviors and preferences differ widely within each group; consequently, a wide range of opportunities should be provided for each. Although urban blacks as a group tended to participate more heavily in urban-oriented activities and expressed preferences for developed sites and opportunities to meet people, there are most likely significant numbers of urban blacks who used wilderness resources and strongly supported the preservation of these areas and the associated opportunities for solitude. The group means presented and discussed are intended only as broad guides to policy because they were formed by aggregating the behavior of diverse members of each group.

IMPLICATIONS FOR MANAGEMENT

Chicago households, particularly blacks, devote a significant amount of their outdoor recreation time to activities close to home. Consequently, efforts to enhance the recreation opportunities for Chicago residents, and particularly blacks, should give significant attention to nearby resources. This includes the maintenance of public parks in urban neighborhoods as well as nearby recreation areas.

Second, the limited black participation in activities that ordinarily take place far from an urban environment poses a difficult question for managers and planners, particularly in light of limited knowledge of the reasons for such behavior. Should they accept these differences as due to cultural differences (i.e., adopt the ethnicity perspective) or undertake programs to break down barriers to wider recreation participation by blacks (i.e., adopt the marginality perspective)? Below are some possible means of increasing and enhancing the experiences of urban blacks in rural environments as a guide for those circumstances where it appears appropriate to do so.

1. Give particular emphasis to areas close to cities -- perhaps county, state, and federal areas near urban areas. This will reduce barriers posed by travel, provide opportunities for group outings, and make a wider range of opportunities available for urbanites.

2. Provide high-quality opportunities for activities that appear to be especially popular with urban blacks, such as bicycling, swimming, fishing, and off-road vehicle riding.

3. Provide means for catering to large groups as well as opportunities for reservations by churches and other social groups.

4. Provide increased levels of facility development and maintenance.

5. Initiate education, information, and interpretive programs aimed at enhancing the experiences of urban blacks in a natural environment.

A component of these programs might be aimed at public school children and their teachers.

The above suggestions assume that it is an appropriate policy to make a wider range of recreation opportunities available to the urban black population. However, we should not assume that blacks *ought to behave like whites*. We could as easily argue that urban whites should be encouraged to act like urban blacks and spend an increased portion of their leisure time close to home -- with the resulting benefits of reduced travel costs and increased opportunities for large group outings.

The strong black orientation to *developed sites* and *meeting people* suggests that efforts to enhance recreation opportunities for blacks should give particular attention to developed sites and opportunities for social interaction. This often points toward large, developed areas. Strong black preferences for well maintained and litter free areas appear consistent with such opportunities. Whites, on the other hand, are more likely to prefer preserved sites and the opportunities to avoid large groups. These needs are more likely to be met at small, undeveloped sites where maintenance and litter may not be significant considerations in relation to other site attributes.

Some support was found for both the marginality and ethnicity explanations for black/white differences in recreation behavior, suggesting that managers give careful attention to the specific needs associated with both social class and ethnic differences both within and between these population groups in public involvement sessions and other efforts to more fully understand urban needs.

Finally, limited knowledge to guide efforts in this area calls for careful evaluations of the effectiveness of those undertakings aimed at enhancing the recreation opportunities for urban blacks.

IMPLICATIONS FOR RESEARCH

The set of activities included in this study limits the implications that can be drawn from the analysis. With the strong orientation of Chicago households, especially blacks, to urban activities it would be desirable if subsequent research aimed at urbanites would include additional urban-based activities such as picnicking, observing plants and animals, attending outdoor events, fishing, walking/hiking, and participating in sports. It also may be useful to extend the analysis beyond outdoor recreation to a wider range of leisure activities.

Although the focus on households in the present study is useful, it would be helpful also to have information on which individuals in the household participated in particular activities. The composition of the household also is likely to be important in explaining individual behavior. Is it a nuclear family, extended family, single-headed household (of which gender), etc.? This would allow for a more detailed analysis that goes beyond participation to the types of leisure groups and the meaning of leisure in the family environment.

Although actual recreation behavior reveals preferences, it is also useful to know what activities individuals would like to engage in if they could. Such an effort would have to be carefully designed to present participants with the full range of options available to them, including those that they have never experienced, so that their choices would not be constrained by existing knowledge, resources, and participation patterns. It could begin by intensively interviewing small groups of urban blacks to obtain realistic and complete responses and perhaps follow the general format of *focus group* sessions commonly used in market research.

Although it is useful to identify activities engaged in and those that are preferred, it is at least as important for managers to know the preferred settings or environments for these activities. Many of the issues faced by recreation resource planners and managers concern the management of settings. Furthermore, the limited questions concerning preferences for site development and social interaction used in this study suggest significant black/white differences that appear to have implications for resource management. This information would be useful in efforts to plan for and manage specific recreation areas. Replicating the work by Schroeder and Anderson (1984) concerning preferences for and perceptions of urban parks with urban black subjects might be particularly effective. Numerous opportunities also seem to exist for making use of market research techniques.

Exploring reasons for the strong urban orientation of Chicago blacks and the low level of black participation in many nonurban activities may provide significant guidance for recreation resource planning and management. It may be that Chicago blacks engage heavily in outdoor recreation activities not included in this study, such as picnicking, or prefer nearby urban resources for a number of other reasons, including a desire to participate in large family or other social groups. Perhaps blacks prefer intensively managed open spaces and sports facilities such as are often found in Chicago parks. On the other hand, the urban-based recreation behavior of black households may be the result of limited resources for travel, fear of discriminatory behavior, lack of skills and equipment for rural-based activities such as primitive camping, or lack of knowledge of rural opportunities. If barriers are limiting the participation and enjoyment of black households, these barriers should be identified and programs developed to remove them. Like the effort suggested above, this undertaking might best be accomplished with in-depth interviews or small group discussions rather than a large survey such as the one that formed the basis of this study.

Further efforts to identify the ethnic differences in recreation behavior could benefit from (1) considering additional urban groups such as Hispanics and Asians, and (2) using additional concepts and variables to reflect ethnicity (as suggested by Hutchison 1987, 1988). Hispanic and Asian communities are becoming increasingly significant urban populations in Chicago and elsewhere. In addition, including other ethnic groups in the analysis would provide new perspectives on inter- and intra-group differences. Limited research has been conducted on the attributes of ethnic subcultures that influence preferences for recreation activities and environments. It is important that this research be concerned with cultural influences on preferences for site attributes as well as recreation activities.

Because evidence indicates that much of the recreation activity of Chicago residents is at the neighborhood level, subsequent research should emphasize recreation behavior at that level. This is particularly important in research on ethnic groups because many Chicago neighborhoods are dominated by a single ethnic group. Such studies would be particularly useful if they would identify specific recreation areas or parts of those areas that are used by each group as well as the attributes of users and nonusers toward the management of those areas. This effort would build on the work of Klobus-Edwards (1981), Joseph (1980), and Woodard (1988).

Much can be learned also from research that evaluates the effectiveness of policies and programs aimed at increasing and enhancing the recreation experiences of urban blacks and other groups. Such research must focus on how individuals perceived and responded to these efforts.

In summary, this study has supported and extended a number of previous findings and moved us a little closer toward identifying differences in the recreation patterns of urban ethnic groups and understanding those differences. It has suggested some directions for management and research aimed at enhancing the opportunities available to urban blacks. However, much more needs to be learned about the preferences of this and other urban ethnic groups before we can develop comprehensive guides for recreation programs aimed at serving diverse urban ethnic groups.

ACKNOWLEDGEMENTS

The authors are indebted to the Illinois Department of Conservation and Southern Illinois University for the data used in this study.

REFERENCES

Antunes, G. and C.M. Gaitz. 1975. Ethnicity and participation: Study of Mexican-Americans, blacks, and whites. *American Journal of Sociology* 80:1192-1121.

Babchuk, N. and A. Booth. 1969. Voluntary association membership: A longitudinal analysis. *American Sociological Review* 34:31-4.

Babchuk, N. and R. Thompson. 1962. Voluntary associations of negroes. *American Sociological Review* 27:647-655.

Cheek, N.H., D. Field and R.J. Burdge. 1976. *Leisure and Recreation Places.* Ann Arbor, MI: Ann Arbor Science Publishers, Inc.

Craig, W. 1972. Recreational Activity patterns in a small negro urban community: The role of the cultural base. *Economic Geography* 48:107-115.

Dorsey, A.H.H. 1972. *A Survey Study of the Comparative Status of Understanding and Reasoning in Conservation Concepts by Ninth Grade Students in the Public Schools of South Carolina.* Ph.D. Thesis, University of Virginia, 123 pp.

Enosh, R., D. Christiansen, D. Staniforth and R.B. Cooper. 1975. *Effects of Selected Socio-Economic Characteristics on Recreation Patterns in Low Income Urban Areas: Part II.* Madison, WI: Recreation Resources Center, University of Wisconsin-Extension. Department of Agricultural Economics, Madison, WI.

Hauser, P.M. 1962. Demographic and ecological changes as factors in outdoor recreation. *Trends in American Living and Outdoor Recreation.* ORRRC Study Report 22, Washington D.C.: U.S. Government Printing Office.

Hutchison, R. and K. Fidel. 1984. Mexican-American recreation activities: A reply to McMillen. *Journal of Leisure Research* 16:344-349.

Hutchison, R. 1987. Race, ethnicity, and urban recreation: Blacks, whites, and hispanics in Chicago's public parks. *Journal of Leisure Research* 19:205-222.

Hutchison, R. 1988. A critique of race, ethnicity, and social class in recent leisure-recreation research. *Journal of Leisure Research* 20:10-30.

Joseph, A. 1980. *Race and Class in Chicago Parks.* Chicago IL: North Central Forest Experiment Station, 58pp.

Kellert, S.R. 1984. Urban Americans perceptions of animals and the natural environment. *Urban Ecology* 8:209-228.

Klobus-Edwards, P. 1981. Race, residence, and leisure style: Some policy implications. *Leisure Sciences* 4:95-112.

Kornegay, F.A. and D.I. Warren. 1969. *A Comparative Study of Life Styles and Social Attitudes of Middle Income Status Whites and Negroes in Detroit.* Detroit, MI: Detroit Urban League.

Meeker, J.W. 1971. Red, white, and black in national parks. *The North American Review* Fall:3-7.

Metro, L.J., J.F. Dwyer, and E.S. Dreschler. 1981. *Forest Experiences of Fifth-Grade Chicago Public School Students.* Research Paper NC-126, St. Paul, MN: U. S. Department of Agriculture, Forest Service, North Central Forest Experiment Station, 6p.

O'Leary, J.T. and P.J. Benjamin. 1982. *Ethnic Variation in Leisure Behavior: The Indiana Case.* Sta. Bulletin 349. West Lafayette, IN: Purdue University Department of Forestry and Natural Resources, Agricultural Experiment Station, 45p.

Olsen, M.E. 1970. Social and political participation of blacks. *American Sociological Review* 33:682-697.

Peterson, G.L. 1977. Recreational preferences of urban teenagers: The Influence of Cultural and Environmental Attributes. *Children, Nature, and the Urban Environment: Proceedings of a Symposium Fair.* USDA Forest Service General Technical Report NE-30, p. 113-121. Broomall, PA: USDA Forest Service, North Central Forest Experiment Station.

President's Commission on Americans Outdoors. 1987. *Americans Outdoors: The Legacy, the Challenge.* Washington, D.C.: Island Press.

Schroeder, H.W. and L.M. Anderson. 1984. Perceptions of personal safety in urban recreation sites. *Journal of Leisure Research* 16:178-194.

Washburne, R.F. 1978. Black under-participation in wildland recreation: Alternative explanations. *Leisure Sciences* 1:175-189.

Washburne, R.F. and P. Wall. 1980. *Cities, Wild Areas, and Black Leisure: In Search of Explanations for Black/White Differences in Outdoor Recreation.* USDA Forest Service Research Paper INT-249. Ogden, UT: Intermountain Forest and Range Experiment Station, 13 pp.

Wendling, R.C. 1981. Black/white differences in outdoor recreation behavior: State-of-the-art and recommendations for management and research. *Proceedings of the Conference on Social Research in National Parks and Wildland Areas.* March 21-22, 1980, Gatlinburg, TN:Great Smoky Mountains National Park, 106-117.

Williams, J.A., N. Babchuk and D.R. Johnson. 1973. Voluntary associations and minority status: A comparative analysis of anglo, black, and Mexican-Americans. *American Sociological Review* 38:637-646.

Woodard, M.D. 1988. Class, regionality, and leisure among urban black Americans: The post-civil rights era. *Journal of Leisure Research* 20:87-105.

Yancey, W.L. and J. Snell. 1971. *Parks as Aspects of Leisure in the Inner-City: An Exploratory Investigation.* Paper presented at the American Association for the Advancement of Science Meetings in Philadelphia.

CHAPTER 5

SOCIAL ENCOUNTERS AS A CUE FOR DETERMINING WILDERNESS QUALITY

Steven D. Moore
School of Renewable Natural Resources
University of Arizona

James W. Shockey
Department of Sociology
University of Arizona

Stanley K. Brickler
School of Renewable Natural Resources
University of Arizona

The outdoor recreation production model of Brown (1984) proposes that the output of resource management (with regard to recreation) is recreational opportunities. When combined with consumer inputs such as time, skills, and experience, recreation opportunities lead to recreation behavior which eventually results in recreation experiences. Experiences, in turn, are the basis from which people derive outdoor recreation benefits. Recreation opportunities at a particular setting may be viewed as bundles of setting attributes (Clark and Stankey 1985), attributes being the raw material from which visitors build experiences. This relationship between attributes and experiences is the basis of the Recreation Opportunity Spectrum (ROS) model (Brown and Driver 1978, Clark and Stankey 1979) which is currently the framework for managing recreation on many federal lands.

People thinking of visiting a wilderness area may conceive that it will have certain kinds of attributes and, accordingly, that certain kinds of experiences may be derived in the area. For example, potential visitors may conceive that wilderness X receives few visitors and that there they should be able to derive an experience of solitude. The conception that people bring to wilderness may be described as a schema (Gardner 1987, Lakoff 1987): *an idealized cognitive representation of what wilderness, or even a particular wilderness, is like* (Moore 1989:18). Wilderness schemata are constructed from past experiences and socialization processes.

As hypothesized by Hendee, Stankey, and Lucas (1978), if a visitor arrives at an area and the real attributes do not match the idealized attributes of his or her wilderness schema, the visitor may fit a new schema (e.g. *non-wilderness* or *park*) to the area. In this manner, the visitor could continue to have an enjoyable recreational experience (though not the one originally conceived). Support for this *product shift* hypothesis has come from a longitudinal study of boaters on the Rogue River (Shelby, Bregenzer and Johnson 1986). Between 1977 and 1984 the density of use on the river increased and the boaters became much more likely to describe the area as *semi-wilderness* or *undeveloped recreation* rather than *wilderness*.

In this paper we explore the product shift hypothesis from another angle and hypothesize that increased density of use will cause visitors to perceive that a variety of attributes of the wilderness area have changed, regardless of whether they have in reality. Specifically, we test the hypothesis that higher levels of social encounters will prompt visitors to not only report lowered experiences of solitude, but also lowered evaluations of physical and biological characteristics of the wilderness. In other words, we examine whether social encounters act as a cue that causes people to re-evaluate the schema applied to a wilderness area.

To test this hypothesis, ratings of eight dimensions of a wilderness setting were compared against reported numbers of social encounters. Under our hypothesis, we predicted that each of these dimensions would be influenced by social encounters. The dimensions were *sense of solitude, feeling of freedom, sense of discovery, feeling of untamed wilderness, sense of security, feeling of danger, feeling that no one had ever been there before,* and *feeling of unspoiled wilderness.* The number of groups met or seen during the wilderness visit was used as the social encounter measure.

Besides examining bivariate relationships between the experience dimensions and social encounters, we also tested two additional hypotheses. In hypothesis two, we propose that relationships between ratings on the experience dimensions and social contacts should be affected by the amount of experience the visitor has in the particular setting. Presumably, experienced visitors should have a more realistic schema concerning an area. Thus, if a person had visited the wilderness area one or more times during the recent past, he or she should have a reasonably good idea of what the area is like and how many encounters to expect. Accordingly, more experienced visitors should be less affected by encounters than inexperienced visitors. Hammitt, McDonald and Noe (1984) describe such an effect for a population of river recreationists.

Hypothesis three proposes that social contact is the primary cue used by visitors to re-evaluate their wilderness schema. Statistically, this hypothesis suggests that the effect of social encounters on visitors' ratings of non-social dimensions should remain significant even if encounters with unacceptable amounts of physical and biological impacts are controlled in the analysis. If supported, this hypothesis would indicate that people who did not encounter more non-social impacts than they prefer would still downgrade their rating of the physical and biological setting because of social encounters. In short, real or perceived increases in environmental impacts do not have to be present to effect a product shift.

THE DATA SET

The data base for this paper came from a mail questionnaire survey of visitors to Aravaipa Canyon Wilderness in Arizona. From April 1987 to March 1988, questionnaires were mailed each month to a random sample of people who had reserved permits to visit Aravaipa Canyon during the previous month. The names and addresses of these individuals were obtained from permit records provided by the Bureau of Land Management (the agency responsible for managing the wilderness area). The sampling process provided a stratified random sample of an annual cross-section of wilderness visitors. Eight hundred permit holders were contacted during the sampling process and 664 (83 percent) responses were received.

The four questions used in the following analyses asked respondents to (1) rate the quality of eight dimensions of the wilderness setting; (2) report numbers of social encounters; (3) report the number of visits taken to the area during their lifetime; and (4) indicate whether various environmental impacts were at acceptable levels or more prevalent than preferred. The eight dimensions (which were described previously) were rated on a five-point scale ranging from *very strong* to *weak*. Social encounters were reported as the number of groups met or seen during the most recent visit. This question was also answered on a five-point scale, each category representing a different degree of social contact (e.g., no other groups, one to two groups, three to five groups, six to ten groups, and more than ten groups). Categories of some of these variables were collapsed in the following analyses to allow sufficient cell counts for loglinear analysis. Experience was reported as the number of lifetime visits. This continuous variable was dichotomized into *0-1* and *2 or more* visits for multinomial logit analyses. A dichotomous environmental disturbance item was constructed from items in the questionnaire. It measured whether the respondent had encountered *more than preferred* versus *acceptable amounts* of seven types of impacts: damaged trees or other vegetation; manure from livestock; human feces or toilet paper on the ground; litter; rock fire rings; evidence of campfires (charred logs and ash); and low flying aircraft.

RESULTS

To test the first hypothesis (that visitors use social encounters as a cue to *fit* a schema to a wilderness area), the ratings of eight dimensions of the wilderness setting were compared separately against reported numbers of groups met or seen during a wilderness visit using several loglinear models. The first, or independence, models did not fit (at p < .05) the data in five cases (*sense of solitude, feeling of freedom, feeling of untamed wilderness, feeling that no one had been there before*, and *feeling of unspoiled wilderness*) thus indicating an association in these bivariate comparisons.

Having determined that a relationship exists in these cases, an adequate description of its pattern or form is required. Another loglinear model posits that the association between one of the wilderness dimensions and the number of groups met or seen is the same or uniform in all parts of the bivariate table. Analogous to the assumed relationship in linear regression, as each higher level of a variable is considered, the chances of observing respondents in one higher (or lower) level of the second variable are constant. If the uniform association model fits the data well, then, a very simple description of the relationship's pattern is possible. This description is accomplished with a single odds ratio, which describes the adjacent category association in each 2 x 2 subtable of the larger table. An odds ratio greater than one indicates a positive association between two variables (as they were scaled for analysis); an odds ratio less than one indicates a negative association. An odds ratio of one indicates no association.

Four of the dimension-encounter relationships can be summarized with uniform association, where all of the adjacent-category odds ratios are equal throughout Table 1. The fifth relationship -- *feeling of untamed wilderness* -- could not be so readily simplified and is not discussed further.

In each of the four relationships characterized by uniform association, higher levels of social encounters were associated with a greater likelihood of downgrading ratings of the wilderness dimensions (ie., a negative association -- see Table 1). For example, if a visitor saw one to two groups during a wilderness visit, his or her odds of rating the feeling of solitude *very strong* versus *strong* were 37 percent lower than a visitor who encountered zero groups. Analogous statements can be made for the other relationships, where the effect of social encounters was less pronounced, but still significant.

These results generally support the first hypothesis: social encounters caused visitors to change the way they conceived of the wilderness area. With greater numbers of social encounters, not only did visitors perceive a lessened sense of solitude, but they also perceived lessened feelings of freedom, that no one had been there before, and of unspoiled wilderness. Because of social encounters, people fit a new schema to Aravaipa Canyon Wilderness, a schema that was something less than *pristine*.

Hypotheses two and three were tested by using multinomial logit models to predict ratings of two of the setting dimensions with three independent variables. The two dimensions were *sense of solitude* and *feeling of unspoiled wilderness*. The independent variables were social encounters, lifetime visits, and impacts encountered (see the data section for a description of how these variables were defined). Logit models can be thought of as analogous to regression models where the dependent variable is dichotomous. With a logit model, however, the dependent variable is actually the natural log of the odds that a respondent is observed in one category rather than the other category. In the multinomial logit models estimated here, the dependent variables have three rather than two categories, so that two logit equations are predicted simultaneously.

Hypothesis two (that experience would mediate the setting dimension-contacts relationship) was tested with both dimensions as the dependent variable. Hypothesis three (that social contact was the primary cue used by visitors to effect a product shift) was tested with the model that had *feeling of unspoiled wilderness* as the dependent variable. This variable was assumed to primarily measure respondents' perceptions of physical and biological attributes of the setting.

In the two models all associations between the independent variables were controlled. Accordingly, the results presented in Tables 2 and 3 represent the direct effects of each of the independent variables on ratings of the dimensions, regardless of the level of the other variables. As before, in both models, the relationship between the dependent variables and social contacts was modelled as a uniform association. Also, the relationships between the dependent variables and the other independent variables (experience and impacts) were modelled as linear contrasts. These models more parsimoniously fit the data than corresponding models lacking the uniform association and linear contrast assumptions. Greater parsimony was accomplished without a significant loss in fit. Furthermore, the models permitted summarization of the direct effects in the models with single loglinear parameters. (As with the bivariate, uniform association models

Table 1.   Ratings of four wilderness setting dimensions versus number of groups met or seen: uniform association models.

Experience	Odds Ratio	L^2	DF^a	p
Sense of solitude	.6254	3.044	5	.693
Feeling of freedom	.7559	11.182	8	.192
Feeling that no one had been there before	.8205	8.503	5	.131
Feeling of unspoiled wilderness	.8292	10.540	8	.229

[a]Degrees of freedom vary because some categories were collapsed to accommodate situations of sparse data.

Table 2. Multinomial logit equations for the odds of indicating a very strong versus moderate to none, strong versus moderate to none, and very strong versus strong sense of solitude.

	Logit Coefficients		
	Very strong vs. moderate to none	**Strong vs. moderate to none**	**Very strong vs. strong**
Intercept	.716[a]	.811[a]	.009[b]
Number of groups met or seen			
0	1.002[a]	.501[a]	.501[a]
1-2	.000	.000	.000
3 or more	-1.002[a]	-.501[a]	-.501[a]
Lifetime experience			
0 visits	.110[b]	.055[b]	.055[b]
1 or more visits	-.110[b]	-.055[b]	-.055[b]
Encounters with impacts			
OK	-.007[b]	-.004[b]	-.004[b]
>than preferred	.007[b]	.004[b]	.004[b]
	Odds Ratios Relative to Reference Categories[1]		
Number of groups met or seen			
0	*	*	*
1-2	.37[a]	.61[a]	.61[a]
3 or more	.13[a]	.37[a]	.37[a]
Lifetime experience			
0 visits	*	*	*
1 or more visits	.80[b]	.89[b]	.89[b]
Encounters with impacts			
OK	*	*	*
>than preferred	.99[b]	1.00[b]	1.00[b]

[1]The asterisk (*) refers to the reference category.
[a]$p < .001$
[b]$p < .400$

Table 3. Multinomial logit equations for the odds of indicating a very strong versus moderate to none, strong versus moderate to none, and very strong versus strong feeling of unspoiled wilderness.

	Logit Coefficients		
	Very strong vs. moderate to none	**Strong vs. moderate to none**	**Very strong vs. strong**
Intercept	-1.356[a]	-.390[b]	-.966[a]
Number of groups met or seen			
0	.302[c]	.151[c]	.151[c]
1-2	.000	.000	.000
3 or more	-.302[c]	-.151[c]	-.151[c]
Lifetime experience			
0 visits	-.195[d]	-.097[d]	-.097[d]
1 or more visits	.195[d]	.097[d]	.097[d]
Encounters with impacts			
OK	.461[e]	.230[e]	.230[e]
>than preferred	-.461[e]	-.230[e]	-.230[e]
	Odds Ratios Relative to Reference Categories[1]		
Number of groups met or seen			
0	*	*	*
1-2	.74[c]	.86[c]	.86[c]
3 or more	.55[c]	.74[c]	.74[c]
Lifetime experience			
0 visits	.68[d]	.82[d]	.82[d]
1 or more visits	*	*	*
Encounters with impacts			
OK	*	*	*
>than preferred	.40[e]	.63[e]	.63[e]

[1]The asterisk (*) refers to the reference category.
[a]p<.001
[b]p<.009
[c]p<.110
[d]p<.160
[e]p<.002

described before, associations between the dependent variable and the independent variables could be summarized with one odds ratio.)

The results of the multinomial logit models provide no support for hypothesis two and, at best, very limited support for hypothesis three. In both of the multinomial logit models, lifetime experience, as defined in this study, had no significant effect on ratings of the *sense of solitude* and *feeling of unspoiled wilderness* (see Table 2 and 3). For the solitude model, social encounters retained a significant (p < .001) and substantial effect on ratings of the dimension over both categories of the experience variable. The effect was nearly identical to that of the bivariate model: visitors who encountered one to two groups during a wilderness visit had odds of indicating a *very strong* versus *strong* feeling of solitude that were only 61 percent as high as the odds of visitors who had encountered zero groups. People who encountered three or more groups had odds that were 37 percent as high as the odds of people who encountered zero groups.

With regard to hypothesis three, the relatively weak relationship between the feeling of unspoiled wilderness and social encounters was significant only at p < .11 when the influences of experience and exposure to environmental impacts were controlled (Table 3). Encounters with environmental impacts exerted a fairly strong and statistically significant (p < .002) influence on ratings of unspoiled wilderness. People who encountered more impacts than they preferred had odds of indicating a *very strong* versus *strong* feeling of untamed wilderness that were 63 percent the size of the odds of people who encountered acceptable amounts of impacts.

SUMMARY AND DISCUSSION

Three hypotheses were proposed and tested in this study. First, we proposed that higher levels of social encounters will prompt visitors to not only report lowered experiences of solitude, but also lowered evaluations of physical and biological characteristics of the wilderness. This hypothesis was generally supported. In addition to causing lowered ratings of the sense of solitude in Aravaipa Canyon Wilderness, social encounters also resulted in a lowered rating of the feeling of unspoiled wilderness. Ratings of two additional, primarily social, dimensions of the setting were also affected by social encounters. Ratings of four other dimensions were unaffected by social contact.

Second, we advanced the hypothesis that experience in the wilderness area should mediate that relationship between dimension ratings and social encounters: experienced visitors should be less affected by social contacts than inexperienced visitors. This hypothesis was unsupported. Experienced and inexperienced visitors were equally affected by social encounters. The lack of an effect, though, could be explained by the construction of the variable used to represent experience. Perhaps the *zero* versus *one or more* dichotomy was insufficient to reflect the cognitive input that is required to become familiar with an area. Further analyses could look at different segments of the experience continuum.

Finally, we asserted that if social encounters were a primary cue in causing a product shift, relationships between social contacts and ratings of physical and biological dimensions of the wilderness setting should remain even after controlling for exposure to environmental impacts. This hypothesis was unsupported at generally accepted standards of statistical significance ($p < .05$). Exposure to unacceptable amounts of environmental impacts was the primary cue that led to downgrading of the feeling of unspoiled wilderness perceived by visitors. Further research would be required to determine whether people who had more social encounters perceived more environmental disturbance and whether such disturbance actually existed.

This result does, however, support research conducted in other settings regarding the influence of environmental disturbances on the perceptions of visitors. Vaske, Graefe and Dempster (1982) found environmental disturbances to have the largest effect of four independent variables on perceived crowding in a wildland area. Bultena, Field, Womble and Albrecht (1981) reported a similar relationship, with encounters with human wastes, toilet paper, campfire rings, litter, horse waste, cut trees or bushes, hiker-made trails, and hiker-made campsites correlating well with felt crowding at Mount McKinley National Park. Similar results were found by Lee (1975) at Yosemite National Park.

CONCLUSION

Context is an important variable that influences how people are perceived and how social behavior affects observers of the behavior (Schneider, Hastorf and Ellsworth 1979). In wilderness, social encounters are relatively unique and memorable, and, accordingly, are likely to be a focal point of attention. The results of this study suggest that social encounters are an important factor considered by people when constructing and changing their conception of a wilderness area. From a managerial viewpoint, this notion implies that a degree of economy can be achieved in managing wildlands to produce certain kinds of recreation opportunities: some attributes influence the perceptions of visitors more than other attributes. In terms of efficiency in producing opportunities, the manager can focus on these *key* attributes (such as social encounters). The Limits of Acceptable Change (LAC) system (Stankey, Cole, Lucas, Petersen and

Frissell 1985) provides a good structure for incorporating such attributes (termed *indicators* in the LAC nomenclature) into a wilderness management plan.

The results also underscore the importance of cognitive processes in defining the wilderness product. Using key attributes as cues, visitors determine how to classify a wilderness and how to interpret experiences in that setting. The upshot of this perceptual process is the well known maxim that wilderness is a place that is assigned qualities and meanings by people (Nash 1982). From a recreation management point of view, then, the job of the manager is to discover and consider how the meanings and perceived qualities are influenced by the attributes encountered by visitors.

REFERENCES

Brown, P.J. 1984. Benefits of outdoor recreation and some ideas for valuing recreation opportunities. In G. L. Peterson and A. Randall (Eds.), *Valuation of Wildland Recreation Benefits.* Boulder, CO: Westview Press, 209-220.

Brown, P.J. and B.L. Driver. 1978. The opportunity spectrum concept and behavioral information in outdoor recreation resource supply inventories: A rationale. In *Integrated Inventories of Renewable Natural Resources.* USDA Forest Service, General Technical Report RM-55. Fort Collins, CO: Rocky Mountain Forest and Range Experiment Station, 24-31.

Bultena, G., D. Field, P. Womble and D. Albrecht. 1981. Closing the gates: A study of backcountry use limitation at Mount McKinley National Park. *Leisure Sciences* 4:249-267.

Clark, R.N. and G.H. Stankey. 1985. Site attributes -- a key to managing wilderness and dispersed recreation. In R.C. Lucas (Ed.) *Proceedings, National Wilderness Research Conference.* USDA Forest Service General Technical Report INT-212. Ogden, UT: Intermountain Research Station, 509-515.

Clark, R.N. and G.H. Stankey. 1979. The Recreation Opportunity Spectrum: A framework for planning, management and research. USDA Forest Service General Technical Report PNW-98. Seattle WA: Pacific Northwest Forest and Range Experiment Station.

Gardner, H. 1987. *The Mind's New Science: A History of the Cognitive Revolution.* New York: Basic Books.

Hammitt, W.E., C.D. McDonald and F.P. Noe. 1984. Use level and encounters: Important variables of perceived crowding among non-specialized recreationists. *Journal of Leisure Research* 16:1-8.

Hendee, J.C., G.H. Stankey and R.C. Lucas. 1978. *Wilderness Management.* Miscellaneous publication 1365. Washington, D.C.: U.S. Department of Agriculture, Forest Service.

Lakoff, G. 1987. *Women, Fire, and Dangerous Things: What Categories Reveal About the Mind.* Chicago, IL: The University of Chicago Press.

Lee, R.G. 1975. *The Management of Human Components in the Yosemite National Park Ecosystem.* Yosemite National Park, CA: The Yosemite Institute.

Moore, S.D. 1989. *Leisure Stereotypes: Person Perception and Social Contact Norms in a Wilderness Area.* Ph.D. Dissertation. Tucson, AZ: University of Arizona.

Nash, R. 1982. *Wilderness and the American mind.* New Haven, CT: Yale University Press.

Schneider, D.J., A.H. Hastorf and P.C. Ellsworth. 1979. *Person Perception.* New York: Random House.

Shelby, B., N. Bregenzer and R. Johnson. 1986. *Product Shift on the Rogue River Between 1977 and 1984: Empirical Evidence from a Longitudinal Study.* Paper presented at the First National Symposium on Social Science in Resource Management. Corvallis, OR: Oregon State University.

Stankey, G.H., D.N. Cole, R.C. Lucas, M.E. Petersen and S.S. Frissell. 1985. *The Limits of Acceptable Change (LAC) System for Wilderness Planning.* USDA Forest Service General Technical Report INT-176. Ogden, UT: Intermountain Forest and Range Experiment Station.

Vaske, J.J., A.R. Graefe, and A.B. Dempster. 1982. Social and environmental influences on perceived crowding. In F.E. Boteler (Ed.), *Proceedings: Third Annual Conference of the Wilderness Psychology Group.* Morgantown, WV: West Virginia University, 211-228.

CHAPTER 6

WHAT MAKES A RECREATION SPECIALIST? THE CASE OF ROCKCLIMBING

Steve Hollenhorst
West Virginia University

Quality experiences for one set of outdoor recreationists may not be quality for others, implying the need for variability in management's approach to satisfying the needs of users (Driver and Brown 1978, Haas, Driver and Brown 1980). The difficulty lies in predicting in advance how and why recreationists will relate to and prefer particular outdoor recreation opportunities. To overcome this problem, managers must be able to accurately classify recreationists based on predictable behavior and preference patterns.

While not identical, user characteristics, behaviors, and preferences do follow fairly predictable patterns. The literature supports the concept of progressive and predictable patterns of change in participation style and intensity over time. Parameters where this has been found to occur include motives for participation (Donnelly, Vaske and Graefe 1986), locus of control, privacy orientation, and levels of arousal (Knopf 1983:217), experience (Schreyer and Lime 1984), and social group structure (Heywood 1987).

RECREATION SPECIALIZATION

Among these parameters, recreation specialization has been proposed as one useful method for classifying outdoor recreationists. Bryan (1977:175) defines recreation specialization as a *continuum of behavior from the general to the particular, reflected by equipment and skills used in the sport and activity setting preferences*. Reportedly a significant dimension in understanding differences in the behavior and preferences of recreationists, specialization has been used to explain progressive and predictable patterns of change in participation over time. Since specialists define quality differently than do novices, classification of recreationists based on specialization enables managers to match specific preferences and behaviors with setting attributes that can be manipulated to facilitate quality opportunities (Ewert and Hollenhorst 1989).

As specialization increases, users become more particular about setting attributes and are more dependent upon the natural qualities of the resource base (Bryan 1977, Hammitt and McDonald 1984, Schreyer and Beaulieu 1986). More specialized users are more sensitive to crowding (Graefe, Donnelly and Vaske 1985), disturbances (Hammitt and McDonald 1983, Lucas 1985), and management restraints (Wellman, Roggenbuck and Smith 1982). Social contexts tend to shift from family and friends to peers of similar skills and interests (Bryan 1977). Specialized users also are more likely to be displaced (Roggenbuck, Wellman and Smith 1980), that is, to make a decision to change recreation behavior because of adverse changes in the recreation environment (Anderson and Brown 1984).

Typically, researchers have used complex combinations of variables to measure specialization. These indices have included indicators of the amount, type and location of prior participation, environmental preferences, social contexts, expenditures, equipment, and commitment. A primary question underlying this study was the usefulness of expertise as a surrogate measure of specialization for one group of outdoor recreationists: rockclimbers. It was hypothesized that expertise would be highly correlated with variables traditionally used to construct specialization indices.

EXPERTISE

While often referred to as an important dimension of specialization, skill level has been the focus of little research. This could be largely because of the difficulties associated with quantifying a recreationist's skill in a given activity. Studying rockclimbers enabled us to overcome this difficulty.

As with other risk recreation activities such as whitewater boating, mountaineering, and SCUBA diving, rockclimbers use a standardized difficulty rating system to quantify level of participation. By recording the difficulty rating of the climb completed by the subject during unobtrusive observation, a consistent and behavioral measure of specialization can be obtained.

The notion of a behavioral measure of specialization is well supported in the literature. Participant satisfaction results, in part, from perceptions of competence and self-sufficiency (Atkinson and Feather 1966, Bryan 1977, Dustin, McAvoy and Beck 1986, Gunn and Peterson 1978, Nash 1985, Sax 1980). Dustin *et al.* (1986) suggest that outdoor recreationists participate in part for a sense of competence. This search for competence continues as an individual gains experience and skills (Atkinson and Feather 1966). For instance, expert whitewater kayakers would likely find a slow moving river boring and unenjoyable. They require activity settings that allow them to participate in a fashion suitable to their high level of expertise.

Several authors propose promotion of recreationist self-sufficiency as a primary goal of recreation professionals (Dustin *et al.* 1986, Gunn and Peterson 1978, Nash 1985, Sax 1980). Under this principle, recreationists should be provided with opportunities for growth and development through a system of increasingly challenging, complex, and novel recreation environments. At some point, recreationists should be allowed to experience the activity setting with autonomy and self-sufficiency. It is through self-sufficiency that feelings of competence, and ultimately enjoyment, arise.

Expertise is a significant factor in the acquisition of these competence and self-sufficiency perceptions. The approach may also provide a more objective and behavioral bases for classifying users into meaningful subgroups (Ewert and Hollenhorst 1989).

PURPOSE OF THE STUDY

The purpose of the study was to determine the relationship between expertise and variables traditionally used to construct specialization indices. The study explored the ideas that recreationists can be classified on a continuum of expertise, and that distinctly different participant characteristics, behaviors, and preferences attend each level. Identification of these types of patterns would have descriptive and predictive utility regarding the user's orientation to and behavior in a particular outdoor recreation activity. Such information would be useful in management decisions intended to improve the quality of the recreation experience for these visitors.

Rockclimbers were an attractive population given the current rise in adventure recreation participation. Factors that point to growing popularity include growth in overall numbers of participants (Ewert 1985, Darst and Armstrong 1980), proliferation of recreational and educational programs and organizations (Ford and Blanchard 1985), greater expenditures for risk recreation opportunities and equipment (Bishoff 1985), and increased legislation and regulation affecting risk recreationists (McEwen 1983, McAvoy and Dustin 1985).

METHODS

The sample consisted of 84 rockclimbers observed at four sites in Ohio and Minnesota during the summer of 1987. Using observational techniques proposed by Webb, Campbell, Schwartz and Sechrest (1966), Hanna and Silvy (1977), and Burrus-Bammel and Bammel (1983), unobtrusive observations of climbers encountered at these sites were recorded.

Quantifying the expertise demonstrated by climbers was straightforward given the difficulty rating systems used in the activity. A rating from 5.0 (very easy) to 5.14 (most difficult) is assigned to virtually every completed climb in North America. This rating is published in climbing journals and local climbing guides. The difficulty of routes at the study sites ranged from 5.0 to 5.12, allowing climbers ample opportunity to choose routes suitable to their ability and preferences.

Upon encountering a climber, the difficulty rating of the route was recorded. To control for testing effects, subjects were not approached until after completing the climb. At that time, they were asked to participate in the study. If they agreed, the difficulty rating was recorded for the previously completed climb. Subjects were then asked to complete a short questionnaire.

To control for the confounding effect of risk, only *top-rope* climbers served as potential study subjects. In a top-rope arrangement, protection is pre-set at the top of the climb using trees or other solid fixtures as anchors. This is much safer than lead climbing where protection is placed as the leader ascends the route. The level of risk in top-rope climbing is constant from climb to climb, regardless of the difficulty. By eliminating the effects of different levels of risk, the relationship between expertise and the indicator variables could be more clearly analyzed.

Study sites were contrasted in terms of the social construct of use density and the environmental construct of naturalness. Two sites were characterized by low use and two by relatively high use. In each of these groups, one site was characterized by minimal evidence of human influence, modification, and development. The other site exhibited significant evidence of these activities.

RESULTS AND DISCUSSION

Descriptive Statistics

The mean expertise level of study subjects was 5.74 (Table 1). A 5.7 or 5.8 climb can be viewed as moderately difficult climbing, especially when top-roped. It was expected that the mean expertise level would be in this range.

The rather high frequency of rockclimbing participations per year, both on-site (16.7) and overall (28.1), is somewhat surprising. Given a seven month climbing season at these sites, these frequencies translate into one rockclimbing participation per week, suggesting that this population comprises rather dedicated and frequent participants. These frequencies also translate into one on-site rockclimbing participation every 1.5 weeks, suggesting that this population is comprised largely of climbers who live close enough to visit the site on a regular basis.

Mean years of both on-site and general rockclimbing experience were surprisingly low; 4.2 and 6.4 years, respectively. This may be a result of the recent growth in popularity of rockclimbing. Considering the mean population age (28.5 years), most participants apparently began rockclimbing in their early twenties.

Finally, 69 (82 percent) of the study subjects were male and 15 (18 percent) were female. From a test of the proportions, it can be concluded that significantly more men than women climb at these sites (Z = 5.89, p < .0001). From 90 percent confidence intervals on the proportion (p) of males, it can be concluded that between 77 percent and 87 percent of the climbers at these sites are men. This high proportion is consistent with previous studies which have found that many outdoor recreation activities continue to be composed primarily of male participants (Hammitt, McDonald and Hughes 1986).

Correlations

Results of the correlation analyses indicated a significant relationship between expertise and the following indicators of specialization: years of on-site rockclimbing experience, years of overall rockclimbing experience, frequency of on-site rockclimbing participation, frequency of general rockclimbing participation, participation in other risk recreation activities,

Table 1. Expertise Level, Various Measures of Experience Use History, Number of Other Risk Recreation Activities Engaged, Age and Sex of Rockclimbers (N = 84)

Variable	Mean	Standard Deviation
Expertise Level	5.74	.3
Participations/Year (Overall)	28.10	19.9
Participations/Year (On-Site)	16.70	16.0
Years of Participation (Overall)	6.42	4.0
Years of Participation (On-Site)	4.16	4.1
Number of Other Risk Activities	3.32	1.7
Age	28.48	7.9
Sex (0 = female, 1 = male)	.82 (82% male, 18% female)	

use density of the site, and the social context of participation (Table 2). No relationship was indicated between expertise and the naturalness of the site, age, and use of technical equipment.

Rockclimbers appear to move through a predictable pattern of skill development related to years of experience and frequency of participation. However, expertise was more strongly correlated with frequency of participation, both on-site and overall, than with years of experience. In terms of both years and frequency of participation, overall experience in rockclimbing was more strongly correlated with expertise than was on-site experience.

As expertise increases, behaviors change and certain attribute preferences become more specific. The extremely high correlation between expertise and social context suggests that the more skilled climbers become, the more likely they are to join elite social worlds of other climbers and participate less often with friends and family. Experts are also more likely to take part in other risk recreation activities.

The negative association between expertise and the use density of the site suggests that as expertise of climbers increases, the more they are sensitive to and likely to be displaced by crowding. While it appears novices are willing to fight crowds and wait in line to climb a route, these conditions are highly distasteful to the expert.

Table 2. Correlations Between Expertise Level and Other Measures of Recreation Specialization (N = 84)

Recreation Specialization Indicators	Correlation with Expertise Level
Social Contexts	.67 *
Frequency of Participation (Overall)	.64 *
Frequency of Participation (On-Site)	.56 *
Years of Participation (Overall)	.37 *
Years of Participation (On-Site)	.31 *
Participation in Other Risk Activities	.35 *
Density of Site	-.22 *
Naturalness of Site	.06
Age	.04
Use of Technical Equipment	.04

* p < .05

Contrary to research on other populations, expertise was not associated with an increase in resource dependency. While Bryan (1977:182) found that the more specialized the trout fisher, *the more . . . enjoyment is linked to the nature and setting of the resource*, expertise level did not indicate this with rockclimbers. While attribute preferences may become more specific as expertise increases, naturalness is not among these attribute preferences. When a climber makes a decision about where to climb, the important considerations are the specifics of the route and the rock at the site, lack of crowds, and opportunities for preferred social interactions. Naturalness is largely inconsequential to the decision.

No correlation was found between expertise and age. It appears that the physical nature of rockclimbing may favor younger climbers, allowing them to perform at expert levels without years of experience. Thus, for the age range of this population (15-47 years) the effects of age on expertise are largely ameliorated.

Specialization theory also suggests that experts are more likely to use technical equipment. Technical equipment used by climbers includes perlon ropes, sewn harnesses, chalk, and climbing shoes. Contrary to specialization theory, non-specialists were found to be just as likely to use this equipment. The purchasable nature of this variable may make it a poor indicator not only of expertise, but of specialization overall.

Regression Analysis

In order to insure linearity and equal variance, pure error tests and a visual check of data plots were performed on the dependent variable, expertise, by all the indicator variables. In every case, linearity and equal variance can be assumed. No transformations were required.

The eight indicator variables found to be significantly associated with expertise were then forced into the multiple regression equation describing expertise level (Equation 1). This final reduced model accounted for 77.6 percent of the variance in expertise level.

While some of the remaining variation may be due to random differences between study subjects, it is likely that a yet unidentified indicator variable might explain some of this variability. Given the physical and strenuous nature of rockclimbing, it is possible that this unidentified variable relates to the physical fitness, strength, and agility of the participant. Physically strong and agile individuals may exhibit higher expertise levels than less fit individuals, all other factors being equal.

Equation 1.   Prediction of Expertise

$$Y = \alpha + .008(X1) - .121(X2) + .004(X3) + .003(X4)$$
$$+ .0002(X5) + .003(X6) - .075(X7) - .021(X8) + e$$

Where: Y =   Expertise Level (skill)

α =   5.748 (constant)

$X1$ =   Use Density of the Site (Crowding)

$X2$ =   Social Contexts of Participation

$X3$ =   Frequency of Participation (On-Site)

$X4$ =   Frequency of Participation (Overall)

$X5$ =   Years of Participation (On-Site)

$X6$ =   Years of Participation (Overall)

$X7$ =   Participation in Lead Rockclimbing

$X8$ =   Participation in Other Risk Activities

e =   Error

Management Implications

The findings suggest that expertise can provide managers with a simple and effective surrogate measure of recreation specialization. By knowing the expertise level of rockclimbers, managers can infer frequency of participation, preferred social environmental settings, sensitivity to crowding, and the likelihood of participation in other risk recreation activities. By also developing an inventory of geological, biological, and social attributes of available resources, management decisions can be made in matching user preferences and behaviors with appropriate resource supplies.

Standardized difficulty rating systems are used in many outdoor recreation activity areas, including whitewater boating, mountaineering, SCUBA diving, downhill skiing, and ski touring. In these cases, managers are provided with an objective, observable, and behavioral basis for classifying recreationists into meaningful subgroups.

REFERENCES

Atkinson, J. and N. Feather. 1966. *The Theory of Achievement Motivation.* New York: John Wiley.

Anderson, D. and P. Brown. 1984. The displacement process in recreation. *Journal of Leisure Research* 16:61-73.

Bishoff, G. (ed.). 1985. National outdoor outfitters market report. *National Outdoor Outfitters News* 10:10-13.

Bryan, H. 1977. Leisure value systems and recreation specialization: The case of trout fishermen. *Journal of Leisure Research* 9:174-187.

Bryan, H. 1979. *Conflict in the Great Outdoors.* University of Alabama, Bureau of Public Administration, Social Study No. 4.

Burrus-Bammel, L. and G. Bammel. 1984. Applications of unobtrusive methods. In J. Peine (Ed.), *Proceedings of Workshop on Unobtrusive Techniques to Study Behavior in Parks.* Atlanta, GA: National Park Service, Science Publications Office.

Darst, P. and G. Armstrong. 1980. *Outdoor Adventure Activities for School and Recreation Programs.* Minneapolis, MN: Burgess Publishing Co.

Donnelly, M., J. Vaske, and A. Graefe. 1986. Degree and range of recreation specialization: Toward a typology of boating related activities. *Journal of Leisure Research* 12:81-95.

Driver, B. and P. Brown. 1978. The opportunity spectrum concept and behavioral information in outdoor recreation resource supply inventories: A rationale. In *Integrating Inventories of Renewable Natural Resources: Proceedings of the Workshop.* USDA Forest Service General Technical Report RM-55, 24-37.

Dustin, D., L. McAvoy and L. Beck. 1986. Promoting recreationist self-sufficiency. *Journal of parks and recreation administration* 4:43-52.

Ewert, A. and S. Hollenhorst. 1989. Testing the adventure model: Empirical support for a model of risk recreation participation. *Journal of Leisure Research* 20.

Ewert, A. 1985. Emerging trends in outdoor adventure recreation. *Proceedings: 1985 National Outdoor Recreation Trends Symposium II.* Athens, GA: National Park Service, 155-164.

Ford, P. and J. Blanchard. 1985. *Leadership and Administration of Outdoor Pursuits.* State College, PA: Venture Publishing Inc.

Graefe, A., M. Donnelly and J. Vaske. 1985. *Crowding and Specialization: A Reexamination of the Crowding Model.* Paper presented at the National Wilderness Research Conference, Fort Collins, CO, July 23-26.

Gunn, S. and C. Peterson. 1978. *Therapeutic Recreation Program Design: Principles and Procedures.* Englewood Cliffs NJ: Prentice-Hall.

Haas, G., B. Driver and P. Brown. 1980. Measuring wilderness recreation experiences. In *Proceedings of the Wilderness Psychology Group.* Durham, NH, 20-40.

Hammitt, W. and C. McDonald. 1983. Pest on-site experience and its relationship to managing river recreation resources. *Forest Science* 29:262-266.

Hammitt, W., C. McDonald and J. Hughes. 1986. Experience levels and participation motives of winter wilderness users. In: R. Lucas (Comp.), *Proceedings-National Wilderness Research Conference: Current Research.* Fort Collins, Co. General Technical Report INT-212. Ogden, UT: Intermountain Research Station, 553p.

Hanna, J., and V. Silvy. 1977. *Visitor Observation for Interpretive Programming.* Washington, D.C.: National Park Service, Office of Interpretation.

Heywood, J. 1987. Experience preferences of participants in different types of river recreation groups. *Journal of Leisure Research* 19:1-12.

Knopf, R. 1983. Recreational needs and behavior in natural settings. In I. Altman and J. Wohlwill (Eds.), *Behavior and the Natural Environment.* New York: Plenum Press, 205-240.

Lucas, R. 1985. *Influence of Visitor Experience on Wilderness Recreation Trends.* Paper presented at the National Wilderness Research Conference, Fort Collins, CO, July 23-26.

McAvoy, L. and D. Dustin. 1985. Regulating risk in the nation's parks. *Trends* 22:27-30.

McEwen, D. 1983. Being high on public land: Rock climbing and liability. *Parks and Recreation* 18:46-50.

Nash, R. 1985. Proceed at your own risk. *National Parks* 59:18-19.

Roggenbuck, J., J. Wellman and A. Smith. 1980. *Specialization, Displacement, and Definition of Depreciative Behavior Among Virginia Canoeists.* Final Report. Blacksburg, VA: Dept. of Forestry, VPI and State University.

Sax, J. 1980. *Mountains Without Handrails.* Ann Arbor MI: University of Michigan Press.

Schreyer, R. and J.T. Beaulieu. 1986. Attribute preferences for wildland recreation settings. *Journal of Leisure Research* 4:231-247.

Schreyer, R. and D. Lime. 1984. A novice isn't necessarily a novice - the influence of experience use history on subjective perceptions of recreation participation. *Leisure Sciences* 6:131-150.

Webb, E., D. Campbell, R. Schwartz and L. Sechrest. 1966. *Nonobtrusive Research Measures in Social Sciences.* Chicago: Rand McNally.

Wellman, J., J. Roggenbuck, and P. Smith. 1982. Recreation specialization and norms of depreciative behavior among canoeists. *Journal of Leisure Research* 14:323-340.

CHAPTER 7

CAMPER SATISFACTION WITH CANADIAN PARK SERVICE CAMPGROUNDS

Rick Rollins
Lakehead University
Thunder Bay, Ontario, Canada

Doug Chambers
Western Region, Parks Canada
Calgary, Alberta, Canada

Measuring recreation satisfaction is an important element in the effective marketing of leisure opportunities, including those found in National Park settings. From a practical management perspective it is desirable to be able to measure how people evaluate recreation settings or experiences. Further, it is important to be able to measure the factors affecting or shaping recreation satisfaction. For example, to what extent do factors such as crowding, scenic beauty, or litter, mold the recreation experience in a national park setting? To what extent can park managers shape recreation satisfaction by manipulating or controlling certain elements of outdoor recreation settings to maximize user satisfaction? From a more theoretical perspective, the study of recreation satisfaction has contributed to the development and testing of theory in human/environmental relations (Propst and Lime 1982).

The purpose of this study was to develop and test a strategy for measuring camper satisfaction with frontcountry campgrounds (those easily accessible by car) of National Parks in Alberta and British Columbia. The measurement of camper satisfaction is an essential element of the *Visitor Activity Management Process* (VAMP), a strategy recently developed to define the social science data required in the development of management plans for Canada's national parks (Parks Canada 1985). More specifically, this study was designed to assist the Canadian Park Service (CPS) in identifying or substantiating management concerns, that could ultimately assist management activities, such as the allocation of resources to maintenance, capital expenditures or information services. Further, to make valid comparisons of visitor perceptions between campgrounds, or to measure change over time at one or more campgrounds, it was essential to establish standard survey procedures.

Recreation satisfaction research has been strongly influenced by theories developed for understanding job satisfaction, particularly those articulated by Lawler (1973). As with job satisfaction, overall satisfaction with a recreation experience is shaped by a number of factors (Shelby 1980), called source satisfactions in this chapter. The relationship between overall satisfaction and the various source satisfactions is typically described in terms of discrepancy theory or fulfillment theory (Lawler 1973). Discrepancy theory states that overall satisfaction is determined by the differences (ie discrepancies) between the factors describing what was experienced, compared to what was expected. Fulfillment theory suggests that overall satisfaction is shaped by the extent to which the various experience factors are fulfilled or satisfied. Comparisons of these two approaches have yielded similar results in terms of ability to explain or predict overall satisfaction (Dorfman 1979, Cockrell 1981, Rollins 1985). The fulfillment approach was used in this study because it is somewhat easier to develop in a short questionnaire, and is easier for managers to interpret.

A number of concerns that have been raised with recreation satisfaction research (Heberlein 1977, Probst and Lime 1982) need to be discussed with respect to this study. The first concern is with sampling bias. Campers tend to select settings that match their preferences, so when surveys are conducted on site, the sample tends to include only campers who are satisfied with prevailing conditions. Where conditions have changed in a campground (e.g., higher use levels), potentially unsatisfied campers may select other campgrounds and so will not be included in the sample. To counter this problem, preference data are needed from non-users as well as users, but this is a difficult and sometimes costly undertaking.

Another concern is the tendency of subjects to rationalize that they must be satisfied, regardless of their actual experience. This pattern of responses is predicted from Festinger's theory of cognitive dissonance (Shaw and Costanzo 1978), which suggests that people strive to maintain consistency in their thoughts and actions. In a situation where a campground differs somewhat from a camper's expectations, cognitive dissonance theory predicts that such a camper may feel the need to have a positive attitude about the campground in order to maintain consistency between thoughts (i.e., level of satisfaction) and actions (investment of time, money and effort to visit the campground). Hence, rather than being disappointed with the conditions of a campground, and expressing dissatisfaction, campers may feel the need to report high levels of satisfaction with the chosen site.

A related concern is the social desirability effect (Edwards 1957) which suggests that people will tend to provide socially desirable responses, particularly when an interviewer is present to record the subject's responses.

This effect can be reduced through anonymous interviewing procedures. For example, in this study subjects were provided with instructions to complete and return the questionnaire (anonymously) to a drop-off box near the campground entrance.

Perhaps for similar reasons, the context of an interview appears to have some influence on responses. For example, many researchers have noted differences in levels of satisfaction when people are interviewed on-site, compared to mail surveys completed at a later date when campers return home (Peterson and Lime 1973, Rollins 1985).

Some researchers have postulated that recreation behavior is motivated by the desire to achieve a variety of psychological states, such as solitude or stress release (Gramann and Burdge 1981). When these goals are blocked, we attempt to reassert control over the situation. This behavior constraint model suggests that if campers are not able to stay in their preferred campground, then they will report lower levels of satisfaction, regardless of actual campground conditions encountered.

Another related concern has been described as product shift. This may occur if conditions in a campground change over time, (e.g., when facilities deteriorate). Campers may shift their frame of reference (i.e., their expectations) and report that they are satisfied, although the experience (i.e., product) has changed. This product shift concern suggests that repeat or returning campers would be more likely to experience a product shift, and be just as satisfied as campers visiting a campground for the first time, in a situation where conditions have changed.

Finally, satisfaction research is limited by the ability of subjects to identify and gauge the significance of those variables or factors that shape overall satisfaction. Models of recreation satisfaction (e.g., Shelby 1980) tend to assume that people can rationally explain the reasons for their behavior. However, in their critique of attribution theory, Nisbett and Ross (1980) have provided convincing evidence of our inability to correctly attribute all the reasons for our actions.

Although the primary purpose of this research was to develop an approach for measuring camper satisfaction that could feed directly into management decisions, it was possible to examine some of the more general concerns with satisfaction research, as described above. The cognitive dissonance (rationalizing) issue was addressed by hypothesizing that people who have selected a campground as their primary destination, will be more satisfied than other campers. Presumably people visiting a campground as a primary destination will be inclined to report higher levels of satisfaction because they have invested some effort to select and visit that campground.

The product shift effect was examined when the responses of repeat visitors were compared with the responses of first time visitors. Our hypothesis is that repeat visitors will express levels of satisfaction that are equal to or greater than the satisfaction of first time visitors, because repeat visitors will be prepared to shift their frame of reference if conditions in the campground were not as expected.

The attribution concern was examined by assessing how well source satisfactions predicted overall satisfaction. Stated as an hypothesis, the sum of source satisfactions should be positively correlated with overall satisfaction.

The behavior constraint hypothesis predicts that campers who feel constrained in their campground selection by being denied their first choice campground, will be less satisfied than campers who are successful in gaining admission into their first choice campground.

METHODS

This study was undertaken at frontcountry campgrounds in Glacier, Yoho and Elk Island National Parks. These National Parks are located on major Canadian highways in Alberta and British Columbia, and receive substantial use by people as primary holiday destinations, or as secondary attractions by people seeking convenient overnight accommodation. During randomly selected days in July and August of 1987, campers were randomly selected as they arrived at frontcountry campgrounds in the three parks. Park staff briefly explained the purpose of the questionnaire to the camper, and instructed the camper to return the completed questionnaire to a drop-off box near the entry kiosk, at the camper's convenience. This procedure was aimed at reducing the inconvenience to subjects, providing a degree of confidentiality, and maintaining cost-effective data collection. It was important to discuss and practice these procedures with park staff, to reduce the possibility of interviewer bias or sampling bias. Response rates ranged from 60 to 75 percent using these procedures.

Overall satisfaction was measured with a three-item semantic differential scale (Osgood, Succi and Tannenbaum 1957). The three questionnaire items consisted of bipolar adjectives (good-bad, unpleasant-pleasant, satisfied-unsatisfied) separated by a seven point scale. Positive responses were coded from +1 to +3, negative responses were coded from -1 to -3, and neutral comments were coded as 0. The responses to the three items were summed, such that overall satisfaction as expressed in this scale could vary from -9 (extremely negative) to +9 (extremely positive). The reliability of the scale was 0.93, using Cronbach's alpha.

Sources of recreation satisfaction were developed for the questionnaire by reviewing previous studies, interviewing park staff, and conducting a series of pilot studies during the summer of 1986 (Rollins 1987). These source satisfaction items related primarily to characteristics of the setting: environmental, social and managerial factors that were potentially under management control. Psychological motives, such as challenge, solitude or learning, were not probed in this study since the relationships between motive satisfactions, satisfactions with setting characteristics, and overall recreation satisfaction are complex and less manageable (Clark and Stankey 1978).

The final form of the questionnaire contained 29 items measuring source satisfaction, as listed in Table 1. Subjects were asked to indicate how satisfied they were with each of the source satisfaction items, using a seven point scale, ranging from extremely unsatisfied (scored as -3) to extremely satisfied (scored as +3). A composite scale, called sum of source satisfactions (SSS) was formed by adding the responses to these items.

RESULTS

The application of these procedures is illustrated in Table 1, describing the mean levels of satisfaction with Elk Island National Park. It is apparent from these data that the following areas could be addressed to improve camper satisfaction: quality of camping space, price of campsite, quality of picnic tables, quality of firepits, quality of firewood, access to telephone, quality of waterfront, quality of playground, level of crowding, and noise. These items had a mean satisfaction rating of 1.5 or lower, certainly an arbitrary criterion, but one that does reflect a degree of dissatisfaction when the range of responses are examined.

The attribution hypothesis was tested by computing the correlation coefficient between overall satisfaction and source satisfactions (SSS), as illustrated in Table 2. The value of Pearson's r is significant and positive for each of the campgrounds in the study, as predicted by the fulfillment theory of recreation satisfaction. However, the r^2 values do not exceed 40 percent, indicating that source satisfactions do not explain or account for a great deal of the variability in overall satisfaction. Clearly there is some imprecision in the approach used here to identify and measure the sources of camper satisfaction. Further, some of this apparent imprecision may be a reflection of a somewhat narrow pattern of positive responses evident in the standard deviations of the overall satisfaction scale. The correlations between source satisfactions and overall satisfaction may be underestimated due to this lack of variability in overall satisfaction.

Table 1.   Mean Source Satisfactions at Elk Island National Park

Item	Mean Satisfaction[a]	Standard Deviation
Quality of water front	1.4	1.56
Quality of playground	1.5	1.37
Quality of cooking shelters	2.3	1.41
Access to telephone	1.4	1.60
Quality of host program	2.5	1.42
Proximity to other park features	1.8	1.36
Quality of interpretation	2.3	1.43
Ease of registering	2.4	1.02
Safety of campground	2.3	1.01
Enforcement of rules	2.3	1.24
Courtesy of attendants	2.6	0.98
Access to garbage facilities	2.4	0.90
Access to drinking water	2.1	1.42
Adequacy of parking	1.9	1.74
Quality of camping space	1.1	1.82
Price of campsite	0.5	1.81
Quality of picnic tables	1.4	1.52
Quality of firepits	1.3	1.70
Access to firewood	2.1	1.41
Quality of firewood	0.9	1.95
Level of crowding	1.2	1.94
Noise level of other campers	1.9	1.50
Behavior of other campers	2.1	1.36
Amount of litter	2.4	1.01
Amount of scenic beauty	2.2	1.15
Amount of bugs/insects	1.0	1.75
Quality of toilet facilities	2.0	1.39
Noise from cars/trains	1.5	1.62
Amount of good weather	0.9	1.84

[a]Satisfaction responses were recorded on a 7-point scale, ranging from -3 (extremely unsatisfied) to +3 (extremely satisfied).

Table 2.   Overall Camper Satisfaction By Campground

Campground	N	Overall Satisfaction[a]	Standard Deviation	r[b]	r²
Mountain Creek	158	6.3	1.3	0.53	0.28
Illecillewaet	127	7.7	1.4	0.63	0.39
Kicking Horse	354	6.9	1.2	0.42	0.17
Hoodoo Creek	240	6.8	1.6	0.58	0.35
Chanceller Peak	245	6.8	1.4	0.49	0.24
Takakkaw	76	7.4	1.5	0.46	0.21
Lake O'Hara	148	7.2	1.3	0.59	0.35
Elk Island	156	5.4	2.3	0.59	0.35
OVERALL	1159	6.8	1.4	0.53	0.28

[a]Overall satisfaction computed from a 3-item semantic differential scale, such that satisfaction can vary from -9 (extremely negative) to +9 (extremely positive).
[b]Correlation between overall satisfaction and the sum of source satisfactions, an index formed by summing the responses to 29 items measuring satisfaction with campground conditions (see Table 2).

Table 3 summarizes the results of the remaining hypotheses. Campers staying in a first choice campground were more satisfied than people forced to stay in a second choice campground, as suggested in the behavior constraint hypothesis. One explanation for this result is that for people who did not select the campground as a first choice, their choice has been constrained, leading to diminished satisfaction. Alternatively, the second choice campground may not fit the expectations or preferences of the camper, and satisfaction will diminish.

Repeat visitors reported higher levels of satisfaction, as predicted by the product shift hypothesis. Alternatively, this result may be due to an improvement in campground conditions, as perceived by repeat visitors.

Finally, campers who have selected the campground as their major destination were more satisfied than campers visiting the campground as a secondary attraction. This result suggests that campers who have visited a campground as a major destination, have made such a strong prior commitment to the campground that they are psychologically predisposed to report high levels of satisfaction, as predicted by cognitive dissonance theory. A second interpretation of these findings is that these campers have taken more care in selecting a campground suited to their needs or preferences.

Table 3. Overall Camper Satisfaction By Context

Context	N	Overall Satisfaction[a]	r[b]
Overall	1159	6.8	0.53
Campground Selection[c]			
First choice	971	6.9*	0.54
Not First choice	173	6.3*	0.48
Familiarity[c]			
First time visitor	776	6.5*	0.55
Repeat visitor	376	7.4*	0.46
Destination[c]			
Campground is Primary Destination	313	7.3*	0.55
Campground is not Primary Destination	829	6.6*	0.51
Camping Style[d]			
Tent	569	6.7	0.59
Van	100	6.8	0.58
Trailer	181	6.9	0.49
Motorhome	190	7.0	0.42
Social Group[d]			
Camping Alone	326	6.6	0.55
With Friends	188	6.9	0.58
With Family	575	6.9	0.51
With Friends and Family	56	6.4	0.47
With an Organized Group	14	7.4	0.76

[a]Overall satisfaction measured with a 3-item semantic differential scale, varying from -9 (extremely negative) to +9 (extremely positive).
[b]Correlation between overall satisfaction and the sum of source satisfactions, an index formed by combining the responses to 29 items measuring satisfaction with campground conditions.
[c]Statistical comparisons between group means tested with student's t-test (p=.05).
[d]Statistical comparisons between group means tested with analysis of variance (p=.05).
*Indicates significantly different group means (p=.05).

Since these front-country campgrounds are used by people employing a variety of different camping styles, it seemed appropriate to examine camper satisfaction from this perspective, as well. As Table 3 indicates, camper satisfaction does not seem to vary by camping style. Tests for differences in levels of satisfaction by camping style were not significant, using analysis of variance procedures. Apparently these campgrounds are adequately designed and managed to accommodate a variety of camping styles, although this interpretation should be weighed carefully with data from non-users.

Another consideration in this analysis was the nature of the social group. The definition of social group used in this study considered 5 categories of social group, as indicated in Table 3. Using analysis of variance to test for significant differences, the results indicated that social groups did not differ in terms of their overall satisfaction.

In order to better understand the nature of recreation satisfaction, the source satisfaction variables were re-examined using factor analysis (with varimax rotation), a procedure for identifying patterns or structures within a set of variables. Factor analysis was used in this study to determine if the 29 source satisfactions could be collapsed or summarized into a smaller number of factors that would make interpretation simpler.

In this analysis, five factors emerged, although, as a rule of thumb, only the four factors with eigenvalues of 1.00 or higher should be considered. Items with factor loadings of 0.40 or higher are retained in Table 4. Using these criteria, most of the 29 source satisfactions have been combined into a smaller number of interpretable dimensions. For example, Factor 1 was labeled *campground surroundings*, since the variables that load on factor 1 seem to reflect such a dimension (e.g., quality of waterfront, quality of playground).

In the next step of this analysis, an index was formed for each factor by summing the responses for all of the items that load on each factor. For example, the seven items loading on the first factor were added together to form a single index, which could vary from -21 to +21. Reliability estimates of these scales ranged from 0.60 to 0.86.

Each of these factor indices were found to be significantly correlated with overall satisfaction, with r values ranging from .17 to .33. Next, stepwise multiple regression analysis was used to determine the cumulative effect of these factors in shaping overall satisfaction. As indicated by the multiple R values in Table 3, all the factors and items, with the exception of campfire characteristics, were significantly related to overall satisfaction. This analysis demonstrates that campers tend to perceive and evaluate campgrounds in terms of at least four of these five dimensions. It is likely that in this multiple regression procedure, the dimension of campfire characteristics was highly correlated with one or more of the other factors, with the result that campfire characteristics failed to emerge as a unique independent variable in terms of explaining overall satisfaction.

Subsequent research should begin with a consideration of these factors to determine if the list of source satisfactions could be enlarged or modified to better describe these dimensions, and improve upon the understanding and prediction of camper satisfaction. For example, follow-up studies would begin by asking campers to consider campsite characteristics, campground surroundings, etc. and to describe their likes and dislikes. By focusing on these specific dimensions, it is possible to assist campers to identify the factors influencing satisfaction (and address the attribution concern raised earlier).

Table 4.   Item Analysis of Source Satisfaction Items

Item	Factor Loading	Eigen-value	Alpha	r	R
Factor 1: Campground Surroundings(4)		7.99	.86	.17	.409
Quality of water front	.659			.37	
Quality of playground	.680			.32	
Quality of cooking shelters	.449			.29	
Access to telephone	.542			.11	
Quality of host program	.738			.27	
Proximity to other park features	.652			.33	
Quality of interpretation	.764			.30	
Factor 2: Campground Services(3)		1.62	.75	.26	.398
Ease of registering	.619			.18	
Safety of campground	.667			.35	
Enforcement of rules	.528			.30	
Courtesy of attendants	.703			.35	
Access to garbage facilities	.538			.24	
Access to drinking water	.458			.29	
Factor 3: Campsite Characteristics(1)		1.12	.68	.33	.331
Adequacy of camping area	.683			.36	
Quality of camping space	.741			.53	
Price of campsite	.501			.30	
Quality of picnic tables	.466			.32	
Factor 4: Campfire Characteristics(0)		.77	.60	.20	
Quality of firepits	.618			.27	
Access to firewood	.601			.25	
Quality of firewood	.672			.24	
Factor 5: Negative Conditions(2)		2.60	.75	.31	.375
Level of crowding	.636			.41	
Noise level of other campers	.826			.34	
Behavior of other campers	.847			.33	
Amount of litter	.700			.31	
Amount of scenic beauty	.592			.43	
Amount of bugs/insects	.422			.25	
Items Not Loading on a Factor					
Quality of toilet facilities(4)				.23	.395
Noise from cars/trains(6)				.28	.406
Amount of good weather(5)				.17	.401

Numbers in parentheses indicate order of entry into stepwise multiple regression equation.
r = Simple correlation with overall satisfaction.
R = Multiple correlation with overall satisfaction.

Also found in Table 4 are Pearson correlations, computed between the amount of satisfaction with each source (e.g., safety, price) and overall satisfaction. All correlations are significant, and vary from 0.11 to 0.53. This result verifies that each source satisfaction used in this study is related to overall satisfaction.

SUMMARY

This chapter has described a method for measuring camper satisfaction, and the factors influencing camper satisfaction, drawing on fulfillment theory of recreation satisfaction. The fulfillment approach was supported through correlational comparisons between scores for overall satisfaction and scores for source satisfactions (the factors thought to influence overall satisfaction). More research is needed to better explain and model these relationships.

Several hypotheses were developed to provide further insights into our understanding of recreation satisfaction. However, these hypotheses were tested with a correlational research design, lacking somewhat in the rigorous controls of a true experimental research design (Isaac and Michael 1981). Other interpretations of the hypotheses are possible , as indicated in the discussion of results. Nevertheless, the testing of the hypotheses described in this chapter provides a useful theoretical framework for interpreting satisfaction data.

Although camper satisfaction in this study was generally high, the case of Elk Island Campground was presented to illustrate how managers can identify problems in campgrounds not rated as highly by campers. Concerns identified by campers could be addressed by making improvements; or alternatively, attempts could be made to provide campers with better information regarding campground characteristics and availability. Factor analysis was illustrated as a technique for reducing a large array of satisfaction variables into a smaller number of meaningful dimensions. This simplified the interpretation of questionnaire results and suggests where to begin to look for other elements influencing camper satisfaction.

This kind of information is useful to the Canadian Park Service, in the short term, for routine monitoring of camper perceptions; in the medium term, for preparing area plans and redevelopment projects; and, in the long term, for management planning and policy development. This data collection was achieved very inexpensively by using park staff to administer the questionnaire. This procedure appeared to enhance the public's regard for the Canadian Park Service, since campers often stated they appreciated being asked for their opinion. Further, these procedures stimulated a commitment of park staff to the evaluation process, and to the implementation of changes if required.

In summary, this study should be viewed as part of a larger research effort,that includes a national household survey developed by the Canadian Park Service to better understand the camping market in Canada (Hewson 1989). This combination of household survey and campground survey provides a good opportunity to understand the views of a wide range of people: from this campground study the views of current campers were collected: and from the household study, information is collected from people who used to camp in CPS campgrounds, people who have never camped in CPS campgrounds, and non-campers.

REFERENCES

Clark, R.N. and G. Stankey. 1978. *The Recreation Opportunity Spectrum: A Framework for Planning, Management and Research.* U.S.D.A. Forest Service General Technical Report PNW-98.

Cockrell, D.E. 1981. *Motivation, Satisfaction and Social Influence in Wild River Recreation.* Unpublished doctoral dissertation, University of Idaho.

Dorfman, P. 1979. Measurement and meaning of recreation satisfaction. *Environment and Behavior* 11:483-510.

Edwards, A.L. 1957. *The Social Desirability Variable in Personality Assessment and Research.* New York: Dryden Press.

Gramann, J.H. and R.J. Burdge. 1981. The effect of recreation goals on conflict perception: The case of waterskiers and fishermen. *Journal of Leisure Research* 13:5-27.

Heberlein, T.A. 1977. Density, crowding and satisfaction: *Proceedings: River Recreation Management and Research Symposium.* U.S.D.A. Forest Service General Technical Report NC-28.

Hewson, P. 1989. Toward an agency marketing framework. Paper presented at *Visitor Management Strategies Conference*, University of Waterloo, 1989.

Isaac, S. and W.B. Michael. 1981. *Handbook in Research and Evaluation.* Edits, San Diego: R.R. Knupp.

Lawler, E. 1973. *Motivations in Work Organizations.* Monterrey, CA: Brooks/Cole Co.

Nisbett, R.E. and L. Ross. 1980. *Human Inference.* Englewood Cliffs: Prentice-Hall.

Osgood, C.E., G. Succi and P. Tannenbaum. 1957. *The Measurement of Meaning.* Urbana, IL: University of Illinois Press.

Parks Canada. 1985. *Management Process for Visitor Activities.* Unpublished report.

Peterson, G.L. and D.W. Lime.   1973.   Two sources of bias in the measurement of human response to the wilderness environment. *Journal of Leisure Research* 5:66-73.

Propst, D. and D. Lime. 1982. How satisfying is satisfaction research? A look at where we are going. *Forest and River Recreation: Research Update*. St. Paul, MN: U.S.D.A. Forest Service Miscellaneous Publication 18, 124-133.

Rollins, R. 1985. *Measuring Recreation Satisfaction Within A National Park Setting: The West Coast Trail Area Of Pacific Rim National Park*. Unpublished doctoral dissertation. University of Washington, Seattle.

Rollins, R. 1987. *Performance Assessment of Natural Park Campgrounds*. Unpublished Parks Canada report.

Shaw, M.E. and P.R. Costanzo. 1978. *Theories in Social Psychology*. New York: Mcgraw-Hill.

Shelby, B.   1980. Crowding models for backcountry recreation.   *Land Economics* 56:43-55.

CHAPTER 8

RECREATION OPPORTUNITY SPECTRUM REEVALUATED: ITS APPLICATION TO THE EASTERN U.S.

Richard J. Lichtkoppler
National Park Service
Denver Service Center

Howard A. Clonts
Department of Agricultural Economics
and Rural Sociology
Auburn University

The Recreation Opportunity Spectrum (ROS) as a recreational land classification system has gradually evolved over the years into a procedure either used or considered by governmental agencies in planning long-term use of the natural resource base. The ROS now serves as an official instrument by which recreational activities in national forests are integrated into the regular multiple use planning and management procedures, (USFS 1986). Wagar (1951) was one of the first to advocate a systems approach to recreational planning that would incorporate resource inventories and classifications as a part of the planning process. Later, recreational diversity as well as human presence in the environment was recognized as having an impact upon the recreational environment while in turn also being affected by the recreational environment (Wagar 1963, 1964). Recreational diversity continued to be advocated (Krutilla 1967) along with a systems approach to recreational planning (Brown, Dyer and Whaley 1973). Work by Brown, Driver, and McConnell (1978) furthered the development of an inventory and classification system for recreational planning and management. Clark and Stankey (1979) described the essence of the ROS system adopted by the Forest Service.

In 1980, both the U.S. Forest Service (USFS) and the Bureau of Land Management (BLM) adopted the ROS as the system to be used for inventorying, planning, and managing the recreational resources under their control. Since these two agencies are entrusted with stewardship of the majority of the nation's public lands, the ROS will, in some form or another, be applied throughout all regions of the United States. The ROS is now being implemented in many parts of the country as well as foreign countries such as Australia. For their own use in implementing ROS, the USFS compiled the *1986 ROS BOOK* as a means to provide coordination between ROS theory and its practical application.

The ROS is based upon the principle of diversity. The objective is to provide a diverse range of recreational opportunities on public lands in order to satisfy a wide range of recreational demands. A key assumption of the ROS concept is that quality in outdoor recreation can best be insured by providing such diversity (Clark and Stankey 1979).

Underlying ROS is the assumption that people seek satisfactory recreational experiences by participating in preferred recreational activities in a preferred environmental setting. To provide varied recreational opportunities on the public lands, as well as to protect the resource upon which they depend, the land managing agency applies the ROS criteria (a mix of physical, social, and managerial parameters) to match specific recreational opportunities with compatible resource qualities. Using the ROS system, land areas are identified as belonging to one of six classes depending on the level of existing or planned development and human influence. These classes are, in order of decreasing development and human influence: urban (U), rural (R), roaded natural (RN), semi-primitive motorized (SPM), semi-primitive non-motorized (SPNM) and primitive (P) (USDA Forest Service 1986).

A primary management objective under the ROS system is to manage the resource base to either maintain the present ROS classification or to manage it in a manner designed to bring about a change in the classification according to the ROS criteria. Classification maintenance and changes are planned in order to meet the demand for recreational experiences and provide a wide range of diversity in the opportunities available. Criteria for delineating ROS classes were developed and presented in the *ROS Users Guide* (USDA Forest Service 1982). The characteristics chosen were remoteness, size, evidence of humans, user density, and managerial regimentation and noticeability.

NEED FOR THE STUDY

The ROS criteria were originally developed and applied in the western U.S. However, the ROS as designed is perhaps unsuited for the eastern forests. The physical and biological attributes of eastern forests have few sites that are distant from some sort of human development or influence upon the land. However, the topography and dense vegetation of most eastern forests provide an effective buffer between development and primitive areas. For example, a primitive recreational experience is available without meeting the remoteness criteria established for the primitive classification for the ROS in the West. If the original criteria were applied, the ROS framework would not reflect the recreational diversity which is to be found in the forests of the eastern U.S. In fact, eastern wilderness areas, for the most part, would not qualify as primitive under those ROS criteria. This is true even for many designated wilderness areas such as the Sipsey Wilderness in the Bankhead National Forest, the subject of this study.

Historically, most work with the ROS has focused on inventorying the resource and then applying the classification system to the resource base. These two steps provide a substantial basis for analyzing the supply of recreational resources and their associated recreational opportunities. However, the ROS was modified for this study because in its original form it did not adequately identify the existing recreational resource supply in the study forest.

The ROS system recognizes that change is a part of the natural environment and that human activity can accelerate and intensify change. But the ROS does not clearly define the amount of change that is allowable within a class before reclassification is necessary. The technique known as Limits of Acceptable Change (LAC) provides a means to evaluate the boundaries of change as they apply to recreational land use. The focus of the LAC is establishing standards on the amount of change to be tolerated before the quality of the recreational opportunity offered in a ROS class is affected (Stankey, Cole, Lucas, Petersen and Frissell 1985).

In light of the inadequacies of the ROS as described above, the authors sought a meaningful way to revise the system criteria to reflect the characteristics of an eastern forest. Thus, the LAC framework was incorporated in the ROS system to add a dynamic dimension to forest recreational management. The resource manager should be able to identify the impact of alternative land uses on recreational use. The modified ROS/LAC procedure facilitates integration of a recreational program into the overall land and resource management plan for a forest or other land management unit.

The research objective on which this chapter was based was limited to the modification of criteria used to delineate ROS classes in the eastern U.S. so that eastern forests could be more appropriately classified for recreational opportunities. Incorporation of the LAC within the ROS provided a methodology for estimating the amount of change required before altering the ROS classification.

METHOD

The Bankhead National Forest (Bankhead/BNF) in Alabama was chosen for study because it exhibits the greatest variety of forest recreational opportunities of all the National Forest units in Alabama. Within the Bankhead are representative selections of the recreational opportunities available through-out the southeastern region. Also, it contains sites that meet the criteria of all ROS classes in use by the USFS, as modified for this study. Visitor demands on forest resources determine the diversity of activity needs which must be addressed under a multiple use concept. The ROS is a means of classifying resource supplies to meet those demands. Thus, an indication of recreational activities pursued in the forest and the degree of satisfaction that visitors have with those resources provides forest managers with a measure of success obtained in forest planning.

Socioeconomic data and travel patterns of visitors to the BNF were collected in personal interviews (N=596) during 1987-88. Respondent characteristics and observed forest use patterns were used to develop a representative assessment of forest visitors on an annual basis. A random sampling procedure stratified by season and by day of the week allowed identification of use patterns on a seasonal and daily basis. The sample was further stratified by recreation site to provide a representative sample of the various ROS classes within the forest. Interviews with forest visitors were conducted using a version of the Public Area Recreation Visitor Survey (PARVS) instrument (USDA 1985). Demographic information on age, sex, race, and education were obtained. Additional data were collected on income level, distance and time traveled, place of trip origin, size of visiting party, main activity, and trip expenditures. The only restriction on data solicitation was that respondents were at least 12 years old, otherwise respondent selection was done in a random manner.

A detailed account of respondents' recreational activities and the ROS classes in which the respondents' pursued them was solicited. Information on visitation to a particular ROS setting was indicated by the location of the visitor's main activity within the forest. In some cases this may have been a different ROS class than where the particular interview was actually obtained. While there were indications of flexibility in movement of the respondents about the forest, a high percentage of the interviews were conducted at their primary destination.

In addition to the visitor survey, field work was conducted to more accurately define ROS classes and their applicable limits. The LAC framework was used to develop subjective, but quantifiable, measures of the various classes for use in redefining the ROS criteria to better coincide with eastern forest characteristics. Since change is a part of the ROS system, the LAC concept provides a means by which change can be monitored. This is the value of integrating the LAC concept with the ROS. Thus, by using the LAC, land managers can identify physical limits of resource change that delineate one ROS classification from another.

LAC terminology, values, and criteria were developed for use in determining the ROS classifications into which the forest resources could be assigned, Table 1. Specific criteria applicable to the more populous and intensively developed eastern U.S. were identified by modifying characteristics and associated criteria already developed and presented in the *1986 ROS Book* (USDA Forest Service 1986). The five characteristics of forest recreational areas shown in Table 1 were identified as important in determining the appropriate ROS class designation for a particular area within the Bankhead. Each characteristic was given a range of numeric values (0 to 25) and specific definitions (criteria) were developed and associated with the values. The characteristics or indicators used in this study to integrate the LAC concept with the ROS system were: 1) access, 2) development, 3) user density, 4) vegetation, and 5) environmental change[1].

As seen in the composite version of the ROS/LAC modification, the changes incorporate the intent of the criteria first developed for the ROS in the western regions. Indicator characteristics for this study were chosen and refined because they can be utilized, albeit in a somewhat subjective manner, by field personnel with a minimum of training. Furthermore, changes in these characteristics indicate changes induced by, or contributing to, the recreational use of an area. Such changes may affect the ROS classification, and subsequently the planning and management of an area. As such, the characteristics are indicators of the amount of use and the overall condition of a particular area.

Information on the frequency of visitation and user density at various locations within the forest provided the basis for initial decisions in reclassifying areas under the ROS. Existing and potential high impact areas were determined and classified according to tolerable use limits under the LAC. Thus, total forest use could be evaluated and management plans established to both protect the resource from overuse, and to provide visitors with satisfactory recreational experiences.

Visitor demographic characteristics also guided the ROS reclassification process. Clear distinctions were observed in, for example, travel distances, age, sex and education of visitors and the forest areas and activities selected for recreation. The three *Primitive* ROS areas, identified as Roaded Natural under the original ROS scheme, were favored by a significant proportion of individuals in all socioeconomic categories, Table 2. The apparent motivation for this user group was to achieve a wilderness experience. Such an experience was possible in the Sipsey Wilderness, even though at no point in the Wilderness would one be more than one and a half miles from an existing road. This was possible because of the dense forest vegetation which muffled sound and limited visual contact. In addition, the size of the Wilderness was sufficient to adequately disperse visitors so that the limits of change associated with Primitive classes were acceptable. Thus, the area clearly should be classified as much less

Table 1. Composite Presentation of Recreation Opportunity Spectrum Classes and Limits to Acceptable Change Values and Terminology

ROS Class	Value	Access	Development	User Density	Vegetation	Environmental Change
	25	Primary highway	Intensively developed area	Intensive use area	Intensively altered area	Intensively changed
R	23	Primary or secondary highway	Very highly developed area	Very heavy use area	Very severely altered area	Very severely changed
	20	Secondary highway	Highly developed area	Heavy use area	Severely altered area	Severely changed
RN	18	Secondary road	Significantly developed area	Significant use area	Significantly altered area	Significantly changed
	15	Improved light-duty road	Moderately developed area	Moderate use area	Moderately altered area	Moderately changed
SPM	13	Unimproved dirt road	Lightly developed area	Frequent use area	Obviously altered area	Obviously changed
	10	Jeep trail	Developed access area	Slight use area	Slightly altered area	Slightly changed
	9	Way				

Table 1. Continued

ROS Class	Value	Access	Development	User Density	Vegetation	Environmental Change
SPNM	8	Primary horse trail	Trail development area	Noticeable use area	Noticeably altered area	Noticeably changed
	7	Horse trail				
	6	Primary foot trail				
	5	Foot trail	Minimally developed area	Minimum use area	Minimally altered area	Minimum change
	4					
P	3	Visible game trail	Unobtrusively developed area	Unobtrusive use area	Unobtrusively altered area	Unobtrusive change
	2	Game trail				
	1	Passable area				
	0	Impassable area	Undeveloped area	Non-consumptive use area	Insignificantly altered area	No change

Table 2. Percentage of Respondents by Socioeconomic Characteristic

Characteristic

ROS Class	Percent Male	Age Groups				Education		Income[a]					
		20	21-40	41-60	Over 60	12 yrs. or less	Some college	10	10-19	20-29	30-39	40-49	50
Rural	49	22	50	22	6	67	33	14	29	27	15	6	9
Roaded Natural	56	19	46	21	13	62	38	22	33	12	18	10	4
Semi-Primitive Motorized	77	10	63	18	9	64	36	8	26	25	25	4	12
Semi-Primitive Non-Motorized	100	4	52	28	16	58	42	9	36	18	23	5	9
Primitive	92	10	65	15	10	40	60	13	33	19	15	8	12
Forest	62	18	54	21	8	62	38	14	30	24	18	6	9

[a] In thousands of dollars

populated and/or altered than a Roaded Natural classification would indicate. Assignment of a Primitive classification was easily accomplished under the revised criteria.

Economic theory requires that supply be matched against demand for an equilibrium to be determined. Accurate identification of recreational resource supply is a necessary first step. Refining the ROS and combining it with LAC merges economic and carrying capacity theory with applied resource management and provides resource managers with a tool necessary for the accurate identification of that supply. Estimates of demand derived via visitor characteristics and use provide the data needed for estimating the *market* equilibrium in forest resource use. Supply is easily quantified once ROS areas are defined and mapped. Several procedures are available to further refine that equilibrium so that the net benefits and costs of a forest recreation program may be determined.[2]

The forest ROS map, Figure 1, was redrawn after each area of the forest was assessed for potential recreational use and sample sites within areas evaluated with respect to current physical conditions (LAC). Once use patterns were established following the sampling period, the revised ROS classes were reevaluated to determine if use was consistent with the LAC criteria. Consistency was achieved in all forest areas.

RESULTS

By redefining the ROS criteria using the methodology described above, the supply of recreation resources in the Bankhead National Forest could more accurately be assessed, Figures 1 and 2. Also, by incorporating the LAC concept, a framework for monitoring and evaluating change was established that is consistent with the ROS.

Using the original ROS criteria (O-ROS), as presented in the *1986 ROS BOOK*, the Bankhead can be classified into just two ROS classes. There are three developed campgrounds and one picnic area which fit the criteria for the rural (R) ROS class. The rest of the forest would be categorized as roaded natural (RN), Figure 1. Application of the modified criteria (M-ROS), as developed for this study, allowed identification of five distinct classes. Under this format some areas and sites classified as RN under the O-ROS format were reclassified as SPM, (SPNM), or (P), under the M-ROS format, Figure 2. Evaluation of LAC indicated that significant change was not occurring at the selected survey sites during the study period. This was expected due to the limited time covered by the research. However, change would be expected when the ROS areas are evaluated over longer time periods.

Comparison of selected visitor travel patterns by ROS class as determined by the two classification schemes was enlightening. For example, under the O-ROS criteria there was little variability in visitor's travel time or travel distance by ROS class, Table 3. However, the M-ROS framework provides five classes within which planning and management of the resource may occur. Thus, it is logical to analyze these travel patterns in the revised

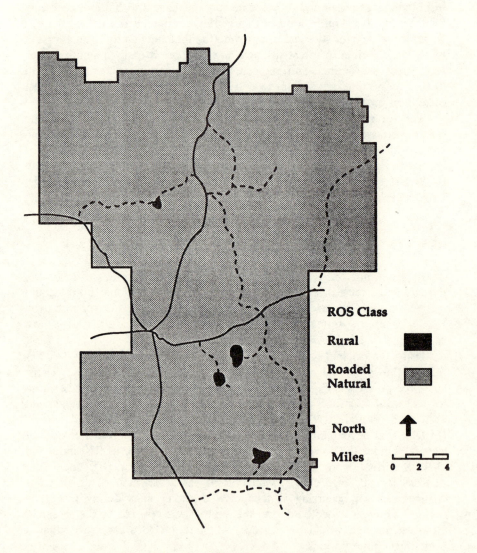

Figure 1. Bankhead National Forest Original ROS Criteria

context.   An examination of the travel variability revealed a significant difference for travel time and distance, Table 4.   Importantly, the primitive ROS area of the forest was shown to contribute a significant proportion of the variation in these two characteristics, Table 5.   Redefinition of the ROS classes showed that the effect of travel time/ distance was confounded when the original classes were used.   Properly accounting for the dispersal of visi-

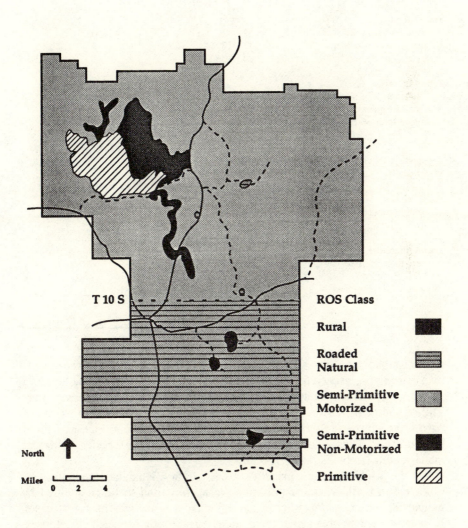

Figure 2.   Bankhead National Forest Revised ROS Criteria

Table 3.   Distribution of Survey Respondents by Travel Time and Distance and by Original and Modified ROS Criteria (in percentages).

	R	RN	SPM	SPNM	P	Total Forest
Respondent Distribution Under Original ROS Criteria						
Travel time						
one hour or less	33	32				65
more than one hour	17	18				35
	50	50				100
Travel distance						
less than 25 miles	14	15				29
25 - 50 miles	22	18				40
more than 50 miles	14	17				31
	50	50				100
Respondent Distribution Under Modified ROS Criteria						
Travel time						
one hour or less	33	7	12	5	8	65
more than 1 hour	17	2	5	2	8	35
	50	9	17	7	16	100
Travel distance						
less than 25 miles	14	4	6	2	3	29
25 - 50 miles	22	3	8	3	4	40
more than 50 miles	14	2	5	2	8	31
	50	9	19	7	15	100

tors throughout the forest via the modified ROS procedure showed a relatively strong preference for more primitive conditions, especially by the *local* population, who are likely to exhibit more intensive use patterns over time. This of course means that it may be necessary to enforce LAC criteria if the conditions which justify the revised ROS classes are to continue as such in the future.   Thus, the importance of the revised categories in forest management becomes more obvious.

If the wilderness and primitive areas of the Bankhead are typical of other eastern wilderness or primitive areas, they tend to be frequented by individuals with characteristics which differ from other general forest users. It is important in managing these areas to account for such differences. Managing such areas in the same manner as semi-developed campgrounds

Table 4. Chi-Square Coefficients for Test of Significance of Travel Time and Distance for Respondent Distribution Under Original and Modified ROS Classes.

	ROS Class					
	R	**RN**	**SPM**	**SPNM**	**P**	**X^2**
Chi-Square Coefficients by Original ROS Criteria.						
Travel time						
one hour or less	0.021	0.021				
more than one hour	0.038	0.039				
						0.120
Travel distance						
less than 25 miles	0.061	0.061				
25 - 50 miles	1.137	1.145				
more than 50 miles	0.920	0.926				
						4.250
Chi-Square Coefficients by Modified ROS Criteria						
Travel time						
one hour or less	0.021	0.771	0.430	0.320	3.825	
more than one hour	0.038	0.419	0.791	0.590	7.041	
						15.247[*]
Travel distance						
less than 25 miles	0.061	4.162	0.418	0.684	6.051	
25 - 50 miles	1.137	0.656	0.158	0.160	2.245	
more than 50 miles	0.920	1.090	1.134	0.118	16.255	
						35.249[*]

[*]Significant at $p < 0.05$.

or picnic areas is likely to result in inappropriate actions which may be deleterious to either the forest resource or visitor satisfaction. In this context, proper identification and specification of the supply of recreational resources is important for good planning and management. Likewise, knowing the characteristics of potential visitors to various ROS areas establishes demand components such as tastes and preferences, income, and use frequency. Thus, there is now opportunity for more accurate management of forest resources to provide the range of multiple uses desired. Timber production and harvesting may proceed while either protection or expansion of recreational areas favored by various user groups

Table 5.   Chi-Square Coefficients for Test of Significance of Travel Time and Distance by Grouped ROS Classes.

	Modified ROS Classes-Grouped		X^2
	All others	Primitive	
Travel Time			
one hour or less	0.742	3.825	
more than one hour	1.366	7.041	
			12.974*
Travel distance			
less than 25 miles	1.046	6.051	
25 - 50 miles	0.389	2.245	
more than 50 miles	2.816	16.255	
			28.804*

*Significant at $p < 0.05$.

is pursued. This was especially evident in areas contiguous to the designated Sipsey Wilderness.   For example, current land use   provides for off-road-vehicle (ORV) use adjacent to the wilderness. Visitor interviews revealed that both ORV and non-ORV visitors preferred other arrangements. Also, the LAC indicated that changes resulting from ORV use were not compatible with long term maintenance of the primitive or semi-primitive, non-motorized ROS designation the area merits. Simple relocation of incompatible uses under the M-ROS plan should resolve that dilemma and provide more effective resource management.

DISCUSSION AND RECOMMENDATIONS

Use of a modified ROS-LAC format allowed more accurate identification and classification of recreational resources of the Bankhead than was possible otherwise. It also provided better measurement of the variability among alternative recreational areas in the national forest.   Field work confirmed that the greater diversity of recreational opportunities indicated by the modified format do indeed exist and would not have been accounted for in the original ROS scheme. Similarly, incorporating the LAC concept allowed dynamic measurement to be integral to the ROS process so that change is monitored and incorporated into data made available to resource managers.   In addition, interviews stratified by the modified classification system provided a basis for more accurate estimates of visitor types and visitor preferences for recreation as well as impacts they may have on the resource base. More accurate identification of forest recreational resources which would be compatible with particular kinds of recreational use has obvious policy implications. Thus, the revised ROS (M-ROS) helps to identify areas of the forest which may be most suitable for future recreational development.

Travel time and distance by forest visitors clearly illustrated the difference in results possible when the same data were analyzed using two different classification systems. Relatively strong differences in visitor patterns of travel to wilderness and primitive areas as well as the socioeconomic background of individuals frequenting those areas demonstrated the value of establishing greater diversity in eastern forest ROS classes. The attraction of more primitive areas for certain types of individuals showed the importance of planning based on selected potential visitor populations. In a separate report, forest visitor numbers were estimated using such characteristics. That research showed that demands on each ROS class could be estimated by general population and forest user characteristics (Lichtkoppler 1989).

For example, the M-ROS allowed identification of the Sipsey Wilderness as a primitive area. This identification was not possible under the O-ROS framework. It is important to be able to identify such recreational diversity, as diversity is the key to planning and management under the ROS system. Analysis of data regarding the time and distance traveled by visitors to this area indicated that these visitors had different travel patterns and socio-economic characteristics than other forest visitors. Research findings such as these have implications for resource valuation models as well as the ongoing, practical, forest management considerations.

As expected, the modifications proposed in this chapter enabled the ROS system to conform to the facts of the situation at the Bankhead. To this end, the use of the LAC concept and its associated methodology can help in monitoring changes in the resource base and provide systematic input into the ROS process. Information collected through a regular program of field work including photo inventories, site inspection, and site evaluation would provide necessary data for use in integrating LAC with the ROS, enabling it to become a more viable part of the total land management program.

The ROS is an evolving system. Implementation is not meant to be governed by hard and fast rules which do not allow for the needs of dynamic situations. It is designed to be a systematic approach to the problem of integrating recreational planning and management into the overall land management plan for public lands. This modification of the ROS will aid land managers in accomplishing that task. As such, the job ahead is to continue to provide recreational diversity while balancing human wants and needs with the conservation of the resource base upon which they depend.

NOTES:

1. Because of the length of these materials, they are not presented here in detail. Copies may be obtained by contacting the author.

2. Such procedures may include travel cost and contingent values to estimate demand and opportunity costs of timber versus recreation to estimate supply values.

REFERENCES

Brown, P.J., B.L. Driver and C. McConnell. 1978. The opportunity spectrum concept and behavioral information in recreation resource supply inventories: Background and application. In G.H. Lund, V.J. LaBau, P.F. Ffolliott and D.W. Robinson (Tech. Coords.), *Integrated Inventories of Renewable Natural Resources: Proceedings of the Workshop*. General Technical Report RM-55, U.S. Department of Agriculture, Forest Service. Fort Collins, CO: Rocky Mountain Forest and Range Experiment Station, 73-81.

Brown, P.J., A. Dyer and R. Whaley. 1973. Recreation research - so what? *Journal of Leisure Research* 5:16-24.

Clark, R.N. and G.H. Stankey. 1979. *The Recreation Opportunity Spectrum: A Framework for Planning, Management, and Research*. General Technical Report PN-98. U.S. Department of Agriculture, Forest Service, Pacific Northwest Forest and Range Experiment Station.

Krutilla, J.V. 1967. Conservation reconsidered. *American Economic Review* 57:777-86.

Lichtkoppler, R.J. 1989. *The Recreation Opportunity Spectrum and the Recreational Use of Bankhead National Forest*. Ph.D. Dissertation, Auburn University.

Stankey, G.H., D.N. Cole, R.C. Lucas, M.E. Petersen and S.S. Frissell. 1985. *The Limits of Acceptable Change (LAC) System for Wilderness Planning*. General Technical Report INT-176. U.S. Department of Agriculture, Forest Service, Intermountain Forest and Range Experiment Station.

U.S. Department of Agriculture. Forest Service. 1982. *ROS User's Guide*.

U.S. Department of Agriculture, Forest Service. 1985. *Public Area Recreation Visitor Survey (PARVS)*. Athens, GA: Southeastern Forest Experiment Station.

U.S. Department of Agriculture. Forest Service. 1986. *1986 ROS BOOK*.

Wagar, J.A. 1963. *Campgrounds for Many Tastes*. Research paper INT-6. U.S. Department of Agriculture, Forest Service, Intermountain Forest and Range Experiment Station.

Wagar, J.A. 1964. *The Carrying Capacity of Wild Lands for Recreation*. Society of American Foresters, U.S. Department of Agriculture, Forest Service, Washington, D.C., Monograph 7.

Wagar, J.V.K. 1951. Some major principles in recreation land use planning. *Journal of Forestry* 49:431-5.

III

RECREATIONISTS, LOCAL POPULATIONS, AND AGENCIES

CHAPTER 9

CUSTOMARY AND TRADITIONAL KNOWLEDGE IN CANADIAN NATIONAL PARK PLANNING AND MANAGEMENT: A PROCESS VIEW

Robert Graham
Department of Recreation and Leisure Studies
University of Waterloo

Robert J. Payne
School of Outdoor Recreation
Lakehead University

The Canadian Parks Service[1] currently administers 34 national parks and national park reserves, one national marine park and one national marine park reserve, five heritage rivers, nine heritage canals, two co-operative heritage areas, and 83 national historic parks and sites. The agency is charged with the responsibility of protecting significant examples of Canada's natural and cultural heritage and with encouraging public understanding, appreciation and enjoyment of these areas.

Nelson (1978) and La Forest and Roy (1981) have described Parks systems and management planning as top-down, relatively autonomous, and conservative. Conspicuously absent from the overall planning framework utilized by the CPS in the late 1970s and early 1980s is a systematic and integrative process of addressing when and how to include an understanding of the needs of people and the relationship of those needs to national parks (Nilsen 1987).

Recent program policy and management directives that have tried to address the importance of developing a better awareness of the interdependent roles and relationships between people and parks include the requirement for an environmental impact assessment (Parks Canada 1981), socio-economic impact assessment and regular reviewing and monitoring regional integration of potential parks or proposed changes within an existing park (Parks Canada 1983). In spite of these changes, linkages between scientific and customary users' environmental knowledge to develop data to: (1) support the establishment of a park, (2) enhance a management plan, or (3) review a park's ongoing management, have been very limited (Rueggeberg 1988).

Andrews (1988), in a recently published bibliography, provides an overview of the international contribution of indigenous and customary ecological knowledge to resource management, scientific research and state-based resource management systems [e.g., parks and protected areas]. The listings represent approximately 250 studies, monographs and books developed over the last two decades. Sibbeston (1987) suggests that growth in the use of this type of expertise and in the recognition of its important contribution to society is seen in the texts of national conservation strategies, particularly the sections which recognize the legitimacy of local-level resource knowledge and management abilities.

While scientific knowledge of resources is important in selecting, planning and managing a protected area, conservation can only succeed by consent. The recognition that local level inputs and shared management are essential to the long term conservation and preservation of areas, is widely noted (e.g., IUCN 1980, Canada 1986b, United Nations 1987). But as Holling (1978:12) suggests, ". . . perceptions determine the methods we use and the solutions we see . . ." According to Berkes, research with a focus on customary and indigenous knowledge is implemented as a ". . . series of steps or levels of inquiry: documenting the ecological knowledge and capabilities of groups, . . . identifying local patterns of resource use, . . . ascertaining how the existing patterns of resource use are internalized and monitored by a community [and] . . . describing the environmental philosophies of users" (1988:8).

International studies documenting the capability of customary and indigenous users' ecological knowledge to influence the outcomes of heritage area planning and management indicate change in the approach of managers and planners in a number of areas. Boundary delineation and zoning based on the protection of valued religious or cultural heritage sites, customary law and traditional activities has occurred in Papua New Guinea, Panama, the Philippines and Australia (Eaton 1984, White 1984, Wright, Housel and DeLeon 1985, and Cobourg Peninsula Sanctuary Board 1987). As a contributor to natural resource inventories and data base development, informal ecological knowledge complements and expands scientific information in areal, regional and site-specific biophysical inventories and monitoring programs (e.g., Nietschman 1984).

Identifying patterns of resource harvesting and other on-going uses within and adjacent to protected areas has often represented a mechanism to initiate communication patterns through which exchanges of scientific and behavioral information can occur. If the communication is only one way and dedicated solely to data development, failing to lead to meaningful involvement in planning and management, considerable resentment against acceptance for the park and its staff and limited involvement in long-term planning and management programs may result (e.g., Weaver 1984, Baldwin 1985, Stenmark 1987 and Caulfield 1988).

Research that ascertains customary law and local resource management systems in protected area planning and management is found in articles by Foran and Walker (1985) and Thomas (1987). Recognition and support for local systems involving self-management of a resource represent an important basis to develop both natural resource and visitor management strategies. The park's resource management guidelines and those of the local community system should be viewed not as two ends of a continuum, but as inseparable. Both the agency's suggested approach to resource management and the local system will be needed to learn how the area has changed, is currently changing and how it can best be managed in the future.

Describing the environmental philosophy of users can help identify appropriate visitor opportunities, potential programs of cultural and natural heritage interpretation and education, risk and public safety requirements. Two American studies of protected areas in the South Pacific and Arizona illustrate that understanding local environmental philosophies can increase the level of the agency's sensitivity in responding to local customs, communication patterns and on-going lifestyles (Thomas 1987, Mitchell 1987).

In Canada, indigenous and customary users' knowledge was used to develop inventory, conservation and management strategies for whales in the Arctic, to resolve the humpback-fishermen conflict in Newfoundland (Lien 1985:231-240), to foster sea bird conservation on the north shore of the St. Lawrence (Blanchard 1985:219-230) and to strengthen local fisheries management (Lamson and Hanson 1984, Pinkerton 1989). In each of these cases, central network customary users or indigenous people contributed in a two-way communication through which it was possible to synthesize users' knowledge of natural science, culture, wildlife behavior and their preferences for management scenarios. Development of these communication channels and networks increased conservation of the targeted species and agency-user trust and understanding.

This chapter addresses two of the emerging socio-political issues in establishing Canadian parks and in their on-going management planning: the recognition of informal knowledge (i.e., traditional, ecological knowledge and customary users' knowledge) as a legitimate source of data in systems and management planning; and the identification of mechanisms that will develop long-term and interactive partnerships between professional managers, customary users and indigenous peoples.

These issues will be addressed by the following questions:

(1) Why should the knowledge and capabilities of customary (Dasmann 1974, U.S. Congress 1980) and indigenous peoples (Freeman 1979) be considered in park selection, planning and management?

(2) How can this knowledge be integrated with formal data in the planning and management of potential and existing protected areas?

(3) How might the Canadian Parks Service develop improved institutional arrangements between managers and users of the resource?

Section One describes the assumptions related to the types of formal knowledge needed to establish Canadian national parks and to guide their subsequent planning. Section Two defines and describes customary and indigenous knowledge and evaluates its actual and/or potential impact on scientific information used in park planning. Section Three briefly suggests several non-hierarchical alternatives that Parks might consider to ameliorate relations between management and its publics.

CANADIAN PARKS SERVICE PLANNING SYSTEM

The primary goal of terrestrial national parks is the preservation of a park's natural conditions, aiming for the highest level of protection for heritage areas in Canada today. In marine parks, emphasis is placed on the conservation of renewable resources, maintaining the area's marine environmental quality through a series of horizontal memoranda of understanding with other federal, provincial and municipal agencies, and on protecting critical natural and submerged cultural and heritage resources.

Parks' comprehensive systems planning process guides terrestrial and marine park NACS identification and park establishment. Both processes begin with the Parks Systems Division or its representative reviewing published scientific information and speaking with scientists and provincial or territorial departments responsible for resource management. The terms of reference for these regional analysis studies usually prohibit the investigator from contacting the public at large including representatives of customary users, environmental groups, and stewardship associations (Lerner 1986). Parks feels that contact with these groups may give rise to unrealistic expectations, criticism about who or what groups were or were not contacted and/or later difficulty in land assembly or park designation.

Media commentary about political cronyism and the exclusion of competitive ideas and philosophies from similar discussions surfaced in a recent marine regional study (Parks Canada 1985c) and led to misunderstandings and misrepresentations among all parties (CLAMP 1984, CBC 1987). Regional analysis studies, the first step in systems planning, aim to identify preliminary or candidate natural areas of Canadian significance (potential NACS or preliminary areas) that have the potential to include a national park. These preliminary areas are redefined and studied in greater detail in a series of subsequent regional field trips. Areas identified as being significant are then listed in a registry for potential designation and conservation by other federal, provincial or environmental organizations.

Potential national parks are selected, with the involvement of governments and the interested public, from each region's list of confirmed NACS. In the systems planning process, the interdependence of local people and resources is not acknowledged until a shopping list of potential areas in their region is defined in a report and delineated on a map. Undoubtedly, time is saved in not identifying knowledgeable marine and coastal customary users or in not documenting their environmental knowledge, values and cultural heritage. But in building a decision to permit long-term limited use of an area such as a national park or national marine park, an understanding of how local residents and customary users see, value and explain their immediate environment is recognized by numerous scholars and agencies as a significant key to the acceptance of a park proposal and the successful on-going management and monitoring of the site (Freeman 1979, Johannes 1982, Weaver 1984, UNESCO 1984, Jacobs 1985, IUCN 1985, Shannon 1987, Thomas 1987, Francis 1987, Rueggeberg, 1988).

To develop an understanding of the natural resource in the proposed or existing park and to monitor and evaluate park-specific objectives for the protection, conservation and preservation of natural and cultural resources, Parks developed a problem solving process which collects predetermined scientific information. These data are used to provide feedback on the biophysical state of the resource and changes in natural systems and to gather comments on management allocation and use prescriptions (i.e., *Natural Resource Management Process* [NRMP] Parks Canada 1978). As a component of the overall planning and management framework for parks, the NRMP is primarily concerned with the management of natural resources.

The companion process [*Management Process for Visitor Activities* or VAMP] provides a decision framework in which to plan, develop and operate services and facilities, to assess regional integration of a park, to evaluate visitor market potential, and to identify interpretive and educational opportunities for the public to understand, enjoy and appreciate heritage.

The framework also considers the public safety implications of proposed and ongoing visitor opportunities and allows the agency to evaluate its effectiveness in meeting public needs. VAMP is a pro-active, flexible and conceptual framework -- one whose features facilitate integration of social science information with the development of the systems planning process of the agency and the management plan for a park (Parks Canada 1985a, Payne, Graham and Nilsen 1986, Graham, Payne and Nilsen 1988).

The VAMP framework requests in several stages of the process that a planner or manager document the informal and indigenous knowledge of customary users and stakeholders (Lerner 1986). The profiling of these users and their knowledge and values can be incorporated into both system and management planning of parks. However, collection of this information is dependent on the initiative, ability and resources of individuals responsible for the application of VAMP and the willingness of user groups to share their knowledge and information.

In keeping with the 1979 National Parks Policy and the 1986 National Marine Parks Policy, the Canadian Parks Service is:

> . . . committed to involving local aboriginal people in the establishment, management and operation of new parks . . . Specific policies on how this commitment is to be applied have been evolving very slowly as discussions and negotiations have proceeded with the native peoples concerned, within and outside the land claims forum (Environment Canada, Parks Service 1987:1).

However, federal policy at present is to have ". . . the Minister retain ultimate stewardship for national parks management." Furthermore, ". . . involvement of any group; in park management will continue to be advisory in nature" [except] ". . . in issues affecting land claims [where] original peoples can be involved as members of a joint advisory and/or decision making body" (Parks Canada 1986, East 1987:4, Rueggeberg 1988:3).

Through land claims agreements, customary use considerations are becoming an active dimension of public participation in park planning and management. Land claims have recently affected the site selection and boundary delineation of several northern national parks (Canada 1984, Canada 1986a). Customary users' knowledge does not, however, seem to be a direct input in NACS identification and new park establishment. However, after a park is established there is growing recognition by the Parks Service that park sites involving claims of native people, the agency must involve customary users in matters of a strategic nature (i.e., development and review of management plans). The 1989 Memorandum of Understanding between the Conseil de Bande de Mingan and the Canadian Parks Service about cooperative planning of Mingan National Park Reserve

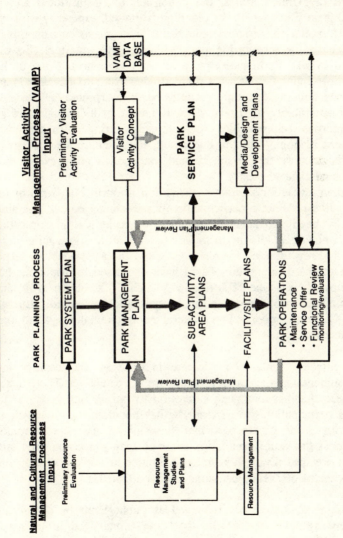

Figure 1. Park Management Process (Source: Environment Canada, Canadian Parks Service 1989b. Adapted from: Payne Graham and Nilsen, 1986)

represents a significant move towards sharing decision making power with customary users (Environment Canada, Canadian Parks Service 1989a).

Unlike the United States, the dimension for institutional and public participation in Canadian Parks planning is limited, especially with respect to policy formulation, program administration (e.g., systems planning) and the legal basis for scrutinizing park administrative matters (Sewell and O'Riordan 1976). Participation as a means of monitoring and evaluating management techniques or as a point of departure to develop long-term constituency building has only recently been interpreted by Parks as an ongoing responsibility of the agency. It feels that individuals and groups have numerous opportunities to comment during both systems and management planning, but the end result, the establishment and planning for a park, is considered to be beyond the public's grasp except in cases involving land claims issues.

Canadian legislation *permits* participation to occur but *does not* require it (Lucas 1976). Public participation in park management planning has traditionally been restricted to pre-emptive issue identification through advisory committees. Issue formulation and information gathering have traditionally been reserved for planners within the agency. With respect to systems planning, some within Parks have expressed the opinion that the systems function is a type of normative planning (Ozbehkan 1969) and the extent of public involvement at this level should be limited. Lucas, in a review of Canadian provincial and federal environmental legislation and case law, commented:

> . . . citizens' rights to participate in decisions by resource and environmental management agencies are not extensive. There is also evidence that agencies with discretion to permit opportunities for public participation are generally either not doing it effectively or not doing so at all. In particular, participation has been extremely limited at the issue formulation stage of agency decision processes. There are also few rights or opportunities in implementation and enforcement of agency decisions (Lucas 1976:102).

Although large areas are managed as public lands by a multitude of government agencies in Canada, that land is managed in trust for the Crown. Rather than land management agencies planning and managing areas in terms of a public trust doctrine, ownership is vested in the Crown and efforts to jointly plan and manage a terrestrial area are extremely difficult to implement. Although Gougeon found that the Canadian Parks Service made considerable effort to involve the public in planning his extensive review of Parks Canada public participation programs, he concludes that:

. . . public involvement is a time consuming, costly, and sometimes obstructionist and controversy creating activity that challenges the bureaucratic structure status quo entrenched in professionalism and administration . . . partnership will not be fully achieved without difficulties and opposition (Gougeon 1985:184).

The opportunities for direct public involvement (i.e., power sharing) in any decision involving Canadian national parks in Canada are limited and access to the courts and litigation are not an effective course of action for resolving environmental disputes. Other mechanisms for participation in protected area designation, planning and management within Canadian Parks Service programs *are* possible, but the extent of involvement and the role of each citizen depends a great deal on the particular decision and its political context.

The IUCN working group on traditional ecological knowledge, and the UNESCO, Man and the Biospheres [MAB] Committee (Francis 1985) and several independent authors, have encouraged planners and managers to include formal and informal sources of knowledge as part of the initial collection of baseline data about a region (Freeman 1979, UNESCO 1984, McNeely and Pitt 1985, IUCN 1985). Parks' current practice of communicating with some customary user groups tends to rely on formal public participation forums and paper-pencil surveys to capture user and interest group informal knowledge about a site. This approach is often perceived by rural communities as ignoring customary forms of communication and local systems of resource management.

Oral cultures and systems of ". . . interdependence and face to face problem solving techniques . . ." are often greeted with considerable reservation by those who suggest that formal meetings and submitted briefs are the accepted method of influencing a decision (Bradshaw and Blakely 1979:15).

However,

. . . between the physical environment and empirically observable behavior there exists a social system, a set of cultural norms and knowledge which define[s] and [or] evaluate[s] portions of the physical environment relevant to the people involved and structure[s] the way people will use [and react to] this environment in their daily lives (Gans 1968:5).

This, therefore, is not a problem of information not being available, but of the need for Parks to carefully assess the benefits of customary and indigenous knowledge in systems and management planning.

CUSTOMARY AND INDIGENOUS KNOWLEDGE
AND PARK PLANNING

Interest in indigenous knowledge (or traditional ecological) and customary users' environmental knowledge and its relationship to conservation planning and management was once considered a narrow area of scholarship, of interest only to a few anthropologists, ethnographers and cultural geographers. Today, international conferences[2] often include sessions devoted to customary users' knowledge. These sessions are dedicated not only to the review and comparison of methodologies and results, but also to the increasing interest among scientists in its application to management.

Dasmann defines customary users as native peoples, local residents and local area resource users ". . . who have a long history of use or occupancy of areas [and] a familiarity [with] their species, communities and ecological processes" (1976:356). The potential contribution of this familiarity with natural history and cultural information to conservation was initially identified by Margules (1958). He noted that in evaluating potential natural areas, (especially where knowledge of environments is difficult to acquire, inadequate or missing), amateur naturalists, local property owners and others intimately familiar with the area can provide information and expertise that may have gone unnoticed.

People develop a unique stock of knowledge or a conceptual structure about their environment through a series of regular occupational or leisure exposures to observable cues and behaviors among each other and objects of attention in the environment (Newell and Simon 1972). The amount and content of environmental knowledge held by an individual group member (user) is often based on: (1) social system and cultural norms (Gans 1968); (2) whether an individual is a novice or master (McCarl 1980); (3) perceptions of some users as central actors/specialists in a network (Mailo and Johnson 1988); or (4) the role played by a leader (Feit 1988). Expressions of this knowledge are evident in a number of forms: jargon and narrative (verbal expressions); on-site activity patterns; preferences for specific micro-and-macro site attributes for an activity; knowledge of the resource (natural history and/or cultural heritage); the canon of work (i.e., informal knowledge used to get the job done); local names for flora and fauna; and song, writings and way finding (Meinig 1970, Bunkse 1978, Freeman 1979, McCarl 1980, Clark and Downing 1984, Hufford 1986).

Dasmann encouraged planners and managers not to separate native peoples and other users' environmental and cultural knowledge of a region in the planning and management of heritage areas. Those who have ". . . maintained the ecological conditions that today are favorable to the establishment of nature reserves . . ." should be involved in their selection, establishment, planning and ongoing management (Dasmann 1984:668).

Indigenous knowledge (traditional ecological knowledge) as defined by Dasmann (1974), is a form of customary users' knowledge. However, in the opinion of others, traditional ecological knowledge includes all of the above noted characteristics related to customary users' knowledge, but also embraces several differences.   Indigenous knowledge, according to Chambers, is:

> . . . knowledge located in people and only rarely written down. Knowledge refers to the whole system of knowledge, including concepts, beliefs and perceptions, the stock of knowledge, and the processes whereby it is required, augmented, stored and transmitted (1983:85).

Most important in this definition is the emphasis placed on the role this knowledge has played and continues to play in sustaining the culture of native peoples. Indigenous environmental knowledge is imprinted over time on a culture and passed from one generation to the next with minor adjustments that are sometimes related to the interaction between the knowledge base and continued sustainable use of the environment (Howes and Chambers 1980, McNeely and Pitt 1985).   This type of informal knowledge is often expressed in strong local traditions, mores, customs, decision making, reliance on compatible use and stewardship of local lifeways, culturally defined places and an intimate and extensive knowledge of the area and its resources. The importance of these culturally defined resources to the culture and identity of traditional peoples should not be underestimated by protected area planners and managers (Howes and Chambers 1980, Weaver 1984).

To some resource managers, politicians and planners, indigenous environmental knowledge sometimes appears to be unscientific, restricted to a very limited area and difficult to compare to formal scientific data. Howes and Chambers comment:

> . . . it seems that when indigenous knowledge and scientific stocks of knowledge come together, synthesis does not occur. One of two things happen; either the two sets of knowledge are isolated from each other . . . or indigenous knowledge is ignored and squeezed out as inferior (1980:332).

The following case studies illustrate the current leading applications of customary and indigenous knowledge to protected area systems and management planning (Parks Canada 1985b) in Canada today.

CASE STUDIES

Existing Canadian park systems and management planning emphasizes a top-down synoptic approach to developing proposals for new parks and heritage areas. Much emphasis in developing these plans is placed on scientific knowledge from the natural sciences and some information from the social sciences. To date, none of the existing plans or system planning studies have provided direct input for informal environmental knowledge except in matters affecting indigenous people's land claims.

Policy affecting marine parks, which are new in Canada, promotes a potential for broader public participation and involvement in their establishment and planning (Environment Canada, Parks 1986 § 1.2). Thus, indigenous and customary users' informal knowledge could begin to represent a new and important contribution to area identification, site selection and on-going management.

At present, one national marine park and one national marine park reserve are designated: Fathom Five (Tobermory, Ontario on Lake Huron), and the marine area around South Moresby (Queen Charlotte Islands, British Columbia). The former is in the beginning stages of management planning while the latter will not commence management planning until the federal Department of Energy, Mines and Resources completes studies of hydrocarbon potential in the adjacent marine areas. Three sites are proposed as candidate parks: Lancaster/Eclipse Sound [Lancaster Sound in the Northwest Territories], West Isles [an area located adjacent to the Canada-U.S. border between Maine and New Brunswick] and the Saguenay [the confluence of the St. Lawrence and Saguenay rivers in Quebec] (Map 1).

Approximately 22 federal acts (administered by eight federal departments, including the one within which Parks is administratively located), 20 provincial and territorial acts and in some areas municipal and native councils' land use and waste disposal regulations, seek to maintain marine environmental quality (Cornwall, Higgins and Karau 1988, Coté 1989).

Protecting the marine environment in a park and controlling impacts will be a co-operatively shared tri-level governmental responsibility.

Because the Parks Service cannot own and directly manage the surface of the water, the activities that occur on it and the flora and fauna in the water column, the approach to public participation, the collection and in some cases the use of informal environmental knowledge in developing these plans (e.g., the preparation of fisheries management plans for marine parks), will be directed by a partnership of parks and other involved department(s). All of the other seven departments involved in reviewing potential sites and on-going planning and management of marine resources require face to face communication, joint decision making and regular discussions with customary users and indigenous peoples before they can change sea use patterns.

Thus, Parks' major role in selecting, planning and managing potential marine parks will be: (1) proactive leadership related to horizontal responsibilities across the other seven federal departments, (2) regional integration of the park with provincial/territorial/local governments, customary users, and indigenous peoples, and (3) coordinating national responsibilities related to a variety of international marine environmental quality commitments.

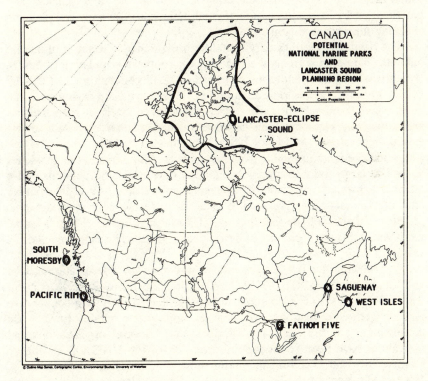

Map 1. Potential National Marine Parks in Canada and Lancaster Sound Planning Region. (Source: Environment Canada, Parks (1987) and Northwest Territories, Northern Land Use Planning Commission (1988))

In the marine parks policy the terms *co-operative management* and *consultation* are used to describe relationships with customary users and traditional peoples. Both of these terms offer interpretation and flexibility to the local manager, especially in the marine setting. In developing marine parks, the agency will be faced with different administrative responsibilities, an extremely dynamic and changing ecosystem, and recognition of the need to create both conservation and preservation objectives for the marine park(i.e., where appropriate, sustainable use of the marine area will continue). These broader program objectives, expressed in policy, offer much hope that customary and indigenous environmental knowledge can be used to strengthen both marine park systems and management planning.

In the case of the proposed marine park for the Saguenay (Map 1), the Quebec region of Parks concluded that effective management of the park would depend on the identification of regional use and impacts and participation by its related customary and indigenous users in area planning and long term management.

The Saguenay Fjord estuary contains a truly remarkable series of marine habitats. The area is frequented by the only southern population of beluga (white whales) whose endangered status and small population size (250-700 animals) has received worldwide attention. They have been described as the most polluted animals on earth. Background toxic levels in some animals are sufficiently high that their carcasses qualify as hazardous waste under existing federal law (McMillan 1988). The unique mixing of fresh and salt water and the large upwelling in the area attract blue, fin and minke whales as well as large concentrations of seabirds. Spectacular fjordal cliffs and a trapped saltwater sea combine to create an unusual yet representative combination of geological and coastal land forms and oceanographic features. In spite of the fact that the St. Lawrence Estuary has substantial industrial, agricultural and urban development, it has maintained much of its wild state.

In reviewing the IUCN's ten marine protected area designations (Salm and Clark 1984:236-241), UNESCO's Marine Biosphere Reserve concept with its emphasis on conservation, sustainable development and cooperative and collaborative planning, seemed an appropriate model to increase conservation for the Saguenay Fjord estuary. Several organizations and individuals have been reviewing the extension of the UNESCO Biosphere Reserve Program to coastal and marine environments (e.g., UNESCO 1984, IUCN 1988, Kenchington, Agardi, Dobbin, Foster, Hanson, Broadus, Gable and Gains 1988). MAB sites acknowledge that:

. . . people constitute an essential component of the landscape and seascape . . . [and] their activities are fundamental for its long term conservation and compatible use . . . [People] are encouraged to participate in management [of the MAB site] and this ensures a stronger social acceptance of conservation activities (UNESCO 1984:2).

One looks in vain for an overarching management structure that gives a MAB site its reality. Instead, one finds a very loosely defined structure, composed of local people who wish to have their area managed from an eco-system perspective. Local committees can quickly identify environmental issues that they would like to see addressed. Usually these issues lie at the margin of several government agencies which until confronted together in a public forum, contemplate taking little action. The management committee thus serves as a communications framework through which mistrust and apathy among groups and individuals can be dissipated (Francis 1985, Payne and Graham 1988). Therefore, the role of Parks, in turn, becomes one of advising and serving rather than directing.

In reviewing the marine MAB concept, Parks opened communications with a committee of U.S. and Canadian scientists interested in a combined international marine MAB demonstration project. Although this project is still very much in a preliminary stage of its evolution, discussions of the concept with customary and indigenous users encouraged a broader dialogue among area users than had occurred during the systems planning phase of the project (Pippard 1987).

During the aforementioned stage of this project (area identification and regional analysis), the World Wildlife Fund (Canada) funded a special workshop to clear the air about what was and was not proposed for the area. This was the first time the Canadian Parks Service, concerned scientists and customary users, had an opportunity to discuss their visions for the area. In its opening statement to the meeting, Parks made clear that this workshop was not the usual way of doing things and that no precedents were to be set by this meeting. At the end of the day, members of the workshop concluded that information provided by Parks about the area was ". . . missing pertinent factual information and knowledge available through customary and indigenous users . . . [and] that to continue to use existing literature to develop an understanding of the area . . . is viewed as a critical pitfall in the marine park planning process" (Pippard 1987:15-16).

It would be inappropriate not to mention that loose organizational structures, like MAB committees, rely on volunteers whose time and attention can be diverted. But over time and in other countries (e.g., United Kingdom's voluntary marine nature reserves: Graham and Huff 1985 or the Caribbean - ENCAMP: Towle 1985) exchanges of information between local systems of resource conservation and state conservation programs have led to a refinement of knowledge, respective skills and management techniques for marine protected areas.

In the case of the Lancaster Sound region of the Northwest Territories (NWT), the Land Use Planning Commission (LUPC) decided that if the proposed land use plan is ". . . to protect and promote the existing and future well being of the permanent residents and communities of the planning region, taking into account the interests of all Canadians," then the documentation of indigenous knowledge of the land, land fast ice and sea would enable the commission to readily identify community issues and concerns about current use of the region and visions of a desired future (NWT-LUPC 1988:1). Commission staff embarked on a series of face-to-face communications with community leaders and knowledgeable people throughout the region. The informal knowledge drawn on maps and recorded on tape represents one of the most important data sources used in developing the plan.

Scientific data about the region available through government, industry and other organizations were then combined with their uses, concerns and desires. Integration of the two forms of knowledge was accomplished through a series of community discussions and meetings with interested individuals and groups. An initial draft was further developed to reconfirm defined interest zones and their sensitivity to access and use. The second draft plan is currently being reviewed in meetings with communities, governments, industries and interest groups (NWT-LUPC 1988).

The Lancaster Sound Planning Region is a roughly triangular area of approximately 1.5 million square kilometers in the Canadian Arctic archipelago (Map 1). It is a region of remote communities, ecosystems of national and international importance and an abundance of non-renewable resources. Wildlife, the land, the ice and the sea are vital to the culture, as well as the economic and physical well being of the Inuit in this area, a people who have sustained their existence for thousands of years using defined systems of local resource management and intimate knowledge. In attempting to develop a land use plan for this area, planners and managers felt that the commission would have to use a community-based approach to planning.

In implementing this approach they decided to willingly seek out and document customary and indigenous knowledge of the region. This cast the LUPC in the role more of a receiver than a sender of information and committed it to a process of collaborative planning (joint decision making) and monitoring (Mills 1988).

Although northern regional land use planning is still evolving, the LUPC has recommended that to achieve a sustainable future, three principles should guide planning of this area: conserve, communicate and then consider development.[3] One of the major recommendations for all proposed projects in the region, whether it be protected area selection or proposed hydrocarbon development, is that communities and proponents initiate planning with a face-to-face ". . . exchange [of] their [scientific] information and community knowledge . . . as often as is possible" (NWT-LUPC 1988:45). It is only through these exchanges that mutual respect for knowledge contributed by different actors can develop and be used to build a vision for the region.

Lessons from both case studies reinforce the fact that sea use and northern land use planning have similar tasks: how to allocate use in a seemingly vast area where loss of quality space or a perceived increase in competition for limited and valued community-managed areas poses the greatest question. Those involved in the Saguenay and the Lancaster Sound Region planning projects have described their experiences as *decision building under uncertainty* and argue that proposed conservation and sustainable use strategies in such situations can only begin to be successful if planners looked to informal sources of information to complement existing data, and move away from the synoptic or rational model of planning.

CONCLUSION

Canadian national park managers and planners have tended to implement systems and management planning with an ecological rationale rather than looking to both the human factor, natural history and cultural information. If, in the next few years, expansion of the Canadian National Parks Systems occurs in the north and in marine and coastal settings, then the agency will be faced with limited scientific information upon which to justify the selection of NACS and potential parks. The current rational, comprehensive approach to systems and management planning assumes full information of the biophysical environment, but accepts the fact that the information requirements for natural science data will be met with the best available and affordable information.

Planners in this situation will either try to *satisfice* [i.e., develop sufficient data in reports to satisfy decision makers or to solve the immediate problem] or move to another planning model (Simon 1957). Neither scientific information (formal knowledge) nor traditional environmental knowledge (informal knowledge) can by themselves effectively aid in planning and managing these resources. It will be necessary to integrate both systems of knowledge and their respective approaches to resource management (state and local systems management) if the site is to meet its long term conservation and preservation objectives. The cases discussed and the review of other international examples of heritage area planning suggest that the Canadian Parks Service should begin to carefully evaluate its current use of a rational synoptic model in systems and management planning.

In conclusion, we wish to suggest a few tentative responses to the three questions posed at the beginning of the chapter.

(1)   Why should the knowledge and capabilities of customary and indigenous peoples be considered in park selection, planning and management? The top-down synoptic planning processes relied on by Parks' systems and management planners will be increasingly difficult to implement in the North and in marine settings.   The emerging planning and management paradigm in both environments is one in which visions of the future are developed through co-operation and collaboration.   Transactive models (Freidman 1987) and their use of bottom-up approaches to identify issues and build decisions seem to be the most successful in establishing protected areas.

If it is accepted that long term conservation of these areas can only succeed by consent (Miles 1982), then developing an understanding of indigenous and customary users' knowledge, skills and abilities is a first step to building communication and trust with these groups. The literature and case studies revealed that these groups are able to effectively identify and describe resource issues, local resource management systems, community patterns of resource use, valued micro-and-macro site attributes, natural resource ecosystem information and sites related to their traditions and culture -- the significance of which might not be understood by those not residing in the community.

This information, when combined with existing formal knowledge, may also enhance the heritage value of the proposed or existing protected area and develop a greater awareness of ecosystem dynamics among both the agency and users.

(2)   How can informal environmental knowledge be integrated with formal data in the planning and management of potential and existing parks? Parks' use of customary and traditional expertise to aid in the implementation of regional analysis research, NACS confirmation studies and management planning can be implemented through the requirements and activities of VAMP (Parks Canada 1985a: 2-3 and 26). The knowledge, skills and abilities of customary uses and indigenous peoples can be documented, if they so wish, to provide unique opportunities for visitors to experience their heritage.

When customary knowledge is collected at the same time as initial resource studies and with the co-operation of these groups, the data can contribute effectively to discussions regarding park selection and establishment.   In systems planning, the Preliminary Visitor Activity Evaluation Analysis, if implemented, could be used initially to develop an understanding of customary and indigenous peoples' knowledge as it relates to: opportunity assessment, identifying existing patterns of use and potential visitor opportunities. In the north and marine settings, there are numerous hazards and risks which the indigenous user and customary user can identify and suggest ways to manage. Enriched interpretive messages, public education opportunities and a greater understanding of the region may be developed from informal ecological knowledge. The data can also support the development of the required marine park preliminary management concept which is stated in policy but has yet to be followed (Environment Canada, Parks 1986: § 1.2.5 and 1.2.9, Mondor 1988).

During management planning, customary and indigenous knowledge can be used to contribute to the data requirements of both the NRMP and VAMP.

(3) How might the Canadian Parks Service develop and improve institutional arrangements between managers and users of the resource? Implementing the Preliminary Visitor Activity Evaluation as a contributor to the process of regional analysis and NACS identification studies would include the informal ecological information of customary and indigenous users. The documentation of existing environmental knowledge and capabilities represents a first step in improving relationships between the agency and user groups.

The process of documentation involves development of a two-way communication network through which both types of information can be shared and commented upon. More important, the development of this network represents how Parks can re-establish communication with specific customary users at any later point in the planning process.

Finally, Parks should carefully assess the potential contribution that the MAB model could make to facilitate the establishment of parks and their ongoing planning and management, particularly in the north and in marine areas.

ACKNOWLEDGMENTS

The opinions expressed are those of the authors, as are any errors or omissions. We would like to acknowledge Per Nilsen and Robert Gougeon of Environment Canada, Parks, Richard Lawrence and the anonymous reviewers who helped with editing and providing suggestions to strengthen the chapter. The Canadian Parks Service and Social Sciences and Humanities Research Council (Canada) must be acknowledged for their support of a portion of this research, but none of the comments or opinions expressed are representative of its policy and direction on these issues.

NOTES:

1. Between 1962 and 1988, Canada's national parks agency changed its name on several occasions. In this chapter, the agency will be referred to as either the Canadian Parks Service (CPS), its most recent name, or Parks.

2. Freeman (1988) cites, as evidence of this trend, recent scientific congresses hosted by the Ecological Sciences and Marine Sciences divisions of UNESCO, the International Association of Biological Oceanographers, the International Union of Biological Sciences, and the National Research Council Meetings on Common Property Management (Freeman and Cabyn 1988).

3. Development is defined as the use of resources today without damaging the prospects for future generations (NWT-LUPC 1988:25).

REFERENCES

Andrews, T.D. 1988. Selected bibliography of native resource management systems and native knowledge of the environment. In M.M.R. Freeman and L.N. Carbyn (Eds.), *Traditional Knowledge and Renewable Resource Management in Northern Regions.* Gland, Switzerland and Edmonton, Alberta: IUCN and Boreal Institute for Northern Studies 105-124.

Baldwin, C. 1985. Management of the Dugong: An endangered marine species of traditional significance. In J. Lien and R. Graham (Eds.), *Marine Parks and Conservation: Challenge and Promise.* St. Johns: MRI Publishing and the National and Provincial Parks Association of Canada, II, Vol. 2, 241-254.

Berkes, F. 1988. Environmental philosophy of the Chisasibi Cree people of James Bay. In M.M.R. Freeman and L.N. Carbyn (Eds.), *Traditional Knowledge and Renewable Resource Management in Northern Regions.* Gland, Switzerland and Edmonton, Alberta: IUCN and Boreal Institute for Northern Studies 7-21.

Blanchard, K. 1985. Seabirds of the Quebec northshore. In J. Lien and R. Graham (Eds.), *Marine Parks and Conservation: Challenge and Promise.* St. Johns: MRI Publishing and the National and Provincial Parks Association of Canada, II, Vol. I, 219-230.

Bradshaw, T.K. and E.J. Blakely. 1979. *Rural Communities in Advanced Industrial Society: Development and Developers.* New York: Praeger Publishers.

Bunkse, E.V. 1978. Commoner attitudes towards landscape and nature. *Annals of the Association of American Geographers* 68:551-556.

CBC. 1987. Canadian Broadcasting Corporation. Land and sea television series.

Canada. 1984. *The Western Arctic Claim: The Invialuit Final Agreement.* Ottawa: Department of Indian and Northern Affairs.

Canada. 1986a. *Agreement Between Her Majesty and the Cree Band of Fort Chipewyan.* Ottawa: Department of Indian Affairs and Northern Development.

Canada. 1986b. *Regulatory Reform Strategy.* Ottawa: Regulatory Affairs Secretariat of the Privy Council Office.

Caufield, R. 1988. The role of subsistence resource commissions in managing Alaska's new national parks. In M.M.R. Freeman and L.N. Carbyn (Eds.), *Traditional Knowledge and Renewable Resource Management.* Gland, Switzerland and Edmonton, Alberta: IUCN and Boreal Institute for Northern Studies, 55-64.

Chambers, R. 1983. *Rural Development: Putting the Last First.* London: Longman.

CLAMP. 1984. Citizens League Against Marine Parks Newsletter 1:1.

Clark, R. and K. Downing. 1984. Why here and not there: The conditional nature of recreation choice. In G. Stankey and S. McCool (Eds.), *Proceedings - Symposium on Recreation Choice.* Ogden: USFS Intermountain Research Station, General Technical Report INT 184, 61-70.

Cobourg Peninsula Sanctuary Board. 1987. *Gurig National Park Plan of Management.* Winnellie: Conservation Commission of the Northern Territory.

Cornwall, G., P. Higgins and P. Karu. 1988. *Canadian Legislation Pertaining to the Prevention and Control of Marine Pollution.* Paper presented at the Canadian conference on marine environmental quality. Halifax, Nova Scotia, February 29 - March 3.

Coté, R. 1989. *Marine Environmental Quality.* Ottawa: Science Council of Canada.

Dasmann, R.F. 1974. Difficult marginal environments and the traditional societies which exploit them: Ecosystems. *Survival International News* 11:11-14.

Dasmann, R.F. 1976. *Environmental Conservation .* New York: John Wiley.

Dasmann, R.F. 1984. The relationship between protected areas and indigenous peoples. In J.A. McNeely and K.R. Miller (Eds.), *National Parks, Conservation and Development.* Gland, Switzerland: IUCN, 667-671.

East, K. 1987. *Joint Management of Canada's Northern National Parks.* Draft report. Winnipeg: Prairie and northern region Canadian Parks Service.

Eaton, P. 1984. Conservation land tenure and conservation in Papua, New Guinea. In J. McNeely and D. Pitt (Eds.), *Cultural Conservation: The Human Dimension in Environmental Planning.* Gland, Switzerland: IUCN, 181-191.

Environment Canada, Parks. 1986. *National Marine Parks Policy.* Ottawa: Ministry of Supply and Services.

Environment Canada, Parks. Canadian Parks Service. 1987. *Terms of Reference for Report on the Involvement of Aboriginal People in National Parks in Other Countries.* Ottawa: Parks.

Environment Canada, Parks. Canadian Parks Service. 1989a. *Memorandum of Understanding Between the Conseil de Bande de Mingan and the Canadian Parks Service.* Ottawa: Parks.

Environment Canada, Parks. Canadian Parks Service. 1989b. *Getting Started: A Guide to Service Planning.* Ottawa: Visitor Services and Interpretation.

Feit, H.A. 1988. Self management and state management: Forms of knowing and managing northern wildlife. In M.M.R. Freeman and L.N. Carbyn (Eds.), *Traditional Knowledge and Renewable Resource Management in Northern Regions.* Gland, Switzerland and Edmonton, Alberta: IUCN and Boreal Institute for Northern Studies 72-91.

Foran, B. and B. Walker. 1985. Cooperatively managed parks in the northern territory: The evolutionary process. In *Science and Technology for Aboriginal Development.* Canberra: CSIRO.

Francis, G.R. 1985. Biosphere reserves: Innovations for cooperation in the search for sustainable development. *Environments* 17:23-36.

Francis, G.R. 1987. Assessment of socio-economic ramifications. *Hydrobiologia* 149:125-129.

Freeman, M.M.R. 1979. Traditional land users as a legitimate source of environmental expertise. In J.G. Nelson, R.D. Needham and D.L. Mann (Eds.), *The Canadian National Parks Today and Tomorrow Conference II, Ten Years Later.* Waterloo: Department of Geography Publication Series No. 12, 11, Vol. I, 345-349.

Freeman, M.M.R. and L.N. Cabyn (Eds.). 1988. *Traditional Knowledge and Renewable Resource Management in Northern Regions.* Gland, Switzerland and Edmonton, Alberta: IUCN and Boreal Institute for Northern Studies.

Friedman, J. 1987. *Planning in the Public Domain.* Princeton: Princeton University Press.

Gans, H.J. 1968. *People and Plans.* New York: Basic Books.

Gougeon, R.B. 1985. *Modifying the Impact of Resource Development: Externalities and Public Involvement in Parks Canada.* Unpublished master's thesis. University of Ottawa.

Graham, R. and D.W. Huff. 1985. Voluntary and co-operative management in marine conservation: England, Scotland and Wales. *Environments* 17:111-126.

Graham, R., R.J. Payne and P.W. Nilsen. 1988. Visitor management in Canadian national parks. *Tourism management* (March): 44-62.

Holling, C.S. 1978. *Adaptive Environmental Assessment and Management.* New York and IIASA: John Wiley and Sons.

Howes, M. and R. Chambers. 1980. Indigenous technical knowledge: Analysis, implications and issues. In D. Brokensha *et al.* (Eds.), *Indigenous Knowledge System and Development.* Boston: University Press of America 329-340.

Hufford, M. 1986. *One Space, Many Places.* Washington: American Folk Life Center.

IUCN. 1980. *World Conservation Strategy: Living Resource Conservation for Sustainable Development.* (Also with the United Nations Environment Program, the World Wildlife Fund, the Food and Agricultural Organization and the United Nations.) Gland: IUCN.

IUCN. 1985. *Draft Programme on Traditional and Informal Knowledge for Conservation.* In IUCN occasional newsletter of the commission on ecology's working group on traditional ecological knowledge. Morges, Switzerland: IUCN.

IUCN. 1988. *Policy for Marine Conservation and Establishment of Marine Protected Areas.* (Draft). Morges, Switzerland.

Jacobs, P. 1985. A sustainable society through sustainable development: Toward a regional development strategy in Northern Quebec. *Landscape Planning* 12:267-283.

Johannes, R.F. 1982. Traditional conservation methods and protected marine areas in Oceania. *Ambio* 11:258-261.

Kenchington, R.A., T. Agardi, J. Dobbin, N. Foster, A. Hanson, J.M. Broadus, F. Gable and A.G. Gains. 1988. *Marine Conservation and Biosphere Reserves.* Draft discussion paper. Woods Hole: Marine Policy Centre, Woods Hole Oceanographic Institute.

La Forest, G.V. and M.K. Roy. 1981. *Report on the Special Inquiry on Kouchibouguac National Park.* Ottawa and St. Johns, New Brunswick: Government of Canada and the Province of New Brunswick.

Lamson C. and A. Hanson. 1984. *Atlantic Fisheries and Coastal Communities.* Halifax: Dalhousie University Press.

Lerner, S.C. 1986. Environmental constituency building: Local initiatives and volunteer stewardship. *Alternatives* 13:55-60.

Lien, J. 1985. Teaching fishermen about whales. In J. Lien and R. Graham (Eds.), *Marine Parks and Conservation: Challenge and Promise.* St. Johns: MRI Publishing and the National and Provincial Parks Association of Canada, 231-240.

Lucas, A.R. 1976. Legal foundations for public participation in environmental decision making. *Natural Resources Journal* 16:73-102.

Mailo, J.R. and J.C. Johnson. 1988. *Determining and Utilizing Communication Networks in Marine Fisheries: A Useful Management Tool.* Unpublished paper presented to 41st Annual Meeting of the Gulf and Caribbean Institute. St. Thomas, USVI, November, 1988.

Margules, C. 1958. Biology conservation, cited in R.F. Johannes, Traditional conservation methods and protected marine areas in Oceania. *Ambio* 2:258-261.

Meinig, D.W. 1970. Environmental appreciation: Localities as humane art. *Western Humanities Review* 25:1-11.

Miles, E. 1982. *The Management of Marine Regions: The North Pacific.* Berkeley: University of California Press.

Mills, H. 1988. *Northern Land Use Planning.* Presentation to the Round Table Lecture Series, Heritage Resources Centre, University of Waterloo, Waterloo, Ontario.

Mitchell, J. 1987. Planning at Canyon de Chelly national monument. *Cultural Resources Management Bulletin* 10:19-21, 30.

Mondor, C. 1988. *Planning for National Marine Parks.* (Draft unpublished paper.) Workshop on National Marine Park Planning. Ottawa: The Canadian Parks Service.

McCarl, R. 1980. Occupational folklore. In E. Iring (Ed.), *Folk Groups and Folklore Genre: An Introduction.* Logan: Utah State University Press, 71-87.

McMillian, T. 1988. Notes from a speech by the Honorable T. McMillan, Canadian Minister of the Environment. The Graves Lecture. New Haven, CT: Yale University.

McNeely, J.A. and D. Pitt (Eds.). 1985. *Cultural Conservation: The Human Dimension in Environmental Planning.* London: Croom Held.

Nelson, J.G. 1978. Canadian national parks and related reserves: Development, research needs and management. In J.G. Nelson, R.D. Needham and D.L Mann (Eds.), *International Experience with National Parks and Related Reserves.* Waterloo: Department of Geography Publication Series No.12, 43-87.

Nelson, J.G. 1987. National parks and protected areas, national conservation strategies and sustainable development. *Geoforum* 18:291-319.

Newell, A. and H. Simon. 1972. *Human Problem Solving.* Englewood Cliffs: Prentice Hall.

Nietschman, B. 1984. Indigenous peoples, living resources and protected areas. In J.A. McNeely and K.R. Miller (Eds.), *National Parks, Conservation and Development,* Gland: IUCN, 333-343.

Nilsen, P.W. 1987. *Visitor Activity Management in Northern National Parks: An Exploratory Study.* Unpublished master's thesis in Recreation and Leisure Studies. Waterloo, Ontario: University of Waterloo.

Northwest Territories Land Use Planning Commission. 1988. *The Lancaster Sound Regional Land Use Plan.* (Second Draft.) Yellowknife: Northwest Territories Land Use Planning Commission.

Ozebekhan, H. 1969. The emerging methodology of planning. In J. Jantsch (Ed.), *Perspectives of Planning.* Paris: OECD, 63-80.

Parks Canada. 1978. *Natural Resource Management Process.* Ottawa: Natural Resources Division, National Parks.

Parks Canada. 1981. *Manual on the Application of the Environmental Assessment Review Process Within Parks Canada.* Ottawa: Resource Conservation Branch.

Parks Canada. 1983. *Directive 2.2.1, Socio-economic Analysis in Management Plans for National Parks.* Ottawa: Socio-Economic Branch.

Parks Canada. 1985a. *Management Process for Visitor Activities.* Ottawa: Visitor Services and Interpretation, National Parks.

Parks Canada. 1985b. *National Parks Management Planning Process.* Ottawa: Policy and Planning, National Parks.

Parks Canada. 1985c. *West Isles Feasibility Study.* A report prepared for Parks Canada and Tourism New Brunswick. Halifax and St. John: Environment Canada, Parks Canada.

Parks Canada. 1986. *Native Involvement in National Parks: A Discussion Paper.* (Draft). Winnipeg: Prairie and northern region office, Parks Canada.

Payne, R.J., R. Graham and P. Nilsen. 1986. *Preliminary Assessment of the Visitor Activity Management Process (VAMP).* A technical report prepared for Visitor Services and Interpretation. Ottawa: National Parks.

Payne, R.J. and R. Graham. 1988. Implementing citizen participation in Canada: Single and multiple actor cases. In L. S. Bankert and R. Warren Flint (Eds.), *Environmental Dispute Resolution in the Great Lakes Region: A Critical Appraisal.* Buffalo: Great Lakes Program, State University of New York. Great Lakes Monograph No. 1, 67-78.

Pinkerton, E. (Ed.). 1989. *Co-operative Management of Local Fisheries.* Vancouver: University of British Columbia Press.

Pippard L. 1987. *Workshop on the Proposed Saguenay National Marine Park.* A report prepared for Environment Canada, Parks and World Wildlife Fund, Canada. Ottawa: National Parks Branch, Environment Canada, Parks.

Rueggeberg, H. 1988. *Involvement of Aboriginal People in National Park Management.* A report prepared for Environment Canada, Parks. Ottawa: Environment Canada: Canadian Parks Service.

Salm, R. and J.R. Clark. 1984. *Marine and Coastal Protected Areas: A Guide for Planners and Managers.* Columbia: State Printing.

Sewell, W.R.D. and T.O. O'Riordan. 1976. The culture of participation in environmental decision making. *Natural Resources Journal* 16:1-12.

Sibbeston, N. 1987. Economic development and renewable resources in the Northwest Territories. In J. Green and J. Smith (Eds.), *Native People and Renewable Resource Management.* Edmonton: Alberta Society of Professional Biologists 153-157.

Shannon, M. 1987. Forest Planning: Learning with people. In M.L. Miller, R.P. Gale and P.J. Brown (Eds.), *Social Science in Natural Resource Management Systems.* Colorado: Westview Press 233-247.

Stenmark, R.J. 1987. National parks and protected areas in the Arctic: Alaska. In J.G. Nelson, R. Needham and L. Norton (Eds.), *Arctic Heritage: Proceeding of a Symposium.* Ottawa: ACUC, 513-528.

Simon, H. 1957. *Administrative Behavior.* New York: Macmillan.

Thomas, W.J. 1987. Marine protected areas and customary rights. In *Coastal Zone '87: Proceedings of the Fifth Symposium on Coastal and Ocean Management.* Washington: American Society of Civil Engineers, VI, Vol. 3, 35555-35567.

Towle, J.A. 1985. Management analysis of the eastern Caribbean natural area management program (ENCAMP). In J. Lien and R. Graham (Eds.), *Marine Parks and Conservations: Challenge and Promise.* St. Johns: MRI Publishing and the National and Provincial Parks Association of Canada, II, Vol. II, 117-126.

UNESCO. 1984. Action plan for biosphere reserves. *Nature and Resources* 20:1-12.

United Nations. 1987. *Our Common Future: World Commission on Environment and Development.* (Bruntland commission). New York: Oxford University Press.

U.S. Congress. 1980. *Alaska National Interest Lands Conservation Act of 1980.* Public Law 96-487. Washington: U.S. Congress.

Weaver, S.C. 1984. *Progress Report: The Role of Aboriginals in the Management of Cobourg and Kakadu National Parks, Northern Territory, Australia.* Unpublished report. Darwin, Australia.

White, A.T. 1984. *Marine Parks and Reserves: Management for Philippine, Indonesian and Malaysian Coastal Reef Environments.* Unpublished doctoral dissertation, University of Hawaii.

World Wildlife Fund, Canada. 1985. *Whales Under the Ice.* Toronto: World Wildlife Fund, Canada.

Wright, R.M., B. Housel and C. De Leon. 1985. Kuna Yala: Indigenous biosphere reserve in the making. *Parks* 15:25-27.

CHAPTER 10

DISTINGUISHING RECREATION FROM SUBSISTENCE IN A MODERNIZING ECONOMY

Ronald J. Glass
Northeastern Forest Experiment Station

Robert M. Muth
U.S. Forest Service

Robert Flewelling
University of North Carolina

Throughout history, humans have relied on renewable natural resources for their sustenance. The few activities engaged in for *sport* (such as falconry or fox hunting) were generally reserved for wealthy or powerful social elites. For most of the world's population, however, hunting, fishing, and gathering served either to provide the mainstay of their food supply, or as significant supplements to resources procured through herding and primitive agriculture. With the advent of industrialization and urbanization, however, household sustenance needs were increasingly met by wage employment and, more recently, by government transfer programs. Thus, for many people in modern societies increasingly less dependent on the personal harvest of fish and wildlife for sustenance, recreational values gradually replaced subsistence as the primary motivation for engaging in hunting and fishing activities.

Today, natural resource policymakers, managers, and most social scientists tend to believe that the use of renewable natural resources for subsistence has all but disappeared in modern industrial societies. Most hunting and fishing regulations in the United States, for example, are designed to manage recreational and commercial uses of fish and wildlife, rather than to provide for users more appropriately characterized by a subsistence orientation. This view has been subscribed to and incorporated into the operating assumptions of resource management agencies as well as interest groups such as conservation organizations, professional societies, sportsmen's groups, and commercial associations. However, an increasing body of research (Barsh 1982, Gladwin and Butler 1982, Lichens 1977, Muth, Ruppert, and Glass 1987, Muth and Glass 1989, Rattner 1984, Victor and Burrell Research and Consulting *et al.* 1981) suggests that rural subpopulations in industrialized North America continue to rely on fish, wildlife, and plant resources for sustenance, although their harvesting activities are managed under policies governing recreational use, commercial use, or Native-American rights.

As ideal-type abstractions, recreational users and subsistence users constitute significantly different groups. In most rural areas of the industrialized world, however, there are probably very few households totally dependent on the direct consumption of natural resources for physical survival. Instead, resource-dependent households are apt to drift in and out of the cash economy as necessity dictates, and as opportunities for employment present themselves. Rather than providing a threshold for survival, subsistence production, by supplementing income from the cash economy, serves to enhance the socioeconomic well-being of otherwise economically-marginal households.

The example of southeast Alaska illustrates the changes wrought by the forces of modernization on traditional subsistence lifestyles. Historically, the indigenous residents of this region were highly dependent upon the harvesting and direct consumption of fish, wildlife and other natural resources (Oberg 1973, Suttles 1968). In retrospect, there is little difficulty distinguishing the basic characteristics of subsistence from recreation in the society that existed in southeast Alaska prior to Euro-American contact. In fact, among the aboriginal Indian peoples of southeast Alaska, fish and wildlife resources were invested with spiritual importance -- the idea of using fish and wildlife for *fun* or for *sport* was not only highly proscribed, it was antithetical to their world view.

Subsistence production has become more and more intertwined with both the private and public sectors of the cash economy (Glass 1987). Although subsistence resources continue to contribute significant quantities to household food budgets, increased affluence has reduced the dependence of most households on natural resources for direct consumption as a basis of physical survival. In the contemporary period, fulfillment of psychological, social, and cultural needs and values through participation in subsistence activities are often cited as being equally or more important than providing material goods for physical survival. These less tangible benefits and satisfactions resulting from subsistence activities among contemporary rural populations are often similar to those derived from recreation participation.

If it were not for policy implications, the distinction between recreation and subsistence would not be an important issue in Alaska. The contribution that participation in an activity makes to the overall well-being of people is certainly more important than its arbitrary categorization. However, both state and federal laws pertaining to fish and wildlife management in Alaska specify subsistence as a priority use over recreational and commercial uses when fish and wildlife populations are in danger of over-harvest. Determining who should qualify as subsistence users under these laws and regulations is an extremely complex and controversial issue.

It is the intent of this chapter to examine the conceptual bases of both subsistence and recreation, and to consider the appropriateness of traditional precepts within the context of a relatively affluent, modernizing economy. As an example of a traditional subsistence community that has undergone considerable modernization, harvest and sociodemographic data are examined for the community of Yakutat, located in southeast Alaska. While sample size is limited (50 households out of a total population of 181), the data provide insights regarding personal use of natural resources in a modern, rural community, and the difficulties in distinguishing recreation from subsistence in this situation.

CONCEPTUAL DISTINCTIONS
BETWEEN RECREATION AND SUBSISTENCE

Although both subsistence and recreation are commonly used terms in the research and policy literature, they tend to be conceptually imprecise. Traditionally, subsistence had been viewed as representing the minimum standard for physical survival, and recreation was regarded as little more than the activities engaged in for play or relaxation during periods of leisure time. Today, however, the main body of social science literature views both of these terms in a much broader context. Although definitions of subsistence remain imprecise (Albrecht 1972, Schneider 1982), discussions of subsistence often reference the psychological, social, economic, and/or cultural aspects of subsistence societies -- societies in which the household is the basic unit of production. Although some authors still subscribe to the minimal standard criterion, the conceptualization of subsistence has been broadened beyond simple physical survival to one in which subsistence provides for the minimum basic needs of life including social, mental, and customary needs (Harmon 1987, Sharif 198, Wharton 1963). Still, other authors consider subsistence as representing a traditional lifestyle, or standard of living above minimal levels, and refer to the survival level as the minimum standard (Berger 1985, Brody 1981, Scott 1976, Usher 1976).

In terms of recreation, considerable effort has been put forth to distinguish it from other activities besides subsistence and to develop more-encompassing definitions of it. With the tensions and stresses inherent in industrial society, it is becoming increasingly appreciated that recreational activity is an essential part of modern life, and not merely a form of frivolous, leisure-time activity (Nash 1975, Yukic 1963). Problems that have been encountered in defining it are expressed by Clawson and Knetsch

". . . In a deeper psychological sense, recreation refers to the human emotion in inspirational experience arising out of the recreation act; we use the latter to stand for the whole. Recreation contrasts with work, which is done primarily to earn money or otherwise to provide the *necessities* of life, or what have come to be so considered, for one's self and one's family. It also contrasts with the mechanics of life, such as eating, sleeping, housekeeping, and personal care. There is no sharp line between recreation and all other activities. The same activity may be work at some times and recreation at others" (1969:6).

Other authors have attempted to differentiate recreation from other activities through behavioral characteristics (Driver and Tocher 1969). This approach has been useful with respect to distinguishing recreation from some other activities, but has not proved to be effective with respect to drawing a distinction between recreation and subsistence.

In spite of these conceptual and definitional problems, interpretations of recreation have been expanded significantly to include a variety of meanings, benefits, and functions relevant to contemporary lifestyles (Burch 1965, Hendee 1974, Kelly 1981). But the difficulty cited in distinguishing recreation from other activities -- even work -- emphasizes the problems in making a distinction from subsistence. Characteristics often attributed to subsistence, such as labor intensity and self-containment within kinship, tribal, or community groups, are not mutually exclusive from recreational participation. As observed by Neumeyer and Neumeyer (1958) with respect to recreation: " . . . The form, the stimulus, and the spread of recreation are all conditioned by the social situation. Enjoyment is enhanced by company. Much recreation is carried on in the immediate primary groups, chiefly the home, the small play groups, the local institutions, and the community. Yet it is the social aspect that frequently is overlooked, or at least is not fully understood and appreciated" (1958:19).

When sufficient income is available from alternative sources to provide sustenance, the distinction between subsistence and recreation appears to relate more closely to the social meaning, motivational forces, and anticipated payoffs that provide incentives to pursue fish, wildlife, and other resources. In the absence of knowledge of these meanings, motivations, and payoffs, differentiating between recreational hunters whose objective is to secure meat (as described by Hendee 1974 and Kellert 1978), and subsistence hunters who reap self-actualizing benefits from participation itself, is very difficult to accomplish on a functional basis.

In Alaska, attempts to provide legal definitions distinguishing subsistence from other uses of natural resources have been less than totally successful. Subsistence behavior is often mistakenly associated with Alaska Natives (Indians, Aleuts, and Eskimos alone), but the Alaska State constitution does not permit discrimination on the basis of race. Furthermore, Natives in southeastern Alaska have shared in the modernization and increased affluence of the region. State and federal laws ascribe subsistence rights to both Alaskan Natives and non-Natives as subsistence users of resources. Rather than differentiating on the basis of ethnicity or income, rural residency and traditional use are the legal criteria most often applied to differentiate those with subsistence dependency from others.

In its deliberations regarding the allocation of lands to restrictive land management designations such as National Parks, the United States Congress recognized the traditional dependency that many Alaskan residents have for fish, wildlife, and other natural resources. Despite considerable controversy, subsistence use was given statutory definition in the Alaska National Interest Lands Conservation Act (ANILCA) which was signed into law in 1980 (a similar definition is contained in a corollary state subsistence law). In ANILCA (U.S. Congress 1980), subsistence is defined as:

> . . . the customary and traditional uses by rural Alaska residents of wild, renewable, resources for direct personal or family consumption as food, shelter, fuel, clothing, tools or transportation; for the making and selling of handicraft articles out of nonedible by-products of fish and wildlife resources taken for personal or family consumption; for barter, or sharing for personal or family consumption; and for customary trade (1980:16).

Both state and federal law rely heavily on *customary and traditional uses* and rural residency to differentiate subsistence from other resource uses. While they may be politically expedient, these criteria do little to distinguish subsistence from recreation in a modernizing society. Customary and traditional use refers to the past, and rural residency by Alaskan standards is hardly a meaningful distinguishing characteristic in terms of dependency on the direct consumption of natural resources.

Besides its importance in satisfying economic needs, legally defined subsistence activities provide a range of benefits that involve psychological, social, and cultural payoffs. In these situations, the distinction between recreation and subsistence is often unclear.

Psychological importance. For many people, whether motivated by subsistence or recreational considerations, resource harvest serves as an in-kind supplement to household income. For many rural residents, however, the opposite is true: cash serves as a means by which to supplement subsistence lifestyles--lifestyles which are preferential to full-scale participation in the cash economy. From a psychological perspective, the opportunity to harvest fish and wildlife resources contributes to a sense of self-reliance, independence, and the ability to provide for one's self--values that social surveys indicate as reasons why many non-Native people migrate to or remain in Alaska (Alves 1980, Muth and Glass 1989). Obviously, these values may pertain to both subsistence as well as recreational harvesters of fish and wildlife.

Social importance. From a social perspective, subsistence harvest and sharing contribute to the cohesion of kinship groups (Langdon and Worl 1981, Oberg 1973), as well as to the solidarity of occupational and friendship networks. This cohesiveness, however, is not unlike the bonding that takes place among recreationists reported in studies conducted in the lower 48 states (Scheuch 1960, Burch 1965, West and Merriam 1970). Additionally, however, subsistence distribution and exchange networks may contribute to the stability of resource-dependent communities as resource sharing extends to multiple households, some of which may contain the elderly, the widowed, or the infirm. Charnley 1983, Fall, Foster and Stanek 1983, Muth in press).

Cultural importance. Harmon (1987) has convincingly argued that human cultural diversity is a desirable social objective, and that renewable natural resources should be sensitively managed to promote continued subsistence opportunities that facilitate cultural diversity. Resource use contributes to the maintenance of traditional cultural and sub-cultural systems within modern societies as well as in developing countries. Natural resources are used in traditional rituals and ceremonies, as well as to reinforce a variety of institutional aspects of social life, such as norms of obligation, wealth and status hierarchies, and respect. Tlingit Indians in southeast Alaska, for example, continue into the present day to distribute deer meat and salmon at community potlatches. Continued access to subsistence resources by populations culturally dependent on them will help ensure the vitality of those cultural systems.

Economic importance. Several attempts have been made to assess the monetary value of domestically-produced food in non-agricultural subsistence economies (Nowak 1977, Usher 1976). Generally, these studies have found that subsistence resources constitute significant contributions to household incomes when compared on a substitution basis with equivalent goods purchased through commercial markets. In modernizing societies, however, cash incomes from employment and social welfare programs are playing increasingly important roles in traditional communities. By supplying a variety of household needs, however, resource harvest supplements income and adds to the standard of living regardless of the level of monetary income and benefits of public programs. In addition, homemade handicrafts made from indigenous resources (e.g., beaver-fur hats, spruce roots crafted into baskets, etc.) are produced for barter, or for sale in commercial outlets.

It is important to note that here, too, these same values may accrue to resource harvesters who may not fit conventional definitions of subsistence (Gladwin and Butler 1982, Rattner 1984).

CONTEMPORARY VILLAGE ALASKA

With respect to the range of services that are presently available in rural southeastern Alaska communities, the situation more closely resembles that of many rural areas in the *lower 48* than the primitive, isolated conditions that existed in the recent past. While many communities are geographically isolated, they have access to many of the same services that are available in more urban environments. Both traditionally, and under present state regulations governing fish and game use, Yakutat is a subsistence community. Yet, the forces of modernization have drastically altered the extent to which its residents are dependent on the direct consumption of natural resources for physical survival.

Yakutat is located on Monti Bay off the Gulf of Alaska, 212 air miles northwest of Juneau. While there are no road connections to outside points, there are 48 miles of roads maintained by the state and another 43.5 miles maintained by the USDA Forest Service. With a population of 561 (U.S. Bureau of Census 1980) and a total of 181 households, there were 348 cars and trucks registered in the community in 1984. The community also has a deep water port with regular barge service to Washington state and daily jet service to Anchorage, Juneau, and points outside.

Modernization of Yakutat is further evidenced by the public utilities and other services that are available. Most homes have commercial electricity, telephones, and television sets. Mail is delivered and out-of-town newspapers are available on a daily basis. The city proper has centralized water and sewage systems as well as garbage pick-up. Public education is available through the 12th grade and selected college courses are available locally through off-campus programs of the University of Alaska and Sheldon Jackson College.

Yakutat can be best described as having a three-sector economy with public (government), private (market), and *subsistence* components (Glass 1987). Only the contributions of the private and public sectors are expressed in monetary terms, and estimates for the latter are incomplete since they do not include some public services which are not readily measured in monetary terms. In this case, the *subsistence sector* refers to that portion of the community's standard of living that can be attributed to the harvest and direct consumption of natural resources.

The available information indicates that the residents of Yakutat enjoy relatively high monetary incomes as well as high levels of consumption of non-marketed natural resources (Glass 1987). At the community level, the 1984 mean annual household income was between $37,000 and $48,000 at the 95 percent confidence level. For the sample households alone, the mean household income was $42,500 and the median was $40,000. Even allowing for Alaska's inflated economy by U.S. standards, these income levels were higher than the national average for the same time period. For instance, a moderate budget for a family of four in Anchorage was estimated at 26 percent higher than required to maintain the same standard elsewhere in the United States (Leask 1984). Costs in Anchorage can be expected to be considerably lower than Yakutat for most imported goods due to economies of scale and greater competition, but locally produced goods would likely be cheaper in Yakutat.

The extent to which a mixed economic system has replaced traditional subsistence dependency is well demonstrated by examining the amounts of household income derived from various sources. Nearly one-third of all monetary income comes directly from government employment, and private sector economic activity is stimulated by additional public investment. The magnitude of state involvement is demonstrated by expenditures in capital improvements that exceeded $15 million during the seven-year period beginning in 1980, or $26,755 on a per capita basis. These expenditures not only provided services to the community but also stimulated additional direct and indirect employment and income. In addition, unemployment benefits are paid to local residents ($133,386 during 1984), and most of these occur during the winter months when other sources of income become scarce and resource harvesting activities are curtailed by inclement weather and resource scarcity. Yakutat residents also benefit from other social programs on the state and federal level, as do other U.S. citizens and Alaskan residents.

Although interrelated with the public sector, the private sector makes a substantial contribution to the Yakutat economy. In fact, two-thirds of the total household income for the community is from the private sector. It is noteworthy that the largest contributor to private sector income, commercial fishing, relies on publicly owned and managed resources. During 1984, commercial fishing contributed approximately a quarter of total income. This estimate reflected gross income, so production costs must be subtracted to make these figures comparable with income from other sources. Other major sources of income from the private sector were retail trade, logging, and construction.

Despite the community's relative affluence, Yakutat residents are quite active in hunting and fishing, and harvest large quantities of fish, wildlife, and other natural resources for personal use. In fact, data provided by the Alaska Department of Fish and Game indicate that Yakutat has one of the highest resource-harvest rates for personal use of any community in southeast Alaska. During 1984, the average harvest per household was reported at over 1,100 pounds. Furthermore, data from the Yakutat survey suggest that the sharing and distribution system associated with the traditional subsistence lifestyle is clearly operative, although no information is available regarding quantities that change hands.

Harvesting natural resources for household consumption is clearly interrelated with the private and public sectors of the economy. Monetary income from these latter two sectors provides the basis to invest in more efficient resource harvesting equipment. Thus, power boats, sonar devices, and gill nets enable people to more efficiently harvest salmon than was possible with traditional techniques and gear. Food preservation is also most often accomplished by freezing or canning rather than by the traditional methods such as air drying. All of this has made rural residents more efficient and less dependent on the harvest of natural resources for physical survival, but they have also become more intertwined with the private and public sectors of the economy.

A good example of interaction that occurs among the components of Yakutat's economy involves the harvesting of salmon. A publicly-owned and managed resource is harvested for three basic purposes; commercial, recreation, and subsistence. In Yakutat, a major source of salmon for personal use is commercial fishing, whereby fish commercially harvested are withheld from the market but are distributed for community consumption instead. Aside from the allocation of commercially caught salmon to personal use, the same gear is often used by those having subsistence permits. With respect to subsistence fishing, Mills and Firman (1986) observed: "Set gill nets were placed in the rivers often at the same locations and by the same individuals who commercially fished" (1986:80).

DISCUSSION

On the basis of conventional concepts, subsistence appears clearly distinct from recreation. Subsistence involves those efforts necessary to assure physical survival, whereas recreation refers to a use of the leisure time that is available after the basic necessities of life are provided. However, contemporary definitions of both subsistence and recreation have much broader scopes. The payoffs attributed to subsistence are much broader than the fulfillment of basic physical needs, and they have psychological, social, and cultural, as well as economic, manifestations.

Likewise, the benefits attributed to contemporary participation in recreational activities encompass a similarly broad, and often overlapping, range of benefits.

In southeastern Alaska, modernization has created a situation whereby people can support themselves through means other than the harvesting of natural resources for personal consumption. While some may supplement their incomes through resource gathering, and others may prefer to harvest natural resources to satisfy basic physical needs, for the majority of households there are alternative means of securing food, clothing, shelter, and other basic requirements. Both the public and private sectors of the economy provide income producing opportunities, and public sector social programs provide support as well as assuring a basis for survival during the worst of times.

Although other payoffs are often emphasized, the importance of resource harvesting should not be hastily dismissed in the context of contemporary concepts of subsistence. Particularly in Alaska, economies tend to fluctuate considerably, both seasonally and over longer times. At the very least, resource harvesting provides a means of improving standards of living and providing additional security during periods of economic downturns (Muth, in press). While contemporary interpretation of subsistence concentrate on psychological and sociocultural implications, the provision of quality food and other necessities of life directly from the natural resource base add to social well-being for many rural Alaskan residents, even if they are no longer absolutely essential for survival.

If subsistence is considered solely a means of satisfying basic needs for physical survival, much of the hunting, fishing, and other forms of resource gathering that occurs in southeastern Alaska is outside of this realm. Rather, the most relevant payoffs are psychological and sociocultural in nature, and these parallel the kinds of payoffs often attributed to recreational participation. On the other hand, the basic motivation for resource gathering may be to provide the means for physical survival, even though alternative means of support may exist. In this case, the contemporary resource gathering may more closely approach the traditional meaning of subsistence.

There are several interesting policy questions that relate to levels of resource dependency in contemporary society. The justification for designating qualified, rural residents as priority users of certain resources might be questioned if these individuals have alternative sources of support. On the other hand, there may be a legitimate social concern that rural residents have priority access to limited resources so that they might benefit from participation itself in resource gathering activities. In terms of social equity, it appears extremely important that no one is disenfranchised from such opportunities, but the criteria to effectively provide access to resources may vary from those stipulated under existing laws and regulations.

From a social welfare perspective, the primary concern is the contribution that resource harvesting activities provide individuals or communities in attaining respectable standards of living--and not whether a given activity might most appropriately be labeled subsistence or recreation. Food, clothing, and shelter are certainly components of the standard of living and may be provided wholly or in part through direct consumption of natural resources. But the benefits derived from interaction with nature and associated group activities are also contributors to the standard of living and quality of life. As a result, attempts to distinguish recreation from subsistence on strict disciplinary bases[1] have not been fruitful. While interdisciplinary approaches have the potential to provide a better understanding of subsistence, there is still likely to be considerable overlap with the benefits consistent with the broader definitions of recreation.

During a time when rural Alaskans are subjected to drastic changes in lifestyles and value systems brought about by rapid modernization, the psychological, social, and cultural payoffs of resource gathering activities can be more critical than its material rewards. An understanding of the motivations and anticipated payoffs of resource gathering is extremely important in assessing the impacts on rural communities by exogenous factors, such as commercial resource development activities, or competition for fish and wildlife by outsiders. If material dependency is the primary concern, a reduction in fish and wildlife populations might have a deleterious effect if the commitment of additional time and effort in harvesting activities cannot compensate for reductions in resource harvest levels due to changes in habitat or increased hunting and fishing pressure. On the other hand, a situation where participation itself provides the primary payoffs would not likely be as severely impacted by fish and wildlife population reductions if these populations were maintained at a threshold level that would induce their pursuit. In this case, other factors such as the intrusion of outsiders could pose a greater threat through their impact on sociocultural and psychological processes.

In closing, it should be recognized that not all Alaskan communities have developed three-sector economies to the extent achieved by Yakutat. In fact, southeastern Alaska has undoubtedly modernized much more rapidly than more remote portions of the state. While three-sector economies exist in communities throughout Alaska, direct consumption of natural resources undoubtedly makes a more critical contribution to physical survival in areas where resource bases are less competitive in the market. Even with a significant public sector of the economy, fish, wildlife, and other natural resources are likely to make a major contribution to the enhancement of local standards of living.

NOTES:

1. Disciplines pertinent to the distinction between recreation and subsistence include psychology, sociology, anthropology, and economics.

REFERENCES

Albrecht, H. 1972. The concept of subsistence. *Zeitschrift fur Auslandische Landwirtschaft* 11:274-288.

Alves, W. 1980. *Residents and Resources: Findings of the Alaska Public Survey on the Importance of Natural Resources to the Quality of Life in Southeast Alaska.* Anchorage, AK: University of Alaska, Institute of Social and Economic Research.

Barsh, R.L. 1982. The economics of a traditional coastal Indian salmon fishery. *Human Organization* 41:170-176.

Berger, T.R. 1985. *Village Journey: The Report of the Alaska Native Review Commission.* New York: Hill and Wang.

Brody, H. 1981. *Maps and Dreams.* New York: Pantheon Books.

Burch, W.R. Jr. 1965. The play world of camping: Research into the social meaning of outdoor recreation. *American Sociological Review* 70:604-612.

Charnley, S. 1983. *Moose Hunting in Two Central Kuskokwim Communities: Chuathbaluk and Sleetmute.* Technical Paper No. 76. Juneau, AK: Alaska Department of Fish and Game, Division of Subsistence.

Clawson, M. and J.L. Knetsch. 1969. *Economics of Outdoor Recreation.* Baltimore: Johns Hopkins Press.

Driver, B.L. and S.R. Tocher. 1970. Toward a behavioral interpretation of recreational engagements, with implications for planning. In B.L. Driver (Ed.), *Elements of Outdoor Recreation Planning.* Ann Arbor: University of Michigan, 9-21.

Fall, J.A, D.J. Foster and R.T. Stanek. 1983. *The Use of Moose and Other Wild Resources in the Tyonek and Upper Yentna Areas: A Background Report.* Technical Paper No. 74. Juneau, AK: Alaska Department of Fish and Game, Division of Subsistence.

Gladwin, C.H. and J. Butler. 1982. Gardening: A survival strategy for the small, part-time Florida farm. *Proceedings, Florida State Horticultural Society* 95:264-268.

Glass, R.J. 1987. *Subsistence as a Component of the Mixed Economic Base in a Modernizing Community.* Paper presented at the Arctic Science Conference, American Association for the Advancement of Science -- Arctic Division, Anchorage, AK.

Harmon, D. 1987. Cultural diversity, human subsistence, and the national park ideal. *Environmental Ethics* 9:147-158.

Hendee, J.C. 1974. A multiple-satisfaction approach to game management. *Wildlife Society Bulletin* 2:104-113.

Kellert, S.R. 1978. Attitudes and characteristics of hunters and anti-hunters. *Transactions of the 43rd North American Wildlife and Natural Resources Conference*, 412-423.

Kelly, J.R. (Ed.). 1981. *Social Benefits of Outdoor Recreation.* Urbana,IL: Leisure Behavior Research Laboratory, Department of Leisure Studies, University of Illinois. Report submitted to the Director of Recreation Management. Washington, D.C: U.S.D.A. Forest Service.

Langdon, S. and R. Worl. 1981. *Distribution and Exchange of Subsistence Resources in Alaska.* Technical Paper No. 55. Juneau, AK: Alaska Department of Fish and Game, Division of Subsistence.

Leask, L. 1984. Prices and incomes - Alaska and the U.S. 1980-1984. *Alaska Review of Social and Economic Conditions, Vol. XXI, No. 2.* Anchorage, AK: University of Alaska, Institute of Social and Economic Research.

Lichens, A.B. 1977. A case study in fish management on the Deschutes River. In E. Wchwiebert (Ed.), *Columbia River Salmon and Steelhead.* Washington, D.C.: American Fisheries Society 115-120.

Mills, D.D. and A.S. Firman. 1986. *Fish and Wildlife Use in Yakutat, Alaska: Contemporary Patterns and Changes.* Technical Paper No. 131. Juneau, AK: Alaska Department of Fish and Game, Division of Subsistence.

Muth, R.M. In press. Community stability as social structure: The role of subsistence uses of natural resources in southeast Alaska. In R.G. Lee, W.R. Burch, Jr. and D.R. Field (Eds.), *Community and Forestry: Continuities and Natural Resources Sociology.* Boulder, CO: Westview Press.

Muth, R.M. and R.J. Glass. 1989. Wilderness and subsistence-use opportunities: Benefits and limitations. In H.R. Freilich (compiler), Wilderness Benchmark 1988: *Proceedings of the National Wilderness Colloquium.* General Technical Report SE-51. Asheville, NC: U.S.D.A. Forest Service, Southeastern Forest Experiment Station, 142-155.

Muth, R.M., D.E. Ruppert and R.J. Glass. 1987. Subsistence use of fisheries resources in Alaska: Implications for Great Lakes fisheries management. *Transactions of the American Fisheries Society* 116:510-518.

Nash, J.B. 1975. *Philosophy of Recreation and Leisure*. Dubuque, IA: Wm. C. Brown Company Publishers.

Neumeyer, M.H. and E.S. Neumeyer. 1958. *Leisure and Recreation*. New York: The Ronald Press.

Nowak, M. 1977. The economics of Native subsistence activities in a village of southwestern Alaska. *Arctic* 30:225-233.

Oberg, K. 1973. *The Social Economy of the Tlingit Indians*. Seattle: University of Washington Press.

Rattner, S.E. 1984. *Diversified Household Survival Strategies and Natural Resource Use in the Adirondacks: A Case Study of Crown Point, New York*. Masters Thesis, Cornell, University, Ithaca, NY.

Scheuch, E.K. 1960. Family cohesion in leisure time. *The Sociological Review* 8:37-61.

Schneider, W. 1982. Subsistence in Alaska: A look at the issue over time. In P.G. Cornwall and G. McBeath (Eds.), *Alaska's Rural Development*. Boulder, CO: Westview Press, 169-180.

Scott, J.C. 1976. *The Moral Economy of the Peasant*. New Haven: Yale University Press.

Sharif, M. 1986. The concept and measurement of subsistence: A survey of the literature. *World Development* 14:555-557.

Suttles, W. 1968. Coping with abundance: Subsistence on the northwest coast. In R.B. Lee and I. DeVore (Eds.), *Man and the Hunter*. Chicago: Aldine Publishing Co 56-68.

U.S. Congress. 1980. *Alaska National Interest Lands Conservation Act*. P.L. 96-487, 94 Stat. Washington, D.C.: U.S. Government Printing Office.

U.S. Department of Commerce, Bureau of the Census. 1980. 1980 U.S. Census. Washington, D.C.: Department of Commerce.

Usher, P.J. 1976. Evaluating country food in the northern Native economy. *Arctic* 29:105-120.

Victor and Burrell Research and Consulting, J.E. Hanna Associates, Inc., and Hough, Stansbury, and Michalski, Limited. 1981. *Methods for Assessing the Socioeconomic Impact of Acid Rain on Canada's Fisheries*. Report prepared for Canada Department of Fisheries and Oceans, Toronto, Canada.

Wharton, C.R. Jr. 1963. The economic meaning of subsistence. *Malayan Economic Review* 8:46-58.

West, P.C. and L.C. Merriam, Jr. 1970. Outdoor recreation and family cohesiveness: A research approach. *Journal of Leisure Research* 2:251-259.

Yukic, Thomas S. 1963. *Fundamentals of Recreation*. New York: Harper and Row.

CHAPTER 11

THE RECREATIONAL OPPORTUNITY SPECTRUM AS A CONFLICT MANAGEMENT TOOL

Steven E. Daniels
Department of Forest Resources
Oregon State University

Richard S. Krannich
Department of Sociology
Institute for Social Science
Research on Natural Resources
Utah State University

Managing dispersed wildland recreation is far less structured than either the management of more developed recreation or the production of forest commodities. Although this may be inevitable given the diversity of activities, settings, and participants involved in dispersed recreation, the lack of structured recreation management approaches can make it appear as though wildland recreation management is capricious or insubstantial. Under such circumstances, differences between the expectations of recreators, other resource users, and resource managers can contribute to incompatible use patterns, dissatisfaction, and conflict.

Responding to the need for more structured approaches to managing dispersed recreation, the USDA Forest Service developed the Recreation Opportunity Spectrum (ROS), which characterizes and classifies different dispersed recreation settings, therefore facilitating recreation management. In this chapter we discuss ways that ROS management guidelines can limit the potential for conflict among resource users with divergent orientations toward forest management. Following a brief overview of conflict in recreation, we consider how the ROS system can help to mitigate this conflict, and examine ways in which an incorrect and idiosyncratic ROS interpretation, illustrated by resource management planning on one National Forest[1], may exacerbate conflict.

The Recreation Opportunity Spectrum: Some Background

The Recreation Opportunity Spectrum (ROS) is a cornerstone of USDA Forest Service recreation management. It provides a framework for stratifying and defining six classes of outdoor recreation environments, activities, and experiential opportunities: Primitive, Semi-Primitive Non-motorized, Semi-Primitive Motorized, Roaded Natural, Rural, and Urban. These six categories are differentiated by both physical and human determinants of recreation opportunity (USDA 1986).

With the possible exception of motorized recreation, the ROS system does not provide for management interventions to either limit or encourage the pursuit of particular types of recreation in particular places (Manning 1985). Nevertheless, the ROS system recognizes that diversity is important in recreation planning (Manning 1987), because users exhibit differing values, objectives, backgrounds, and experience preferences. In addition, a wide variety of landforms, facilities, and vegetative characteristics interact with recreator needs and preferences. The ROS system addresses the diversity of recreation settings and user characteristics by providing relevant management guidelines which consider both land capabilities and recreator needs.

The role of diversity in landforms as a factor influencing aesthetics and recreation was raised many years ago by F. L. Olmstead, Jr. (Stevenson 1977), as well as by Leopold (1921), and Marshall (1933, 1938). However, relatively little research was focused on this topic prior to the 1960s. Manning's recent review (1987) shows that social scientists became increasingly aware of the complexity of recreation management *vis-a-vis* the diversity of settings during the mid to late 1960s (Wagar 1966, King 1966, Shafer 1969). During that period, there were efforts to develop classification schemes to *zone* wildland as a function of its recreational potential (Carhart 1961, ORRRC 1962). Efforts to classify and quantify the role of diversity increased the recognition that no single recreation facility or setting could fulfill the entire range of recreation demands (Manning 1987), and that a systems approach to recreation management was needed to achieve a better match between the diversity of recreation settings and demands (Stankey 1974).

The design of the ROS reflected insights derived from research concerning the social-psychological dimensions of recreation (Buist and Hoots 1982). Major contributions to this body of research include the work of Clark and Stankey (1979), Brown, Driver, and McConnel (1978), Brown, Driver, Bruns, and McConnel (1979), and Driver and Brown (1978). These early efforts addressed both the major issues involved in applying social science research findings to recreation management and the special problems that confront the application of such principles in the multiple use context of federal land management.

Perhaps the most important aspect of the ROS's development for our purposes is the incorporation of recreation opportunity as a function of both recreator activity and the physical setting (Driver, Brown, Stankey, and Gregoire 1984). This interaction between activity and setting is at the core of the ROS's value as a land management system. Although management efforts can influence activities, management of settings is often more straightforward and more consistent with the mandates and orientations of federal land management agencies. Moreover, land management affecting the setting also affects recreational opportunity, and may therefore indirectly influence activities.

For example, the number of other people that recreators engaged in a given activity (hiking, for example) can see without feeling crowded is much lower in a primitive setting than in more developed settings. This is closely related to recreators' expectations about the types of experience that they will have in various settings (Schreyer and Roggenbuck 1978). Accordingly, social-psychological carrying capacities and preferred management options differ according to both setting characteristics and recreators' expectations. In general, the more primitive the setting, the fewer human impacts are necessary to degrade the setting and the recreational opportunities.

The ROS system recognizes these differences in sensitivity by incorporating evidence of humans along with size and remoteness as criteria when classifying recreation settings. Accordingly, the criteria related to evidence of human activities are more stringent in more primitive areas. Although these criteria do not explicitly address the diversity of recreation preferences or expectations, implicitly they recognize the correlation between relatively pristine and remote settings and experiential expectations involving low levels of human activity and environmental modification.

Conflict in Outdoor Recreation

There is an extensive literature indicating that conflict management is inherent in recreation management, and that the conflict between particular recreation goals and other recreation or non-recreation goals is much more complex than it initially appears. The sources of this conflict are as diverse as the types of recreators and recreation activities present in wildland settings.

Conflict in the arena of outdoor recreation can briefly be defined as *goal interference attributed to the behavior of others* (Hammitt 1988). Perhaps the most useful typology of conflict in recreation was presented by Jacob and Schreyer (1980), who attempted to systematically define and study basic causes of conflict situations. In their typology goal interference *per se* does not constitute conflict; attribution of the interference to another's behavior is also required.

Concomitant with goal interference is goal incompatibility, which occurs when different groups attempt to achieve mutually exclusive or contradictory goals. Many recreational activities impair the ability of others to recreate, or at least limit the degree to which others will be satisfied with their recreation experiences. For example, recreation activities pursued by off-highway vehicle (OHV) users, whose goals include rapid travel and an emphasis on action and excitement, may be incompatible with those of backpackers, whose activity involves slow, quiet travel and who are more likely to prefer solitude and opportunities to observe the environment. Clearly this sort of goal incompatibility can lead to goal interference, and reduced satisfaction on the part of participants who find that the presence and activities of others conflicts with their recreation objectives. An objective of recreation management should be to minimize the former to prevent the latter.

The ROS system is not a panacea for resolving all recreation management problems. As with any system that utilizes a limited number of measurable variables, the ROS does not consider many unique attributes of specific recreation settings. For example, ROS classifications do not address such things as the presence or absence of hiking trails, game and nongame animal species, streams or lakes, or other features that may facilitate or restrict certain recreation activities[2]. However, if properly applied, the ROS system has considerable potential for reducing goal incompatibility through: 1) spatial separation and 2) the establishment of clear expectations about physical settings and the quality of experiences.

Spatial separation has obvious value in conflict management in recreation, but it goes beyond merely separating recreators from other persons or activities that are potentially incompatible. The potential for some activities to produce discrepancies between recreation goals and experiences may diminish over time or distance, but the degree to which this occurs differs across recreation activities. For example, horseback riding has limited effects on other recreation beyond the immediate area surrounding the trails used, although effects of horseback riding on the physical characteristics of wilderness trails, and therefore on the experiences of other users, may persist for several days. Therefore, spatial separation of horseback riding and hiking or other uses may be relatively unimportant as a strategy for limiting recreation conflict. In contrast, effects of motorized off-highway vehicles (OHVs) extend over a broad area due to the transmission of noise, and may result in goal interference among other recreators whose use occurs concurrently. In this instance, spatial separation of activities may represent a highly effective strategy for limiting recreation conflict.

The ROS system can therefore reduce some, but not all, forms of recreation conflict because it facilitates management that spatially separates types of users whose concurrent use of the same or adjoining areas is likely to produce goal incompatibility. This is particularly evident when considering the distinctions between the Primitive or Semi-Primitive Non-Motorized ROS area designations and the ROS classifications in which roads and motorized activity are very evident. Since goals are in part a function of setting, and the ROS directly addresses the nature of recreation settings, it has the ability to separate at least some types of goal-incompatible recreationists.

ROS management may also reduce goal incompatibility by establishing or reinforcing expectations about settings and the type and quality of recreation experiences available in particular settings. The average forest user is unaware of the ROS system, because the ROS classification boundaries are not designated by signs or markers. Certainly there are very few recreators who would plan an outing with the thought, *I'd like to get in a day of Semi-Primitive Non-Motorized recreation.* Based on a number of experiences, however, recreationists eventually associate certain attributes with particular areas. For example, hikers in pursuit of quiet and solitude will seek out, and return to, an area where they expect that few other people will be encountered and where motorized vehicles will not be present. Such experience preferences are more likely to be satisfied in areas which are classified under ROS as Primitive or Semi-Primitive Non-Motorized, rather than in areas classified as Roaded Natural.

Thus, land management that adheres to conditions that are consistent with established ROS standards contributes to a certain stability of the recreation opportunities that are available in particular settings, and thereby reinforces compatibility between recreationists' goals and expectations and their experiences in those settings. In contrast, if recreationists seeking solitude and a relatively pristine natural setting arrived at their favorite site only to find a timber sale or newly-erected oil rig, or if they read of such development in the local paper, it is clear that their goals and expectations regarding the recreation setting would differ from those being pursued by the resource management agency. This kind of situation is an important source of conflict and public dissatisfaction regarding management of public wildlands.

The expectations of groups that are more knowledgeable about resource management issues than average recreators can also be affected by the ROS management system. Interest groups, whether they are concerned with preservation and conservation in a general sense (e.g., Sierra Club and Wilderness Society), the promotion of a particular activity (e.g., Trout Unlimited and OHV clubs) or resource development (e.g., logging and mining entities), frequently devote considerable effort and resources to maintain their familiarity with National Forest management policies. Such groups often pay particularly close attention to systems like ROS, which provide a common basis for shared expectations about resource management activities and decisions.

If consistently[3] applied, the ROS can establish and reinforce these groups' expectations about recreation management, and can therefore reduce disagreement. For example, in a forest with both Roaded Natural (RN) and Primitive (P) areas, resource development activities involving significant environmental alterations would ordinarily be more acceptable in the former areas, where there is already relatively widespread evidence of human activity and environmental alteration.   Those interested in resource development should anticipate that neither preservation-oriented interest groups nor the Forest Service will be likely to support extensive development in the P areas. Similarly, the preservation groups will be more likely to accept responsible resource development in the RN areas.   This suggests that a clear understanding of the acceptable behavior in different areas, shared in common by divergent interest groups and by resource managers and *fostered by a consistent application of ROS*, will facilitate land management for recreation and other outputs.   Under such circumstances, the potential for misunderstanding, unfulfilled expectations, dissatisfaction, and conflict should be lower.

Inconsistent application of the ROS system, however, will not provide guidance to the interested publics, and they will not clearly understand the basis for management decisions regarding the provision of recreation *vis-a-vis* the other uses of public lands.   Such circumstances provide a context in which conflict is much more likely to emerge.   Theories of individual participation in social movements linked to public controversies and conflict episodes stress that perceived *common grievances* and shared ideologies often are key elements of such situations (see Smelser 1963, Walsh and Warland 1983). Discrepancies between resource management expectations that may be based on ROS standards and actual management actions can give rise to collective perceptions of discontent or grievance, which in turn can contribute to the resource mobilization process among groups and organizations. The emergence of such responses and resulting conflict is particularly likely when there are pre-existing organizational structures and networks that provide a basis for collective response (see Turner 1981), as is often the case when controversies emerge over natural resource management issues on public lands.

An Illustrative Case Involving One Forest's Interpretation of ROS

Some of the problems that can result from inconsistent application of the ROS system are illustrated by a recent proposal for an exploratory oil well on land administered by a forest in the Forest Service's Region 2 (Colorado and eastern Wyoming)[4]. As indicated by Figure 1, the proposed well site is located in an area previously designated by the forest as providing Semi-Primitive Non-Motorized (SPNM) recreation opportunities. The upper sections of the proposed access route to the well site are also surrounded by lands classified as SPNM, while lower sections of the route are in an area designated as Semi-Primitive Motorized (SPM). A wilderness area boundary is located roughly one to one and one-half miles southwest of the well site and access corridor.

Of particular interest is the location of the well and upper access route segments within an area designated as SPNM. Existing management directions in the current Land and Resource Management Plan for this forest specify that the area is to be managed to emphasize SPNM recreation opportunities, and that all roads are to remain closed to motorized use. Although abandoned roads and tracks in the area built in the 1960s during previous petroleum exploration activities are still visible, all motorized vehicles, including snowmobiles, are currently prohibited from traveling beyond the area designated as SPM.

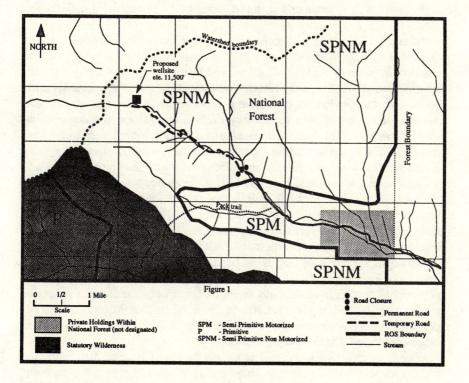

Figure 1.   Study Area Recreation Opportunity Spectrum Classes

Under the ROS system, evaluation of a resource development proposal such as this would usually begin by determining whether the well, access road development, and presence of motorized project equipment would be incompatible with the existing SPNM designation and related management directives. The areas affected by these incompatible activities would then be evaluated, and the number of acres and area boundaries where SPNM recreation opportunities were not compatible with the proposed oil exploration would be delineated. Since ROS designations simply represent management guidelines rather than legal mandates to restrict use, incompatibility would generally not represent a basis for denial of the drilling permit. However, if such a project was permitted, the area surrounding the well and access route might be redesignated, probably to either SPM or RN, depending largely on the level of project activity and whether the public could operate motor vehicles on the newly constructed road. Such a redesignation would need to be maintained at least during the exploratory activities, and perhaps longer as a result of either subsequent production developments or the time needed to fully implement reclamation efforts.

In contrast to such a conventional approach, this particular forest adopted a much different and highly idiosyncratic interpretation of the relationship between ROS designations and resource development proposals. In unstructured interviews with the authors, the recreation management planner on this Forest stated that the proposed well site and access road were not inconsistent with the existing SPNM designation for surrounding lands. This interpretation is unusual, since both the well site and access road would substantially alter the recreation setting as human activity increased, structures were built, and motorized equipment was used.

This forest determined that the SPNM designation was consistent with the proposed exploratory oil well activities, so long as the access road through the SPNM area could not be used by motor vehicles operated by the public. This interpretation implied that a fairly extensive resource development activity could be permitted within areas currently designated for non-motorized recreation (P or SPNM), as long as no public motorized recreation use occurred. If taken to the extreme, such an interpretation might imply that a major roadway could be constructed to support extensive project vehicle and equipment use in P or SPNM areas, yet would not identify such activities as inconsistent with the ROS designation so long as public motorized access was prohibited.

The reasons for such an atypical interpretation of ROS on this forest are difficult to determine. However, they appear to have emerged only recently, since Environmental Assessments conducted for earlier petroleum exploration proposals on the Forest adopted a more conventional approach to applying ROS to the decision-making process. The forest's interpretation apparently evolved following personnel shifts, particularly when an individual trained only in resource economics rather than recreation management was assigned to act as recreation staff officer. Circumstances such as staffing shifts, different training backgrounds of recreation staff, and variations in the degree of familiarity with the basic premises upon which the ROS system is based may all contribute to inconsistent interpretation and application of ROS guidelines.

The manner in which the ROS was interpreted may also reflect increased pressures on the National Forest to accommodate petroleum development. In addition to regional and national political and economic pressures for expanded oil exploration and development, the local socioeconomic setting also may influence agency response. The area encompassed by this forest has a long history of economic dependence on oil and gas activities, and the local economy might be devastated by the curtailment of petroleum development. More than one-third of the land within this forest is currently classified as SPNM, thus creating a potentially significant barrier to petroleum development. Such constraints can be more or less ignored if the current ROS interpretation on this forest prevails.

Regardless of the causal factors influencing this forest's interpretation of ROS guidelines, the situation clearly reflects a significant departure from the approach adopted by other forests under similar conditions. More careful and consistent delineation of Forest Service policies and more stringent training and programs to enhance management familiarity with ROS guidelines and the principles on which they were founded are apparently warranted.

The Effect of Inconsistent ROS Interpretation on Conflict

The sort of inconsistency evidenced by this forest's interpretation of the ROS guidelines has several implications regarding conflict. First, and most obviously, it may eliminate the potential for the ROS to reduce conflict. As noted previously, the two primary strengths of the ROS system as a conflict minimizer are spatial separation and expectation development, and this forest's interpretation fails to accomplish either. Disregarding or misinterpreting the role of setting in the recreation experience means that the forest will permit adjacent or overlapping activities with incompatible demands on the setting. Such circumstances represent an obvious recipe for conflict.

Indeed, this forest's interpretation of ROS guidelines could increase conflict.[5] There are a number of dimensions along which conflict could be increased, including:

recreator vs. recreator
recreator vs. resource developer

recreator/interest groups vs. agency
personnel vs. agency
development proponents/third party contractors vs. agency

Recreator-recreator conflict could be exacerbated because recreation activities that substantially alter the natural setting could be allowed to occur in areas that were either historically or explicitly managed for other recreation uses, e.g. the use of OHV's in a previously untrampled area. Recreators would then be in conflict with each other, as some types of recreational activities and their environmental impacts would lead to goal incompatibility and interference for others.

Recreator-agency conflict could arise both because of recreator concerns about incompatibility of competing resource uses and because the forest would appear to have established, and then ignored, a system for recreation management. Many recreators may not ordinarily be aware of established ROS designations for specific areas. However, the potential incompatibility of ROS designations and resource development proposals is frequently brought to the public's attention through documents and public input processes involved in the preparation of Environmental Assessments and Environmental Impact Statements required under the National Environmental Policy Act of 1969 (NEPA). If enhanced public awareness includes a perception that management guidelines are being ignored, recreators and other interest groups might logically assume that if the forest exhibits such inconsistency when addressing internal matters, it is also likely to be inconsistent in its dealings with other people or situations. Under such circumstances, the credibility of the Forest's recreation management plan, and indeed its entire management direction, are likely to be questioned.

Conflicts between recreators or other interest groups favoring the preservation of wildland recreation resources and resource development interests are common wherever public land management involves efforts to conform to multiple use mandates. However, inconsistent ROS applications could help to exacerbate such conflict. Recreation-oriented interest groups are more likely to mobilize their resources and actively oppose resource development proposals that are perceived as highly incompatible with the existing recreation resources of an area, and which may interfere with their goals for recreation participation. Such conflicts will tend to become especially rancorous when a highly valued recreation resource is threatened, when some segments of the public depend heavily on that resource for either recreational or economic opportunities, and when there are organized or emergent groups which can readily mobilize resources to litigate or otherwise oppose development proposals (see Turner, 1981).

Internal personnel-agency conflict could also increase, because this forest interprets the ROS differently than other National Forests. Personnel assigned or transferred to this forest must reconcile their experiences with ROS guidelines with this unusual approach. A newly-appointed recreation manager would inherit the management decisions of his or her predecessor, and may become involved in projects that s/he would not have approved or would have implemented differently. Finally, some analysts suggest that the Forest Service has a strong pro-commodity bias (Twight 1983, Clary 1986, O'Toole 1988), which causes disaffection among Forest Service personnel in non-timber or non-extractive specialties. This forest's interpretation of the ROS guidelines seems to confirm those criticisms. The forest seems to be saying *You can argue for whatever ROS classifications you like, but we can still make any environmental modifications we choose because we interpret how ROS guidelines should be applied.*

Finally, conflict is likely to increase between either third-party consultants and the forest or development proponents and the forest.[6] Recent staffing cuts experienced by the Forest Service have resulted in increased reliance on third-party consultants to perform a number of services. Perhaps the most significant of these is preparing environmental documents pursuant to NEPA. Consultants conducting recreation assessments usually have experience with several forests and are familiar with the ROS guidelines; their analyses and products therefore are shaped by the prevailing Forest Service procedure, and difficulty can arise when any single forest is a notable *policy-outlier*. As a result, it can be more difficult to establish mutually acceptable procedures and expectations, or the consultants' recommendations may be inconsistent with the forest's objectives. Neither outcome is beneficial.

CONCLUSIONS

Although it would be foolish to suggest that resource managers should ignore the need for unique and innovative responses to the needs which arise in individual forests and specific resource contexts, our analysis suggests that a consistent interpretation of the ROS guidelines is anything but foolish. The ROS facilitates management of recreation resources by standardizing management and recreator expectations, and therefore can reduce conflict among a variety of interest groups.

This chapter's description of one forest's idiosyncratic interpretation of the ROS guidelines shows the extent to which divergence from orthodox ROS standards can not only eliminate the potential benefits of the system, but can also create significant negative impacts. Although it is important that ROS not be interpreted so rigidly as to preclude site-specific planning or effective multiple-use management, allowing forests to apply ROS as they choose implies that the system does not have a scientific basis, and that the guidelines can be interpreted on an ad hoc basis. This situation exposes the Forest Service to charges of inconsistency, or even duplicity.

Clearly more consistent policy directives are needed if such problems are to be avoided. Among the steps which need to be considered are the implementation of more rigorous training programs to ensure that agency personnel responsible for recreation management are familiar with ROS guidelines and with the conceptual and empirical foundations upon which they are based. Additional specification of the guidelines themselves may also be in order, particularly to clarify the degree to which certain conditions are inherently inconsistent with various ROS area designations. Only if these and other sources of inconsistency and confusion are resolved can the conflict-minimization potential of ROS be fully realized.

NOTES:

1. This Forest, located in the northern section of the Rocky Mountain region, is not identified in this chapter to protect the anonymity of individuals who provided information or were involved in the implementation of management decisions and interpretations.

2. We appreciate comments by Steve Kellert prompting us to clarify this point.

3. We are defining consistency to mean both uniformity in application and application that complies with the theory which underlies the ROS system. Our discussion may not apply to cases where the ROS system is applied uniformly but incorrectly.

4. Information regarding the application of ROS guidelines on this National Forest was obtained in the course of the authors' participation as members of an Interdisciplinary Team investigating the impacts of a proposed project. This case is not in any sense set forth as representing how ROS application problems may emerge in varied forest management situations. In fact, our experience from similar projects on several other National Forests suggests that this case is in fact quite atypical, but that it provides a useful illustration of how improper interpretation and application of the ROS can add to rather than reduce resource management problems.

5. The proposal that raised the concerns discussed in this chapter was terminated prior to substantial public involvement or project implementation. As such, many of the potential conflicts outlined here did not arise, although proponent/contractor communication with the Forest was hindered by the latter's ROS interpretation.

6. There is also the potential for consultant vs. developer conflict, but that is not really ROS-related nor is it the Forest's problem.

7. This is paper no. 2538 of the Forest Research Laboratory, Oregon State University. This research was also supported by the Utah Agricultural Experiment Station, Utah State University, and approved as paper no. UAES 3662.

REFERENCES

Brown, P.J., B.L. Driver and C. McConnel. 1978. The opportunity spectrum concept and behavioral information in outdoor recreation resource supply inventories: Background and application. In H.G. Lund *et al.* (Technical Coordinators), *Integrated Inventories of Renewable Natural Resources: Proceedings of a Workshop.* USDA Forest Service General Technical Report RM-55. Fort Collins, CO: Rocky Mountain Forest and Range Experiment Station, 73-84.

Brown, P.J., B.L. Driver, D.H. Bruns and C. McConnel. 1979. The outdoor recreation opportunity spectrum in wildlife recreation planning: Development and application. In *Recreation Planning and Development: Proceedings of the First Annual National Conference, Vol. II.* New York: American Society of Civil Engineers.

Buist, L.J. and T.A. Hoots. 1982. Recreation Opportunity Spectrum approach to resource planning. *Journal of Forestry* 80:84-86.

Carhart, Arthur H. 1961. *Planning for America's Wildlands.* Harrisburg PA: The Telegraph Press.

Clark, R.N. and G.H. Stankey. 1979. *The Recreation Opportunity Spectrum: A Framework for Planning, Management, and Research.* USDA Forest Service General Technical Report PNW-98. Portland, OR: Pacific Northwest Forest Experiment Station, 32 pp.

Clary, D.A. 1986. *Timber and the Forest Service.* Lawrence, KS: University Press of Kansas.

Driver, B.L. and P.J. Brown. 1978. The opportunity spectrum concept and behavioral information in outdoor recreation resource supply inventories: A rationale. In H.G. Lund *et al.* (Technical Coordinators), *Integrated Inventories of Renewable Natural Resources: Proceedings of a Workshop.* G. USDA Forest Service General Technical Report RM-55. Fort Collins, CO: Rocky Mountain Forest and Range Experiment Station, 24-31.

Driver, B.L., P.A. Brown, G.H. Stankey and T.G. Gregoire. 1984. The ROS planning system: Evolution, basic concepts, and research needed. Unpublished manuscript. Fort Collins, CO: Rocky Mountain Forest and Range Experiment Station.

Hammitt, William E. 1988. The spectrum of conflict in outdoor recreation. Presented at *Benchmark 1988: A National Outdoor Recreation and Wilderness Forum*, Tampa, FL, January.

Jacob, G.R. and R. Schreyer. 1980. Conflict in outdoor recreation: A theoretical perspective. *Journal of Leisure Research* 12:368-380.

King, D.A. 1966. *Activity Patterns of Campers*. St. Paul, MN: North Central Forest Experiment Station, Research Note NC-18, 42 pp.

Leopold, A. 1921. The wilderness and its place in forest recreational policy. *Journal of Forestry* 19:718-721.

Manning, R.E. 1985. Diversity in a democracy: Expanding the recreation opportunity spectrum. *Leisure Sciences* 7:377-399.

Manning, R.E. 1987. *Studies in Outdoor Recreation: A Review and Synthesis of the Social Science Research in Outdoor Recreation.* Corvallis, OR: Oregon State University Press.

Marshall, R. 1933. The forest for recreation. In *A National Plan for American Forestry*. Washington, D.C.: Senate Doc. 12, 73rd Congress, 1st Session.

Marshall, R. 1938. *The People's Forest*. New York: H. Smith and R. Haas.

O'Toole, R. 1988. *Reforming the Forest Service*. Washington, D.C.: Island Press.

Outdoor Recreation Resources Review Commission. 1962. *Outdoor Recreation for America*. Washington D.C.: U.S. Government Printing Office.

Schreyer, R. and J.W. Roggenbuck. 1978. The influence of experience expectations on crowding perceptions and social-psychological carrying capacities. *Leisure Sciences* 1:373-393.

Shafer, E.L. Jr. 1969. *The Average Camper Who Doesn't Exist*. Broomall, Pennsylvania: Northeastern Forest Experiment Station, Research Paper NE-142, 54 pp.

Smelser, N. 1963. *Theory of Collective Behavior*. New York: The Free Press.

Stankey, G.H. 1974. Criteria for the determination of recreational carrying capacity in the Colorado River Basin. In A.B. Crawford and D.F. Peterson (Eds.), *Environmental Management in the Colorado River Basin.* Logan, UT: Utah State University Press, 82-101.

Stevenson, E. 1977. *Park Maker: A Life of Frederick Law Olmstead.* New York: MacMillan.

Turner, R.H. 1981. Collective behavior and resource mobilization as approaches to social movements: Issues and continuities. In L. Kriesberg (Ed.), *Research in Social Movements, Conflict and Change.* Greenwich, CT: JAI Press, 1-24.

Twight, B.W. 1983. *Organizational Values and Political Power: The Forest Service versus the Olympic National Park.* University Park, PA: The Pennsylvania State University Press, 139 pp.

USDA Forest Service. 1986. *The 1986 ROS Book.* Washington, D.C.: U.S. Government Printing Office.

Wagar, J.A. 1966. Quality in outdoor recreation. *Trends* 3:9-12.

Walsh, E.J. and R.H. Warland. 1983. Social movement involvement in the wake of a nuclear accident: Activists and free riders in the TMI area. *American Sociological Review* 48:764-780.

CHAPTER 12

PUBLIC RECREATIONAL ACCESS: A NATIONAL STUDY OF POLICIES AND PRACTICES OF PRIVATE LANDOWNERS

Brett A. Wright
George Mason University

H. Ken Cordell
USDA Forest Service
Southeastern Forest Experiment Station

Tommy L. Brown
Cornell University

Considerable concern has been expressed in recent years that private recreational open space is decreasing through conversion and closure (Brown, Decker and Kelley 1984, Guynn and Schmidt 1984, Wright and Kaiser 1986). The Soil Conservation Service (1982) estimates that about one million acres of rural lands are converted for urban, residential, transportation and other built-up purposes annually. Moreover, additional amounts of the remaining private open space are being closed and/or posted to deny public recreational access (Brown *et al.* 1984, Wright, Kaiser and Fletcher 1988, Cordell and Wright 1989).

The problem is magnified because decreases in the supply of available recreational open space come during a period of increasing public demand for outdoor activities and federal retrenchment in management and acquisition of public lands for recreation. For this reason, the President's Commission on Americans Outdoors (1987) suggested the need to encourage private landowners to open more lands for recreation. Therefore, it is important that the federal government monitor trends in recreational access to private lands on a national and regional basis to ascertain whether sufficient public and private acreage is available to meet the nation's demands for outdoor recreation opportunities.

The objectives of this analysis and chapter are to (1) describe the varying degrees of recreational access, (2) estimate the availability of private lands for recreation nationwide and (3) develop a profile of private landowners and the private land base. Data were derived from a survey of 11,687 rural landowners who participated in the 1986 National Private Land

Ownership Study (NPLOS) conducted by the U.S. Forest Service, Southeastern Forest Experiment Station, Athens, Georgia.

RURAL LANDOWNERS' ACCESS DECISIONS

Wright *et al.* (1988) reported that landowners' decisions regarding recreational access were not purely dichotomous choices, but choices of the degree to which the public was allowed or restricted access. Understanding the different degrees of access to private lands enables researchers to more accurately estimate land availability and recreational opportunities.

Policy alternatives included *prohibition, exclusion, restriction, open* and *fee (leasing).* Landowners who adopt *prohibitive* access policies totally preclude recreation. Reasons for prohibiting recreation may include land-use conflicts, loss of privacy, or an attitudinal bias toward the appropriateness of the activity. Hunting has been especially susceptible to land closures due to owners' anti-hunting attitudes (Brown *et al.* 1984., Wright *et al.* 1988).

Landowners adopting an *exclusive* policy purchase or own land because of the exclusive rights that a person receives to the attributes of that property. These owners, in effect, reserve recreation opportunities for their own personal enjoyment (Gramman, Bonnicksen, Albrecht and Kurtz 1985).

The distinction between a policy of exclusion and one of prohibition is very important. To understand, one must examine the reasons why landowners limit access to their lands. Using hunting as an example, prohibitionists preclude access because they do not believe in hunting. Exclusionists, on the other hand, limit access because they want to maintain wildlife resources for their exclusive use and enjoyment.

Property owners who expand access to their lands to include personal acquaintances maintain a *restrictive* policy. Restrictive policies vary by degree, but generally are grounded in the acquaintanceship between the landowner and the recreationist. Thomas and Adams (1982) found that 60 percent of Texas hunters found access through such friendship and kinship networks.

Those persons allowing individuals who are not personal acquaintances to recreate on their properties without imposing a fee, practice an *open* access policy. However, owners may require recreationists to obtain written or verbal permission prior to entering their lands.

In contrast to landowners who allow recreation without charge are those who assess a *fee* for access rights. Assessing a fee for recreation takes many forms. It may involve a written contract, formal lease, or a verbal agreement between two parties. Compensation to landowners may be in the form of money, services, or other considerations valuable to the landowner.

Past tendencies of researchers to base supply estimates on posting practices and to view these posting practices as synonymous with prohibition are suspect (Brown *et al.* 1984). Many landowners who post their properties do so at least partly to control access and may allow recreational activities if permission is requested. Posting practices are important, both in terms of the intent of landowners and how these practices are perceived by recreationists, but are by no means indicative of the supply of rural recreation opportunities.

Past research suggests that five primary factors or domains influence landowners' values, beliefs and attitudes, thus forming the bases for access policies. The first domain involves landowners' beliefs about recreationists, both as individuals who landowners know and as a group that they perceive collectively. Inappropriate behavior by recreationists is a major disincentive for allowing access (Rounds 1973, Brown 1974, Holecek and Westfall 1977). Ninety-seven percent of New York landowners who restricted access in 1972 reported a behavior-related reason contributed to their decisions to restrict access. Brown and Thompson (1976) found that landowners' policies are determined not only by their personal experiences, but also by the experiences of friends and neighboring landowners.

A second factor which influences owners' access decisions is liability. Landowners' fear of liability includes more than being found liable for recreational injuries occurring on their property. It involves the threat of being sued as well (Kaiser and Wright 1985, Kozlowski 1986). Psychological stress, lost time and the expense of litigation, and the adverse publicity accompanying a court case are other major disincentives.

Another sphere of influence in access decisions is the owners' attitude regarding the appropriateness of the activity to be carried out on their property (Rounds 1973, Brown 1974). Hunting is especially susceptible to attitudinal biases as anti-hunting attitudes seem to be increasingly important factors in decisions to close lands, especially as land ownership changes and larger proportions of rural landowners have urban backgrounds. Snowmobiling, off-road vehicle use, camping, and other activities which are perceived to have resource impacts, also may be susceptible to attitudinal biases.

Resources attributes, especially current land uses being employed by owners, also are possible determinants of access policy (Durrell 1969, Ryder and Boag 1981). Some agricultural practices, such as row cropping and livestock operations, often are not perceived as compatible with allowing recreation. In addition, owners' recreational uses of their property have been found to be negatively correlated with public access. Brown, Decker and Kelley (1983) found that the more active the landowner is in wildlife-related activities, the greater the likelihood that he/she would limit access. Gramman *et al.* (1985) termed this an attitude of *exclusivity* and others have suggested it poses . . . *the toughest access problem of all to resolve* (Wildlife Management Institute 1983:3).

Finally, the opportunity for landowners to derive income or other compensation in exchange for permitting access may be increasingly more prominent in landowners' decisions. Leasing lands for hunting has a long history in Texas (Pope, Adams and Thomas 1984) and other areas of the south, and for hunting waterfowl in Maryland (Brunori 1987). As demand for hunting and other outdoor recreational activities increase relative to the diminishing supply of lands available to the public, increasing numbers of landowners will turn to fee policies.

Socioeconomic and demographic characteristics are also correlated to some degree with access decisions. Age, sex, education and whether landowners reside on their property have been found to be correlated with posting and access policies (Holecek and Westfall 1977, Brown *et al.* 1984, Wright *et al.* 1988), but these factors have low predictive power, limiting their utility in statistical modeling of owners' access decisions (Wright and Fesenmaier 1988).

METHODS

The National Private Land Ownership Study was a Forest Service survey of nonindustrial, private rural landowners owning a minimum of 20 acres. Master tax rolls available in county tax appraisal offices, were used as sampling frames from which to obtain names and addresses of eligible landowners. Tax rolls are generally accepted as the best available sampling frames for rural ownership surveys. Using the National Outdoor Recreation Supply Information System's county-level data files (USFS 1987), counties with high population densities (>200 persons/mile^2) or high concentrations of government-owned land (>50 percent) were eliminated. Of 3,107 counties in the contiguous United States, 338 were *too urban* and 162 had *too much government land* to be included. After eliminating ineligible counties, there was a total of 2,556 counties from which to draw the national sample.

Counties were randomly selected using a grid matrix system to ensure even geographic distribution of counties chosen within each state. From each county, a stratified random sample of 25 names was chosen from the master tax rolls. County samples consisted of 3 strata of persons owning 20 to 99 acres, 100 to 499 acres and more than 500 acres, ensuring equal representation of large and small landowners.

The mail survey instrument was designed, pretested and mailed to the sample of landowners in 1986, following closely the procedures outlined by

Dillman (1978). The primary purpose of the survey instrument was to solicit information regarding the characteristics and management of private rural lands. Access policies respondents currently enforced on their properties and the amount of acreage affected by each were also collected. Other data regarding potential determinants of those policies also were collected.

As a result, 4,856 questionnaires were returned, producing an effective response rate of 37 percent for useable questionnaires. Possible non-response bias was accounted for in two ways. First, in a pretest conducted statewide in Georgia prior to implementation of the national sample, selected response items were compared between respondents and non-respondents. Data for a sample of 100 non-respondents were obtained through phone interviews. General means and frequencies compared between these two groups of sampled landowners indicated that policy, management and ownership circumstance variables were not significantly different. Response proportions among owner characteristics however, were found significantly different between these two groups. Thus, the second correction for non-response bias was to weight the data base, using forest inventory data from the U.S. Forest Service, the National Resources Inventory from the Soil Conservation Service, and other published reports providing regional characteristics. Applying these weights made the NPLOS data set as nearly proportional to that of the national population of landowners as possible.

Because a disproportionate random sample resulted, the above post sample weighing was required. Individual case data within the NPLOS data base were weighted to reflect population-to-sample ratios, allowing the extrapolation of findings to regional and national estimates.

Frequency analyses provided a general description of landowners and their properties. Regional comparisons of landowners were made among the four U.S. Forest Service macro regions (Fig. 1) using a one-way analysis of variance and Duncan's Multiple Range Test ($\alpha = 0.05$). National estimates of private lands available for recreation were calculated.

RESULTS AND DISCUSSION

The Owners

Respondents were predominately male (79.6 percent) and slightly less than 58 years of age. The overwhelming majority of respondents was white (96.1 percent) and married (82.1 percent); family size averaged 2.6 people. Landowners' occupations varied greatly, however, 45 percent were retired. Landowners reported earning an average of $35,303 in total family income for 1985.

Educational attainment was relatively high--58 percent of the property owners graduated from high school and had gone on to complete some college work. Further, 15.6 percent had obtained a college degree and another 14.9 percent had completed some graduate work.

Private land ownership across the U.S. appears to be family-oriented. Eighty-six percent of landowners reported owning their lands either solely (38.4 percent) or as part of a family ownership (47.7 percent) and had owned that property for 23 years. Further, 38 percent resided on their land and 90 percent lived within a 20 mile radius of their property.

Regional differences among rural landowners were found with several variables. Respondents in the Southern region were significantly older (59.5 years) than landowners in all other regions (p < 0.017). Family incomes in 1985 were highest among persons from Pacific Coast ($42,872) and Southern ($39,321) regions (p < 0.001). Accordingly, landowners in the Pacific

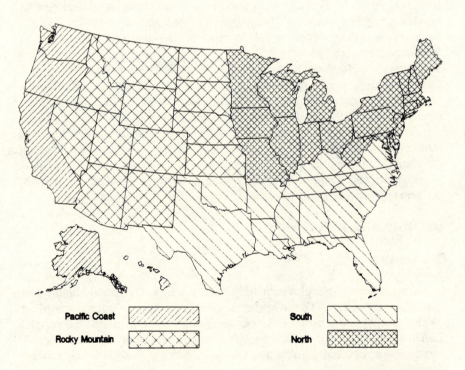

Figure 1.   RPA Outdoor Recreation and Wilderness Assessment Regions

Coast region made more money from their lands in 1985 ($12,399) than landowners in other regions (p < 0.001). Southern owners were least dependent on their lands as sources of income ($5,058). No significant differences were found among landowners in different regions regarding amount of property taxes paid in 1985.

Motives for owning rural lands appear to be changing. Four out of 10 respondents rejected crop agriculture as an important reason for owning rural land. Crop agriculture was reported as the least important ownership objective of all reasons posed to the respondents. Landowners did report that making money from *Fee Hunting, Fishing, and other Recreation* (95 percent), *Growing Timber for Sale* (68 percent) and *Investment Potential of the Land* (61 percent) were very important reasons why they owned their properties.

The Land

Respondents owned an average of 183 acres. Those from the Pacific Coast and Rocky Mountain/Great Plains regions owned the largest tracts of land (M = 310 acres and 304 acres, respectively) which were significantly larger (p < 0.001) than tracts owned by eastern landowners. Southern and Northern landowners owned tracts of 163 acres and 131 acres, respectively.

Cropland was reported as the largest single land use across the nation (M = 63 acres), even though many owners rejected agriculture as an important ownership objective. This was followed closely by land in forests (M = 53 acres), pasture (M = 31 acres) and range (M = 25 acres). Forty-two percent of respondents used these lands for grazing livestock, primarily beef cattle (83 percent).

Regionally, Pacific Coast landowners reported the largest amounts of land in forests (M = 76 acres) as compared to Rocky Mountain/Great Plains owners who averaged only nine acres of timber. Amount of area in forests in the Rocky Mountain region was found to be significantly smaller (p < 0.036) than forest area in other regions. Landowners in the Rocky Mountain region joined those from the Pacific Coast in having significantly more rangeland (M = 71 acres, M = 91 acres, p < 0.001) and row crops (M = 96 acres, M = 102 acres, p < 0.001) than owners from eastern regions. Rocky Mountain owners also possessed significantly more acreage in pasture (M = 112 acres, p < 0.001). No other regional disparities regarding land uses were found.

Recreation was another common use of land, even though few landowners were found to be physically altering the landscape to enhance recreational opportunities. Ninety-three percent of the respondents' properties accommodated recreation in some manner. Overall, hunting was reported by owners as the activity most compatible with private land resources (88 percent). In general, dispersed forms of outdoor recreation were perceived as being the most appropriate. Driving off-road vehicles (79 percent), shooting (77 percent), photography (77 percent), nature study (75 percent), hiking (73 percent), birdwatching (72 percent), picnicking (72 percent), riding horses (71 percent), and camping (65 percent) were reported as being compatible activities by a majority of property owners. Water-related activities such as fishing (47 percent), swimming (39 percent), canoeing (32 percent), and boating (30 percent) were much less compatible (only 30 percent of the respondents reported owning surface water). The degree to which private landowners allow recreation is a question of high priority to recreation and natural resource planners.

Recreational Access Policies

As suggested by past research, recreational access policies adopted by private landowners in this study took several forms. Results regarding access policies are presented according to the number of landowners adopting a specific policy and, more importantly, the amount of land affected by that policy. Some properties were closed to recreation. Others were maintained for exclusive recreational use by owners or were restricted to invited guests. Still others were opened to the general public, either for a fee or free. Furthermore, landowners often controlled implementation of these policies by posting their properties. Even though posting is not a policy, in and of itself, it does have a significant impact on perceptions of land availability.

Posting Practices

Thirty-three percent of respondents (n = 1,431) posted at least a portion of their lands against trespass. Of these, 85 percent posted *all* of their properties. In general, it appeared landowners did not bother with selective posting; that is, posting only a particular section of their lands. On average, owners posted 232 acres.

Pacific Coast owners reported the highest incidence of posting (39.6 percent). Southern owners were second (34.4 percent), followed by landowners from the Northern region (33.2 percent). Respondents from the Rocky Mountain/Great Plains (RM/GP) region posted the least of all regions (23.7 percent). When this practice is viewed in relation to total acreage owned, however, respondents from the Rocky Mountain region posted significantly more land (M = 648.66 acres) than did other landowners (p < 0.001). Conversely, northern owners reported posting the smallest number of acres (M = 125.58 acres) which was significantly smaller than amount of land posted in all other regions (p < 0.001).

Of owners who posted their lands, only 14 percent of the landowners prohibited all recreational access. Eighty percent of posting landowners provided recreational access for members of their families, and 65 percent allowed only friends and neighbors to use their lands. Additionally, 19.2 percent posted their properties to protect rights of persons leasing their lands for recreation, and another 8.1 percent allowed the general public to use their lands, as long as they asked permission.

Prohibitive Policies

Very few landowners proscribed all recreation (< five percent). Landowners from the Southern region showed the highest propensity to close their land (six percent), even though differences found among owners closing their properties from each region were marginal. Numbers of persons closing their lands varied from 3.5 percent of respondents in the North to six percent in the South. This, in effect, closed only five percent of total land owned by respondents. Table 1 shows the effects of respondents' policies on total acreage under access policies.

Exclusive Policies

Thirty-eight percent of respondents reported closing a total of 206,910 acres of land to all but personal recreation. This figure represented 25 percent of the respondents' total land base.

Approximately 40 percent of owners in the North, South, and Pacific Coast regions reported excluding access to all but family members on some portion of their land. Only 22 percent of Rocky Mountain owners indicated they reserved land for private recreation. Acreage affected by these policies was greatest in the Pacific Coast region. Thirty-nine percent of the respondents' acreage in that region was operated under a policy of exclusion (Table 1).

Restrictive Policies

Easily the most common policy enacted by landowners, policies predicated on the acquaintanceship between the landowner and the recreationist affected 44 percent of the acreage sampled nationwide (369,813 acres). Over half the acreage owned by respondents from the RM/GP region (52 percent) was operated in such a manner. Northern and Southern owners dedicated 46 percent and 43 percent of their acreage, respectively, to this type of policy. Less than 30 percent of the acreage in the Pacific Coast region was managed under a restrictive policy.

Fee Policies

Only five percent of all landowners in the sample indicated they leased any portion of their properties for recreation (< six percent of total acreage). Those found to be operating land under this policy reported leasing an average of 253 acres. Approximately 60 percent of these owners leased to clubs or groups of individuals. Slightly less than 40 percent leased to individuals and very few leased lands to government agencies.

The largest number of landowners undertaking a fee recreation policy was found in the Southern region (seven percent). Between two percent and three percent of owners in the other regions charged for recreational access to their properties. Southern owners also dedicated the largest amount of land to fee recreation (23,062 acres).

Motivations for leasing were mostly consistent among all landowners. Respondents reported monetary reasons for adopting a leasing policy, such as *helping to pay taxes* and gaining *additional income*. Other perceived advantages were lessees' enhanced *stewardship of the land* (32 percent) and their ability to aid in *controlling trespass* (32 percent).

Table 1.   Distribution of Land Controlled Under Specific Recreational Access Policies Adopted By Nonindustrial, Private Rural Landowners Sampled (Percent of Total Acreage in Region).

Policy	North	South	RM/GP	Pacific Coast	U.S.
Prohibitive	7,479 (3%)	17,216 (6%)	7,445 (3%)	5,703 (5%)	37,843 (5%)
Exclusive	53,289 (25%)	77,847 (28%)	30,196 (13%)	45,578 (39%)	206,910 (25%)
Restrictive	99,183 (46%)	119,911 (43%)	115,892 (52%)	34,827 (30%)	369,813 (44%)
Leased	4,543 (2%)	23,062 (8%)	1,562 (< 1%)	14,280 (12%)	43,447 (5%)
Open	50,927 (24%)	35,499 (13%)	64,805 (29%)	16,380 (14%)	167,610 (20%)
Total[a]	215,421 (100%)	273,535 (100%)	219,900 (100%)	116,768 (100%)	825,624 (100%)

[a] numbers may not sum due to rounding errors.

Overwhelmingly, hunting was the most common type of lease. Forty-seven percent of the fee policy holders leased their lands for hunting, a majority (60 percent) indicating that big game was the primary type of hunting, even though other types of hunting were allowed under conditions of most leases. These activities generated an average of $531 per landowner per year. Fees charged for hunting leases ranged from less than $10 to a high of $8,000 per year. Twelve percent of these persons indicated they would lease additional land (M = 115 acres), if the right incentives were provided. Other recreational activities appear to be insignificant in terms of revenue generation. Nationally, 53 million acres were estimated to be leased as described above.

Open Policies

Twenty-five percent of the respondents allowed the general public to use 167,610 acres of their lands for recreation. This equated to roughly 20 percent of total acreage owned by all persons in the sample. Nationwide, a total of 230 million acres was estimated to be operated under an open policy.

Greatest regional disparities regarding open access were found in the East. Thirty-one percent of Northern owners allowed a portion of their lands to be used by people other than personal acquaintances for recreation. In contrast, less than 13 percent of Southern landowners allowed open access.

Rocky Mountain landowners reported the largest percentage of lands open to the public. Slightly less than 29 percent of lands in this region were open to public recreation (64,805 acres). Twenty-four percent of Northern lands were open as well. Southern and Pacific Coast landowners reported the smallest percentages of total land available to the public under this policy (13 percent and 14 percent, respectively).

National Estimates

By applying the weighted percentage of total acreage under each of the five access policies identified in the study, to the total amount of private farm and ranch land in each region, statistical inferences were drawn. Estimates of the amount of land available for recreation can be seen in Table 2.

Of the estimated 1.21 billion acres of land in nonindustrial, private ownership in the United States, approximately 63.1 million acres are closed to recreation. Furthermore, over 295 million acres are closed to all but exclusive use of owners. This, in effect, decreases the supply of private land available for recreation of most Americans by almost one-third (30 percent).

The largest blocks of recreational lands are operated under policies based on familiarity. Access to 47 percent of private land base was estimated to be restricted to persons who were personally acquainted with the owner. Over 568 million acres of land fell under this policy.

Land available to persons without friendship and/or kinship networks to draw upon for recreation amounted to approximately 23 percent of the land in private ownership. Slightly more than 53 million acres were estimated to be operated under some form of leasing arrangement and approximately 230 million acres were open to the public. Persons gaining access to this open acreage may be required to obtain prior permission of the owner (either written or verbal) in order to use these lands, but generally, these lands were open to the general public.

Activity-Specific Policies

Beyond the five general policies, some landowners mandate policies that are activity-specific. Wright and Fesenmaier (1988) noted that landowners may be more restrictive with hunting access to certain species (e.g., small

Table 2.   Estimated Total Acreage of Private, Nonindustrial Land Available for Recreation by Access Policy[a].

Policy	North	South	RM/GP	Pacific Coast	U.S.
Prohibitive	11,857 (4%)	27,377 (6%)	13,361 (4%)	10,557 (13%)	63,152 (5%)
Exclusive	84,614 (26%)	123,789 (30%)	54,241 (14%)	32,365 (40%)	295,009 (24%)
Restrictive	156,310 (48%)	188,041 (44%)	206,731 (55%)	17,891 (22%)	568,973 (47%)
Fee	5,923 (2%)	34,719 (8%)	3,194 (<1%)	9,500 (12%)	53,336 (4%)
Open	66,663 (20%)	53,658 (13%)	97,799 (26%)	11,544 (14%)	229,664 (19%)
Total[b]	325,367 (100%)	427,584 (100%)	375,326 (100%)	81,857 (100%)	1,210,134 (100%)

[a] in thousands of acres
[b] numbers may not sum due to rounding errors.

game hunting was allowed but deer hunting prohibited). Failure of past research to capture activity specific access policies of landowners was a weakness in attempts to better understand landowner policy behaviors.

By eliminating landowners who indicated their lands were not appropriate for each activity and then calculating the allow/disallow ratio for all persons having resources compatible with each activity, a better idea of landowners' acceptance of different activities was gained. Inasmuch as hunting was perceived to be the activity most suitable to private lands, it was the activity most often allowed. Sixty-seven percent of landowners who permit public access allowed hunting on their lands (Table 3). Non-consumptive activities such as photography, birdwatching, nature study, hiking, and picnicking also were allowed by a majority of respondents.

However, even though the majority of owners with open lands felt their lands were highly compatible with shooting, camping, and off-road vehicle use, these activities were prohibited by over 65 percent of landowners. Perceptions of dangers and/or resource damages associated with these activities may provide some explanation for landowners' intolerance of these pastimes.

CONCLUSIONS

Based on results of this study and related research to date, several points become readily evident. First, the private land resource is vast, but it seems threatened as a natural resource because of development pressures. Population increases and resultant urban expansion will require an increasing amount of rural land be converted to urban uses. Estimates of up to 1.5 million acres of rural lands being converted to nonagricultural uses annually have been made in the past (Resources for the Future 1983, PCAO 1987).

Second, farm and forest incomes are decreasing. Less than 20 percent of respondents' total family incomes for 1985 were generated from their lands (M = $6,778). Therefore, reasons reported by respondents for owning rural lands appear to be changing from the traditional agricultural-related ownership objectives. *Making money through fee recreation, growing timber for sale,* and *investments* were reported as the most important reasons for owning rural lands. *Raising livestock, living in a rural environment,* and *crop agriculture* were much less important to today's landowners.

While it appears that landowners possessed a latent desire to generate income through the outdoor recreation potential of their properties, this desire has not come to fruition for a majority of the landowners. Only five percent of the owners were actively charging fees for outdoor recreation, and the overwhelming majority of this activity was for hunting. Other forms of outdoor recreation seem to be limited in their income earning potential thus far.

Table 3.　Study Landowners' Receptivity to Selected Recreational Activities (Percent Allowing Access).[a]

Activity	North	South	RM/GP	Pacific Coast	U.S.
Hunting	72	64	64	60	67
Photography	69	57	63	66	64
Birdwatching	66	53	63	60	61
Nature Study	65	52	60	62	60
Hiking	64	51	60	55	59
Picnicking	54	48	52	53	51
Fishing	50	53	43	47	51
Horseback Riding	51	43	63	52	50
Shooting	36	31	36	34	34
Camping	34	30	45	29	33
Swimming	22	26	19	30	24
ORV Driving	31	15	19	14	23
Canoeing	24	19	19	17	21
Boating	16	12	7	15	14

[a]Based only on landowners who indicated owning resources compatible with respective activities.

But, the number of landowners adopting a fee recreation policy has increased since 1977. Motivations for leasing were consistent among all landowners. Monetary reasons, such as *helping to pay taxes* and gaining *additional income* were prevalent. Other perceived advantages were lessees' enhanced *stewardship of the land* and their ability to aid in *controlling trespass*. Fee recreation may increase owner incomes and conserve natural resources.

Data suggest that the number of persons adopting a fee policy could increase to 11-15 percent of all landowners (the equivalent of 115 million acres) if the right incentives were provided. However, inconsistencies in governmental policies send mixed signals to landowners regarding leasing.

First, few states have offered tax breaks or any other incentives, to property owners who allow public recreation on their lands, whether for free or fee. Second, state laws designed to encourage access by eliminating fear of legal liability for recreational injury have been largely ineffective in convincing landowners that there is little risk.   Protection afforded under state recreational use statutes, now enacted in 49 states, is unknown to a majority of landowners.   This has tremendous implications for state and federal recreation and natural resource agencies. Also, protection afforded by these laws may be inconsequential compared to the fear and burdens of being taken to court, on which these statutes have no effect.   Having to pay lawyer fees, time away from work and anxieties associated with litigating court cases are major disincentives in and of themselves. Further, the vast majority of these statutes predicate insulation from liability on free access. Landowners who choose to assess a fee for access lose their protection in most states.

Legal liability notwithstanding, another major factor in land closures is the behavior of recreationists.   Public ignorance resulting from this disassociation with the land will undoubtedly continue to negatively affect recreationist behavior.   As property damages, litter, trespass and other problems persist, land closures and increasing restrictions on access will become more severe.

Also, it is highly likely that there will be major turnovers in land ownership over the next 10-15 years: 45 percent of the landowners are retired. New owners are likely to bring on even more strict access policies. As this progresses, ownership for reasons of exclusive resource use, will probably increase. This will, in effect, lock up many recreation resources and further polarize those persons who can afford to purchase land for recreation and those who cannot.

IMPLICATIONS FOR RESEARCH AND POLICY

The National Private Land Ownership Study is among the most comprehensive of research efforts to date, directed at documenting the supply of private, nonindustrial lands, particularly with respect to land available for outdoor   recreation.   Through this study, a better understanding of individuals who own rural lands and reasons for that ownership is gained. Furthermore, estimates of the amount of land in various land uses, leasing practices currently undertaken by landowners, and amount of land controlled under specific recreational access policies are established.

However, now that NPLOS has established the benchmark from which researchers can monitor changes in the private recreation estate, more in-depth studies of factors associated with landowner behavior, particularly access policy behavior, need to be conducted. This research must go beyond merely understanding the *what* and *how much* of recreational access to private lands, to a greater understanding of *why* landowners adopt specific access policies.

Furthermore, more knowledge regarding the recreational carrying capacities of these lands needs to be obtained. To this point, most recreation supply research has concentrated on refining the methods of estimating the quantity of land available for recreation. These efforts have not addressed the question of the quality of recreational opportunities. Additionally, a deeper understanding of recreation-related problems experienced by landowners, their attitudes toward providing recreational access, and preferred incentives is prerequisite to undertaking programs to encourage additional access in the future. To date, no research at the national level has attempted to model landowner access decisions. Several agencies, such as the U. S. Forest Service, work closely with states in providing assistance to private woodland owners. However, these programs have mostly focused on encouraging private owners to manage timber and to make it available for commercial harvest. While some of these programs show private landowners how their recreation or wildlife objectives can be integrated with timber management, there are no Forest Service programs explicitly aimed at increasing public outdoor opportunities on nonindustrial private lands. In the future, increased funding for assistance for recreation management or the diversion of funds away from other programs will be needed. This study has helped to identify roles for the Forest Service and other public agencies in working to provide assistance and perhaps to provide direct incentives to private landowners for opening their lands for public recreation. In the East especially, increased public access to private lands will be essential to maintain current levels of available recreation opportunities since public lands in this part of the country are scarce. Federal and state forestry agencies' involvement and experience as forest managers, with their longer-term public interest perspective, place them in a position to greatly affect future recreation supply. Without public sector involvement, serious shortages of certain recreation opportunities will likely occur in the future. These shortages will be especially critical near urban areas where open space is being developed at a rapid rate. Private land access will be needed to help address future recreation opportunity shortages, since public lands cannot meet all of the projected demands.

REFERENCES

Brown, T.L. 1974. New York landowners' attitudes toward recreation activities. *Transactions, North American Wildlife and Natural Resources Conference* 39:173-179.

Brown, T.L. and D.Q. Thompson. 1976. Changes in posting and landowner attitudes in New York State 1963-1973. *New York Fish and Game Journal* 23:101-137.

Brown, T.L., D.J. Decker and J.W. Kelley. 1983. Posting in New York: 1980 update. *New York Fish and Game Journal* 30:121-139.

Brown, T.L., D.J. Decker and J.W. Kelley. 1984. Access to private lands in New York: 1963-1980. *Wildlife Society Bulletin* 12:344-349.

Brunori, C.R. 1987. Maryland's waterfowl resource: A best case example of noncommodity values. *Valuing Wildlife: Economic and Social Perspectives.* Boulder: Westview Press, pp. 143-153.

Cordell, H.K. and B.A. Wright. 1989. Public recreational access to private lands: An update on trends and the foreseeable future. *Trends* 26:15-18.

Dillman, D.A. 1978. *Mail and Telephone Surveys: The Total Design Method.* New York: John Wiley and Sons, Inc., 321 pp.

Durrell, J.S. 1969. Hunter - landowner relationships. *Transactions North American Wildlife Natural Resource Conference* 34:179-185.

Gramman, J.H., T.M. Bonnicksen, D.F. Albrecht and W.B. Kurtz. 1985. Recreational access to private forests: The impact of hobby farming and exclusivity. *Journal of Leisure Research* 17:234-240.

Guynn, D.E. and J.L. Schmidt. 1984. Managing deer hunters on private lands in Colorado. *Wildlife Society Bulletin* 12:12-19.

Holecek, D.F. and R.D. Westfall. 1977. *Public Recreation on Private Lands - The Land Owner's Perspective.* East Lansing, MI: Michigan Agricultural Experiment Station. Research Report No. 335, 12 pp.

Kaiser, R.A. and B.A. Wright. 1985. Recreational use of private lands: Beyond the liability hurdle. *Journal of Soil and Water Conservation* 40:478-481.

Kozlowski, J.C. 1986. The challenges: Legal views on liability. Proceedings, Recreation on Private Lands: Issues and Opportunities. A Workshop convened by the Task Force on Recreation on Private Lands, Washington, D.C., pp. 27-30.

Pope, C.A., C.E. Adams and J.K. Thomas. 1984. The recreational and aesthetic value of wildlife in Texas. *Journal of Leisure Research* 16:51-60.

President's Commission on Americans Outdoors. 1987. *President's Commission on Americans Outdoors: The Legacy, The Challenge.* Washington, D.C.: Island Press, Inc., 426 pp.

Resources for the Future. 1983. *Outdoor Recreation for America.* 1983. Washington D.C.: Resources for the Future, Inc., 42 pp.

Rounds, R.C. 1973. *Public Access to Private Land for Hunting in Colorado.* Unpublished Ph.D Dissertation. University of Colorado, 240 pp.

Ryder, J.P. and D.A. Boag. 1981. A Canadian paradox - private land, public wildlife: can it be resolved? *Canadian Field Naturalist* 95:35-38.

Thomas, J.K. and C.E. Adams. 1982. *An Assessment of Hunters' Attitudes and Preferences Concerning Texas Wildlife and Wildlife Regulatory Policies.* College Station, TX: Texas A & M University, Agricultural Experiment Station, 419 pp.

U. S. Forest Service. 1987. *National Outdoor Recreation Supply Information System.* Athens, GA: SE Forest Experiment Station, Data file.

U. S. Soil Conservation Service. 1982. *National Resources Inventory.* Washington, D.C.: U.S. Soil Conservation Service, Data file.

Wildlife Management Institute. 1983. *Improving Access to Private Land: A Path to Wildlife.* Washington, D.C.: Wildlife Management Institute, 13 pp.

Wright, B.A. and R.A. Kaiser. 1986. Wildlife administrator's perceptions of hunter access problems: A national overview. *Wildlife Society Bulletin* 14:30-35.

Wright, B.A. and D.R. Fesenmaier. 1988. Modeling rural landowners' hunter access policies in East Texas. *Environmental Management* 12:229-236.

Wright, B.A., R.A. Kaiser and J.E. Fletcher. 1988. Hunter access decisions by rural landowners: An East Texas example. *Wildlife Society Bulletin* 16:152-158.

IV

TOURISM

CHAPTER 13

ARE MOUNTAIN TOURISM AND FORESTRY INEXTRICABLY LINKED? A DISCUSSION WITH EXAMPLES FROM THE SWISS ALPS

Martin F. Price
Environmental and Societal Impacts Group
National Center for Atmospheric Research

Over the past hundred and fifty years, the basis of the economies of most communities in the Alps and other temperate mountain regions, such as the Rocky Mountains, has changed irrevocably. In the mid-nineteenth century, local economies in both regions depended on primary activities. In the Alps, agriculture and forestry had supported local communities in a subsistence economy for centuries. In the Rocky Mountains, European settlement was just beginning, spurred on by discoveries of minerals and seemingly inexhaustible supplies of land which could be exploited for agriculture and timber.

At the same time, other attributes of these mountain regions were being discovered, usually by people who did not live locally. Mountains began to be recognized as beautiful places where people could escape from urban environments and regain their health. By the late nineteenth century, some small communities had developed into health spas and tourist centers. The economic power of tourism in these regions continued to increase through the first half of this century, but it was not until after World War II that tourism became the basis of the economy of most communities, as it is today.

The primary resource on which the mountain tourist economy depends is the landscape (Krippendorf 1984), which includes three major components: mountain peaks, forests, and the valley bottoms that include settlements, agricultural land, and often lakes and reservoirs. Within this landscape, the forests have a multiple significance. First, they partition the landscape, acting as an esthetic or *passive* recreational resource. Second, they are important for active recreation, providing an environment for hiking and skiing trails. Third, they protect watersheds and limit the occurrence of natural hazards (avalanches, rockfalls, and floods), thus ensuring the survival of mountain communities and infrastructure.

Yet, as financial and human resources have been, and are, increasingly diverted from forest management and utilization to providing services in the tourist sector, the development of mountain tourism may paradoxically be endangering its future.

The reason is that forests have to be continually managed if they are to provide their critical protective functions in the long term, with management activities at levels which permit regeneration and ensure that forests include trees with a diverse range of ages and, if possible, species (e.g., Mayer 1976a). In an economy in which forestry to provide timber is important, the provision of the protective functions is almost inevitable with harvesting at a level which permits long-term production of timber. This is the traditional concept of sustained-yield forestry (Clawson and Sedjo 1984). Over-cutting leads both to inadequate future supplies of timber and to potential loss of the protective functions. Hence, there is considerable incentive for forest managers to limit harvests to a sustainable level. However, when few resources are put into forestry, inadequate harvesting levels can also endanger the protective functions. If stands are not thinned, relatively thin trees develop which become increasingly susceptible to natural hazards. Few new trees can start growing in the dark conditions in such stands. In addition, if trees reach a certain age and are not removed, they are increasingly likely to be attacked by pests and diseases; a risk which increases when the trees in a stand have similar ages. All of these characteristics decrease a forest's ability to provide the protective functions. Thus, in an economy where forests are much more important for their protective, esthetic, and recreational qualities than for providing wood, a new concept of sustained-yield forestry is necessary (Wiebecke and Peters 1984). Such a concept would recognize that minimum, rather than maximum, harvesting levels must be set and implemented to supply all of the desired outputs.

THE SWISS ALPS AS A CASE STUDY

This chapter aims, first, to describe the co-evolution of forestry and tourism in the Swiss Alps over the last two centuries and, second, to assess the need for changes in relationships between the two sectors and propose mutually-beneficial changes. As similar developments in forestry and tourism have taken place in other temperate mountain regions, many of the proposed changes may be relevant to these regions.

The chapter is based on a comparative study of the Swiss Alps and Colorado Rocky Mountains (Price 1988b), and draws heavily on research in two of the *test areas* of the Swiss Man and the Biosphere (UNESCO) program: Aletsch (in Canton Valais) and Davos (in Canton Graubünden) (Figure 1). As the communities of the Swiss Alps exhibit great geographic, historical, and socio-economic diversity, these areas are not necessarily representative of the region as a whole. However, they provide good examples of both socio-economic trends and forestry policies and practices found throughout the region.

FORESTS IN THE TRADITIONAL ALPINE ECONOMY

The forests of the Swiss Alps were, and still are, mainly owned by local people, either as individuals or as members of communes and cooperatives. In the traditional economy, trees were used to provide leaves for fodder and wood for fuel, construction, building fences, and many other agricultural purposes. In addition, the sale of wood, for construction, woodworking, and charcoal, both within Switzerland and abroad, provided the main source of income for many communes well into the present century (Leibundgut 1956).

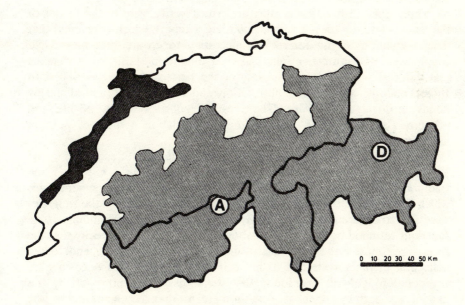

Figure 1.   Switzerland, showing the location of the Jura highlands (dark shading) and Alps (light shading) and the MAB test areas: Aletsch (A) and Davos (D). Also shown are the boundaries of Canton Valais and Canton Graubünden

The inhabitants of the Swiss Alps have recognized the connection between the productive and protective functions of their forests since at least the late 13th century, when the first orders prohibiting certain or all uses within communal forests were imposed. Subsequently, communes placed increasing limitations on the use of forests and wood as awareness of the effects of deforestation grew; but ever greater areas of forest were cleared for grazing, local use, and profit (Tromp 1980). A principal effect was to lower timberline throughout the Alps by 200-300 metres (Langenegger 1984a).

FORESTRY AND TOURISM FROM 1800 TO 1876

In the early 19th century, encouraged by the earliest Swiss foresters and stimulated by natural catastrophes, many of the mountain cantons passed legislation regulating the use of the forests (Price 1988a). At the same time, tourism was beginning to become an important economic force in some communities, such as Davos, which began its development as one of the first health-resorts in the 1850s (Bernard 1978).

Three dates in the 19th century are critical with regard to the forests of the Swiss Alps. In 1861, Landolt published a report, which concluded that strict regulation of the forests was necessary to ensure that they could supply wood and protective functions on a long-term basis, and recognized that deforestation affects the beauty of the landscape (Tromp 1980). In 1868, Landolt's linkage of deforestation and flooding was underlined by floods throughout the Alps. These caused substantial loss of life and property (Bloetzer 1978), making forestry legislation a topic of political importance.

In 1876, the federal Forest Police Law came into effect, placing the mountain forests under federal superintendence. The law follows the traditional concept of sustained-yield forestry, requiring management plans which emphasized timber harvesting, rather than specifying the activities necessary to ensure the forests' survival as viable ecosystems fulfilling all the functions required by human populations. Two key articles specify that the forest area must not be decreased and that livestock grazing and fodder collection in the forests had to be limited. The latter was necessary for regeneration; Landolt had found that the forests' long-term viability was endangered both by annual use one-third greater than increment and by lack of regeneration (Tromp 1980).

FORESTRY AND TOURISM FROM 1876 TO 1950

The "Belle Epoque"

After 1876, there were significant decreases in both grazing and logging, which was much better regulated by the cantons' forest services, and generally concentrated on individual or small groups of trees rather than large areas. In Davos, harvests decreased from the high levels of the mid-19th century, and afforestation projects were started (Günter 1980).

During the *Belle Epoque*, from the late nineteenth century until 1914, tourism expanded rapidly in the few existing centers, substantially increasing demands for wood for construction and fuel. Davos became a center for summer and winter sports as well as a health-resort, with rapidly increasing numbers of hotels, guests, and inhabitants; the population grew five-fold from 1870 to 1910 (Keller and Kneubühl 1982). However, most communities in the Alps were only marginally influenced by tourism, remaining relatively self-sufficient rural communities, with a permanent valley settlement and seasonally-inhabited summer settlements and alpine pastures above. Such was the case with Aletsch, which was not easily accessible until the construction of the Furka-Oberalp railway in 1915, and had little accommodation until after World War II (Mattig and Zeiter 1984).

1914 through 1945

After the *Belle Epoque* ended, the number of visitors to Switzerland did not again reach the 1910 peak until well after the end of World War II (Mattig and Zeiter 1984). In spite of variable demand, Davos remained an important health-resort, diversifying into a wide range of recreational and cultural activities which permitted most hotels and sanatoria to stay open. After a sharp decrease at the beginning of World War II, visitation rose sharply (Keller and Kneubühl 1982).

While tourism in the Alps generally stagnated or declined between 1914 and 1945, the consumption of Swiss timber increased (Affolter 1985), and forestry remained important in the mountain economy (e.g., Auer 1956). In Davos, where over half of the jobs were in the service sector by 1929 (Keller and Kneubühl, 1982), harvests from the forests were about two-thirds of increment (Günter 1980). In Aletsch, harvests were often higher than the sustained yields defined in management plans until 1947, especially during the 1930s and 1940s, when demand for sale was high (Price 1988b). In both areas, in spite of prescriptions in management plans, harvesting tended to concentrate on the sites which were most accessible and had the best quality timber.

THE POST-WAR DEVELOPMENT OF TOURISM AND FORESTRY

The economy of the Swiss Alps changed rapidly after World War II, stimulated by increases in income, vacation time, and car ownership and improved transport networks. The result was a rapid growth in tourism until the mid-1970s, since when it has slowed down (Messerli 1983). Some of these trends have had serious negative consequences for the maintenance and use of the mountain forests. Tourism has provided jobs which offer equal or better remuneration and benefits for less physical effort than jobs in forestry (Schwingruber 1985). The development of transport networks has been important, both in permitting oil to substitute for wood as the major fuel source in the Alps, and in stimulating the international flow of timber.

Tourism

From 1950 to 1978, the number of hotel beds in the Swiss Alps doubled. The supply of self-catering facilities grew even faster: from 1966 to 1978, beds increased three-fold in number. Many settlements now have more second homes than permanent residences. Between 1950 and 1980, the number of cable-cars increased from 29 to 424; ski lifts from 250 to over 1,300 (Bridel 1984).

Aletsch provides an excellent example of the rapid development of tourism (Mattig and Zeiter 1984). Until 1950, the summer settlements of Riederalp and Bettmeralp were accessible only on foot. From 1951, both were accessible by cable-car, and capacity and demand for access and accommodation increased greatly (Figure 2). In the villages in the valley below, accommodation capacities increased ten-fold from 1950 to 1980. There has been a corresponding change in employment. Until 1960, the primary sector accounted for over half of the area's jobs. By 1980, the service sector accounted for over half of the jobs, and agriculture for only 13 percent; many of these people work part-time in tourism.

The development of tourism in Davos has also been substantial, though not as meteoric. From 1950 to 1980, the number of beds more than doubled. The capacity of ski-lifts and cable-cars also expanded rapidly until 1973 (Figure 3). Expansion has since been limited by the mid-1970s recession, new environmental laws, and regional competition. From 1947 to 1957, visitation declined. Numbers rose subsequently, but have levelled off since 1973. Employment in the primary sector has continued to decrease in importance, and was 4 percent in 1980, when the service sector accounted for 77 percent of jobs (Price 1988b).

Forestry

Post-war Swiss forestry has been characterized by few positive trends. The number of full-time positions in public forests has steadily declined from 12,000 in the 1950s to just above 7,000 (BAF 1985). Until 1980, wood prices rose far more slowly than wages. In the 1980s, wood prices generally decreased (Affolter 1985). Though wages have risen, they are no higher than in other industries requiring people with a low level of training. Thus, in a country with unemployment under one percent, wages in forestry, the industry with the highest national accident and death rates, cannot compensate for the lack of promotion opportunities and year-round employment (BAF 1985). As only half of the people with a basic training

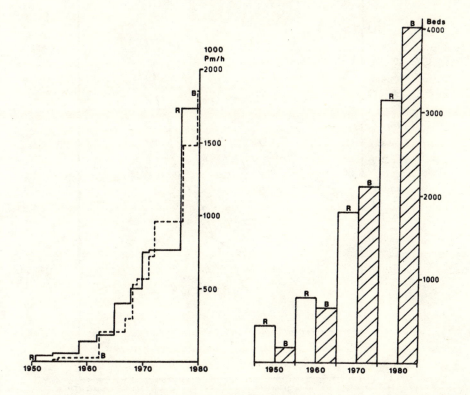

Figure 2.   The growth of uphill transport capacity and accommodation at the resorts of Riederalp (R) and Bettmeralp (B) in the Aletsch test area, 1950-1980. Pm/h = Person-metres/hour

in forestry remain in the profession (Moser, 1985), there is increasing use of contractors, who often use untrained foreign workers and do not do high-quality work since they are employed on a piece-work basis. These trends are for Switzerland as a whole; in the Alps, conditions are generally worse than average, partly because wages are lower (Schwingruber 1985). Furthermore, much of the forestry work in the Alps is still left to farmers, who earn less than lowland farmers (Darbellay 1984) and would rather look for part-time work in the more lucrative and less tiring tourist sector.

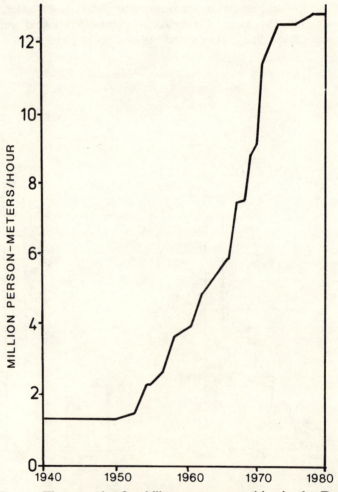

Figure 3.   The growth of uphill transport capacities in the Davos test area, 1940-1980. Ski lifts of all types, cable-cars, and railways are included

Forest management requires not only people, but also access. Over 5,000 km of new roads are needed to provide minimum access to the mountain forests (Ott 1984), which would still leave many areas inaccessible even to helicopter-logging. Lack of accessibility is linked to the steep terrain (Ott 1972) and lack of money. Road building costs have recently grown substantially, both with increasing wages and because roads are being built into more difficult terrain (e.g., Spinatsch 1983). These costs can be partially set off by government grants, but few forest owners have adequate financial resources to pay the residual costs. While improved access increases potential profitability, it still may not permit the mountain forestry industry to become self-sustaining (e.g., Stauffer 1985).

Since 1950, the annual number of hours worked in the mountain forests has decreased, as the full-time labor force has shrunk and the forests' owners need little wood for agriculture, construction, or fuel and can generally not sell it profitably. This trend, combined with the lack of infrastructure, has meant that levels of management have decreased. In the early 1970s, only half of these forests were regularly used, and a quarter irregularly (Ott 1972). Two major consequences of this low level of management have been discussed by foresters for decades (e.g., Bavier 1940, Wieser 1950, Oechslin 1957, Jungo 1969, Ott 1976, Bischoff 1982). The first is a high proportion of even-aged stands of trees which are thin for their age and site conditions (Ott 1972) and therefore are susceptible to natural hazards. The second is a lack of regeneration, stemming both from the first and from increased populations of game animals. In 1876, the year of the Forest Police Law, the federal Hunting Law was also passed. This gave strong protection to game animals by limiting hunting seasons and areas and specifying strict requirements for licenses. As a result, populations of large game animals have increased almost exponentially. These profoundly influence forests by browsing on young trees and debarking older ones. The animals are recognized as a desirable part of the recreational landscape but, like the forests, require strict management to ensure its future.

The recent history of forestry in the test areas displays many of the characteristics found throughout the Alps. In Aletsch, harvests in the 1960s and 1970s were generally well below those prescribed. In the 1980s, harvests have risen, but remain less than a third of increment. The increased harvests are mainly because government subsidies are available to remove spruce trees infested with bark beetles. In one forest district, including five of the communes, this work is done by a forester and his staff; in the other forest district, by contractors. The stands in three-quarters of the forest area consist of trees in one size-class; regeneration is limited, particularly at the lower edge of the forest, where hundreds of deer gather in the winter, and at timberline, where the additional problem of browsing by livestock exists. Many trees have been damaged by rockfall, which usually leads to fungal infection, slower growth, and lower-value wood (Bellwald and Graf 1985).

In Davos, the development of winter tourism led to decreased harvests from the forests, particularly from the mid-1960s, as the farmers who own most of the forests took part-time winter jobs in tourism rather than cutting wood to use and sell. Until 1965, the commune employed three part-time foresters; from 1965 to 1971, two; and from 1971 to 1980, only one. Harvests declined to about a quarter of increment. In 1979, heavy snowfall brought down 120,000 trees, and the commune took on an additional full-time forester to cope with the required harvesting. In 1984 and 1985, the commune voted to employ three full-time foresters, subsidize forestry roads, and pay for the management of all forests in the area, whether owned by individuals or the commune. These decisions provided the basis for a management plan prepared in 1985. Recent harvests have been about two-thirds of increment; 14 part-time laborers, half from Italy, are employed in the summer and fall. Two-fifths of the forest area consists of single-sized stands. There is a serious lack of regeneration, due to both low harvests and substantial browsing by deer (Teufen 1985).

POSSIBLE FUTURE RELATIONSHIPS
BETWEEN FORESTRY AND TOURISM

The trends presented above show that, since 1950, for both the Swiss Alps as a whole and the test areas in particular, tourism has increased immensely in economic and social importance, while forestry has declined steadily. In general, tourism has developed at the expense of forestry. A common example is a road whose construction is subsidized for forestry and is then used to develop, and for access to, tourist facilities, such as ski lifts, accommodation, or hiking trails. Some forestry activities certainly do have negative impacts on tourism, especially where forestry roads cross hiking trails, or logging interferes with the experience of hikers (e.g., noise from chainsaws; newly-cut trees; creation of wide, muddy roads).

The development of tourism has many direct impacts on forestry. Forests are cleared, often from the most productive, accessible low-altitude sites, to allow construction. Ski runs cut through forests increase the danger of windthrow, desiccation and disease; revegetation, especially on modified slopes, is often inadequate to prevent erosion by meltwater and sliding snow. Skiing tends to retard regeneration, as seedlings, saplings, and trees are damaged by skis and machines. These also compact the snowpack, so that snowmelt is later and more rapid, shortening the growing season for seedlings and saplings, and making erosion more likely. Finally, during the short summer, forestry activities have to be scheduled and undertaken so as to minimize impacts on hikers' activities and enjoyment.

While the direct impacts are often locally quite severe, indirect impacts, which are mostly economic, are more widespread and significant in the long-term. One important indirect impact is the change in employment availability and patterns, which decreases the potential and active forestry labor force. A second is that investment in, and the maintenance of, facilities for tourism leads to a lack of resources for forestry. As short-term opportunities have generally outweighed long-term considerations, such development often results in over-capacity and thus to low profits or even losses. Yet, as discussed in the introduction, tourism's long-term survival depends on the protective and recreational functions that forests provide. Improved relationships between tourism and forestry are clearly required. The tourist industry should support forestry, either directly or indirectly, as discussed below. Equally, forestry planning, harvesting, and maintenance must all consider the importance of the forests for tourism.

The principal need of forestry, throughout the Swiss Alps, is to increase maintenance and harvesting levels. Maintenance includes planting, thinning, and the control of game, pests, diseases, and livestock. While the means for undertaking these activities are well-developed (e.g., Mayer 1976a), more flexible planning is needed to achieve the diverse functions of these forests, particularly those related to recreation. Harvesting levels generally need to increase two- to four-fold. At present, much harvesting is compulsory, as a result of physical and/or biological damage, and limited by access. Consequently, harvested areas and volumes usually bear little relationship to those prescribed in management plans.

The increase in forestry activities is necessary to improve forest structure, i.e., provide a more even distribution of trees of different ages, with increased regeneration, more open stands, and lower volumes of standing timber. In general, a greater diversity of tree species would also be preferable (Mayer 1976b). The purpose of these changes is to maximize the forests' ability to withstand natural and anthropogenic stresses, in order to protect societal infrastructure, and to provide both a high-quality environment for passive and active recreation and timber of as high a quality as possible. While these changes are necessary throughout the mountain forests, their importance varies at all scales. The requisite time-frame is long-term: decades or even centuries.

These increased levels of activity require two conditions. The first is to increase the necessary resources, including planning, labor force, access, vehicles, equipment, and machinery. The second is to develop markets, so that the forestry industry can maximize its self-sufficiency, thus minimizing the need for financial support, whether from governments or from other economic sectors such as tourism. Income from sales should be the main source of the necessary resources, ensuring the provision of the non-market functions (i.e., protection, recreation). While market development is considered only tangentially below, the market cannot be improved by import tariffs; in the international flow of wood and wood-products in and out of Switzerland (protected by international trade agreements), such measures would probably hurt rather than help the forestry industry. Stimuli to the industry's development must therefore come from within Switzerland. Many levels of decision-makers and many industries can affect, or be affected by, developments in forestry: including tourism, wood-products, agriculture, transport, construction, and energy (Price 1988a). Thus, while it is not proposed that the tourist industry alone attempts to stimulate forestry, tourism must provide strong support for forestry.

Coordination

The lack of coordination between tourism and forestry is both a symptom and a cause of existing relationships. Increased coordination is essential. Since most forestry work is now done from May to October, a crucial form of coordination is for tourism to provide winter employment to members of the forestry workforce, so they have a reliable year-round income. At present, many do find winter work in tourism, but such work should be explicitly provided; there is considerable competition, for instance from farmers.

A second vital area of coordination is in planning and undertaking all activities affecting mountain forests. Management planning for these forests has changed little over the last century, in spite of the great change in the relative importance of the forests' functions. Though many foresters (e.g., Forstingenieure des Berner Oberlandes 1982) admit the primary functions of mountain forests are protection and recreation, plans primarily consider timber harvesting, and were written without input from individuals in other sectors of the mountain economy. Also, some areas have plans which are so old as to have no current relevance (e.g., the Aletsch plans, dating from 1924 to 1942).

The principal emphasis of most existing plans, in accordance with cantonal regulations, is on sustained yields. In the foreseeable future, harvests in most of the Alps are unlikely to even approach these theoretical levels, for three reasons. First, the workforce is too small. Second, access networks are inadequate to reach much of the forest area. Third, a large part of the annual harvest is unplanned, resulting from physical or biological damage to trees. While likely areas of damage might be predicted from forest surveys - where these exist - timing and extent are essentially unpredictable. Compulsory harvests are sometimes higher than planned yields; but since much of the timber to be removed is rather inaccessible, a disproportionate investment of resources is required. Finally, markets for the greatly increased volumes of timber which would be harvested, if the theoretical yields were produced, might not exist. At present, harvested timber is sometimes turned into chips at the logging site, since the costs of removing it to the valley are too high for a profit to be made.

Various recent changes in planning methodologies explicitly give greater weight to the non-market functions of mountain forests (e.g., Langenegger 1979, 1984b). Flexible planning methods being developed at the Federal Technical School (ETH) in Zürich consider both the complex terrain and the great variety in forest communities and functions. These methods emphasize functional zoning of forests, divided into rational management districts, as a basis for planning. One example is Gordon (1985); such zoning is also proposed for new plans in Valais. Current research at the Federal Forestry Research Institute also stresses flexibility and the involvement of non-foresters in planning and management. This is critical, as the impetus to coordination in planning and management must come from the forestry profession. Yet, in spite of strong public awareness of the threat posed to forests by pollution, general understanding of the long-term public benefits of well-managed forests is still limited. Public information networks on the importance of forests to tourism and society as a whole already exist, at all levels from the local to the federal, but there is still great need for their further development.

Local financial support

While coordination between tourism and forestry is necessary to stimulate the latter, it also requires financial support until it can develop sufficiently to support itself through wood sales. The provision of local financial support is complicated by the fact that, although most of the people deriving their income from tourism are members of the local political commune, they may not own forest as individuals or as members of the local civil commune, cooperatives, or corporations. Equally, not all forest owners live in the same political commune as their forests. Since levels of local financial support for forestry vary enormously throughout the Alps, existing levels will be described, and developments proposed, with reference to the test areas.

In Aletsch, most tourist facilities are above treeline. The forests below are on steep slopes, and are unimportant for skiing or hiking. However, they protect the cable-cars, roads, railway, and valley and slope settlements on which the tourist economy depends. Yet the tourist industry has not invested in the management of the forests. The income the communes derive from tourism is inadequate to plan and pay for the severe backlog in harvesting, maintenance, and road construction. The increased harvests of the 1980s have brought no financial gain; federal subsidies only allow costs to be covered. Thus, local political action appears necessary if tourism is to financially support forestry, perhaps through the imposition of a special tax. The situation is complicated by various factors: the two forest districts both include a number of communes, each of which would vote separately; each commune's forests cross a wide range of altitudes; and some communes own forest within the boundaries of other communes.

In Davos, the commune provides considerable financial support to forestry, as discussed previously, although it owns only 16 percent of the forest area. This results from two factors. The first is a wide awareness of the forests' importance and potential instability, following the substantial damage in 1979 and subsequent public education by the local forester. The second is the commune's good financial health; a result, at least partially, of income from tourism. While this factor is not widespread in the Swiss Alps, the agreement of the commune's citizens to support forestry is an important precedent which other communities could follow.

Improvements in the management and structure of the mountain forests require planning for rationally-bounded areas, rather than historically-demarcated areas such as the Aletsch communes. However, such planning, in which all forestry-related activities are coordinated and priorized, must follow a communal decision that overall management of the forests in a given area is in the public interest and should take precedence over individual concerns. Such a decision would provide a basis for greater, if indirect, financial support of forestry by tourism since general agreement to support forestry would have to be buttressed by funds which would presumably come from a tax on the principal industry of most mountain communities: tourism.

Changes in policy and forestry legislation

Since the 1950s, the financial situation of mountain forestry has become increasingly precarious. Tschannen and Barrand (1985) showed that, on average, forestry enterprises in the Alps lost money, while profits were made elsewhere in Switzerland. For two-thirds of the Bernese Oberland's forests, maintenance and harvesting cannot break even, and the costs of maintaining protective and recreational facilities cannot be covered (Stauffer 1985). As mentioned above, road construction costs are generally prohibitive, even when government grants are provided. Existing grants for harvesting are primarily used to remove timber which is diseased or not easily accessible. Such harvesting results either in deficits or minimal income to forest owners, and the costs of subsequent reforestation and maintenance are again prohibitive.

In view of these extreme economic problems, even the best coordination and a reasonable level of local financial support will not result in the urgently-needed increases in forestry activities. The conclusion, therefore, is that tourism and forestry should work together to ensure that cantonal and federal governments supply the necessary resources. Already, cantonal and federal legislation and policies provide financial assistance to all aspects of mountain forestry (Price 1988a); the level of support and activities covered have increased considerably in recent years (Wandeler 1985). However, existing legislation and policies are generally inadequate, primarily because of their emphasis on preserving the forest area and producing timber, rather than on long-term provision of all forest functions.

The critical lack in existing legislation is that it does not specify that forests must be managed at the minimum level necessary for them to provide their functions in the long term. Consequently, cantonal forest service officials cannot persuade forest owners to do anything in their forests unless it can be shown that their protective function is directly endangered, e.g., by the likelihood of a widespread epidemic of bark beetles, or because trees have been damaged or killed by windstorms, avalanches, or other factors. As nearly all forestry operations lose money, forest owners will not cut or remove trees if they view a nebulous *public* as the only beneficiary. Similarly, they will not invest in new roads, plant trees, or do any maintenance if they see no likelihood of a return on these investments or of a rise in wood prices in the foreseeable future.

To overcome these problems, a new federal forest law has been drafted (Wandeler 1985), and is expected to come into effect in the early 1990s. Its primary goals are to ensure the minimal level of management necessary for the forests to fulfil their functions in the long term, and to provide assistance to forest owners so they do not suffer financial hardship in undertaking activities for the public good. Tourism and forestry have a mutual interest in working together to accelerate the passage of this legislation and ensure the future of the forests, based on the understanding that coordinated planning and management of the forests is essential for both industries and for the future of the communities of the Swiss Alps.

ACKNOWLEDGEMENTS

This chapter is based on research supported by the Swiss Man and the Biosphere program, the U.S. National Science Foundation, and the University of Colorado. The National Center for Atmospheric Research is sponsored by the U.S. National Science Foundation.

REFERENCES

Affolter, E. 1985. Zunehmende Zwangsnutzungen: Holzmarkt und Holzverwendung aus der Sicht der Waldwirtschaft. *Schweizerische Zeitschrift für Forstwesen* 136:805-818.

Auer, C. 1956. Die volkswirtschaftliche Bedeutung des Gebirgswaldes. *Schweizerische Zeitschrift für Forstwesen* 107:319-326.

Bavier, J.B. 1940. Problemstellung in der Gebirgsforstwirtschaft. *Schweizerische Zeitschrift für Forstwesen* 91:161-174.

Bellwald, S. and H. Graf. 1985. *Der Wald im Aletschgebiet: Zustand und Entwicklungstendenzen.* Bern: Schlussbericht zum schweizerischen MAB-Programm 17.

Beratungsstelle für Arbeitssicherheit in der Forstwirtschaft (BAF). 1985. *8. Jahresbericht.* Luzern.

Bernard, P.P. 1978. *Rush to the Alps.* New York: Columbia University Press.

Bischoff, N. 1982. Der Zustand des Gebirgwaldes in der Schweiz. *Schweizerische Zeitschrift für Forstwesen* 133:691-709.

Bloetzer, G. 1978. *Die Oberaufsicht über die Forstpolizei nach schweizerischem Bundesstaatsrecht.* Zürich: Schulthess.

Bridel, L. 1984. Formes et tendances de l'evolution touristique. In E.A. Brugger, G. Furrer, B. Messerli and P. Messerli (Eds.), *Umbruch im Berggebiet.* Bern: Haupt, 203-240.

Clawson, M. and R. Sedjo. 1984. History of sustained-yield concept and its application to developing countries. In H.K. Steen (Ed.), *History of Sustained-Yield Forestry.* Durham, NC: Forest History Society, 3-14.

Darbellay, C. 1984. Mountain agriculture in change. In E.A. Brugger, G. Furrer, B. Messerli and P. Messerli (Eds.), *The Transformation of Swiss Mountain Regions.* Bern: Haupt, 289-316.

Forstingenieure des Berner Oberlandes. 1982. Die Leistungen des Waldes - Erwartungen und Grenzen. *Schweizerische Zeitschrift für Forstwesen* 133:515-536.

Gordon, R. 1985. *Ueberlegungen zur Forsteinrichtung im Gebirgswald, anhand des Beispiels der Gemeinde Tarasp.* Unpublished Diplomarbeit, Institut für Wald- und Holzforschung, ETH.

Günter, T.F. 1980. *Die Wälder der Landschaft Davos.* Unpublished Diplomarbeit, Geographisches Institut, Universität Zürich.

Jungo, J. 1969. Aktuelle forstpolitische Probleme der Schweiz. *Schweizerische Zeitschrift für Forstwesen* 120:1-18.

Keller, P. and U. Kneubühl. 1982. *Die Entwicklungssteuerung in einem Tourismusort.* Bern: Schlussbericht MAB Projekt 4.18.

Krippendorf, J. 1984. The capital of tourism in danger. In E.A. Brugger, G. Furrer, B. Messerli and P. Messerli (Eds.), *The Transformation of Swiss Mountain Regions*. Bern: Haupt, 427-450.

Langenegger, H. 1979. Eine Checkliste für Waldstabilität im Gebirgswald. *Schweizerische Zeitschrift für Forstwesen* 130:640-646.

Langenegger, H. 1984a. Mountain forests: dynamics and stability. In E.A. Brugger, G. Furrer, B. Messerli and P. Messerli (Eds.), *The Transformation of Swiss Mountain Regions*. Bern: Haupt, 361-372.

Langenegger, H. 1984b. Besonderheiten der Forsteinrichtung im Gebirgswald. *Schweizerische Zeitschrift für Forstwesen* 135:469-480.

Leibundgut, H. 1956. Das Problem des Gebirgshilfe. *Schweizerische Zeitschrift für Forstwesen* 107: 297-310.

Mattig, F. and H.-P. Zeiter. 1984. *Die touristiche Wachstumsprozess im MAB-Testgebiet Aletsch*. Fiesch: Druck AG.

Mayer, H. 1976a. *Gebirgswaldbau - Schutzwaldpflege*. Stuttgart: Fischer.

Mayer, H. 1976b. Die Verjüngung des Gebirgswaldes. *Schweizerische Zeitschrift für Forstwesen* 127:14-30.

Messerli, P. 1983. The concept of stability and instability of mountain ecosystems derived from the Swiss MAB-6 studies of the Aletsch area. *Mountain Research and Development* 3:281-290.

Moser, U. 1985. Erhaltung forstlicher Arbeitskärfte zur Pflege des Waldes. *Wald und Holz* 66:692-700.

Oechslin, M. 1957. Aus dem Aufgabenkreis des Gebirgsforstmannes. *Schweizerische Zeitschrift für Forstwesen* 108:651-663.

Ott, E. 1972. Erhebungen über den gegenwartigen Zustand des Schweizer Waldes als Grundlage waldbaulicher Zielsetzungen. *Mitteilungen EAFV, Birmensdorf* 48:1-193.

Ott, E. 1976. Probleme des Gebirgwaldbaus. *Schweizerische Zeitschrift für Forstwesen* 127:138-150.

Ott, E. 1984. Forest potential. In Brugger, E.A. Brugger, G. Furrer, B. Messerli and P. Messerli (Eds.), *The Transformation of Swiss Mountain Regions*. Bern: Haupt, 157-166.

Price, M.F. 1988a. The development of legislation and policy for the forests of the Swiss Alps. *Land Use Policy* 5:314-328.

Price, M.F. 1988b. Mountain forests as common-property resources: management policies and their outcomes in the Colorado Rockies and the Swiss Alps. Unpublished Ph.D. dissertation, University of Colorado, Boulder.

Schwingruber, C. 1985. Ergebnisse 1984 der Lohnerhebung der schweizerischen Forstwirtschaft. *Wald und Holz* 66:811-819.

Spinatsch, P. 1983. Walderschliessung. *Schweizerische Zeitschrift für Forstwesen* 134:517-529.

Stauffer, A. 1985. *Pflege und Nutzung der Bergwälder - Grenzen der Eigenwirtschaftlichkeit*. Birmensdorf: Bericht EAFV.

Teufen, B. 1985. *Wirtschaftsplan für die Wälder der Landschaft Davos*. Kreisforstamt 18 Davos.

Tromp, H. 1980. Hundert Jahre forstliche Planung in der Schweiz. *Mitteilungen EAFV, Birmensdorf* 56:253-267.

Tschannen, E. and P.-A. Barrand. 1985. Die wirtschaftliche Lage schweizerischer Forstbetriebe 1984. *Wald und Holz* 66:761-773.

Wandeler, H. 1985. Die Revision der eidgenössischen Forstgesetzgebung: Stand und Schwerpunkte. *Schweizerische Zeitschrift für Forstwesen* 136:657-664.

Wiebecke, C. and W. Peters. 1984. Aspects of sustained-yield history: forest sustention as the principle of forestry - idea and reality. In H.K. Steen (Ed.), *History of sustained-yield forestry*. Durham, NC: Forest History Society, 176-182.

Wieser, R.F. 1950. Die Erhaltung des Hochgebirgwaldes durch Jungwuchspflege und Durchforstung. *Schweizerische Zeitschrift für Forstwesen* 101:560-565.

CHAPTER 14

PARKS, ABORIGINAL PEOPLES, AND SUSTAINABLE TOURISM IN DEVELOPING REGIONS: THE INTERNATIONAL EXPERIENCE AND CANADA'S NORTHWEST TERRITORIES

Erik Val
Tourism and Parks
Economic Development and Tourism
Yellowknife, N.W.T., Canada

In October 1982 the Third World National Parks Congress, meeting in Indonesia, issued the Bali Declaration which drew international attention to the link between conservation, parks, sustainable development, and the rational use of the world's natural resources (Packard, 1982). In his closing remarks, the Director General of the International Union for the Conservation of Nature and Natural Resources (IUCN) noted that protected areas should provide ". . . lasting benefits to the peoples of a nation and the world. Protected areas are protected *for* people, not *from* people" (Talbot 1982:2).

The six point Declaration identified, among other fundamental principles, the need to take into account the economic, cultural, and political contexts of protected areas when developing park management regimes.

"Recognize the economic, cultural, and political contexts of protected areas; increase local support for protected areas through such measures as education, revenue sharing, participation in decisions, complementary development schemes adjacent to the protected area, and, where compatible with the protected area's objectives, access to resources" (Parks Congress 1982:2).

This principle provides a useful paradigm to examine the role and contribution of parks and tourism to the economies of developing regions and countries. The principle also provides the basic objectives necessary to create a balanced policy for parks establishment, tourism development, and aboriginal people's participation in park and tourism initiatives.

Five years after the Bali Declaration, Nelson (1987) in his nine country comparative analysis of natural parks, conservation strategies, and sustainable development identified the need for more research to understand the relation between indigenous and local people, national parks, planning, and development in hinterland regions around the world. He suggested that "the roles or uses that are made of protected areas in such regions can not only determine the character of the landscape, but also the ways of life and future of the inhabitants" (Nelson 1987:308). This chapter undertakes the research identified by Nelson by studying the relationship between parks, tourism, and aboriginal peoples in Canada's Northwest Territories (N.W.T.). The chapter will examine the underlying geographic, social, political, and economic conditions in the N.W.T. that have led the territorial government to draft an innovative and responsive policy for territorial parks and related tourism development. In order to better appreciate the N.W.T. context, comparisons will be made to a sampling of other developing regions and countries that are also dealing with parks, tourism development, and aboriginal people.

THE RELATIONSHIP BETWEEN PARKS, TOURISM, AND ABORIGINAL PEOPLES

Before examining the northern Canadian and international situation, the relationship between parks, tourism and aboriginal peoples is briefly explored.

In 1986, the President's Commission on Americans Outdoors undertook a comprehensive review of the role that parks, conservation, recreation, and tourism play in the United States. The Commission issued a report which appeals to all levels of government and the private sector to protect more recreational resources and to make them available to more Americans. Gunn (1986) in his submission to the Commission describes the symbiotic linkages between conservation, recreation, and tourism:

"As natural and cultural resources are put in public and non-profit ownership and management for resource protection and *conservation* programs, they increase in popularity. Millions of people take great interest in these assets of the nation and wish to see them, photograph them, and become enriched by them - functions clearly within the ideologies of *leisure* and *recreation*. In the process of doing so, these visitors demand lodging, transportation, food service, and a variety of products and services - functions easily within the ideology of *tourism*" (Gunn 1986: Tourism-3).

Canadian and US examples such as Banff, Jasper, Yosemite, and Yellowstone National Parks come quickly to mind as examples of the co-existence of these phenomena. However, their co-existence has not been without contention and conflict. Both these parks services face the same challenge of balancing resource protection and preservation with public use and enjoyment, the driving force behind recreation and tourism. Some hope of conciliating this conflict may be drawn from the 1987 World Commission on the Environment and Development Report which has refocused attention on the interdependence between environmental and economic planning. In its report, *Our Economic Future*, the Commission spells out the principles of sustainable development, and the need to integrate conservation and development. Tourism and parks offer real opportunities to promote sustainable development initiatives. Gunn points out that pragmatically, " . . . the overlap between these ideologies should force supporters to recognize how much they can gain by greater interface and even collaboration at times" (Gunn, 1986: Tourism-4).

Tourism industry representatives speaking at the 1985 Canadian Assembly on National Parks also recognize the closing of the gap between these ideologies, noting that "tourism represents the opportunity for growth based upon natural resource conservation" (Clarke 1987:26), and "responsible tourism projects depend on a high quality landscape" (Kehm 1982:39).

Related to parks and tourism in developing regions is the role of aboriginal peoples in managing these resources and activities. In Canada's North and around the world the increasing importance of this role is being recognized (Fenge 1986 and 1987, Weeks 1986, Rueggeberg 1988).

Cultural Survival, an interest group of anthropologists, practitioners, and experts on aboriginal peoples, notes that ". . .in the past, most protected areas have been set aside without the advice or consent of local residents", and that ". . . it has become obvious that the exclusion of traditional inhabitants from conservation areas has not always had the desired ecological or conservational effects" (Clay 1985:2).

In her analysis of native people and parks, Weeks (1986) points out that while native people and national parks share a common interest in protecting ecosystems, conflict usually occurs due to the cultural differences between them and the developing agency. To avoid such conflict, she recommends that greater collaboration and understanding between the two groups is needed to successfully develop and manage these resources and activities.

In the Arctic, the Inuit Circumpolar Conference (ICC) also recognizes the need for the greater involvement of Northerners in conservation and development initiatives. The ICC, representing Inuit from Alaska, Canada, and Greenland, emphasizes the importance and role that communities play in developing integrated conservation and development strategies. The ICC's draft conservation strategy recognizes that ". . . Inuit organizations and communities are beginning to confront the need to manage resources in relationship to present and future needs, and they are seriously discussing the problems and potentials related to the commercial development of local resources" (ICC 1988:4).   Jull (1988) in his analysis of Sami political development in Norway identifies the same need for greater native involvement in resource management decision making.

A SAMPLING OF THE INTERNATIONAL EXPERIENCE

Analyzing and comparing factors that influence and shape policy-making has benefits for both the resource manager and academic when developing or understanding the essential purpose, goals, and objectives underlying public policy (Mitchell 1979). A broader understanding based on the review of the international experience can lead to the development of policies that are sufficiently flexible to respond to changing managerial situations and circumstances. Such a review has assisted policy makers in Canada's North in developing a parks and tourism development policy.

Before examining the international experience, a brief review of tourism economics and developing nations is useful. Sessa (1983) describes natural and cultural assets as the raw materials of tourism. As industrialized countries reach their saturation point of these raw materials then greater tourism attention is directed towards developing countries. He argues that tourism in developing countries ". . . reintegrates these otherwise resourceless localities into a higher productivity cycle and higher standard of living" (Sessa 1983:78, 81).

However, drawbacks exist, and they should be recognized when developing a parks and tourism policy. Tourism in many areas around the world is considered seasonal, and investment decisions must be taken recognizing the cyclical nature of the industry, excess capacity at certain times of the year, and marketing for off-season use. Tourism demand is also sensitive to changing economic conditions and international or local events (Culpan 1987). Furthermore, support infrastructure for tourism can be expensive, especially when appealing to a demanding up-scale international market. Other factors to consider when planning for tourism development include the impact on local traditions, environmental impact, stimulation of local consumption and inflationary effect on wages, and profit loses to foreign investors. Some analysts argue that traditionally, tourism profit margins have been low compared to other investment opportunities (Culpan 1987). These potential drawbacks must continually be weighed against the benefits of tourism, such as employment, income, business opportunities, and foreign exchange earnings. Furthermore, these negative impacts emphasize the need to properly plan and manage the growth of tourism in a sustainable manner by understanding the sensitivity of the product (natural and cultural resources), the demand (international adventure tourism) and local concerns (aboriginal peoples).

The parks and tourism policymaking context in Canada's Northwest Territories, in certain respects, is similar to that of other developing countries. Similarities include:

A large or almost exclusive aboriginal population with strong, evolving cultural ties to a land and renewable resource base;

A devolving or recently transferred authority for self-government from either a central authority or former colonial power;

A developing regional or national economy dependant on primary resource extraction with little or no secondary processing or manufacturing, and few long-term local benefits; and

Limited or developing tourism infrastructure (accommodation, transportation, specific tourist services, etc.).

Differences are also relevant when comparing Canada's North to other developing regions. Differences include:

A reasonably reliable source of government funds to develop parks and tourism in the N.W.T. with no pressing requirement to seek international assistance; and

Political change is occurring in the N.W.T. with minimal social upheaval and no military intervention.

Kenya

During and since colonial rule, Kenya has developed a mature adventure-oriented tourism industry, based on wildlife that is protected by large tracts of natural habitat found in the country's national parks. In Kenya, parks and tourism are interdependent and benefit from each other in terms of resource conservation, employment, income, and foreign exchange earnings (Johnson 1986). From 1963 to 1980, tourism, coffee and tea were the top domestic exports of the country. Tourism was also the fastest growing export in terms of foreign exchange earnings, and had the greatest forward and backward linkages to other sectors of the Kenyan economy (Summary 1987). Compared to Canada's North, tourism in Kenya, which has developed since the turn of the century, is considerably advanced in terms of international market share, *brand* name recognition, and tourism infrastructure. However, with time and prudent development, the N.W.T. may in the future enjoy the same success experienced by Kenya. The Kenyan experience points to the role of the national parks as a "tool of national development rather than a bastion of preservation" (Burnett and

Bulter 1987:46). The Kenyan experience also points to the need for greater local involvement, and the country " . . . is experimenting with new management forms encouraging greater integration of parks into its local human environment, and evolution of Kenya's parks into de-nationalized quasi-public corporations controlled by local governments is not inconceivable" (Burnett and Bulter 1987:49-50).

Nepal

Parallels exist between Canada's North today and Nepal's experience in Royal Chitwan Park some 20 years ago. *The Tiger Tops Jungle Lodge*, one of a number of lodges in this park, was conceived on a program of offering a high quality tourism wilderness experience in a protected area. The program has been successful because tourism services in the park are managed by qualified Nepali naturalists who realize the need to protect the wildlife habitat from over-use. Over-use is managed by limiting the lodge room capacity (Johnson 1986). A paper presented at an international workshop on the national parks management in the Himalayas identified the challenges of conducting a commercial tourism operation in accordance with the principles of sustainable development, particularly in meeting basic needs of the local poor (Roberts and Johnson 1985). However, the Tiger Tops group did achieve other sustainable development goals such as sensitivity to culture and tradition, consideration of carrying capacity of the natural resource base, application of appropriate local technology, and income and employment generation. This tourism company recognized from the outset: ". . . the importance of operating in harmony not only with the habitat of the wildlife on which the business depends, but also with the social environment of the Chitwan Valley" (Johnson 1986:12).

More recent examples exist in Nepal such as the integration of tourism ventures into the development of Annapurna National Park. These initiatives are premised on the sustainable use of species, developing optimal, not maximum, tourism opportunities, preservation of the cultural heritage, and assistance to the local people in developing ancillary tourism opportunities (Johnson 1986).

The Nepali experience in establishing national parks and successfully integrating tourism into these protected areas with the involvement of local people is a model to consider when setting the direction for parks and tourism development in Canada's North.

Galapagos Islands

The international experience is not always positive, and much can also be learned from these tourism and parks related problems. Since Darwin visited the Galapagos Islands in 1835, they have been exciting places for scientists and, more recently, tourists to study and observe biological processes and species. In 1939, most of these islands were set aside by Ecuador as a national park to protect the islands' unique natural resources. Since then, tourism has grown in response to international interest in visiting the islands. Growth in tourism and the requirement to visit these islands accompanied by guides has yielded local employment and other related benefits. Some 18,000 tourists visit the island annually from small cruise boats and a few larger vessels. The effect of these tourism benefits has been to make local residents shareholders in the conservation of the park resources. Since the mid-1960s an administrative and management structure has been in place on the island primarily to control use and study the destructive processes of over-use by tourism and feral mammals (Stephenson 1985).

Tourism has also created threats to the islands' natural resources. The natural history of the islands is based primarily on sensitive beach dune systems and volcanic slopes with little topsoil. These landscapes are particularly susceptible to excessive trampling caused by tourism and browsing feral goats. The impact of visitor interaction with breeding and nesting bird colonies and free ranging reptiles is also of concern. The Ecuadorian government, however, does realize the importance of the Galapagos to its tourism economy, which is a major contributor to its foreign exchange earnings. The government, along with other agencies such as the IUCN, the World Wildlife Fund, and the Smithsonian Institute have contributed research monies, but additional management funds are still required. In order to handle the ever-growing number of tourists, park managers recommend a ten percent fee levied on the cost of visiting the park. These additional funds would permit a maximum of 25,000 visitors annually who would be controlled and managed by a warden service, which would be doubled. More boats and money for patrolling, park maintenance, research, and conservation would also be available. Tourism, one of the major threats to the integrity of the islands, could now become their saviour (Stephenson 1985).

The Galapagos experience sends a clear message to Canada's North which is the need to understand the resource base and its capacity to sustain tourism use, and manage this use appropriately in order to conserve the resources, which are the primary attractions in the first place.

Other Experiences

Over the last 20 years, Central America has established protected tropical rainforest areas which have been developed as either Indian Reserves, Biosphere Reserves, World Heritage Sites, or National Parks.

These designations by themselves provide international recognition which attracts tourists from around the world. Examples include protected areas such as Darien National Park in Panama, Guanacaste National Park in Costa Rica, Rio Platano Biosphere Reserve in Honduras, and the Kuna Indian Reserve in Panama. The management and operation of all these protected areas involve extensive local participation by way of employment, training, and developing tourism opportunities. These efforts are assisted by international agencies such as IUCN, World Wildlife Fund, individuals and private corporations. This broad based international involvement provides the appropriate promotion needed to develop a growing tourism economy at a pace consistent with local needs and aspirations (Kamstra 1985, Houseal, MacFarland, Archibold and Chiari 1985, Janzen 1986, Myers 1987, Navarro and Fletcher 1988).

Finally, Greenland's National Park, located in the northeast corner of the island, is also a relevant comparison to Canada's North. As a high arctic park, it is in many respects similar to Northern Ellesmere Island National Park Reserve. The two parks are separated by a 50 km strait at their northern most extremities. Both parks have rich and varied landscapes and wildlife, and experience growing tourism use. International hikers, glacier trekkers, mountain climbers, and kayakers are the specialized adventure tourists who use these arctic parks. These parks are remote, have short visitor seasons, and are expensive destinations. Culturally, the two parks are similar, both have traces of past Inuit and pre-Inuit occupation with no current native settlements. Both parks have been the subject of considerable physical and biological research over the last 30 years (Vibe 1984).

PARKS, TOURISM, AND ABORIGINAL PEOPLES IN CANADA'S NORTHWEST TERRITORIES (N.W.T.)

The review of the international experience provides the basis to examine tourism and parks development in Canada's N.W.T. The balance of the chapter examines the underlying social, political, economic, and geographic factors that influence the making of a territorial parks policy for the N.W.T. The actual draft policy, yet to be finalized, will be presented. Comparisons will be made between the federal and territorial parks systems to illustrate the similarities and differences between their mandates, roles and objectives.

Tourism is an important and growing component of the renewable resource economy of the N.W.T. As the tourism industry grows, so does the importance of federal and territorial parks in Canada's North. The $124 million (1988) tourism industry is a steady contributor to the N.W.T.'s economy. As one of the largest private sector employers, the industry provides over 2,700 permanent and seasonal jobs, representing some 20 percent of the labour force. In contrast to the non-renewable resource sector, tourism offers business and employment opportunities that are compatible with aboriginal peoples' traditional lifestyle. Moreover, tourism creates benefits that are widely distributed throughout the North. In the N.W.T., exceptional growth potential has been identified in the outdoor adventure and cultural tourism markets (Murray 1988). This potential further reinforces the importance of national and territorial parks in the development of the tourism sector. The challenge the Government of the Northwest Territories (GNWT) faces is establishing a parks system that both responds to the long-term tourism needs for the Territories and its aboriginal peoples, as well as conserves those natural and cultural resources which are the primary tourist draw.

Existing National and Territorial Parks in the N.W.T.

National Parks, administered and managed by the Government of Canada, have existed in the N.W.T. since 1922 with the establishment of Wood Buffalo National Park. After a lull of about half a century, the next two national parks were established in 1972. These parks, Nahanni and Auyuittuq, are actually national park reserves to be designated as national parks after the settlement of native land claims. The *National Parks Act* applies to these lands, subject to the right of aboriginal peoples to continue traditional hunting, fishing and trapping activities (R.S., C.N-13, amended 1988, C.48). The newest in the N.W.T. and Canada's most northern national park reserve, Northern Ellesmere Island, was established in 1988 (Map 1).

These northern national parks have sensitive environments, are remote, experience low use, are used primarily for their wilderness resources, and have modest levels of visitor services and infrastructure. These three national park reserves, and Wood Buffalo National Park, occupy a total area of about 80,000 km^2 in the N.W.T. (Table 1).

In contrast to the federal parks system in the N.W.T., the territorial system, administered and managed by the GNWT, is extremely small, only 130.9 km^2 of land, and young, having started in 1970. The majority (80 percent) of the 43 are small wayside or community parks (Table 2). These parks serve primarily local day use and en route travel markets. Blackstone Territorial Park, which opened officially in 1985, is the first and only outdoor recreation park (Map 1). The remaining territorial parks commemorate historic or archaeological sites. Two recently established parks at Kekerten Island and Qaummaarviit in the Eastern Arctic are attractions that play an important role in the tourism economy of the region.

Both the federal and territorial governments are considering new park proposals across the North (Map 1). The federal government is discussing with the Inuit communities of Pond Inlet and Arctic Bay a combined land and marine park proposal for Northern Baffin Island and Lancaster Sound. Negotiations are underway with the Dene/Metis people of Snowdrift on a park proposal for the East Arm of Great Slave Lake. Other potential federal parks in the N.W.T. are located on Banks Island, Bathurst Inlet, and Wager Bay.

Since 1984, the GNWT has been considering four large outdoor recreation park proposals: the Ram Plateau/North Nahanni River located beside Nahanni National Park Reserve, the Campbell Hills/Lake situated south of Inuvik, the Dodo Canyon located on the Canol Trail southwest of Norman Wells, and the Three Rivers Area located 30 km south of Wrigley. These four proposals are at various stages of discussions with the affected communities. Hidden Lake Territorial Park, close to Yellowknife, has been partially developed and awaits designation.

The mandates of federal and territorial parks services are different in certain important aspects. Protection by preservation and conservation is the Canadian Parks Service's primary policy goal. Promoting public understanding, appreciation and enjoyment are related objectives. Developing parks solely for tourism is not part of the national parks mandate:

> "To protect for all time those places which are significant examples of Canada's natural and cultural heritage and also to encourage public understanding, appreciation and enjoyment of this heritage in ways which leave it unimpaired for future generations" (Parks Canada 1982:11).

Table 1.   National Parks and Park Reserves in the N.W.T.

Name	Date Established	Size (km^2)	1987 - 88 use* (No. of Visitors)
Wood Buffalo NP	1922	14,200**	3,398
Nahanni NPR	1972	4,800	810
Auyuittuq NPR	1972	21,500	442
Northern Ellesmere NPR	1986	39,500	86

(Source: Ward and Killham 1987:12 and Canadian Parks Service 1988)
NP = National Park
NPR = National Park Reserve
* April 1, 1987 - March 31, 1988
** N.W.T. portion only; total area is 45,000 km^2

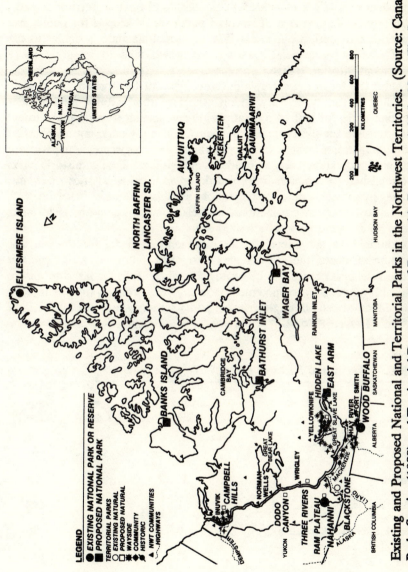

Map 1. Existing and Proposed National and Territorial Parks in the Northwest Territories. (Source: Canadian Parks Service (1988) and Territorial Department of Renewable Resources (1986). Note: The Locations of existing parks are representative and not actual)

The territorial minister of the Department of Economic Development and Tourism (EDT) is mandated to establish and operate territorial parks by the *Territorial Parks Act*. Territorial parks are developed for public use, recreation, and tourism purposes. The territorial mandate is similar to the rest of Canada's provincial park systems which tend to integrate parks development into the tourism economy.

Under the territorial act, five different types of territorial parks may be established. The types vary widely, ranging from natural environment recreation parks for limited recreational use to smaller wayside parks found at the roadside for the travelling public. Community parks are established for the recreational benefit of a community. Outdoor recreation parks are for general recreational use by residents and visitors. Finally, historic parks are established to commemorate historic or archaeological sites or events. Natural environment, outdoor recreation, and historic parks have the potential to be tourist destinations, whereas community and wayside parks tend to be en route or local attractions.

Although the act directs the establishment of parks for tourism and recreation purposes, the GNWT also recognizes that as a tourism *product* or *attraction*, parks must also be protected and carefully managed to ensure sustainable tourism development. As such, " . . . conservation is more a consequence of establishing territorial parks rather than a reason for their creation" (Hamre 1986:4).

Table 2.   Territorial Parks in the N.W.T.

Category	Category (Sites)	% of Total	Size (km²)
Wayside	24	56	29.1
Community	11	26	3.2
Outdoor Recreation	1	1	14.3
Natural Environment Recreation	0	0	0.0
Historic	7	16	84.3
TOTAL	43	100	130.9

(Source: Ward and Killham 1987:171)

PARKS AND TOURISM POLICYMAKING CONTEXT

"The North is Canada's last frontier, but we are not isolated. The Northern frontier is an exciting place of creativity and innovations" (GNWT 1988:8).

The section that described the international experience showed how the N.W.T. is more akin to a developing nation than most other jurisdiction in southern Canada. Geographic, demographic, economic, cultural, and political factors have created a unique policy-making context for developing parks and tourism in the N.W.T.

Geographic Factors

The Northwest Territories is a vast and diverse region of approximately 3.2 million km^2. This immense area constitutes a third of Canada's land mass and spans four time zones. Long travel distances by air and land make the N.W.T. both a remote and expensive tourism destination. Whereas the expense, especially air travel, can be a deterrent, the remoteness is an alluring feature which is increasingly attracting more tourists. Relative to the south, the high cost of travel and services in the N.W.T. tends to draw lower volumes of tourists, who stay longer and spend more when in the North (Murray 1988). Equally important to tourism in the N.W.T. is the natural history and landscape diversity which varies from high arctic desert, to barrenground tundra, to boreal forest. This spectacular diversity provides a wide variety of opportunities for developing tourism attractions and parks in the N.W.T. These attractions and parks, in turn, can draw on many specialized outdoor adventure markets ranging from trophy sport fishing, to trekking, dog sledding and kayaking (Murray 1987).

Demographic Factors

Relative to its size, the population of the N.W.T. is remarkably small. In 1988, 55,000 people lived in 50 cities, towns, hamlets, and hunting camps scattered across the Territories (Outcrop 1988). While a small and dispersed population may appear to be a disadvantage, this wide distribution of communities provides access to many tourism attractions across the North. As tourism in the N.W.T. is relatively new, the work force is still inexperienced and requires training in a wide variety of skills and trades (Murray 1988). The success of tourism is dependent on providing an exceptional experience and high quality service, and therefore training will play a critical role in preparing the workforce.

Cultural and Historical Factors

Native people in the North are beginning to recognize the interest that their traditions and culture generate with tourists. Increasingly, tourists are looking for a mix of high quality natural and cultural experiences (Tourism Research Group 1988). The North has much to offer by way of interesting and unique lifestyles and traditions. Today, three major native groups, the Dene, Metis and Inuit make up 60 percent of the northern population. Seven different languages are spoken across the North, five of which are native. Strong cultural ties to past traditions and renewable resource harvesting are the mainstays of northern aboriginal life. Together with contemporary lifestyles, the North's rich native and non-native archaeology are attractive resources, which, if properly protected and sensitively interpreted, will complement the abundant natural attractions which draw visitors North. Tourism related to cultural experiences will continue to grow and play an important role in developing the tourism economy of the North. Tourism is a part of the northern economy which is consistent with the skills, interests, and traditions of native northerners.

Economic Factors

Tourism continues to make a steady contribution to the N.W.T.'s $1.67 billion economy (Murray 1988). The N.W.T. economy is Canada's fastest growing at 13.4 percent annually, a full 3.5 percent above the national average (Bureau of Statistics 1988). Much of this growth has been concentrated in non-renewable resource development, particularly in the petroleum and mining sectors. This part of the economy is vulnerable to fluctuating world energy and mineral prices. The tourism sector is the fourth largest contributor to the N.W.T. economy after petroleum, mining, and government. Tourism has been resilient and relatively unaffected by downturns in the non-renewable sectors of the economy. Furthermore, relatively little capital is required to enter the industry as an outfitter or guide, and, therefore, considerable potential exists for more Northern involvement and ownership. Since 1982, the sector has experienced continued growth in tourist expenditures and an overall 30 percent increase in the number of non-resident tourists (Table 3).

The potential for market growth in the N.W.T. tourism industry is encouraging. Only some 17 percent of the available North American market for adventure travel to the N.W.T. is currently being captured (Table 4). These findings are based on recent government travel surveys of the Canadian and US pleasure travel markets to Canada (Tourism Canada, 1986a,b,c).

Table 3.   Non-Resident Tourist Travel and Expenditures (June-September
                 1982-1987)

	1982	1984	1986	1987
Number of Visitors	43,800	41,800	52,000	58,000
Estimated Tourist Expenditures $1982 in 000s	39,113	46,000	47,450	50,950

(Source: EDT 1987:4)

As part of the tourism economy, parks make significant contributions by creating seasonal and permanent jobs and generating wages, salaries, and business profits. No specific data are available on the impact of territorial parks, but the Canadian Parks Service has assessed the effect of its four national parks in the N.W.T. and Yukon (Intergroup Consultants 1985). Direct gross domestic product (GDP) in 1983/84 due to park and visitor expenditures in both territories was estimated at $3.4 million creating 120 person-years of employment. The spin-off income and jobs created by indirect and induced expenditures generated an additional $1.5 million and 71 person-years of employment (Intergroup Consultants 1985).

The development of parks will assist in promoting growth in the tourism sector. A system of territorial parks across the N.W.T. will offer an array of tourism destinations that will attract a wide variety of tourists. Furthermore, the establishment of territorial parks provides government an opportunity to assist the private sector in developing the tourism industry. Such assistance includes land and resource protection, as well as financial contributions to facility and infrastructure development (roads, services, information centers, etc.).

Political Factors

As a result of a steady devolution of powers and responsibilities over the past 20 years between the federal and territorial governments, the GNWT has evolved to a cabinet system of government with many powers and responsibilities similar to those of the provinces in the rest of Canada. In the future, new powers and sources of revenue will reduce its dependence on the federal government and increase the GNWT's ability to meet Northern economic and social goals. Although land ownership will probably be retained by the federal government after devolution, increased

Table 4.   Estimated Market Potential for N.W.T. Tourism Products

Outdoor/Adventure Travel Markets	Existing Pleasure Travel Trips Captured	Estimated North American Market Potential	Current N.W.T. Penetration Rate
Fishing/Hunting	5,745	28,000	20.4%
Non-Consumptive Adventure Products	6,195	46,600	13.3%
General Touring Market	14,372	78,636	18.3%
TOTAL	26,312	153,236	17.2%

(Source: Murray 1988:6)

resource management powers will allow the territorial government to set its own resource development priorities, including the establishment of territorial parks.

Over the years the government tradition of public participation will have important implications for how communities are involved in directing the development of tourism and parks. The system of government is unique as it is based on consensus decisionmaking and public consultation. A party system does not exist due to the small population spread across the Territories. This system has led to the creation of many committees and boards at the regional and local levels. While these committees and boards may slow the process of decision making, they have the advantage of greater community and individual involvement in government policy making and planning.

Native Land Claim Factors

Through their land claim settlements, native people will have greater opportunities to become more involved in tourism and parks development. Political and economic powers of native groups across the Territories is growing. The native land claims process, which started 15 years ago, is defining aboriginal rights on matters related to land and resource ownership, renewable resource management, and economic development. With these responsibilities and powers comes new found economic clout based on compensation monies, resource ownership, land title, and revenue sharing. As native organizations across the Territories acquire greater control over wildlife management, they will become increasingly more involved in planning, managing, and operating territorial and federal parks. Native groups have negotiated or are negotiating specific provisions related to their involvement in national and territorial parks development and management. In the case of the Inuit of the N.W.T., special impact and benefit agreements will have to be negotiated with affected native communities as a pre-condition to establishing a park. These agreements would indicate how the park would be developed and operated in terms of local employment, training, business opportunities, and other related socio-economic benefits. Approaches to joint community/government management regimes for parks are also a part of these settlements. Specifically, a national park in the northern Yukon with such a joint management regime has been provided for in the final settlement for the Inuvialuit people of the Mackenzie Delta/Beaufort Sea region. The East Arm of Great Slave Lake may also be set aside as a national park in the future settlement of the Dene/Metis claim in the western N.W.T.

A PROPOSED TERRITORIAL PARKS POLICY

In contrast to 100 years of National Parks policy-making in Canada, the N.W.T. has just begun to draft its territorial parks policy. In 1986, a territorial parks policy was proposed and now is being finalized. As a draft, an opportunity exists to review the policy in the context of those influencing factors discussed earlier.

The Mission of Territorial Parks

Review of the international experience and an understanding of the N.W.T. situation illustrates that the settlement of native land claims, continued native harvesting, community participation in planning and decision making, and federal-territorial co-operation are four guiding principles which must be clearly recognized in a parks policy.

First, all existing or future territorial parks are subject to existing and future land claim settlements. This provision means that territorial park boundaries may be altered as a result of lands selected as part of a settlement. Also, the role of government in managing a park may change as wildlife and renewable resource management boards are established under these settlements.

Second, native people are assured the right to continue to hunt, fish, and trap in territorial parks. This right is provided by the *Territorial Parks Act*, and inherently recognizes the importance of the native harvest in the N.W.T.

Third, no territorial park will be established without community consultations and support. This tenet reflects the N.W.T. tradition of collective decision making and community consultation. Furthermore, the principle creates the added advantage of building immediate credibility with communities at the start of consultations.

Fourth, territorial parks will be established co-operatively with other federal and territorial departments involved in developing and managing conservation areas.

Next, the important role that tourism and parks will play in the development of the N.W.T. economy is built into the parks program mission statement. Specifically, parks are:

> To provide opportunities for tourism and recreation, as well as enjoyment, education, and appreciation of the natural and cultural heritage of the N.W.T.;
>
> To create a focus for marketing the natural and cultural heritage of the N.W.T. as part of its tourism industry;
>
> To offer opportunities for employment and business which take advantage of the skills of native peoples and are compatible with Northern lifestyles; and
>
> To undertake or support the development of services, facilities, and/or programs to attract and manage visitors to territorial parks (EDT 1989:4).

In addition to tourism and economic goals, the establishment of territorial parks will take into account other existing or potential land uses to minimize conflicts with other activities such as traditional land and resource uses, industrial development, and sensitive biological features or historic resources. Another related goal of the parks program will be to provide outdoor recreational and educational opportunities for visitors to the N.W.T. and its residents. Parks will also play a commemorative role in designating historic or cultural resources.

Planning and Managing Territorial Parks

The *Territorial Parks Act* empowers the Minister of Economic Development and Tourism to plan, develop, manage, and operate territorial parks. The international experience and failings of the past illustrate the need for greater community involvement in all phases of parks development. In the past, the government has experienced problems with acceptance of proposals because communities were not involved in the early stages of parks planning and development. In response to the need for greater involvement, community park management committees may be established.

These committees will work jointly with government in researching, planning, developing, managing, and operating parks. These committees will advise the Department of Economic Development and Tourism on biophysical and socio-economic research requirements, designating sites, and preparing park management plans, development schedules, and implementation budgets. The *Territorial Parks Act* allows for the establishment of such committees; and a special agreement would determine the terms of reference for a particular committee.

In the long term, a co-operative approach to parks planning and operations has obvious benefits. These benefits include " . . . building community acceptance which determines the effectiveness of management programs, providing local knowledge of the resource base that may otherwise not be available, and lowering the costs of management by using locally-based monitoring and enforcement" (Rueggeberg 1988:60).

For this approach to succeed, sound principles of community consultation and animation will be practiced. The Minister of Economic Development and Tourism must listen carefully and respond to the views of communities through their management committees. These committees will consist of interest groups who have a stake in park development, such as hunters and trappers associations, native organizations, municipal governments, historical societies, and elders groups. These groups and individuals possess customary and traditional knowledge critical to the development of park and tourism resources. All too often in the past, park agencies have either ignored or not sought out this wealth of information, much of which is either unavailable or too costly to gather using scientific research methods (Graham and Payne 1988).

In sum, the draft policy on community and public consultation and involvement will be based on the following principles:

> Public discussion prior to decisions;
> Clear and accurate information;
> Indication of contentious issues requiring decisions and relevant
>   policies, legislation and agreements;
> Adequate notice and time for public review; and
> Careful consideration of public input (EDT, 1989:10).

Tourism and Territorial Parks: Impacts and Benefits

Territorial parks will be developed to make a positive contribution to nearby communities and their economic base. This policy objective means that the positive and negative consequences of establishing a park will be examined. Such an examination may involve undertaking a socio-economic impact assessment as part of the parks planning process. The assessment would identify positive and negative effects of creating parks on the social and economic make-up of the affected communities. Monitoring and mitigatory measures would also be included in such an analysis.

Practically, the policy will encourage the use of local contractors and employees as much as possible during park construction and operations. Initially, special price and scheduling provisions for contracts will be considered but the long-term objective will be to develop an unsubsidized competitive local service sector. Training will be provided to prepare local people for staff positions and associated business/tourism opportunities.

Basic support facilities to assist guides and outfitters may also be provided in parks. Local business involvement may occur on the basis of privately operated, publicly owned concessions, private developments on leased or licenced lands such as lodges or camps, or subsidized facilities either within or outside of parks. Services such as guiding and interpretation programming would be provided by the private sector on a fee for services/cost recovery basis. Furthermore, the private sector would benefit from the government's marketing and promotional efforts associated with advertizing the tourism potential of territorial parks.

The government's policy commitment is that:

Parks developed as tourist destinations will be marketed and promoted as *brand name* products by creating a competitive position in the consumer marketplace;

Government will encourage private sector involvement by supporting the development of associated park tourism infrastructure and services inside and outside of parks (lodges, outfitting, guiding, etc.); and

When feasible, parks services and facilities provided by either the private or public sector will be developed on a cost recovery and/or fee for service basis (EDT 1989:10).

Park Boundaries and Siting

Determining the boundary and location of territorial parks is linked to the broader policy objective of developing parks as a viable component of a region's tourism economy. The choice of park location will be determined by factors such as: presence of outstanding natural and cultural resources, market demand for natural and cultural attractions, accessibility, existing infrastructure and services, community support, cost of development, other competing or complementary tourism attractions, and a host of other considerations.

Factors considered when developing park boundaries and determining its location would include:

Park Boundary
>   Large enough to include outstanding natural and cultural features
>   and contain most visitors' activities;
>   Adequate buffer from surrounding land uses;
>   Room to accommodate future expansion;
>   Avoid conflicting third party interests;
>   Should correspond to recognizable natural and built features.

Park Siting
>   Location with outstanding natural and cultural features;
>   Adequate development potential for services and infrastructure;
>   and
>   Available public access (air, land, or water) (EDT 1989:11).

Tourism, Territorial Parks, and Conservation

The preceding policy discussion has focused on developing parks for the purpose of tourism and economic growth. As described earlier, conservation is not a parks policy objective unto itself. However, after the decision to establish a park is taken, then conservation and sustainable development are important principles used to guide parks development. The territorial government recognizes that a conservation and a sustainable development approach is required if the tourism resources are to be protected for continued future use.

> To maintain the facilities and opportunities, and thereby to continue to fulfil the mission of the program, the natural and cultural resource base of parks must be conserved. This should not be confused with the purpose of the legislation, which does not provide for the creation of territorial parks for the purpose of conservation of natural resources. In other words, conservation may be a consequence of park designation, but may not be the reason (EDT 1986:11).

An important spin-off of creating parks for economic and tourism reasons will be the conservation of N.W.T. lands and resources.

SUMMARY AND CONCLUSIONS

Political, social, and economic conditions in the Northwest Territories are quickly changing. Devolution of federal authority to the GNWT, settlement of native land claims, a consensus form of government decision making, and an economic focus on developing renewable resources are some of the factors that will direct tourism and territorial parks development in Canada's North. Many of these factors have and will continue to play a similar role in the development of parks and tourism economies in the North and other developing countries and regions around the world.

The Northwest Territories is a region of Canada where new parks will play an important role in developing the tourism economy. If planned carefully and sensitively with Northerners taking into account both resource capabilities and market demands, territorial parks have the potential of becoming sustainable tourist destinations. In the long-term, parks developed for tourism purposes will also make a significant contribution to conservation in the N.W.T. The appreciation and understanding of the wilderness resources that this type of tourism generates will also create the public support needed to protect and conserve these areas.

In the N.W.T. as well as internationally, conservation, parks, and tourism and native peoples are closely related. The sustained development of the tourism industry depends on the conservation of the natural and cultural resources and local involvement. The viability, longevity, and prosperity of tourism and parks depends on a society's ability not only to identify and develop opportunities, but also to conserve its natural and cultural resources.

NOTE

The opinions expressed in this chapter do not necessarily reflect those of the Government of the Northwest Territories.

REFERENCES

Bureau of Statistics. 1986 N.W.T. Census Tables on Mobility, Education and Labour Force Activity. *Newstats*. Yellowknife: Government of the Northwest Territories.

Bureau of Statistics. 1988. *Economic Accounts 1987-1985.* Yellowknife: Government of the Northwest Territories.

Burnett, G.W. and L.M. Bulter. 1987. National Parks in the Third World and Associated National Characteristics. *Leisure Sciences* 9:41-52.

Canadian Parks Service. 1988. *Visitor Attendance Monthly Statistics Report.* Ottawa: Canadian Parks Service.

Canadian Statutes, (R.S., C.N-14 amended in 1988, C.48). *National Parks Act.* Government of Canada, Ottawa.

Clarke, B.B. 1987. Tourism and Parks: A Global Perspective on Tourism. In R.C. Scace and J.G. Nelson (Eds.), *Heritage for Tomorrow, Canadian Assembly on National Parks and Protected Areas.* Vol. 5. Ottawa: Environment Canada 35-40.

Clay, J.W. 1985. Parks and People. *Cultural Survival Quarterly* 9:2-4.

Culpan, R. 1987. International Tourism Model for Developing Economies. *Annals of Tourism Research* 14:541-552.

Department of Economic Development and Tourism (EDT). 1986 and 1989. *Draft Policy for Territorial Parks.* Yellowknife: Government of the Northwest Territories (Unpublished).

Department of Economic Development and Tourism (EDT). 1986 and 1987. *Tourism Facts: A Statistical Report of Tourism Travel in the Northwest Territories.* Yellowknife: Government of the Northwest Territories.

Department of Economic Development and Tourism (EDT). 1988. *An Economic Overview of the Northwest Territories.* Yellowknife: Government of the Northwest Territories.

Fenge, T. 1986. National Parks to Conserve the Northwest Territories? *Parks News.* The Journal of the National and Provincial Parks Association 22:4-8.

Fenge, T. 1987. Conserving Nunavut Through the Settlement of the Inuit Land Claim. *Parks News.* The Journal of the National and Provincial Parks Association 23:20-25.

Government of the Northwest Territories. 1988. *Direction for the 1990s.* Yellowknife: Government of the Northwest Territories.

Graham, R. and R.J. Payne. 1988. Customary and Traditional Knowledge in Canadian National Park Planning and Management: A Process Review. Paper presented at the Second Symposium on Social Science in Resource Management. Urbana-Champaign, IL: University of Illinois.

Gunn, C.A. 1986. Philosophical Relationships: Conservation, Leisure, Recreation and Tourism. In *A Literature Review*, appendix to *The Report of the President's Commission on Americans Outdoors.* Washington, D.C.

Hamre, G.M. 1987. *An Overview of Territorial Parks in the Northwest Territories Tourism Industry 1987.* Yellowknife: Department of Economic Development and Tourism.

Houseal, B., C. MacFarland, G. Archibold and A. Chiari. 1985. Indigenous Cultures and Protected Areas in Central America. *Cultural Survival Quarterly* 9:10-21.

Intergroup Consultants Ltd. 1985. *Economic Performance of Four National Parks/Reserves.* Report prepared for Parks Canada. Winnipeg: Intergroup Consultants Ltd.

Inuit Circumpolar Conference (ICC). 1988. *Inuit Communities and Conservation Strategy, An Overview of Major Issues.* Prepared for the Canadian Department of Fisheries and Oceans. Ottawa: Department of Fisheries and Oceans.

Janzen, D. 1986. *Guanacast National Park: Tropical Ecological and Cultural Restoration.* San Jose, Costa Rica: Editorial Universidad Estatal a Distancia.

Johnson, B. 1986. Conservation, Adventure Tourism and Development: Patterns for Emulation? *Landscape Architectural Review* 22:10-14.

Jull, P. 1988. *Lapland: The Native North in Norway.* Yellowknife: Aboriginal Rights and Constitutional Development Secretariat, Government of the Northwest Territories.

Kamstra, J. 1985. Problems and Progress in the Parks of Latin America. *Parks News* 20:10-14.

Kehm, W. 1987. A Banff Perspective: Visions for 21st Century. In R.C. Scace and J.G. Nelson (Eds.), *Heritage for Tomorrow, Canadian Assembly on National Parks and Protected Areas,* Vol. 5. Ottawa: Environment Canada 23-30.

Mitchell, B. 1979. *Geography and Resource Analysis.* London: Longman.

Murray, D. 1987. *A Product Development Plan for the Northwest Territories Tourism Industry 1987.* Regina: DMCA Consultants.

Murray, D. 1988. *A Needs Assessment of Human Resources and Training Requirements for the Northwest Territories Tourism Industry.* Regina: DMCA Consultants.

Myers, N. 1987. Kuna Indians Building a Bright Future. *Equinox* 8:19-21.

Navarro, J.C. and R. Fletcher. 1988. Preserving Panama's Parks. *The Nature Conservancy Magazine* 38:20-25.

Nelson, J.G. 1987. National Parks and Protected Areas, National Conservation Strategies and Sustainable Development. *Geoforum* 18:291-319.

Outcrop Ltd. 1988. NWT Data Book 1987-88. Yellowknife: The Northern Publishers.

Packard, J.R. 1982. Bali Parks Congress Asks for a World Wide Action Plan. *Parks* 7:1-4.

Parks Canada. 1982. *Parks Canada Policy.* Ottawa: Minister of Supply and Services Canada.

Parks Congress, 3rd World. 1982. *Bali Declaration.* Bali, Indonesia.

Roberts, J.D.M. and B.D.G. Johnson. 1985. Adventure Tourism and Sustainable Development: Experience of the Tiger Mountain Group's Operations in Nepal. Paper presented to an International Workshop in the Management of National Parks and Protected Areas in the Hindu Kush Himalya, May 6-11, 1985, Kathmandu, Nepal.

Rueggeberg, H. 1988. *Involvement of Aboriginal People in National Park Management in Other Countries.* Ottawa: Environment Canada.

Sessa, A. 1983. *Elements of Tourism Economies.* Rome, Italy: Catal.

Stephenson, M. 1985. Galapagos - the Struggle for Survival Continues. *Park News* 20:3-9.

Summary, R.M. 1987. Tourism's Contribution to the Economy of Kenya. *Annals of Tourism Research* 14:531-541.

Talbot, L.M. 1982. Director General of IUCN, Closing Remarks to the Third World National Parks Congress, Bali, Indonesia.

Tourism Canada. 1986a. *Canadian Tourism Attitude and Motivation Study: Detailed Tabulations, Volume I.* Ottawa: Department of Regional Industrial Expansion.

Tourism Canada. 1986b. *Canadian Tourism Attitude and Motivation Study: Detailed Tabulations, Volume II.* Ottawa: Department of Regional Industrial Expansion.

Tourism Canada. 1986c. *U.S. Pleasure Travel Market. Canadian Potential: Main Report.* Ottawa: Department of Regional Industrial Expansion.

Tourism Research Group. 1988. *Adventure Travel in Western Canada.* Ottawa: Tourism Canada.

Vibe, C. 1984. The National Park in Northern Greenland. *Greenland Newsletter.* Greenland: The Commission for Scientific Research in Greenland.

Ward, N.E. and B. Killham. 1987. *Heritage Conservation the Natural Environment.* Ottawa: Environment Canada.

Weeks, N.C. 1986. National Parks and Native Peoples: A Study of the Experience of Selected Other Jurisdictions, with a View to Cooperation in Northern Canada. Beach, ed. In *Contributions to Circumpolar Studies.* Uppsala Research Reports in Cultural Anthropology. 7:84-150.

World Commission on Environment and Development. 1987. *Our Common Future.* Oxford: Oxford University Press.

V

NATURAL RESOURCE RECREATION VALUES

CHAPTER 15

INFORMATION EFFECTS AND BIASES
IN THE TRAVEL COST METHOD

Daniel J. Stynes
Michigan State University

George L. Peterson
USDA Forest Service
Rocky Mountain Forest & Range Experiment Station

Research into recreation valuation procedures has addressed a number of determinants of value in recreation experiences and a host of associated technical problems and biases. An issue that has not been fully recognized or systematically addressed is that of consumer information. Most researchers have assumed that consumers have perfect information about recreation opportunities or have lumped information with travel and other costs incurred in the recreation consumption process.

The development of contingent valuation methods (CVM) has helped direct some attention to the informational properties of recreation markets. Informational aspects of these markets, whether simulated or actual, must be understood in order to predict market behavior and to properly estimate demand. From recent reviews of CVM methods, information has emerged as both a determinant of value and a potential source of bias in valuation procedures (Cummings, Brookshire and Schulze 1984, Mitchell and Carson 1986). In this note we present parallel arguments for the travel cost method. Here too, consumer information is an important, albeit neglected, determinant of value. Information can also represent an important bias in travel cost procedures, if not properly accounted for. Before turning to the travel cost method, we briefly review the treatment of information in CVM studies.

INFORMATION IN CVM STUDIES

Cummings *et al.* (1984) present *information bias* as a major category of problems in CVM studies. Their conception of *information bias* is, however, not well defined, encompassing biases related to starting points, payment vehicles, question sequencing, and the information provided to the respondent. Cummings *et al.* (1984) conclude their review of CVM methods by deriving reference operating conditions (ROC's) for CVM studies based on analysis of the informational properties and services of markets. These ROC's include the need for subjects to understand the commodity to be valued and to have experience in making choices relative to this commodity. Iterative bidding games are recommended because they provide simulated experience with the relevant commodity and market setting, helping subjects to obtain and process relevant information.

Bergstrom and Stoll (1985) more fully capture informational properties of markets through a general model of market decisions based on cognitive processes. They suggest that within the CVM framework, information is more properly viewed as an input to a decision process rather than a *bias* to necessarily be eliminated.

Mitchell and Carson (1989) present a comprehensive typology of response effect biases in CVM studies which helps to more clearly distinguish between information effects and information biases. This distinction is an important one. Choices in CVM studies, like choices in general, will vary with the amount and type of information provided. How attitudes, behaviors, and values respond to variations in information are important research questions to be studied, not *biases* to be eliminated.

A bias may exist in a CVM study, if the market being simulated or the response to an artificial market differs from what would occur in an actual market. In many cases CVM studies are undertaken because no actual market exists. In these cases it is important to understand the market characteristics (including informational characteristics) that are appropriate to the intended application and to capture these properly in the CVM design.

These reviews of CVM methods and the CVM studies on which they are based have begun to draw attention to the informational properties of recreation and amenity markets. Research to date, however, has tended to look at information as a bias stemming from technical issues in questionnaire design rather than a substantive determinant of behavior and attitude. This orientation has shed little light on the informational properties of recreation markets. Our limited understanding of consumer awareness and knowledge of recreation opportunities constrains CVM researchers in correctly simulating recreation markets.

INFORMATION IN TRAVEL COST STUDIES

The travel cost method uses observations from an actual market to estimate a demand curve for a recreation site. References to consumer information in the travel cost literature are scarce. In discussing the treatment of opportunity costs of time, McConnell (1975, p. 332) has noted that a distance variable in the travel cost model may *allow for the filtering effect of distance on information about a site*. Here we will show that it may also introduce a substantial bias.

Talhelm (1973) cites imperfect information as one of three reasons why someone might pass up one recreation site to visit a more distant one. However, like most researchers, he chooses to assume perfect information in order to infer measures of quality or preference for sites from observed travel patterns. The decay of information with increasing distance from a site could also be advanced in support of Smith and Kopp's (1980) suggested spatial limits to the travel cost model.

As in the CVM setting, information is both an important component of the market (a determinant of demand) and a potential source of bias, if not properly taken into account in the estimation procedures. Our purpose in this note is to point out how information may enter as a bias in travel cost procedures, and to urge recreation economists to expand efforts in the economics of information, including the topic of information as a determinant of demand and value.

A SIMPLE TRAVEL COST EXAMPLE: THE AGGREGATE ZONAL MODEL

The simple zonal model serves to illustrate how the failure to properly specify information can introduce a bias in the travel cost procedure. Individual, hedonic and any other variations of the travel cost approach which use spatial variations in travel cost to trace out a demand curve will be prone to similar biases if variations in consumer awareness of recreation areas are not accounted for.

Assume a single unique site (no substitutes) with a surrounding population of 1,000 people distributed uniformly into 10 zones at travel costs of from \$1 to \$10. Further assume the population may be divided into two groups, those aware of the park and those unaware of the park. Assume that awareness of the site decays with travel cost (distance to the park), say the percentage of the population at travel cost p that is aware of the site is given by $a(p) = 100-10p = 10(10-p)$. The population distributions are shown in columns 3 and 4 of Table 1. Assume a known linear per capita demand function $q(p)=10-p$, for the aware population. Those unaware of the park are assumed to have zero demand. Visits from each zone under these assumptions can be generated by applying the hypothesized per capita demand function to the aware population. The results of these calculations are shown in column 5. Total visits that would be observed are 2,850.

Table 1.   Travel Cost Model Example

Zone	Travel Cost(p)	Total Popln	Aware Popln	Visits	q1(p)	q(p)	Q3(0)
1	$1	100	90	810	8.1	9.0	900
2	$2	100	80	640	6.4	8.0	800
3	$3	100	70	490	4.9	7.0	700
4	$4	100	60	360	3.6	6.0	600
5	$5	100	50	250	2.5	5.0	500
6	$6	100	40	160	1.6	4.0	400
7	$7	100	30	90	0.9	3.0	300
8	$8	100	20	40	0.4	2.0	200
9	$9	100	10	10	0.1	1.0	100
10	$10	100	0	0	0.0	0.0	0
TOTAL		1,000	450	2850			4500

NOTES: $q1(p)$ = per capita demand function for full population
= Visits/Total Popln = $(10-p)^2/10$
$q(p)$ = per capita demand function for aware population
= Visits/ Aware Popln = $10-p$
$Q3(0)$ = predicted visits from each zone under full information
= $q(p)^*$ Total Popln

Now assume the role of an economist who is given the data on travel costs (column 2) and visits (column 5). The economist would assemble the population data in column 3 and apply the travel cost method to estimate a demand curve for the site. The per capita demand function using the full population is $q1(p)=q(p)^*a(p)/100 =(10-p)^2/10$. Cranking through the travel cost procedure yields a site demand function Q1 (see Figure 1) and a consumer surplus of $6,825. These are both incorrect because the analyst has mistakenly assumed perfect information.

The correct site demand function is labeled Q2 in Figure 1. This is generated by using the assumed per capita demand function $q(p)= 10-p$ and the aware population in the travel cost procedure. The consumer surplus from this procedure is $10,125. The failure of the assumption of perfect information biases the demand curve downward from Q2 to Q1 and biases consumer surplus downward from $10,125 to $6,825.

In most cases, it is reasonable to assume that awareness of a park will decline with distance from the site. If awareness is not included as a variable in the per capita demand function, part of the decay in per capita visits across zones will be incorrectly attributed to travel costs rather than the lack of homogeneity in awareness across zones. The latter is a violation of the travel cost model assumptions which require that all variables influencing demand be properly specified in the per capita demand function (Rosenthal *et al.* 1984).

The extent of the bias is a function of the degree of correlation between travel cost and awareness. This is another example of an omitted variable problem, with the nature of the bias paralleling points made by Cesario and Knetsch (1970) in regard to time costs, Caulkins, Bishop and Bouwes (1985) in regard to substitute prices and Bockstael and Strand (1987) more generally.

We can carry this example one step further to generate the number of visits, demand, and consumer surplus that would be expected if all consumers were aware of the site. If we assume that people presently unaware of the site will behave like the aware subgroup after being informed, we apply the per capita demand function q(p) to the full population. This procedure generates 4,500 visits at the present fee (column 8 of Table 1), a demand curve given by Q3 in Figure 1, and a consumer surplus of \$14,250. This assumes no congestion costs at the site. If instead we assume the unaware population would not visit the site even if informed, Q1 is the correct demand curve. Figure 1 and Table 2 summarize the results under the three different assumptions about information.

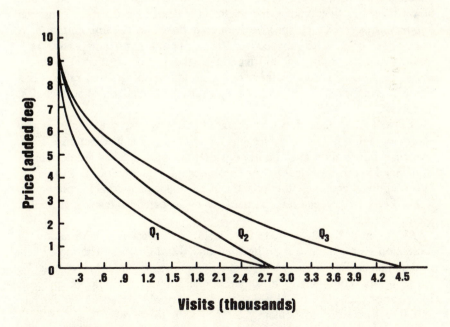

Figure 1.   Demand Curves Under Alternative Assumptions About Consumer Information

Table 2.   Estimates of Visits and Consumer Surplus under Different
                Informational Assumptions.

Assumption	Visits	Surplus	CS/Visit
Assume Perfect Information			
Demand curve = Q1	2,850	$6,825	$2.39
Known Imperfect Information			
Demand Curve = Q2	2,850	$10,125	$3.55
Full Information			
Demand curve = Q3	4,500	$14,250	$3.17

NOTE: Travel cost data in Table 1; Demand curves in Figure 1.

DISCUSSION AND RESEARCH SUGGESTIONS

The example illustrates how consumer information may introduce a bias into estimates of demand and value. In order to estimate the size and nature of the bias in empirical studies and to correct for it, we need a clearer understanding of what consumers know about recreation opportunities and how changes in their knowledge might alter demand and value. Thus, the *information as a bias* perspective is directly linked to the *information as a determinant of demand* perspective. We prefer the latter perspective as it elevates the economics of information to the higher position it deserves within recreation, i.e. as an important determinant of demand rather than simply a pesky problem we can usually ignore or handle via some technical correction.

Considerable research will be required before we can confidently specify consumer information variables in recreation demand functions. First, consumer information must be more widely acknowledged as a determinant of demand worth investigating. As consumer information does not fit neatly into traditional economic theory and can introduce considerable complexity, it has been largely ignored, particularly by researchers favoring revealed preference methods.

While not directly stated, the neglect of consumer information in recreation seems to have been justified on several grounds. The most likely explanation is that information about a site is simply another cost to be borne by the consumer as an inherent part of the consumption process. Information costs, like travel and time costs, vary with distance from the site and therefore were conveniently lumped with these other costs, without recognizing the problems this poses for travel cost analysis. The problem with time costs was recognized early (Cesario and Knetsch 1966) and has received considerable attention over the past decade. We expect that information costs will likewise receive more attention in the future. Information technologies are changing rapidly and their impacts on market structure and behavior are already substantial (e.g. computer stock trading). Further, many of the characteristics of recreation which make it somewhat unique even within the field of resource economics, tend to increase the importance of information as a determinant of behavior. Among these characteristics are the spatial nature of recreation markets, the role of the consumer in producing recreation experiences, and the intangible and service nature of recreation *products*.

Recreation has much in common with health, education, and other areas of activity for which public information programs and information subsidies have been more fully addressed (Gandy 1982). Lack of information about recreation opportunities and inequities in the distribution of this information have been identified in recreation (Godbey 1985, Stynes 1986) and relevant public information programs and/or possible information subsidies have long been part of the recreation policy agenda. For example, *developing an effective communications system to inform recreation users of recreation services* was one of six principal recommendations of the National Academy of Sciences (1969) almost two decades ago. Similar policy and research recommendations have continued to appear, but have not yet captured the attention of economists. An increasing emphasis on marketing in recreation also argues for a better understanding of the role of information in consumer recreation choice. From the marketing perspective, information is one of the needs that providers must meet in order to satisfy the consumer. Information is also a potentially powerful demand shifter in the form of advertising and promotion.

Even if information is lumped with other costs inherent in the consumption process, this doesn't explain why travel and time costs have received so much attention in recreation, while information costs have been largely ignored. Recreation and resource economists are largely following a tradition of neglect of the information topic within economics. Stigler (1961, p. 213) has colorfully characterized information as occupying *a slum dwelling in the town of economics*. Since 1960 more attention has been devoted to the topic, albeit in highly selected areas. In a survey of the topic, Hirschliefer and Riley (1979) divide the information area into two parts: (1) the economics of uncertainty and (2) the economics of information. The first subarea takes uncertainty as given and studies how individuals behave under uncertain conditions, while the latter covers behaviors to reduce or overcome uncertainty. Most applications in resource and recreation economics seem to fall in the area of decisionmaking under uncertainty, e.g., existence, bequest, and option value and studies of risk. The economics of information would appear to also be a fruitful field for recreation economists.

There is a plethora of relevant information-related theories from psychology, consumer behavior, marketing, geography, economics, communications, advertising, and other fields of study, but few of these have been adapted to recreation or tied to traditional recreation demand models. Consumer decision processes are inherently cognitive ones. Better understanding of consumer information search, perception, and information processing should therefore be helpful in formulating improved demand models. Improved measures of consumer knowledge and guidance on how to specify consumer knowledge within recreation demand models are also essential.

In the simple example above, we have treated consumer information as a dichotomous variable and proposed distinct demand functions for the aware and unaware groups. This simple approach seems like a good place to start. Logical extensions include developing higher levels of measurement for the information variables and directly incorporating these within the per capita demand specification. Spotts and Stynes (1985) discuss the complexities of conceptualizing and measuring consumers' familiarity with parks. Demand models that might include higher levels of measurement for information variables pose significant measurement, specification, and estimation problems.

Further complexities are introduced by substitute sites. Demand for any single site is clearly a function of what alternatives the consumer is aware of and what information he or she has about each of these alternatives. Handling of substitutes in recreation demand analysis is a nagging problem with few simple and satisfactory solutions. A clearer focus on consumer awareness and information about recreation opportunities suggests tackling the substitute issue from the consumer's perspective. Discrete choice models appear to have an advantage here, but more attention must be given to the choice sets from which consumers select.

Another way to include cognitive components in travel cost models is to replace physical measures of distance and site attributes with perceptual measures. Most commonly this is done when modeling individual behavior, but it has also been applied in aggregate models (Cadwallader 1981). Since there are clear feedback effects between park information and park visits, development of simultaneous equations and systems models should also shed light on relationships between demand and consumer information over time.

CONCLUSION

Our simple example illustrates two important points. First, failure to take into account consumers' lack of awareness of recreation sites may result in biased estimates of demand and value using the travel cost procedure. If consumer awareness is omitted from the per capita demand function specification, a bias will exist when awareness of the site varies systematically with distance from the site (or more specifically travel cost). For most sites, we expect awareness of a site to decrease with distance. In these cases, travel cost model estimates of demand and consumer surplus will be biased downward. Secondly, given assumptions or data pertaining to spatial patterns of park awareness, estimates of demand and value can be generated for conditions of either perfect or imperfect consumer information. The resulting estimates of demand and value can be used to assess the likely impacts and benefits of changes in consumer information. These kinds of applications open up a major new field for recreation economists.

More explicit consideration of consumer information in recreation demand analysis therefore offers potential to both improve estimates of demand and value under existing conditions and to make use of recreation economic analysis in weighing the benefits and costs of consumer information programs. As both the public and private sectors expand marketing and information programs, travel cost methods and related techniques should once again prove to be quite useful tools. We will, however, need to devote greater attention to how consumer information is handled within our traditional recreation economics toolkit.

REFERENCES

Bergstrom, J.C. and J.R. Stoll. 1985. *Cognitive Decision Processes, Information, and Contingent Valuation.* Natural Resources Working Paper Series, Department of Agricultural Economics, Texas A&M University.

Bockstael, N.E. and I.E. Strand, Jr. 1987. The effect of common sources of regression error on benefit estimates. *Land Economics* 63:9-20.

Cadwallader, M. 1981. Towards a cognitive gravity model: The case of consumer spatial behaviour. *Regional Studies* 15:275-284.

Caulkins, P.P., R.C. Bishop, and N.W. Bouwes. 1985. Omitted cross-price variable biases in the linear travel cost model: Correcting some common misperceptions. *Land Economics* 61:182-194.

Cesario, F.J. and J. Knetsch. 1970. Time bias in recreation benefit models. *Water Resources Research* 6:700-704.

Cummings, R.G, D.S. Brookshire, and W.D. Schulze (Eds). 1986. *Valuing Environmental Goods: A State of the Arts Assessment of the Contingent Valuation Method.* Totowa, NJ: Rowman and Allanheld.

Gandy, O.H. 1982. *Beyond Agenda Setting: Information Subsidies and Public Policy.* Norwood, NJ: Ablex Publishing.

Godbey, G. 1985. A model of nonuse of public leisure services. *Proceedings 1985 National Outdoor Recreation Trends Symposium* Vol II, pp. 90-102. Atlanta, GA: USDI, National Park Service, Southeastern Regional Office.

Hirschleifer, J. and J.G. Riley. 1979. The analytics of uncertainty and information: An expository survey. *Journal of Economic Literature* 17:1375-1421.

McConnell, K.E. 1976. Some problems in estimating the demand for outdoor recreation. *American Journal of Agricultural Economics* 57:330-334.

Mitchell, A.A. (Ed). 1978. *The Effect of Information on Consumer and Market Behavior.* Chicago: American Marketing Association.

Mitchell, R. Cameron and R.T. Carson. 1989. *Using Surveys to Value Public Goods: The Contingent Valuation Method.* Washington D.C.: Resources for the Future.

National Academy of Sciences. 1969. *A Program for Outdoor Recreation Research.* Washington D.C.

Rosenthal, D.H., J.B. Loomis and G.L. Peterson. 1984. *The Travel Cost Model: Concepts and Applications.* Fort Collins, Co: Rocky Mountain Forest & Range Experiment Station General Technical Report RM-109.

Smith, V. K. and R.J. Kopp. 1980. The spatial limits of the travel cost model. *Land Economics* 56:64-72.

Stigler, G.J. 1961. The economics of information. *Journal of Political Economy* 69:213-225.

Spotts, D.M. and D.J. Stynes. 1985. Measuring the public's familiarity with recreation areas. *Journal of Leisure Research* 17:253-265.

Stynes, D.J., D.M. Spotts, and J.R. Strunk. 1985. Relaxing assumptions of perfect information in park visitation models. *Professional Geographer* 37:21-28.

Talhelm, D.R. 1973. *Defining and Evaluating Recreation Quality.* Trans. 38th North American Wildlife & Natural Resource Conference 38:183-191.

CHAPTER 16

NET ECONOMIC VALUE OF HUNTING AND FISHING IN IDAHO

Dennis M. Donnelly
USDA Forest Service
Rocky Mountain Forest and Range Experiment Station

Cindy Sorg-Swanson
USDA Forest Service
Northern Region (R-1)

John B. Loomis
Division of Environmental Studies
University of California-Davis

Louis J. Nelson
Idaho Department of Fish and Game

In the United States and many other countries, recreation is seen as an activity that renews one's spirit, promotes and maintains good health, and promotes understanding of and fellowship with others. Perhaps most importantly, people recreate because they enjoy it. Hunting and fishing as recreation also allows people to experience wild areas and test their outdoor skills. However, hunting and fishing, and recreation in general takes place in a broader framework of overall wildland resource management. Thus, wildlife managers, livestock interests, people interested in the overall environment, wood products companies, and many others make legitimate claims on the wildland ecosystems so necessary to satisfactory recreation, including hunting and fishing.

In order to facilitate the valuation of hunting and fishing as recreation, this chapter reports results of a large study that provides estimates of economic value for fishing and hunting in Idaho. These are estimates of on-site consumptive value and as such do not reflect option value, on-site nonconsumptive value, existence value, or bequest value (Peterson and Sorg 1987). This frame of reference is based on the premise that economic values are important in our society for decisionmaking, even though they are not the only consideration. They are but one component of a group of important items to consider whenever renewable natural resource decisions are made. Thus, the reported results indicate people's willingness to pay for certain hunting and fishing experiences, but the results do not reflect the total intrinsic worth of hunting and fishing in general, of each species, or of particular members of each species.

The first part of the chapter provides concepts about economics and value useful for considering study results. Then, after describing the study approach and methods, we present results based on the travel cost and contingent valuation methods. Finally, we discuss the relationship between values for the individual species considered in the study and indicate how methods and results like these could be useful for management.

VALUATION PRIMER

To provide the reader with a complete package of information, this section briefly summarizes the concepts and principles underlying valuation research described in this chapter. We include material from several sources which would provide additional reading beyond this introduction.

Consumptive values reported here are part of a broader value context (Loomis, Peterson, and Sorg 1984). One way to characterize economic value is to subdivide it into two major categories, expenditure value (economic impact) and efficiency value (willingness to pay, WTP). Expenditure value is determined in part by how much an activity contributes to the national, state, or local economy in the form of cash transactions. Some feel that economic impact value is the only category of economic value relevant in economic analyses of wildlife benefits. However, analyses of renewable natural resource management must also include measures of economic efficiency. Efficiency value is the net economic contribution to society (i.e., to national economic development) of supplying a resource or recreation opportunity.

To further contrast expenditure value (impact) and efficiency value (WTP), consider Figure 1. On an individual basis each of us has some maximum total willingness to pay for a trip to hunt or fish. We form this maximum by considering for example, factors such as total and disposable income, potential satisfaction obtainable not only from the proposed trip but also from alternative activities, and time since our last hunting or fishing trip. This maximum or total willingness to pay may be considered as having two components, what we actually spend (expenditures in a private sector economy), and willingness to pay over and above what we actually pay, i.e., the amount in excess of actual expenditures (labeled Total Consumer Surplus in Figure 1) up to the total willingness to pay . When we do not have to spend the total amount we are willing to pay, the difference is considered to be a net economic benefit accruing to the individual. The sum of such net benefits for all people participating in hunting or fishing is an estimate of aggregate net economic benefits associated with hunting or fishing.

Since net willingness to pay is the amount over and above what we actually spend on a hunting or fishing trip, and is the correct economic value to help answer economic efficiency questions, what then is the nature of and proper use for economic impact or expenditure data? An individual on a fishing or hunting trip spends money for transport, lodging, and gear and supplies. This money is spent at home, en route, and near the hunting or fishing site. The economy of these respective locations gains because money is spent. However, no new wealth is added to the national economy. Money that would have been spent at home is instead spent elsewhere. This money circulates in the economy where it was spent and makes merchants and local sales tax collectors happy. But national net economic development is not increased by these money transactions.

To sum up, every individual has some absolute maximum or total willingness to pay for a good or service based on income constraints,

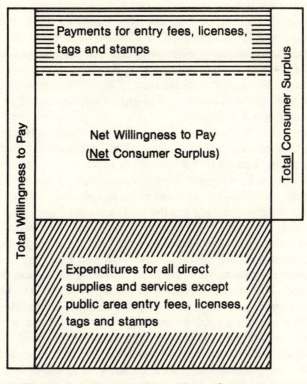

Figure 1. Willingness to Pay and Expenditure Concepts

perceived utility, and alternative needs. Actual expenditure for the good or service makes an *impact* in a local, state, and national economy. Any part of the total willingness to pay not expended, becomes part of net potential willingness to pay and is individually a net benefit. For all individuals involved the sum of net WTP is an aggregate net economic benefit.

One point that may need clarification is how to treat fees charged for recreation. If a private recreation supplier charges fees, for example a rancher charges for hunting access on private property, the fee becomes part of the consumer expenditures impacting the local economy. If, on the other hand, the charge is an entry fee or a license fee for access to publicly provided recreation, the fee is considered part of total consumer surplus, i.e., part of the net willingness to pay in excess of all the consumer's private sector expenses (see Figure 1). This accounting stance results because the fee is simply a cash form of the contribution to public net economic benefits. In effect, the public agency providing recreation has captured part of the individual's WTP and transformed a potential economic benefit to society into a tangible economic benefit to society.

Analysts estimate the magnitude of net economic benefits, which economists call consumer surplus, using two generally accepted methods, the Contingent Value Method (CVM) and the Travel Cost Method (TCM) (References for *both CVM and TCM*: U.S. Water Resources Council 1979, 1983; Desvouges, Smith, and McGiveney 1983; *CVM*: Randall, Ives, and Eastman 1974, Bishop and Heberlein 1979, Brookshire, Randall, and Stoll 1980, Cummings, Brookshire, and Schulze 1986, Mitchell and Carson 1989; *TCM*: Dwyer, Kelly and Bowes 1977, Rosenthal, Loomis, and Peterson 1984, Sorg and Loomis 1985).

The theoretical basis for the TCM is the association between different goods (factors of production) that are used to produce a product. In this instance, the site and travel to the site are two factors generally required to produce recreational hunting and fishing. Accordingly, TCM is based on the premise that an individual's travel cost from an origin to a destination is a proxy for price when estimating the demand curve for hunting or fishing at a particular site, since the site does not have a market price. As travel distances and concomitant costs increase from origins farther away, trips per capita decrease. At some distance, travel cost becomes high enough that visitation essentially ceases from origins at that distance. Analysts use this maximum distance to define the outer boundary of a market area for the given site. Anyone traveling this maximum distance is considered to be expending their maximum total willingness to pay to visit the site. People living beyond the market area consider the price of the good too high to pay, i.e., they do not pay the cost necessary to travel from their homes to a specific site for hunting and fishing. People who travel less than the maximum distance are assumed to be willing to pay the same maximum price as those traveling from the market area periphery even though they are not required to do so. The difference between the total maximum willingness to pay and what is actually paid is the previously mentioned consumer surplus, i.e., net WTP or net economic benefit.

Contingent valuation methods (CVM), also known as bidding game methods, are based on quantifying an individual's preferences for a well defined, often nonmarketed product. In applying the method, CVM relies on mail, personal, or telephone interviews. There are several approaches to eliciting values with CVM. In one typical format, a person responds yes or no to bidding questions specifying a hypothetical payment that increases successively with each round of bidding. In this format, the last positive response in each case determines the maximum WTP for the resource, or the change in the resource being evaluated. Useful results depend on asking well-posed valuation questions of individuals properly sampled from the population of interest.

In summary, TCM makes inferences about value based on actual behavior, i.e., travel from home to an outdoor hunting or fishing site. CVM measures directly what people say they would do contingent upon assumed conditions in a typical hunting/fishing recreation market. CVM techniques may be used in any situation where TCM is applied, plus other valuation situations where TCM is inappropriate. However, CVM's flexibility comes with the price that it may be relatively more cumbersome than TCM in its survey design and data gathering phases. Both methods have their strong and weak points (Sorg and Loomis 1985).

OBJECTIVES AND METHODS

The primary objective of this study was to estimate economic values for specific forms of hunting and fishing in Idaho. In addition, the study was to serve as a prototype whose methodology could be used by other states. (It should be noted that recently the state of Montana completed a study similar to this one reported for Idaho).

Both the travel cost method (TCM) and contingent value method (CVM) were employed in this study. CVM would serve as a related, but different source of values. Values from these two sources would be compared.

Both TCM and CVM estimate a dollar equivalent value for a unit of nonmarketed good or service. Defining the good is part of the process of asking appropriate and relevant questions for the problem at hand. In this study, the relevant question is what is the monetary value of an individual's trip to hunt or fish at a specified site in Idaho. In addition, what is the average per-unit value of this good over the entire set of sites for particular kinds of hunting and fishing. Thus, the product being valued in this study is a trip to a specified site for hunting and fishing.

Most species hunted or fished in Idaho were included in the study. Species considered by themselves were American elk, (Sorg and Nelson 1985), steelhead (Donnelly, Loomis, Sorg, and Nelson 1985), and Idaho's unique species--bighorn sheep, mountain goat, moose, and pronghorn (Loomis and Nelson 1985). Mule deer and white-tailed deer were grouped together (Donnelly and Nelson 1986). Other game species were grouped together more broadly. Waterfowl included 27 species of ducks and geese (Sorg and Nelson 1987). Upland game included cottontail rabbits, pheasant, quail, grouse, wild turkey, and dove (Young, Donnelly, Sorg, Loomis, and Nelson 1987). Cold and warm water fishing included trout, landlocked salmon, sturgeon, various panfish, and bass (Sorg, Loomis, Donnelly, Peterson, and Nelson 1985).

A one percent sample for the study survey was drawn from all persons holding 1982 Idaho hunting and fishing licenses in each of the species categories. This survey, conducted in late 1982 and early 1983, provided TCM data for all species and CVM data for all species except deer and elk. A later survey for deer and elk CVM data was taken for persons holding these licenses in 1983. The survey for each species group was designed to determine among other items, respondent's trip origin; how many trips were taken; which hunting and fishing areas were visited; distances traveled; expenses incurred by category; and the bidding responses for CVM.

Each person in the sample received a letter describing the survey effort and requesting that the respondent fill out an attached form. Each of the study reports cited above contains a copy of the survey form for that particular species. Subsequently, canvassers from the University of Idaho and the Idaho Department of Fish and Game called each respondent and recorded the necessary information. As a result of the combination of mail and telephone contact, the return rate was high, almost 100 percent for each species category. Response numbers ranged from several hundred to several thousand depending on the group.

Analysis for TCM

Once the survey for each species was completed, the typical progression was to perform quality control on the data, do preliminary statistical tests, aggregate the data, run regression analysis to obtain estimated demand curves, and use the demand curves as a basis for estimation of net benefits (WTP) per trip. Iterations of these steps were often necessary.

After raw data were edited and validated, the data were aggregated by hunt/fish site and origin of the traveler. For example, a typical aggregated record would include average values for all data that applied to deer hunters who traveled from Ada County (Boise) to Game Management Unit 1 (all of Boundary County and much of Bonner County in the northern Idaho Panhandle).

These aggregated records for combinations of origin counties and destination Game Management Units contain a variety of information in addition to that collected in the survey. Data of particular interest included distances traveled, substitute relationships, quality variables, county per capita income, and expenditure information.

The two factors that are most obviously associated with demand for a good or service are its price and the ability to pay for it. In this study distance traveled was transformed to price paid to hunt or fish. Distance traveled in each origin-site aggregated record is the average of all the respective responses to a question about round-trip distance traveled from home to the site and return. The proxy quantity for individual income was county per-capita income, since each origin location is a county, and since income questions were not asked of individuals.

Quality of a hunting or fishing area was defined as the potential for harvesting an animal. The potential was measured by an individual sighting or harvesting an animal, or by area success rates the previous year.

Two substitute indices were tried. Both are based on quality and distance (Knetsch *et al.* 1976). The first substitute index is the maximum ratio approach and is the ratio of the substitute area's quality measure to the distance traveled to obtain the potential quality. Since distance traveled is a proxy for price, the ratio in effect measured potential success per dollar spent to obtain hunting or fishing at an alternate site. The best substitute site for the particular area under analysis, and from a specific origin, was the alternate area visited from the same origin that had the greatest ratio of quality per cost. The other substitute index is the sum of ratios approach. Instead of selecting just one best alternate site, the quality/cost ratios were summed for all sites that were visited from an origin and whose ratio exceeded that of the site being analyzed. It was thought that the greater this sum of ratios, the more opportunities would be available in substitute sites.

The model used that incorporates all these relevant variables is called a regional or multi-site model rather than a single site model (Cesario and Knetsch 1976, Knetsch *et al.* 1976). Use of this form of TCM fits the pattern of multiple hunting and fishing areas. A regional model allows the use of the entire data set in the estimation of demand curves. This reduces small sample problems associated with estimating a regression separately for each hunting or fishing site. In the model each site is represented by its level of the quality variable. The substitute relationship, if it exists, between sites is also included. Two functional forms that describe the regional model have been useful in previous work and were candidates in this study to describe the so-called trip (Stage 1) demand curve of TCM analysis, i.e., trips per capita as a function of cost (i.e., price) of traveling to the hunting/fishing site (Dwyer *et al.* 1977:89-91).

Linear Model:

$$TPC = b_o + b_1*(RTDIST) + b_2*(QUAL) + b_3*(INC) + b_4* (SUBS)$$

Exponential (Semi-log-dependent Variable) Model:

$$\ln(TPC) = b_o + b_1*(RTDIST) + b_2*(QUAL) + b_3*(INC) + b_4*(SUBS)$$

where:

TPC = trips per capita, i.e., trips from a given origin to a particular hunting/fishing area, divided by the population of the origin county or counties

RTDIST = roundtrip distance from a particular origin to a particular hunting/fishing area (see Table 1)

QUAL = the quality index of the hunting/fishing area (see Table 1)

INC = per-capita income of the county or counties

SUBS = one of two possible substitute indices.

Regression analysis provided statistical information on which to judge the suitability of these functional forms and their variants to estimate the trip demand curve. These equations became input to a computer program that synthesized an aggregate trip demand curve (Stage 2) for a hunting/fishing area (Dwyer *et al.* 1977:91-94). This computer program further estimated visits, consumer surplus and consumer surplus per trip for each site and for all sites combined. The best functional form for the demand curve was chosen based on the coefficient of multiple determination (R^2), the relevant F-statistic, and on the t-statistics for individual independent variables as well as how accurately the regression predicted visits in the Stage 2 analysis.

Finally, for each species (group) the net benefits on the basis of a trip, a calendar day, and a Wildlife/Fish User Day (WFUD) were computed. A WFUD is the same concept as a Recreation Visitor Day (RVD), i.e., 12 hours of use by one person or one hour of use by 12 persons, or some similar combination of time and people. Further details are in the individual reports cited earlier.

TCM and Unique Species

Unlike all the other species sought by hunters and anglers, Idaho's unique species (mountain goat, bighorn sheep, moose, and antelope) are hunted by individuals who have obtained a permit in a drawing. Anyone desiring a chance of obtaining a unique species permit could enter the drawing, but permits issued are much fewer than the number of applicants. Consequently, demand is not measured only by winners of the drawing who take trips; rather, demand is measured by the number of applicants for the permit drawing (Loomis 1982).

For the unique species, net WTP is estimated by methods similar to those applied to the other species. However, for total WTP, expenditures were approximated for each unique species because willingness to pay for hunting unique species in Idaho was based on permit data rather than actual trips. These approximations were based on the perceived resemblance between hunting unique species and the type of big game hunting for which expenditures were available. For example, antelope hunting is similar to deer hunting in terms of equipment, access, and location. Expenditures for elk hunting were applied to the other three unique species.

Analysis for CVM

The most complex part of applying the CVM in a survey is the order and wording of the bidding questions. A great deal of work was required to reduce or eliminate various kinds of bias that are thought to affect CVM surveys (Hanley 1988, Mitchell, and Carson 1989). The resulting text of the questions for each species is contained in the appendix of the respective detailed reports.

Generally each survey respondent was asked if s/he would pay a percentage (somewhere between zero and 50 percent) more than the current cost in order to continue hunting/fishing at the area s/he visited. The amount of cost increase was raised until the respondent said s/he would pay no more. This high value was recorded.

The average of the high bids for all respondents who visited a given site was considered the mean bid for current hunting/fishing conditions in that management area. This incremental bid is considered the WTP, on average, over and above the amount actually spent on the trip.

User Fees

As noted earlier user fees paid to public agencies are considered to be consumer surplus and are added to WTP to estimate total consumer surplus (Figure 1) (U.S. Water Resources Council 1983). However, Idaho residents pay relatively low license and tag fees for all hunting and fishing activities except the unique species. Since residents' responses made up the bulk of

Table 1. Hunter and Angler Profiles, Idaho Wildlife Study, 1982 Season

Hunting/ fishing activity	Number of days per trip	Number of hours per day	Area quality variable[a]	Number of Licensed people in party	Expenditures[b] (dollars)					Aggregate rnd. trip distance (miles)
					Travel	Lodging	Misc.[c]	Guide	Total	
Upland game[d]	1.15	3.87	6.34	2.37	11.82 (414)[e]	81.94 (17)	10.25 (417)	-	24.03	100
Pheasant	1.12	3.74	6.57	2.33	9.03 (280)	110.17 (6)	8.93 (284)	-	20.15	82
General fishing - cold	1.58	4.53	5.00	2.56	19.20 (386)	64.90 (20)	22.81 (354)	-	37.05	200
General fishing - warm	1.36	4.36	9.79	2.61	13.09 (43)	10.50 (4)	13.31 (42)	-	24.62	154
Waterfowl	1.15	4.52	8.29	2.41	30.38 (183)	39.00 (2)	7.93 (183)	-	38.75	67
Elk	2.84	7.05	4.50	2.70	37.73 (3862)	42.60 (102)	22.47 (3862)	1026.68 (57)	76.47	730

Table 1. Continued

Hunting/ fishing activity	Number of days per trip	Number of hours per day	Area quality variable[d]	Number of licensed people in party	Expenditures[b] (dollars)					Aggregate rnd. trip distance (miles)
					Travel	Lodging	Misc.[c]	Guide	Total	
Deer	1.87	6.58	8.21	2.54	19.05 (5511)	57.70 (54)	11.61 (5511)	1087.06 (16)	34.38	306
Steelhead	1.55	5.34	0.95	2.63	33.15	98.54	33.86	-	72.21	218
Unique Species:										
Bighorn Sheep	8.60									239
Moose	5.90	N/A	N/A	N/A			N/A			113
Antelope	1.90									181
Mountain goat	4.00									441

[a]The measure of area quality depended on the activity. Upland game, pheasant, waterfowl - opportunities to shoot per day; General fishing cold and warm, and steelhead - fish caught per trip; Elk, deer - number of animals seen per trip.

[b]These figures do not include outlays for licenses, tags, fees, or special stamps.

[c]Food, ammunition, incidental items.

[d]Upland game includes pheasant, but pheasant is also reported separately.

[e]Numbers in parentheses are the number of respondents who indicated they incurred expenses in the respective categories.

the data set, and since many residents took several trips, license fees considered as consumer surplus are negligible for all except unique species after being prorated over all trips taken. Consequently, this contribution to consumer surplus was ignored in TCM except for unique species. Unique species were not considered in the CVM portion of the study.

RESULTS AND DISCUSSION

To provide an idea of the nature of the hunting/fishing activities, Table 1 presents profiles for hunters and anglers in Idaho during the 1982 seasons. The number of days per trip varies widely depending on the activity. This is also true for hours per day hunting or fishing. The area quality variables are not directly comparable but do illustrate how the quality variable in each activity's demand equation depended on the nature of the activity. Average number of licensed people in the party varies little between hunting and fishing. Amount of expenditure varies and appears related to the type of hunting or fishing.

The total amount spent on hunting or fishing trips depends partially on the time spent in the field and the distance traveled to the activity. Distances traveled tend to correspond to the availability of the chosen activity. For example, because elk hunting is available in fewer locations compared to deer hunting, elk hunters on average travel longer distances. Figures for expenditures show that some activities, such as elk hunting, are more expensive in terms of the total trip, but costs are spread over many more days than other forms of hunting and fishing (Table 1).

Demand Curve Regressions for TCM

Table 2 shows the specific form of regression that estimates trips per capita relative to the origin population (Stage 1 demand curve). In all cases, distance significantly entered the demand curve regression with a negative sign. The distance variable is always a surrogate for price, so this result agrees with expectations based on economic theory. County per-capita income was positively correlated with trips per capita for general fishing and negatively associated with trips per capita for big game and waterfowl hunting. It was not associated with upland game and pheasant hunting. It appears that average per-capita county income does not clearly relate to the propensity to hunt or fish in the same way as would be expected for individual incomes of those participating in each type of hunting or fishing activity. Thus, the effect of income on participation in hunting and fishing in Idaho, at least as considered in this study, remains unresolved.

Quality for a hunting or fishing area could be measured in several ways, for example, scenic beauty, remoteness, or access to campsites. But logically, the most important aspects of quality relate to the actual or potential harvest of game or fish. The nature of the quality variable in each case (see footnote c of Table 2) reflects the different ways to account for quality in the presence of various species bag limits. For example, the number of deer or elk harvested per hunter is limited, but total harvest in a hunt unit provides information about its quality. In all cases the quality variable in each regression was statistically significant and entered the regression positively correlated with trips per capita. Therefore, as quality of each site increased, so did use of the site measured in trips per capita.

Substitution effects are statistically significant in regressions for upland game and pheasant hunting, for waterfowl hunting, and for steelhead fishing. Substitution effects are marginally significant in the regressions for both cold and warm water general fishing. Neither the elk nor the deer regression has a statistically significant variable for substitute effect. Table 2 (footnote b) tells which of two substitute indices applies to each species. The data did not allow us to rigorously test hypotheses about why particular substitute results occurred for certain species. The authors strongly suggest that future studies of this type include survey questions designed to explore respondents' reasons and motivations for choosing particular hunting/fishing experiences and settings.

Net and Total Willingness to Pay

Results related to this study's principal objective are net willingness to pay (WTP) estimates for trips to hunt or fish for each species or species group considered in the study. Table 3 shows these WTP values per trip and per WFUD for both TCM and CVM. The TCM values range from $360 per trip (not including license fee) for hunting one of the unique species, mountain goat, to about $28 per trip for steelhead fishing. The TCM estimate for elk hunting is about $100 per trip, for deer about $50 per trip. Since values for Idaho's unique species were not estimated via CVM, elk hunting had the highest CVM estimate of those reported, about $93 per trip, and the deer hunting CVM estimate was about $40 per trip.

Net willingness to pay per trip estimated with TCM, plus license fees for unique species (Table 3), was combined with the total expenditure data from Table 1 to provide an estimate of total willingness to pay per trip for the various hunting and fishing experiences. This result, shown in Figure 2, illustrates the ranking of total willingness to pay per trip for the species groups. On the basis of total WTP per trip, the various species rank in the order one might intuitively place them, based on availability of the respective activities in Idaho. In other parts of the United States, individual

Table 2.   Summary of Regressions for Per-Capita Demand Curves

Species results based on hunting/ fishing data	Dependent variable	Intercept	Distance roundtrip	Substitute index[b]	Quality[c]	County per capita income	Misc. terms	Regression statistics
Upland game hunting	1	-8.5706	-0.00529	SUB -0.1365	TSHOOT 0.2653			F = 109.2
Pheasant hunting	1	-8.9341	-0.00526	SUB -0.1676	TSHOOT 0.3057			42.8
General fishing - cold	1	-10.712	-0.00322	ln (SUB) -0.015	TFISH 0.00345 $TFISH^2$ -0.000002	INCOME 0.00134 $INCOME^2$ -0.0000002		83.0
General fishing -	1	-12.647	-0.00275	ln (SUB) -0.0259	TFISH 0.00477 $TFISH^2$ -0.000004	INCOME 0.1937 $INCOME^2$ -0.0000002		32.0
Waterfowl hunting	1	-5.29	-0.0034	SUB -0.0088	TSHOOT 0.0017	INCOME -0.00045		13.9
Elk hunting	1	-3.1102	-0.0016		TOT UNT HARV LAST YEAR 0.001049	INCOME -0.0009924		398.3

Species results based on permit applications	Dependent variable	Intercept	Distance roundtrip	Substitute index[b]	Quality[c]	County per capita income	Misc. terms	Regression statistics
Deer hunting	2	3.098[d]	-0.0024		TOT UNIT HARV LAST YEAR 0.000404	INCOME -0.0008472		232.9
Steelhead fishing	1	-7.6026	-0.00587	ln (SUB) -0.2248	TFISH 0.02174			33.4
Bighorn sheep hunting	3	-5.688	-0.00141		SUCCESS 0.01149	INCOME -0.0006	#PERMITS 0.0195	117.87
Moose hunting	3	-7.92	-0.0032		SUCCESS 0.033 $SUCCESS^2$ -0.0002		#PERMITS 0.0297	57.02
Antelope hunting	3	-6.2890	-0.00323	SUB -0.092	SUCCESS 0.01966	INCOME -0.0003759	#PERMITS 0.003285	186.2
Mountain goat	4	0.000094	-0.00001					4.74

[a] Codes for the form of the dependent variable are: 1 = log natural of trips per capita; 2 = log natural of trips per capita; 3 = log natural of trips per thousand population; 4 = applications per capita.

[b] The particular form of the substitute index is one of the two types discussed in the text for species that had this term significant in the regression: substitute index 1 – Upland/game, Steelhead; substitute index 2 – General fishing -- cold and warm, Waterfowl, and Antelope.

[c] Measures of quality are abbreviated as: TSHOOT = total opportunities per day to shoot for upland game, pheasant, and waterfowl; TFISH = total fish caught per trip at the particular site for cold water and warm water general fishing and for steelhead; SUCCESS = the proportion of hunters with hunting success in a given unit; TOT UNIT HARV LAST YEAR = the number of animals harvested the previous year, in this case 1981.

[d] The positive sign on this intercept value is due to the form of the dependent variable. For deer only, the dependent variable is measured in trips per capita rather than trips per thousand population.

species or species groups might rank differently because changes in hunting or fishing opportunities plus differences in travel patterns and actual cash outlay would certainly contribute to the likelihood of ranking differences.

The following two sections examine possible reasons why the rankings of total WTP per trip in Figure 2 occur as they do.

Unique Species

For the four unique species hunted in Idaho on a limited basis, values reported are for the permit to hunt, not for the hunting trip (Table 3). These scarce permits are awarded by random selection that includes several restrictions based on eligibility for previous hunts. In addition, Idaho residents only may apply for moose hunting. This limitation violates one of the assumptions of the Travel Cost Method because restricting demand and therefore the market area likely results in an underestimate of net willingness to pay for moose hunting (Loomis 1982). The alternative, however, was to not estimate any value for moose hunting.

The large number of permit applications for mountain goat and bighorn sheep relative to available hunting opportunities suggests that hunting these animals is a coveted experience. These animals are typically located in inaccessible mountainous terrain, so a hired guide or outfitter often assists hunters. Even after allowing for a license and fees, plus regular hunting expenses that probably are greater than for elk hunting, and likely the expense of an outfitter, hunters place additional value in the form of WTP on hunting these two species (Figure 2). However, because data were not available about expenses for hunting goats and sheep, elk hunting expenses were used to construct Figure 2.

While elk and moose do not occupy the same ecological niches, the ranges and habitats for both animals overlap somewhat (Idaho Department of Fish and Game 1980a, 1980b). Thus, moose hunting expenses may be more in line with those for elk hunting. The amount of effort, access, and equipment required is likely similar for both species. Expenses for antelope hunting are approximated by those for deer hunting.

Steelhead

Steelhead total WTP holds an interesting position relative to other fishing and hunting activities ranked adjacent to it (Figure 2). Because steelhead fishing sites are located primarily in north-central Idaho, they are scarce relative to general fishing opportunities and also located farther from major population centers. Thus, it is reasonable to assume that total willingness to pay would be found greater in Idaho for steelhead angling than for general fishing. Interestingly though, net willingness to pay for

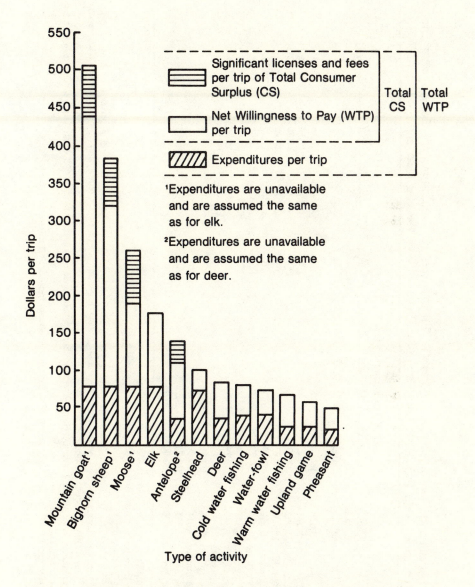

Figure 2. Total Consumptive value per trip (direct expenditures and net willingness to pay based on TCM), Idaho Wildlife Study, 1982 Seasons. Resident License for Antelope in 1982 was $31, for Moose, Bighorn Sheep, and Mountain Goat, $71.

Table 3. Estimates of Net Willingness to Pay (WTP) in Excess of Expenditures for Each Species Group. Estimates Made from 1982 Data Except for Estimates from 1983 for Deer and Elk with CVM.

Hunting/ fishing activity	TCM trips in sample[a]	WTP estimated by TCM per			CVM bids in sample	WTP estimated by CVMe		
		trip[b]	day[c]	WFUD[d]		trip	day	WFUD
Elk hunting	3,636	99.82	35.18	59.87	383	92.54	32.58	55.46
Deer hunting	5,511	50.23	26.86	48.99	579	40.09	19.18	36.08
Steelhead fishing	1,962	27.87	14.29	29.77	258	31.45	20.29	45.60
General fishing-cold	19,033	42.93	25.55	63.87	769	22.52	14.25	37.75
General fishing-warm	6,262	42.18	26.36	63.26	78	16.35	12.02	33.08
Upland game hunting[f]	3,964	34.77	28.50	81.04	420	25.82	22.45	69.62
Pheasant hunting[f]	2,331	28.84	24.44	74.63	285	24.26	21.66	69.50
Waterfowl hunting	1,843	32.79	28.51	75.69	183	16.87	12.05	32.64
Idaho unique species[g]								
Antelope hunting	8,795	73.31	38.58					
Bighorn sheep hunting	1,014	239.00	27.80					
Moose hunting	6,531	112.84	19.12					
Mountain goat hunting	820	360.00	90.00					

[a]Number of applications in the sample for unique species.

[b]A round trip from home to the activity site for hunting or fishing.

[c]Any part of a 24-hour day.

[d]Wildlife and Fish User Day is 12-person-hours afield, i.e., 1 person for 12 hours, 12 persons for 1 hour, or 4 persons for 3 hours, etc.

[e]CVM results for deer and elk are based on the 1983, not 1982, hunting season (Sorge and Nelson 1985, Donnelly and Nelson 1986). CVM values were not estimated for Idaho's "unique" species.

[f]Upland game hunting includes pheasant hunting. Because pheasant hunting data made up a large proportion of the entire upland game data set it was also considered separately.

[g]License and fees are $31.00 for antelope; $71.00 for bighorn sheep, moose, and mountain goat hunting.

steelhead fishing trips, based on the TCM or CVM, is among the lowest found in this study, especially in comparison to other types of fishing. One possible reason could be that actual expenses for steelhead fishing are higher than expenses reported for most other species. For example, jet-boats are necessary to access some steelhead areas. It is certainly possible that the large cash outlay necessary to fish for steelhead, as shown in Table 1, may consume so large a proportion of the individual's total willingness to pay, that an individual's residual or net willingness to pay is relatively small.

Bids for CVM

Reported values based on the CVM approach are generally lower than those based on the TCM approach (Figure 3). In this study, the key CVM questions about willingness to pay typically referred to the last trip. Economic theory suggests that the last (i.e., marginal) quantity obtained of any good is valued less than the first unit of the good. Although not formally tested in this study, the marginal effect could explain why CVM-based values are less in general (except for steelhead fishing; see Table 2 and Figure 3) than those from TCM, which considered all trips an individual made.

VALUE USE AND MANAGEMENT IMPLICATIONS

Value estimates for given hunting or fishing activities are weighted averages over all sites in Idaho where that particular activity took place. The weighing factor is the number of trips by survey respondents to the respective sites. Since survey respondents were randomly sampled, the value estimates reported here would be used most appropriately to evaluate management actions that occur uniformly over all the respective hunting and fishing sites in Idaho and that do not significantly change the proportions of trips to each site. To the extent that a management action concentrates on only some sites, the distribution of trips may be subject to change. In such cases values specific to those particular sites are preferred. Equations for demand relationships estimated in this study can be applied to a specific site or groups of sites. To do this, the user must determine the quality variable value for the site(s) under study. Then by applying the estimation techniques of this or other TCM studies, benefits can be estimated for the base quality level and for contemplated changes. An example of this type of analysis considers the value relationships of forage used by deer, elk, antelope, and/or domestic livestock (Loomis *et al.* 1989). Likewise, changes in substitute site relationships can be tested using those estimated demand curves that include substitute index terms.

The concept of total economic value, as used in this chapter, has two components, efficiency value or total consumer surplus and impact value or expenditures in the private sector. These values can be part of an even broader value framework that includes option, existence, or bequest value concepts (Peterson and Sorg 1987). Determining which component of economic value to use in a management decision depends upon the particular question of interest. If the land planner is concerned with the most efficient use of the land, then efficiency (WTP) values are most appropriate. For example, a decision might require comparing net benefits of timber production to net benefits of elk production.

Net benefit of timber production equals the value of timber harvested less the cost of harvest and subsequent reforestation. Under some circumstances it is possible to also have consumer surplus and producer surplus benefits associated with timber production. These considerations are beyond the scope of this chapter. (See Just, Hueth, and Schmitz 1982 for additional information).

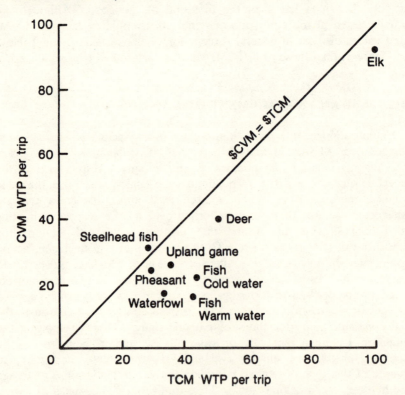

Figure 3. Comparison of Willingness to Pay (in dollars) Expressed via TCM and CVM

The societal benefit of trips for elk hunting is computed as the aggregate amount of hunters license fees plus net willingness to pay per trip in excess of expenditures for the hunting trip, less the cost of providing the hunting opportunity which may be zero if no habitat maintenance is necessary. Further, note that expenditures of individuals for their elk hunting are not used in the calculation because costs the hunter pays in the private sector generally do not reflect cost to the land of providing elk habitat. After the net benefits of each use are computed, the greater net benefit, that for timber or elk, indicates benefits to all of society. It is irrelevant from an economic efficiency stance that benefits from timber production are captured as money returns and that benefits from hunting elk, in the form of hunters net willingness to pay, are not.

Suppose now that the question of interest to the land planner shifts from efficiency to impact on local, state, and national economies. In this case the expenditure information is the relevant value measure to use. The choice in this instance may depend on whether timber production or elk hunting provides more income (expenditures) to the local and state economy. Expenditures associated with timber harvesting may involve harvesting equipment, sawmills, or site maintenance related industries. Hunter expenditures may involve local lodging, taxidermists locally or at home, and miscellaneous expenses such as clothing, food, or equipment. Whichever land use provides more local income activity may be the more desirable. A related consideration is which industry will provide long term stability in the economy in the form of jobs and local financial revenue.

The discussion above considers the two *polar* cases of efficiency and impact. The question of which economic value measure to use is dependent on the issue at hand. More often than not both measures are used in conjunction with one another, plus other considerations, to insure a proper mix of activity which is not only efficient but also provides needed local income.

ACKNOWLEDGEMENTS

Lloyd Oldenburg and others in the Idaho Department of Fish and Game initiated the study and collected data along with personnel of the Cooperative Wildlife Unit at the University of Idaho. The U.S. Fish and Wildlife Service and Bureau Land Management, the U.S. Army Corps of Engineers, and the U.S. Forest Service cooperated in funding. Data analysis was done by personnel from U.S. Forest Service and U.S. Fish and Wildlife Service. Two anonymous reviewers contributed to the content and format of this chapter. Responsibility for presentation of results and conclusions rests with the authors.

REFERENCES

Bishop, R.C. and T.A. Heberlein. 1979. Measuring values of extramarket goods: Are indirect measures biased? *American Journal of Agricultural Economics* 61:926-930.

Brookshire, D.S., A. Randall, and J.R. Stoll. 1980. Valuing increments and decrements in natural resource service flows. *American Journal of Agricultural Economics* 62:478-488.

Cesario, F.T. and J.L. Knetsch. 1976. A recreation site demand and benefit estimation model. *Journal of Regional Studies* 10:97-104.

Cummings, R.G., D.S. Brookshire, and W.D. Schulze (Eds.). 1986. *Valuing Environmental Goods: An Assessment of the Contingent Value Method.* Totowa, NJ: Rowman and Allanheld, 270 p.

Desvouges, W.H., V.K. Smith, and M.P. McGivney. 1983. *A Comparison of Alternative Approaches for Estimating Recreation and Related Benefits of Water Quality Improvements.* Washington, D.C.: U. S. Environmental Protection Agency, Office of Policy Analysis Report EPA-230-05-83-001, EPA Contract No. 68-01-5838, var. pg.

Donnelly, D.M., J.B. Loomis, C.F. Sorg, and L.J. Nelson. 1985. *Net Economic Value of Recreational Steelhead Fishing in Idaho.* U.S. Forest Service, Rocky Mountain Forest and Range Experiment Station Research Bulletin RM-9, 23 pp.

Donnelly, D.M. and L.J. Nelson. 1986. *Net Economic Value of Deer Hunting in Idaho.* U.S. Forest Service, Rocky Mountain Forest and Range Experiment Station Research Bulletin RM-13, 27 pp.

Dwyer, J.F., J.R. Kelly, and M.D. Bowes. 1977. *Improved Procedures for Valuation of the Contribution of Recreation to National Economic Development.* Water Resources Center Report 128. Urbana: University of Illinois, 218 pp.

Hanley, N. 1988. Using contingent valuation to value environmental improvements. *Applied Economics* 20:541-549.

Idaho Department of Fish and Game. 1980a. *Elk Species Management Plan 1981-1985.* Boise: Idaho Department of Fish and Game, 91 pp.

Idaho Department of Fish and Game. 1980b. *Trophy Species Management Plan 1981-1985.* Boise: Idaho Department of Fish and Game, 113 pp.

Just, R.E., D.L. Hueth, and A. Schmitz. 1982. *Applied Welfare Economics and Public Policy.* Englewood Cliffs, N.J: Prentice-Hall, 491 p.

Knetsch, J.L., R.E. Brown, and W.J. Hanson. 1976. Estimating expected use and value of recreation sites, pages 103-115. In C.E. Gearing, W.W. Swart, and T. Var (Eds.) *Planning Tourism Development-Quantitative Approaches.* New York: Praeger Publishers, 221 p.

Loomis, J.B. 1982. Effect of nonprice rationing on benefits from publicly provided recreation. *Journal of Environmental Management* 14:283-289.

Loomis, J.B., D.M. Donnelly, and C.F. Sorg Swanson. 1989. Comparing the economic value of forage on public lands for wildlife and livestock. *Journal of Range Management* 42:134-138.

Loomis, J.B., G. Peterson, and C. Sorg. 1984. A field guide to wildlife economic analysis. *Trans. North American Wildlife and Natural Resources Conference* 49:315-324.

Loomis, J.B. and L.J. Nelson. 1985. *Net Economic Value of Hunting Unique Species in Idaho*. U.S. Forest Service, Rocky Mountain Forest and Range Experiment Station Research Bulletin RM-10, 16 pp.

Mitchell, R.C. and R.T. Carson. Forthcoming. *Using Surveys to Value Public Goods: The Contingent Valuation Method*. Washington, D.C.: Resources for the Future, 463 p.

Peterson, G.L. and C.F. Sorg. 1987. *Toward the Measurement of Total Economic Value*. U.S. Forest Service, Rocky Mountain Forest and Range Experiment Station General Technical Report RM-148, 44 pp.

Randall, A., B.C. Ives, and E. Eastman. 1974. Bidding games for valuation of aesthetic environmental improvements. *Journal of Environmental Economics and Management* 1:132-149.

Rosenthal, D.H., J.B. Loomis, and G.L. Peterson. 1984. *The Travel Cost Model: Concepts and Applications*. U.S. Forest Service, Rocky Mountain Forest and Range Experiment Station General Technical Report RM-109, 10 pp.

Sorg, C.F. and J.B. Loomis. 1985. An introduction to wildlife valuation techniques. *Wildlife Society Bulletin* 13:38-46.

Sorg, C.F., J.B. Loomis, D.M. Donnelly, G.L. Peterson, and L.J. Nelson. 1985. *Net Economic Value of Cold and Warm Water Fishing in Idaho*. U.S. Forest Service, Rocky Mountain Forest and Range Experiment Station Research Bulletin RM-11, 26 pp.

Sorg, C.F. and L.J. Nelson. 1985. *Net Economic Value of Elk Hunting in Idaho*. U.S. Forest Service, Rocky Mountain Forest and Range Experiment Station Research Bulletin RM-12, 21 pp.

Sorg, C.F. and L.J. Nelson. 1987. *Net Economic Value of Waterfowl Hunting in Idaho*. U.S. Forest Service, Rocky Mountain Forest and Range Experiment Station Research Bulletin RM-14, 18 pp.

U.S. Water Resources Council. 1979. *Procedures for Evaluation of National Economic Development (NED) Benefits and Costs in Water Resources Planning*. (Level C); Final Rule. Washington, D.C.: Fed. Reg. 44:72892-72976.

U.S. Water Resources Council. 1983. *Economic and Environmental Principles for Water and Related Land Resources Implementation Studies*. Washington, D. C.: U.S. Government Printing Office, 137 pp.

Young, J. S., D. M. Donnelly, C. F. Sorg, J. B. Loomis, and L. J. Nelson. 1987. *Net Economic Value of Upland Game Hunting in Idaho*. U.S. Forest Service, Rocky Mountain Forest and Range Experiment Station Research Bulletin RM-15, 23 pp.

CHAPTER 17

SCENIC BEAUTY AND RECREATION VALUE: ASSESSING THE RELATIONSHIP

Thomas C. Brown
Rocky Mountain Forest and Range Experiment Station
USDA Forest Service

Merton T. Richards
School of Forestry
Northern Arizona University

Terry C. Daniel
Department of Psychology
University of Arizona

David A. King
School of Renewable Natural Resources
University of Arizona

The importance of forest recreation is formally recognized in legislation such as the Multiple-Use Sustained Yield Act of 1960, and the importance of landscape scenic quality is recognized in the Wild and Scenic Rivers Act of 1968 and the National Environmental Policy Act of 1969. The Forest and Rangeland Renewable Resources Planning Act of 1974 and the National Forest Management Act of 1976 reinforced the mandate to consider recreation and aesthetic resources, and emphasized the evaluation of tradeoffs among competing demands. Taken together, these laws reflect a public desire for more thorough and analytical consideration of recreation and scenic quality in land management.

While scenic beauty is an important resource in its own right, it also derives importance as it contributes to recreational experiences. For example, the scenic beauty of the forest surrounding a campsite, picnic ground, or hiking trail almost certainly contributes to the value of the recreation experiences. The purpose of this chapter is to investigate the relationship between forest scenic beauty and recreation value, in the context of developed camping. The analysis focuses on a survey of campers at forest campgrounds in Arizona. Some of the results of the survey have been reported in previous papers (Brown, Daniel, Richards and King 1989, Daniel, Brown, King, Richards and Stewart 1989). This chapter will provide an overview of these earlier results and report new analyses and comparisons pertaining to the relationship between scenic beauty and recreation value.

Adequate treatment of scenic beauty within the multiple use decision-making process requires, first of all, a reliable method for measuring of the relative scenic beauty of alternative environments. The psychophysical approach to assessing scenic beauty (Zube, Sell and Taylor 1982, Daniel and Vining 1983) offers one such method. The psychophysical approach assesses scenic beauty in terms of the perceptual judgments of observer panels sampled from populations of interest. Observers are asked to indicate their judgments and preferences for different levels of environmental quality represented directly or graphically (e.g., by color slides or prints). Responses of a number of observers are subjected to a psychometric scaling routine and then aggregated to provide a standardized (interval scale) index of preference or perceived quality (Daniel and Boster 1976).

This basic methodology has been applied in a number of environmental assessment contexts (e.g., Daniel, Wheeler, Boster and Best 1973, Kaplan, Kaplan and Wendt 1972, Peterson 1967, Shafer 1964, Shafer and Richards 1974, Zube 1974). Recent applications have shown the method to be useful for gauging the effects of forest management practices on public perception of scenic beauty of forest areas (e.g., Schroeder and Daniel 1981, Benson and Ulrich 1981, Buhyoff, Wellman and Daniel 1982, Brown and Daniel 1984). This research has found high consistency among public groups in their scenic preferences (Daniel and Boster 1976, Brown and Daniel 1986, Schroeder 1984).

Scenic beauty research has not only found consistent scenic beauty preferences; scenic beauty modeling studies have also found consistent relationships between forest characteristics and the scenic beauty of the forest. Controlling for viewer effects by randomly selecting viewers and appropriately scaling their responses, and controlling for the choice of view point by randomly selecting views within each area of interest, these studies have shown that much of the variance in perceived scenic beauty can usually be expressed in terms of standard forestry measurements. For example, in the ponderosa pine type, which is of particular interest for this study, Arthur (1977) and Brown and Daniel (1986) found that 70 to 80 percent of the variance in scenic beauty was accounted for by measurements of overstory, understory, and downed wood.

Scenic beauty research provides a good understanding of the public's relative scenic preferences, but it does not necessarily indicate the assigned value (Brown 1984) of scenic beauty to the public. While it is reasonable to expect a monotonic relationship between perceived scenic beauty and the value of scenic beauty, it is conceivable that the scenic conditions that respondents consistently agree are preferable would be of high value in some real world contexts and of little value in others. Indeed, the very consistent and reliable preferences found in most studies of scenic beauty might not be a good indication of the value to society of scenic beauty in many circumstances.

Brown and Daniel (1984) hypothesized that the strength of the relationship between scenic quality and recreation value could be represented as a continuum. At one extreme, the value of recreation activities such as driving for pleasure and picnicking may be strongly dependent on the scenic quality of the surrounding environment. At the other extreme, the value of recreation activities that have a strong performance element, such as rock climbing or white-water kayaking, may have a lesser dependence on the scenic quality of the surrounding environment.

The value of forest camping experiences surely depends to some extent on the scenic quality of the surrounding forest landscape. At the same time, there are undoubtedly other important factors affecting the value of forest camping. The relationship between recreation value (RV) and scenic beauty (SB) can be conceptualized as:

$$RV = f (SB, X_1, ..., X_n) \tag{1}$$

where X_1 to X_n include such items as other site features (e.g., facilities, lakes, fishing quality), social conditions at the site (e.g., crowding and noise), location, and characteristics of substitutes. The relative contribution of such features, and the unique contribution of each, is of course difficult to determine. Determining the relationship between scenic beauty and the value of a camping experience will require relatively precise assessments of both in the context of specific changes in relevant conditions at forest camping sites.

Economic value, based on willingness to pay, is one measure of assigned value. Individuals indicate their willingness to pay for a wide range of goods via their exchanges of money for goods. Several studies have estimated the economic value of changes in scenic quality.[1] Other studies have estimated the value of changes in dimensions related to scenic beauty, such as forest condition, visual air quality, and tree density. While some of the economic studies assessed property value impacts of trees via appraisals (Peters 1971, Morales, Boyce and Favoretti 1976), and some used indirect methods (the travel cost and hedonic property value methods) to estimate willingness to pay (Michaelson 1975, Leuschner and Young 1978), most, and the more recent, have used contingent valuation.

In contingent valuation, individuals indicate the value they place on goods in the context of hypothetical markets (Cummings, Brookshire and Schulze 1986, Rowe and Chestnut 1982). Typically, respondents are asked for their *willingness to pay* for the goods. Previous contingent valuation studies have evaluated such goods as landscape scenes, recreation opportunities, trust fund memberships, or air quality levels. The goods can be described verbally or represented graphically, as by photographs or computer simulations. The respondent may *bid* different amounts that s/he would be willing to pay in the form of a direct payment, extra taxes, utility bills, or some other *payment vehicle*. A number of variations on the basic format have been used, but the goal is to use responses to the hypothetical market to estimate the economic value of the environmental quality level (or change in level) represented. Contingent valuation provides relatively precise cardinal measures of value that are potentially commensurate with other costs and benefits of environmental change.

Many contingent valuation studies that focused on goods with visual dimensions have used photos to depict the goods (e.g., Randall, Ives and Eastman 1974, Adams, Currie, Herbert and Shikiar 1980, Walsh and Olienyk 1981, Schulze, Brookshire, Walther, MacFarland, Thayer, Whitworth, Ben-David, Malm and Molenar 1983, Crocker 1985, Boyle and Bishop 1988). The use of photographs has the advantage that numerous environments can be represented to respondents without the costly and time-consuming task of actually transporting them to the scene. Although the validity of using photographs in contingent valuation has not been widely tested, numerous studies have found photos to be a valid medium for evaluating scenic quality (e.g., Boster and Daniel 1972, Shafer and Richards 1974, Daniel and Boster 1976, Jackson and Hudman 1978, Shuttleworth 1980, Kellomaki and Savolainen 1984).

Contingent valuation and scenic beauty estimation methods were applied in the present study to assess the effects of forest conditions on campers' estimates of the value of their camping experience and perceptions of the scenic beauty of the surrounding forest. Recreationists were questioned at campgrounds about their current experience, and about alternative forest environments represented on photos. The experiment sought to (1) determine the relative recreation value and scenic beauty of these forest sites, (2) investigate the relationship between measures of recreation value and public perception of scenic beauty in forest campgrounds, (3) compare direct and photo-based measures, and (4) estimate the value of scenic beauty.

USER SURVEY

Ideally, to evaluate the contribution of forest scenic beauty to the value of forest recreation, one would measure the value of recreation at numerous sites, measure the forest scenic beauty and all other relevant characteristics of those sites, and then regress the value estimate on the site characteristics to determine the independent contribution of each characteristic and gain some understanding of interactions among the characteristics. Because of the numerous characteristics that may affect recreation, many sites would be needed to provide sufficient degrees of freedom for the statistical analysis. Such an extensive effort was beyond the scope of this study. However, we did measure recreation value and forest scenic beauty at several different sites -- a sufficient number to allow computation of reliable estimates of correlation between scenic beauty and recreation value. Furthermore, we used responses about photographs of different scenic conditions to obtain a measure of willingness to pay for forest scenic beauty.

Direct personal interviews were conducted during the summer of 1985 with campers sampled at 12 different campgrounds located in ponderosa pine forests of north-central Arizona. Data from two of these campgrounds proved to be inadequate, however, so we only present results for the remaining 10 campgrounds, which are listed in Table 1. Each campground is organized into campsites that contain a picnic table, grill, and place for a vehicle and tent.

The interview contained two main sections, an initial set of questions about the current camping trip, and then questions about areas represented on photos. Two survey instruments were used, which differed only in the second, photo-based, section of the questionnaire. One half of the respondents received the scenic beauty instrument and the other half received the contingent valuation instrument.

The initial questions of the first section covered items such as the length of stay, number of persons in the party, previous trips to the sample site, other destinations on the current trip, and trip expenses. Then, respondents were asked to estimate their own or their household's expenditures for (1) gasoline, (2) food and beverages, and (3) campground and rental fees for the Arizona part of their trip to the campground. The three amounts were summed by the interviewer to obtain a total expenditure per party for the stay at the campground.

After confirming the calculated total expenditure, the respondent was asked *how much more you (your household) would have been willing to spend on this trip before deciding not to come to this campground -- that is, before deciding to do something else or to stay at home.* The sum of total expenditure and the estimate of additional willingness to pay was taken as the respondent's expressed maximum willingness to pay (via incurred expenses) for the current trip to the campground. Because scenic beauty and other site features varied from one campground to the next, and our particular interest in forest scenic beauty was not apparent to respondents, their answers were potentially affected by the full range of site features. The resulting direct estimate of recreation value thus reflects the conceptual model of recreation value depicted in Equation 1.

The second section of the questionnaire was about 35 forest areas depicted on color prints. Each forest area was represented by six 3 x 5 inch prints arranged in a 3 x 2 array on a page of a looseleaf notebook. The 35 areas included the campgrounds where interviews took place, plus ponderosa pine stands on the Coconino National Forest inventoried in 1979 as part of an earlier study (Brown and Daniel 1984). The photos of the campgrounds were taken at randomly selected locations within each campground, with the constraint that the photos did not contain man-made features, such as picnic tables, vehicles, and tents, or people. The photos showed only the forest characteristics of the campgrounds. The photos of the timber stands were also obtained under similar constraints. Six notebooks were used in the interviews, each with the 35 pages arranged in a unique random order.

Although each of the campgrounds where interviews took place was represented among the 35 photo sets, it is unlikely that many respondents recognized their specific campground among the 35 areas. Respondents were not told that their campground was among the photos. The specific interview locations seldom coincided with the photo point of an included photograph. And, by design (via the inclusion of photos of the timber stands), many of the 35 areas were quite similar, making it difficult for respondents to recognize *their* campground among the photos.

The scenic beauty instrument asked respondents to *assign a scenic beauty rating to each forest area*, where *1 = very low scenic beauty, 10 = very high scenic beauty*. After all 35 photographed areas were rated for scenic beauty, respondents were asked to *rate the scenic beauty of the forest area around this campground*. It was made clear that this rating, which we call the *direct* rating, was to apply to the entire campground, and not just the immediate area around their campsite.

Table 1. Sample Size for Each Campground

Campground	Scenic Beauty	Contingent Valuation	Total
Spillway	82	80	162
Canyon Point	97	100	197
Ashurst Lake	54	45	99
Pine Grove	53	52	105
Rock Crossing	51	46	97
Dairy Springs	56	57	113
Whitehorse A	50	46	96
Whitehorse B	96	92	188
Kaibab Lake	79	70	149
Dog Town	38	33	71
Total	**757**	**707**	**1464**

The contingent valuation instrument used the same notebooks of color prints, but asked monetary questions. Respondents were first (1) reminded of the maximum that they said they would be willing to spend to camp at the campground, which was the sum of their expenditures for their trip and how much more they said they were willing to pay before deciding not to come to the campground, and (2) given an opportunity to revise their estimate of total willingness to pay. They were then asked to indicate for each of the 35 areas in the photos *the most you would have been willing to spend on this trip if forest conditions at this campground (all other things being equal) were like the forest areas depicted in the photos.* In essence, for each campground sample, the relationship between recreation value and scenic beauty can be conceptualized as:

$$RV = f \ (\ SB \ | \ X_1, \ ..., \ X_n) \tag{2}$$

where the X vector refers to the same items as in Equation 1. Campers' responses can be taken as an indication of willingness to pay for scenic beauty, *ceteris paribus*.

Scaling of Responses

The scenic beauty ratings of each respondent were individually standardized to yield an index for each of the photographed scenes and for the direct scene. The standardized index, SB, for each campground was calculated individually for each respondent as:

$$SB_{ij} = [(R_{ij} - MR_j) / SDR_j] \ 100 \tag{3}$$

where :

R_{ij} = rating of campground i by respondent j
MR_j = mean rating of the 35 photo sets of respondent j
SDR_j = standard deviation of the 35 photo set ratings of
   respondent j.

For this transformation, the origin and interval size for each respondent's SBs were determined by responses to the 35 photo sets, which were common stimuli for all respondents.

SBs were computed for both the direct scenic beauty ratings (SB^d_{ij}) and for the photo-based ratings (SB^p_{ij}). SBs were averaged across respondents within each campground sample to yield mean direct (SB^d_i) and photo-based (SB^p_i) estimates for each campground for the various respondent groups. And photo-based SBs were averaged across all 10 samples to yield grand mean estimates for each campground ($SB^{p^*}_i$).

Estimates of net willingness to pay based on the contingent valuation responses were derived for each household for the actual experience and for each photo area on a per-person per-trip basis. The actual experience, or *direct*, value was estimated as:

$$CVt^d_{ij} = MORE_j / N_j \tag{4}$$

where:

CVt^d_{ij} = additional willingness to pay per person per trip for the direct experience for campground i and respondent j

$MORE_j$ = respondent j's additional willingness to pay for the current trip

N_j = number of people in the party on respondent j's current trip.

The comparable photo-based estimate of additional willingness to pay was computed as:

$$CVt^p_{ij} = (MAXt_{ij} - EXPt_j) / N_j \tag{5}$$

where:

CVt^p_{ij} = respondent j's net willingness to pay per person per trip for campground i as represented by the photos

$MAXt_{ij}$ = the total expense respondent j was willing to incur for the current trip if the forest had the appearance depicted in photo set i

$EXPt_j$ = actual expenses of respondent j for the current trip

N_j = the number of people in the party, as above.

CVt^p_{ij}, then, was the amount more per person that a respondent estimated his or her household would be willing to spend.

CVs were averaged across respondents within each campground sample to yield mean direct (CVt^d_i) and photo-based (CVt^p_i) estimates of additional willingness to pay for each campground for the various respondent groups. Also, individual CV estimates of Equations 4 and 5 were divided by the number of days per trip (DAYSt) to give additional willingness to pay on a per-person-per-day basis and then averaged across respondents to yield CVd^d_i and CVd^p_i. Finally, individual photo-based CVs were averaged across all 10 samples to yield grand mean estimates for each campground (CVt^{p*}_i and CVd^{p*}_i). To summarize the scaling procedures, Table 2 lists the more important variables.

Before computation of the SB and CV indices, respondents who did not provide a response for each photo set were dropped from the sample. Contingent valuation data were additionally trimmed for respondents who appeared to reject the bidding procedure. The resulting sample sizes are listed in Table 1. The number of campers interviewed at each site varied depending upon the number of campsites and campers visiting during the survey period. The trimming procedure and other details of the methods are described by Daniel, *et al.* (1989).

Forest Scenic Beauty and Recreation Value

Mean number of days per trip spent at the campground (DAYSt) varied from 2.9 to 4 across the 10 campgrounds (Table 3). Length of trip, expenditures (EXPt), and direct estimates of additional willingness to pay (CVt^d and CVd^d) are reported in Table 3 for only the half of the sample that received the contingent valuation instrument (who provided contingent valuation responses for the photo sets). However, these responses are very similar to those of the other half of the sample. Mean expenses per person per trip (EXPt) varied from about $30 at Rock Crossing to about $60 at Pine Grove. On a daily basis, expenses per person varied from about $7 at Dairy Springs to about $14 at Ashurst Lake. Additional direct willingness to pay per trip (CVt^d) varied from a mean of $6.67 at Dairy Springs to $24.61 at Canyon Point. Combining expenses and additional willingness to pay, total direct mean willingness to pay per trip varied from $36.95 at Rock Crossing to $73.91 at Pine Grove.

Table 2. Description of Selected Variables

Name	Description
EXPt	Total estimated expenses per person per trip
DAYSt	Number of days per party per trip
SB^d	Scenic beauty of the surrounding forest (direct)
SB^{p*}	Scenic beauty of the forest depicted in photos, all samples combined
CVt^d	Additional willingness to pay per person per trip for the current experience (direct)
CVt^{p*}	Additional willingness to pay per person per trip if the forest were like that depicted in the photos, all samples combined
CVd^d	Additional willingness to pay per person per day for the current experience (direct)
CVd^{p*}	Additional willingness to pay per person per day if the forest were like that depicted in the photos, all samples combined

As reported in more detail by Daniel *et al.* (1989), photo-based scenic beauty ratings obtained at the different campground samples were highly reliable, and very similar from one sample to the next. And, photo-based estimates of additional willingness to pay obtained at the different campgrounds were very similar across samples. For both measures, two-way analyses of variance indicated that the mean photo-based response across all 35 photo sets did not differ across campground samples, but that the effect of photo-set was highly significant. Furthermore, the 45 pair-wise correlations between the SB^p_i of the 10 samples were all above 0.80, with a median of 0.92, and the corresponding correlations for CVt^p_i were all above 0.78, with a median of 0.93. Because of this close agreement among campgrounds, further analyses of the photo-based measures are based on the grand mean measures of SB and CV (SB^{p*}, CVt^{p*}, and CVd^{p*}, presented in Table 3).

Mean photo-based additional willingness to pay per trip (CVt^{p*}) ranged from minus \$12.80 to \$10.48 (Table 3). A negative estimate indicates that respondents on average were not even willing to pay as much as they actually paid if the forest around their campground were to look like the forest depicted in the respective photo set.

Direct and Photo-based Estimates of Scenic Beauty

Inspection of Table 3 shows that the direct scenic beauty values (SB^d) are all considerably higher than the corresponding photo-based values (SB^{p*}). Similarly, nearly all direct contingent valuation estimates (CVt^d) are greater then their corresponding photo-based estimates (CVt^{p*}). This consistent preference for actual conditions over those depicted on photos was discussedin detail by Brown *et al.* (1989), who suggest that active participation, self-selection, and/or cognitive dissonance elevated the direct responses.

Although the direct and photo-based measures of scenic beauty do not agree on an absolute basis, they are related. The correlation between the two measures is 0.87, and highly significant, across the 10 campgrounds (Table 4). This comparison is a relatively stringent one. Previous comparisons have required each observer to evaluate all sites, where necessary by transporting respondents from site to site. Here, all respondents rated all photos, but the direct judgments were obtained from totally independent samples. The high correlation obtained here indicates that the photos rather accurately depicted the relative scenic beauty of the campgrounds.

Table 3. Mean values for selected variables[1] for 10 campgrounds[2]

CAMPGROUND	EXPt	DAYSt	SB^d	SB^{p*}	CVt^d	CVt^{p*}	CVd^d	CVd^{p*}
Spillway	40.33	3.7	108	-13	17.02	-2.01	6.20	-.58
Canyon Point	46.64	5.2	132	78	24.61	9.60	7.34	3.04
Ashurst Lake	42.35	3.5	70	-58	8.35	-12.80	3.76	-3.65
Pine Grove	60.36	6.3	121	57	13.55	7.10	2.65	2.06
Rock Crossing	30.09	2.9	105	35	6.86	3.30	2.57	.90
Dairy Springs	46.13	6.4	120	70	6.67	10.48	1.77	3.23
Whitehorse A	40.74	3.6	118	17	19.63	3.78	5.94	.95
Whitehorse B	47.79	3.9	136	54	18.16	6.34	5.91	1.79
Kaibab Lake	35.04	3.5	106	20	14.37	3.38	5.72	1.05
Dog Town	33.30	3.2	113	15	12.58	1.81	4.78	.70

[1]See Table 2 for descriptions of variables.
[2]Scenic beauty and contingent valuation estimates from separate samples at each campground.

Direct Estimates

The direct estimates of recreation value were obtained at 10 different sites without any mention to respondents of scenic beauty or forest characteristics. Thus, their responses are expected to reflect the full range of variables that affect recreation value, as depicted in Equation 1. Also, the direct estimate of recreation value was estimated only from the respondents who received the contingent valuation instrument, so that the estimates of SB and CV are from completely separate sets of respondents at each campground.

The correlation between the direct estimates of scenic beauty (SB^d) and recreation value was 0.57, with recreation value expressed on a per-trip basis (CVt^d, Table 4). Assuming no interactions between forest scenic beauty and other site features, this 0.57 correlation indicates that scenic beauty accounts for 33 percent of the variance in recreation value.[2]

The correlation between direct SB and CV drops to 0.29 with CV expressed on a per-day basis (CVd^d). The lower correlation with CV expressed on a per-day basis is expected in light of the positive relationship between scenic beauty and length of stay (DAYSt correlates 0.50 with SB^d,

Table 4). Length of stay tended to be longer at the more attractive campgrounds, so that additional willingness to pay *per day* tended to be lower at the more attractive campgrounds, all else equal.

The direct measures of scenic beauty and additional willingness to pay for camping at the 10 campgrounds indicate that the two measures are related, but that other features of the camping environment probably are at least as important as forest scenic beauty in determining willingness to pay. The 0.57 correlation between the two measures suggests that forest camping probably falls somewhere near the middle of the continuum described abovefor the relationship between scenic quality and recreation value. Forest scenic quality is probably more important to the value of camping than it is to some recreation activities which have a strong performance element, but less important than it is to other activities such as driving for pleasure.

The current study suggests that scenic beauty is not the overriding concern in developed camping, at least given the range of scenic conditions found at the 10 campgrounds in the sample. Studies of the relative contribution of various factors that affect camper satisfaction support this finding. In these studies, campers at developed sites reported that scenic beauty and forest characteristics were usually less important to satisfaction than such factors as feelings of relaxation (Connelly 1987), which would be affected by crowding and noise, and campsite design and facilities (Lime 1971).

Table 4. Pearson Correlations for Selected Variables[1] across 10 Campgrounds

	EXPt	DAYSt	SB^d	SBP*	CVt^d	CVtP*	CVd^d
DAYSt	.79**						
SB^d	.37	.50					
SBP*	.38	.68*	.87***				
CVt^d	.25	.04	.57*	.27			
CVtP*	.31	.64*	.90***	.97***	.30		
CVd^d	-.12	-.34	.29	-.05	.89***	-.01	
CVdP*	.31	.66*	.89***	.98***	.29	1.00***	-.01

[1] See Table 2 for descriptions of variables.
* indicates significance at p < 0.05
** indicates significance at p < 0.01
*** indicates significance at p < 0.001.

Photo-based Estimates

In contrast to the 0.57 correlation between the direct estimates of scenic beauty and recreation value, the correlation between the photo-based estimates of scenic beauty and recreation value was nearly unity. On a per-trip basis, the correlation between scenic beauty (SB^{P*}) and additional willingness to pay (CVt^{P*}) was 0.97, while on a per-day basis (CVd^{P*}) the correlation was 0.98 (Table 4). In each case, the two correlated variables were estimated from separate samples at each campground. Clearly, subject to a linear transformation, the photo-based scenic beauty and contingent valuation measures were essentially identical for the 10 campgrounds.

The photo-based portion of the survey was designed to measure the value of forest scenic beauty to campers. Campers were asked to assume that all features of their camping trip remained unchanged except the surrounding forest, which was depicted in the photo sets. As shown in Table 3, respondents indicated on average a difference in willingness to pay from the least to the most attractive forest conditions among the 10 campgrounds of about $22 per person per trip ($7 per person per day), *ceteris paribus*.

The very high correlation (0.97) between photo-based additional willingness to pay and scenic beauty (CVt^{P*} and SB^{P*}, respectively) indicates an almost perfect linear relationship between the two. Clearly, the contingent valuation and scenic beauty respondents perceived the photo sets similarly, and both were sensitive to the same variations in forest characteristics. It should be clear, however, that this high correlation does not indicate the contribution of scenic beauty to recreation value. Furthermore, the high correlation is not comparable to the correlation between the direct measures of recreation value and scenic beauty (0.57). By design, the former, photo-based, correlation was obtained in the *ceteris paribus* context, where only the forest characteristics changed (as in Equation 2), while the latter was obtained in an unconstrained context, without any mention to the respondents of scenic beauty or surrounding forest characteristics (as in Equation 1).

The very high correlation between photo-based additional willingness to pay and scenic beauty seems remarkable. However, it is probably quite reasonable to expect a high correlation where the value of the overall recreation experience depends at least to some extent on forest scenic beauty. Because only the forest features were varied among the photo sets, respondents were forced to focus solely on this dimension. Indeed, because of the *ceteris paribus* nature of the photo-based survey design, either a strong or weak dependence of recreation value on scenic beauty might produce a high correlation between CV^{P*} and SB^{P*}.

Direct versus Photo-based Estimates of Recreation Value

Another comparison of interest is that between direct (CVt^d) and photo-based (CVt$^{p^*}$) additional willingness to pay. The correlation is 0.30 (Table 4), similar to that between CVt^d and SB$^{p^*}$ (0.27), as would be expected since CVt$^{p^*}$ and SB$^{p^*}$ are nearly perfectly correlated. But this is not a meaningful correlation, because the direct and photo-based contingent valuation estimates are not directly comparable. While CVt^d is a function of all the factors affecting recreation value (as in Equation 1), the CVt$^{p^*}$ is essentially a function of just the forest characteristics (as in Equation 2). The low correlation is probably more the result of this difference than of the fact that one estimate is direct and the other based on photos.

Qualifications

There is a danger with the photo-based contingent valuation procedure that the hypothetical nature of the photo-based exercise allowed for significant hypothetical bias in the responses. Respondents were already removed from reality by their direct contingent valuation response. They were then moved one step further by using that direct response as a base for their photo-based responses. In attempting to respond to each of the photo sets, and to show how their willingness to pay differed among the sets, respondents may have tended to lose sight of the payment aspect of the question and simply use the dollar metric as a ratio scale for indicating differences among the scenes.

Ajzen and Peterson (1988), in a discussion of the theory of reasoned action, point out limitations of contingent valuation approaches. Willingness to pay is an expression of behavioral intent that may or may not reflect an attitude toward a particular object, institution, or event, such as the inherent beauty of a forest scene. They argue that attitudes toward public goods differ from attitudes toward a behavioral construct such as paying for a public good. Because of the quite hypothetical nature of the photo-based additional willingness to pay estimate of this study, the contingent valuation responses may indicate a behavioral intention to pay for the good, or they may be more of a reflection of an attitude toward the good.

Another potential danger with the *ceteris paribus* approach to estimating the value of an attribute of a good is that it may not adequately treat the impact of interactions between the attribute of interest (e.g, forest scenic beauty) and other attributes that are held constant (e.g., camping facilities). Such interactions are only reflected in the resulting estimates of willingness to pay if there is sufficient variation in these other attributes among the different survey sites. The high correlations of the photo-based contingent valuation responses among the 10 campgrounds, reported above, suggest that interactions were minimal, but they might not be for a set of sites that differed more, one from the other, than the sites used in this study.

Of course, the direct contingent valuation survey is also subject to potential problems. Perhaps the principal danger in obtaining responses at several sites is that responses at those different sites may be differentially affected by artifacts of the survey procedures, causing unwanted variation in the direct responses which could have lowered or raised the correlation between CVt^d and SB^d.

CONCLUSIONS

Photos were confirmed as a good proxy for directly viewed scenes in assessing relative scenic beauty of forest areas. However, photo-based scenic beauty judgments were not directly comparable to judgments of directly viewed scenes when observers were actively engaged in recreation. Apparently, active participation in recreation elevates the judged scenic beauty of one's surroundings.

Campers' direct responses indicate that forest scenic beauty is a valuable component of forest camping experiences. Furthermore, in their photo-based responses, campers indicated a substantial willingness to pay for improved scenic beauty at developed campsites. In addition, the very high correlation between photo-based measures of recreation value and scenic beauty indicates that judgments of recreation value and scenic beauty are both responsive to variation in the same features of forest scenes. However, because the contingent valuation respondents were instructed to estimate their willingness to pay for the forest scenes in the photos assuming all other campground features remained the same, the nearly perfect linear relationship between the photo-based measures may significantly exaggerate the degree to which recreation value depends on scenic beauty.

Willingness to pay among recreationists for improved forest scenic beauty is probably stronger the more the recreation context focuses on the forest characteristics versus other features of the recreation experience. Additional research is needed on the relative importance of forest scenic beauty, as compared with other features, across a range of forest recreation activities.

NOTES:

1. Other studies have estimated the economic cost of providing forest scenic beauty. For examples, see Fight and Randall (1980) and Brown (1987).

2. In contrast to this significant correlation between scenic beauty and recreation value measured with contingent valuation, no significant correlation was found between SB^d and recreation value as estimated via the individual zonal travel cost models for each campground. These travel cost models are reported by Richards, King, Daniel and Brown (1989, Table 2).

REFERENCES

Adams, R.C., J.W. Currie, J.A. Hebert and R. Shikiar. 1980. *The Visual Aesthetic Impact of Alternative Closed Cycle Cooling Systems.* Main report NUREG/CR-0989. Richland, WA: Batelle Pacific Northwest Laboratory 75 pp. plus Appendixes.

Arthur, L.M. 1977. Predicting scenic beauty of forest environments: Some empirical tests. *Forest Science* 23:151-159.

Ajzen, I. and G.L. Peterson. 1988. Contingent value measurement: The price of everything and the value of nothing? In G.L. Peterson, B.L. Driver and R. Gregory (Eds.), *Amenity Resource Valuation: Integrating Economics with Other Disciplines.* State College, PA: Venture Publishing 65-76.

Benson, R.E. and J.R. Ulrich. 1981. *Visual Impacts of Forest Management Activities: Findings on Public Preferences.* USDA Forest Service Research Paper INT-262. Ogden, UT: Intermountain Forest and Range Experiment Station 14 pp.

Boster, R.S. and T.C. Daniel. 1972. *Measuring Public Responses to Vegetative Management.* In Proceedings 16th annual Arizona watershed symposium. Phoenix, AZ: Arizona Water Commission 38-43.

Boyle, K.J. and R.C. Bishop. 1988. Welfare measurements using contingent valuation: A comparison of techniques. *American Journal of Agriculture Economics* 70:20-28.

Brown, T.C. 1984. The concept of value in resource allocation. *Land Economics* 60:231-246.

Brown, T.C. 1987. Production and cost of scenic beauty: Examples for a ponderosa pine forest. *Forest Science* 33:394-410.

Brown, T.C. and T.C. Daniel. 1984. *Modeling Forest Scenic Beauty: Concepts and Application to Ponderosa Pine.* USDA Forest Service Research Paper RM-256. Fort Collins, CO: Rocky Mountain Forest and Range Experiment Station 35 pp.

Brown, T.C. and T.C. Daniel. 1986. Predicting scenic beauty of timber stands. *Forest Science* 32:471-487.

Brown, T.C., T.C. Daniel, M.T. Richards and D.A. King. 1989. Recreation participation and the validity of photo-based preference judgments. *Journal of Leisure Research* 21:40-60.

Buhyoff, G.J., J.D. Wellman and T.C. Daniel. 1982. Predicting scenic quality for mountain pine beetle and western spruce budworm damage forest vistas. *Forest Science* 28:827-838.

Connelly, N.A. 1987. Critical factors and their threshold for camper satisfaction at two campgrounds. *Journal of Leisure Research* 19:159-173.

Crocker, T.D. 1985. On the value of the condition of a forest stock. *Land Economics* 61:244-254.

Cummings, R.G., D.S. Brookshire and W.D. Schulze (Eds). 1986. *Valuing Environmental Goods.* Totawa, NJ: Allanheld.

Daniel, T.C., L. Wheeler, R.S. Boster and P. Best. 1973. Quantitative evaluation of landscapes: An application of signal detection analysis to forest management alterations. *Man-Environment Systems* 3:330-344.

Daniel, T.C. and R.S. Boster. 1976. *Measuring Landscape Esthetics: The Scenic Beauty Estimation Method.* USDA Forest Service Research Paper RM-167. Fort Collins, CO: Rocky Mountain Forest and Range Experiment Station 66 pp.

Daniel, T.C. and J. Vining. 1983. Methodological issues in the assessment of landscape quality. In I. Altman and J.S. Wohlwill (Eds.), *Behavior and the Natural Environment.* New York: Plenum Press 6:39-84.

Daniel, T.C., T.C. Brown, D.A. King, M.T. Richards and W.P. Stewart. 1989. Perceived scenic beauty and contingent valuation of forest campgrounds. *Forest Science* 35:76-90.

Fight, R.D. and R.M. Randall. 1980. Visual quality and the cost of growing timber. *Journal of Forestry* 78:546-548.

Jackson, R.H. and L.E. Hudman. 1978. Assessment of the environmental impact of high voltage power transmission lines. *Journal of Environmental Management* 6:153-170.

Kaplan, S., R. Kaplan and J.S. Wendt. 1972. Rated preference and complexity for natural and urban visual material. *Perception and Psychophysics* 12:354-356.

Kellomaki, S. and R. Savolainen. 1984. The scenic value of the forest landscape as assessed in the field and the laboratory. *Landscape Planning* 11:97-107.

Leuschner, W.A. and R.L. Young. 1978. Estimating the southern pine beetle's impact on reservoir campsites. *Forest Science* 24:527-537.

Lime, D.W. 1971. *Factors Influencing Campground Use in the Superior National Forest of Minnesota*. St. Paul, MN: USDA Forest Service Research Paper NC-60, North Central Forest Experiment Station 18 pp.

Michaelson, E.L. 1975. Economic impact of mountain pine beetle on outdoor recreation. *Southern Journal of Agricultural Economics* 7:42-50.

Morales, D, B.N. Boyce and R.J. Favoretti. 1976. The contribution of trees to residential property values, Manchester, Connecticut. *Valuation* 23:27-43.

Peters, C.L. 1971. Shade and ornamental tree evaluation. *Journal of Forestry* 67:411-413.

Peterson, G.L. 1967. A model of preference: Quantitative analysis of perception of the visual appearance of residential neighborhoods. *Journal of Regional Science* 7:19-31.

Randall, A., B. Ives and C. Eastman. 1974. Bidding games for valuation of aesthetic environmental improvements. *Journal of Environmental Economics and Management* 1:132-149.

Richards, M.T., D.A. King, T.C. Daniel and T.C. Brown. 1989. The relationship between travel cost and contingent value estimates of forest recreation value. Unpublished manuscript.

Rowe, R.D. and L.G. Chestnut (Eds.). 1982. *The Value of Visibility: Economic Theory and Applications for Air Pollution Control*. Cambridge, MA: Abt Books.

Schroeder, H.W. 1984. Environmental perception rating scales: A case for simple methods of analysis. *Environment and Behavior* 16:573-598.

Schroeder, H.W. and T.C. Daniel. 1981. Progress in predicting the perceived scenic beauty of forest landscapes. *Forest Science* 27:71-80.

Schulze, W.D., D.S. Brookshire, E.G. Walther, K.K. MacFarland, M.A. Thayer, R.L. Whitworth, A. Ben-David, W. Malm and J. Molenar. 1983. The economic benefits of preserving visibility in the national park lands of the Southwest. *Natural Resources Journal* 23:149-173.

Shafer, Jr., E.L. 1964. *The Photo-Choice Method for Recreation Research*. USDA Forest Service Research Paper NE-29. Upper Darby, PA: Northeastern Forest Experiment Station 10 pp.

Shafer, Jr., E.L. and T.A. Richards. 1974. *A Comparison of Viewer Reactions to Outdoor Scenes and Photographs of Those Scenes*. USDA Forest Service Research Paper NE-302. Upper Darby, PA: Northeastern Forest Experiment Station 26 pp.

Shuttleworth, S. 1980. The use of photographs as an environmental presentation medium in landscape studies. *Journal of Environmental Management* 11:61-76.

Walsh, R.G. and J.P. Olienyk. 1981. *Recreation Demand Effects of Mountain Pine Beetle Damage to the Quality of Forest Recreation Resources in the Colorado Front Range.* A report by Colorado State University to the USDA Forest Service. Fort Collins, CO.

Zube, E.H., J.L. Sell and J.G. Taylor. 1982. Landscape perception: Research, application, and theory. *Landscape Planning* 9:1-33.

Zube, E.H. 1974. Cross-disciplinary and intermode agreement on the description and evaluation of landscape resources. *Environment and Behavior* 6:69-89.

CHAPTER 18

PRESERVATION ATTITUDES AND CONSUMER SURPLUS IN FREE-FLOWING RIVERS

Howard A. Clonts
Department of Agricultural Economics and Rural Sociology
Auburn University

Joy W. Malone
USDA Forest Service

Availability of free-flowing rivers in the United States has been altered radically as dams, waterways, diversions, and other measures have been used to impound or extract water from the natural flow. In the study area covered by this report, the State of Alabama, nearly all major potentially navigable streams have been altered and are no longer free-flowing. Numerous lesser streams also have been dammed for local municipal or industrial water supply needs. Of the nearly 12,000 miles of major rivers and streams in the State, only about 20 percent remain free-flowing. Only few streams of state or regional significance remain free-flowing or virtually free-flowing over their entire course. This study examines citizen attitudes concerning such rivers and provides a measure of the value of a limited public good.

Controversy has erupted periodically over the use and control of the free-flowing rivers as well as the relatively free-flowing stretches of otherwise impounded rivers in Alabama. Efforts periodically are made by public or private interests to change the public good to a private good status with basic points of contention being (1) access to streams and (2) control of stream flow. The object of control is to gain the economic rent such a resource offers.

Difficulties in valuation of public and/or non-market goods such as free-flowing rivers may in part explain why development has progressed so rapidly despite concern of those opposed to loss of natural qualities associated with undeveloped resources. River resources provide a classic example of differences in philosophies and goals for natural resources in the United States (Diamant, Eugster and Duerksen 1984.) Rivers have become a focal point in the increasingly intense *development versus preservation* debate in the United States. Industrial interests, government agencies, and environmental groups are the main participants in this debate. The general public has not been involved and little is known about public attitudes regarding resource conservation issues. Studies dealing with public opinions and attitudes indicate that philosophies of the general public may differ from those of the elected leadership (Arthur 1981). This is especially true if policies endorsed or rejected by legislative bodies are taken as proxies for opinions of those groups. As noted below, data from this study confirm this divergence in attitudes between formal leaders and their constituents.

Historically, U.S. policy makers have favored resource development over preservation. The policy of the United States government regarding resources up to the latter part of the 20th century may be best summed up in a quote by Daniel Webster, *Let us develop the resources of our land, call forth its powers* . . . (quoted in Ashworth 1977). Over the past two decades, however, resource use policies have shifted away from unbridled exploitation as the adverse effects of development policy became clear. Various legislative acts, such as the National Wild and Scenic Rivers Act, the Wilderness Act, and the Endangered Species Act, were aimed at balancing development goals with those of protection and preservation.

More recently, The President's Commission on Americans Outdoors recommended a *2000 by 2000* program for the nation's riverways (Alexander 1987). Through local, state, and national efforts, 2000 river segments should be protected by the year 2000. The program would include reinvigoration of the Wild and Scenic Rivers program and stress a geographical balance of rivers across the country. State river programs would be the backbone of the renewed conservation thrust.

The interest in rivers exemplified by the *2000 by 2000* program indicates that concern still exists over the potential loss of natural resources, especially riverways, in the nation. However, simple interest in protecting rivers is not sufficient justification for delaying development. The economic advantages of development must be balanced with economic advantages of protection, conservation, and, perhaps, preservation. The positive economic consequences of development (jobs, business expansion, tax revenue) are quickly identifiable, but no clear market for natural resource protection exists. Consequently, the demand price for resource preservation tends to be ignored, and the full costs of development are not adequately analyzed. There is, however, in the minds of individuals, an intrinsic value for aesthetic qualities -- a reservation demand for undeveloped resources which is rarely quantified. Reservation demand expresses an individualized philosophy which generally is not established in a market setting or public forum. Yet, opinions are held by individuals as to whether they are satisfied with ongoing public and private resource use and allocation decisions. If a realistic policy for governing the development or protection of resources is ever to be developed, the reservation demand (preservation value) of the public must be determined.

PRESERVATION VALUES AND CONSUMER SURPLUS

Public Goods

The demand for natural resources is derived from consumer demands for products or services which stem from the resources themselves. Values are most easily assigned to those resources for which there is an obvious final product, e.g., petroleum, iron ore, etc. The problem is somewhat different when the resources themselves are viewed as the product or service, e.g., water. A further complication arises when the resource is viewed generally by consumers as a public good.

A public good, as discussed here, is considered as indivisible as well as fully accessible to all consumers (Tietenberg 1988). Common examples of natural resource public goods are natural diversity, national parks, the fish in the sea, and, for this chapter, free-flowing rivers.

The primary distinguishing characteristic of a public good is that individual consumer preferences must be summed vertically rather than horizontally to derive a market demand response curve. With respect to microeconomic theory, the market discrimination model is usually chosen to express demand and price conditions. An efficient market for a public good, thus, requires perfect price discrimination for each consumer since no one is willing to pay again for value or benefit paid by previous consumers or users.

Non-Market Valuation of Natural Resources

In the past, recreational use of an area has been cited as economic justification for development as well as its protection from proposed development. However, earlier studies indicate recreational use alone does not account for the total benefits of resource protection. Additional benefits were suggested by Weisbrod (1964), Krutilla (1967), and more recently by Walsh, Sanders and Loomis (1985), and Cummings, Brookshire and Schulze (1986). These additional benefits are often collectively referred to as preservation values.

The fact that values for natural resources exist above those which are defined in terms of the physical use of a resource give rise to concerns about the attitudes which contribute to intrinsic value. Decisions by policy makers frequently are based on constituent attitudes as much or more than expressed market values. Thus, information concerning recreationists' opinions are as important as recreational use and market conditions. Research procedures which measure both attitudes and values for physical use provide policy makers with far more information on which to base decisions. Such procedures formed the base on which this chapter is established.

Different methods of determining economic value (both use and preservation) of water resources approved by the United States Water Resources Council include the travel-cost method, the unit-day approach, and contingent valuation (U.S. Water Resources Council 1983). The purpose of such procedures relates to the problem of market failure or the absence of markets through which marginal benefits and marginal costs are estimated (Shulstad 1983).

Contingent Valuation - Theory and Practice

When multiple sites, or rather a statewide resource, is being evaluated, the contingent valuation procedure is the best approach. The contingent method has been used to derive a demand schedule for a variety of recreational settings and services (Cummings, *et al.* 1986). The method suggested by Davis (1963) allows recreation planners to decide among several management alternatives for planning services at a recreational site. Contingent valuation essentially is a bidding game that is used to determine the value that users place in recreational services. Values derived in the bidding process then are expressions of consumer preference (attitude) for a site, service, or resource.

A general specification of the contingent valuation model may be considered as:

$$B = f(q,c,t), \tag{1}$$

where B is the bid per time period, (i.e., day, week, year); q represents site quality conditions such as water quality, c is consumer demographic characteristics, and t indicates the number of trips during the period of time evaluated. The model may be made consistent with the theory of consumer choice by assuming that the bid value, B, is consumer surplus per unit $\underline{x}$ (McConnell 1983). That assumption is expressed as:

$$B = CS(q,c\ t)/x, \tag{2}$$

where $CS(.)$ is the consumer surplus function.

However, the list of variables under q or c could be rather extensive, and experience has shown that demographic variables frequently are poor indicators of resource use. Also, site quality indices tend to be correlated with trip number or total visitation. Thus, this simplistic model for contingent valuation tends to be weak with regard to specification. Walsh (1986) argues that the contingent value approach may be viewed in the same light as the travel cost method if an incremental change in quantity (trips per year, etc.) can be determined for the bid values. That is, the model may be specified as equation (3) where Q is the independent variable - number of trips, a is a constant for maximum willingness to pay

$$\text{Total WTP per trip} = a - bQ \tag{3}$$

(Q trips), and b, the rate of change in willingness to pay per unit change in Q. This equation may be restated as:

$$\text{Total WTP per year} = aQ - bQ^2 \tag{4}$$

and the inverse of the demand equation as:

$$\text{Total WTP per year} = a - 2bQ \tag{5}$$

As with the McConnell approach, Walsh assumes multiple trips to a site in a given time period. In the empirical study for this chapter, recreationists were found to have made an average of 8.4 trips to a free-flowing river over a three-year period. Most respondents reported fewer than three trips per year, and many reported only one trip over the three years. In nearly every case, each visit reported by individual respondents was to a different site or even a different river.

Under such conditions, these two consumer surplus models for demand have limited applicability. For special cases with limited visitation, the public good approach is appropriate (Stoll and Johnson 1984, Bradford 1970). Total benefit or consumer surplus may be estimated by the vertical summation of individual values. The slope of the total benefit curve (first derivative) is a compensated demand curve indicating the relation between consumer surplus and increments in recreational activity. If there are no repeat visits to a recreational site, then total benefit is consumer surplus.

Arguments against use of contingent valuation and other non-market value techniques fall primarily on the problem of separability (Milon 1983). Basically, the assumption of separability permits the nonmarket good, which in this case is also a public good, to be considered independent of all other goods in the utility function of an individual. Individuals are assumed to be able to mentally trade off marginal changes in the resource value with monetary units. Milon (1981) also has argued that contingent valuation assumes a particular right of access which may or may not be consistent with an individual's perceived rights to a particular nonmarket good. In other words, bid values in the process assume free access to the resource in question. In the study on which this chapter is based, free-flowing rivers were considered accessible, although, in fact, access was restricted to highway river crossings, specific public use areas, and places where private property was used for access either with or without owner permission.

While such arguments are perhaps valid and impose limits on the procedures for determining demand values, the procedure does uphold the models expressed in equations (1-4) in that attitudes (reservation demands, preferences, or mental trade-offs) contribute to implied consumer surplus and are expressed in values estimated. Unless such attitudes are determined and quantified, policies regarding resource use and allocation tend to be based only on expressed market conditions.

Resources falling into the category of public goods and other nonmarket resources do not have clearly expressed market prices. Policy ignoring the implied consumer surplus will tend to favor individuals and entities in the market who have a particular private interest. With regard to free-flowing rivers, the private interests include private electric power companies, public power generators such as the Corps of Engineers, and special cases where property rights to stream flow have been awarded to private interests on the basis of water law or political concessions. When private interests are the bases for policy decisions, the full cost of river use which includes non-market values and externalities, is not evaluated.

Willingness to Pay

Usefulness of estimating preservation values through contingent valuation of resources lies in the expression of a willingness to pay for both preservation of natural resources and recreational use of the resource base (Randall, Ives and Eastman 1974). A recent survey of Colorado residents indicated a willingness to pay for preservation of the free-flowing rivers of that state. The contingent valuation method was employed to determine respondents maximum willingness to pay for river preservation over and above the expected benefits they would receive if they used the resource. Study results indicated a willingness to pay for preservation of the rivers expressed in three different ways: option, existence, and bequest values (Walsh, et al. 1985).

Option values are placed on the opportunity of future resource use in addition to actual use. Inclusion of option values in demand analysis provides a more socially accurate allocation of resource preservation (Weisbrod 1964). The value that people place on knowing that some areas provide a protected habitat for plants, fish, wildlife, and natural geomor phological features associated with a resource is termed *existence* value (Walsh, et al. 1985). *Bequest* value measures the demand attributed to the satisfaction of providing future generations with the same opportunities as the current generation. These values include preservation of aesthetic, ecological, and recreational aspects of a river for future generations.

Figure 1 illustrates the importance to society of including preservation values in evaluating the total benefits of river protection. The figure shows a hypothetical example of the preservation demand for a free-flowing river. Willingness to pay for river preservation includes any user fees and charges plus any surplus value which may accrue (U.S. Water Resources Council 1983). User fees and charges are represented by line CD on the graph. Triangle BCD represents the surplus, or consumer's surplus, of any (recreational) use of the river at price C (dollars) and E (quantity) visits. Consumer's surplus for river preservation may be defined as the difference between the consumer's maximum willingness to pay and the amount he actually pays to enjoy the river. Including preservation values shifts the demand curve for river preservation vertically. The consumer surplus with the addition of preservation values then becomes the area ACDF. Inclusion of preservation values does not affect the demand curve for a particular use, nor will the addition of preservation benefits diminish the recreational use-value of rivers (Walsh, *et al.* 1985).

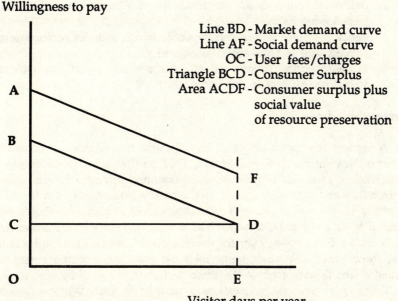

Figure 1.   Preservation Demand for a Free-Flowing River

METHODS

With the historical trends and directives enumerated above as guides, a study was initiated to estimate the perceived value of free-flowing rivers in Alabama and to determine the attitudes of the public (both real and potential consumers) regarding the public good status of rivers in question. Such a determination would provide a basis for setting realistic policy at the state level regarding river use and development, and contribute to other efforts nationwide aimed at understanding the true values of basic natural resources, of which free-flowing rivers are a major component.

Objectives

An empirical analysis of free-flowing rivers in Alabama was conducted in 1986-87 to obtain needed data on recreational use rates, attitudes toward preservation, and values placed on the river resources of Alabama. Specific objectives were to:

1. determine the recreational use of selected free-flowing Alabama rivers;
2. determine attitudes of the residents of Alabama regarding these free-flowing rivers;
3. develop a river recreationists profile which includes socioeconomic data as well as river preferences, and
4. estimate preservation values Alabamians place on selected free-flowing rivers in the State.

Survey Procedures

A random telephone survey of 733 Alabama households was conducted between November, 1986, and March, 1987, to determine attitudes toward preservation, estimates of preservation value, and recreational use rates of 15 free-flowing rivers of Alabama. In the survey, households were identified as either river user or non-user households. River user households were defined as those households which had at least one household member who had visited a free-flowing river for the purpose of outdoor recreation in the past three years. Non-user households did not have a member who had visited a free-flowing river in the same period.

River users were asked questions pertaining to river visitation patterns, recreational activities at the rivers, trip characteristics, and attitudes toward river preservation. Non-users were questioned on why they do not visit free-flowing rivers, and their attitudes toward river preservation. Both groups were asked to put monetary values on specific aspects of river use and protection.   Finally, demographic data were collected from all respondents.

Contingent valuation procedures were used to estimate a proxy demand value for several rivers, or rather the aggregate value (total benefit) of a class of rivers -- those that are free-flowing.

RESULTS

Data collected in the recreational use survey showed that the 15 free-flowing rivers under study are an important recreational resource. Of the 733 households contacted, 14 percent contained one or more members who had visited at least one of the rivers included in the survey. This rate of activity compares with participation rates for the State of 11 percent and 12 percent for freshwater fishing and boating, respectively (Clonts, Smutko and Brothers 1986, Strickland and Roper 1986). Comparisons of sample data with statewide data showed that the sample was representative of the population. Thus, by expanding the sample proportion of river users to reflect statewide use rates, it was estimated that about 570,000 Alabamians used free-flowing rivers as part of their recreational resource base within three years prior to being interviewed. This is a conservative estimate of total use as no attempt was made to quantify use by non-residents.

Socioeconomic Characteristics

Socioeconomic characteristics of both river users and non-users were obtained to develop a profile of each group. Table 1 summarizes the socioeconomic characteristics of user and non-user groups. Mean scores of the two groups were significantly different for most characteristics at either the 0.05 or 0.10 probability level. (A probability level of .10 was necessary because of the strong similarity between user and non-user populations). The data show that river users in Alabama fit the general description of activity oriented recreationists nationwide (Ewert 1985). Rivers visited most frequently by respondents over the previous three years exhibit *mountain environment* characteristics, such as rocky stream beds and banks, and swift water during optimum flow periods. This indicates a user bias toward streams which offer unique opportunities such as white water canoeing or provide a test for special skills such as canoe handling or rock climbing along stream banks. Also, perceived characteristics of the better known rivers, such as being rocky, swift, or dangerous, may explain emphasis on such barriers as lack of access, equipment, skills, and the need for guides.

River users were asked to respond to a series of questions concerning their most recent trip to one of the study rivers. Data were obtained concerning several aspects of recreational trips to free-flowing rivers, such as recreational activities at the river, distance traveled, party size, and trip cost, Tables 1 and 2. The favored activity choices were interpreted as expressing both the aesthetic qualities of rivers and the opportunity for specific recreational pursuits. The act of driving for pleasure along stretches of free-flowing rivers as a favored activity among the majority of respondents is an indication of the high aesthetic value placed on natural environments. Other often specified pursuits were recreational in nature and indicated a value placed on the opportunity for continuation of those activities.

Preservation Values

Preservation values tend to be higher and more significant for areas which are in a natural, undeveloped condition due to the increasing scarcity of such resources (Walsh, *et al.* 1985). Free-flowing rivers fit this description, and because of the irreversibility of water development projects, the number of free-flowing rivers will diminish as more projects are built. Therefore, it is important that the total benefits, including preservation values, be included in the analysis of free-flowing river valuation, and their loss be included as a cost of development projects.

Table 1.   Mean Socioeconomic Characteristics of Survey Respondents.

Characteristic	Unit	River users	Non-users
Age of household head **	yr.	42	47
Respondent education **	yrs.	15	13
Family income	dol.	25-30,000	20-25,000
Occupation			
white collar *	pct.	48	34
blue collar *	pct.	16	27
unemployed, student, homemaker**	pct.	36	38
Travel cost			
food	dol.	18	--
transportation	dol.	13	--
accommodations	dol.	26	--
total[a]	dol.	39	--
Party size	no.	5	

*   Significantly different at 0.05 level
**   Significantly different at 0.10 level
[a]   Weighted average per trip.

Preservation and recreational use values of Alabama's free-flowing rivers obtained in the study indicate that individuals are concerned with protection of free-flowing rivers. The willingness to pay to maintain study rivers in their natural condition averaged nearly $57 per year per household, and totaled $64 million statewide, Tables 3 and 4.

Since each value was determined in a separate bidding procedure and respondents were asked three times to verify the individual and summed values, the total willingness to pay does in fact represent aggregate consumer demand. Net consumer surplus in this case is not a valid measure since most of the sample had no access cost for river use. Thus, while a net benefit could be calculated for the user portion of the sample, it has limited usefulness. Since a portion of the sample had no actual river use, a contingency bid value per trip number would reflect only active river recreationists. Though variation in willingness to pay exists between the two groups, both groups expressed a desire to preserve rivers for the sake of preservation itself. Consistently, the highest dollar values were reported for existence value, indicating many individuals feel preservation for habitat protection is highly important. Both groups also placed relatively high values on protecting rivers for future generations, with bequest values ranked second in order of preservation value. Existence and bequest values accounted for over two-thirds of total preservation value. Among both groups, preservation for the sake of recreational use was valued least. However, recreational option value may have been interpreted by some respondents as an alternate means of expressing recreational use value. Yet, even if the two values are summed, the interpretation remains unchanged.

Table 2. Percentage of River Users Participating in Selected Recreational Activities.

Activity	Respondents participating	Reason for visit	
		primary	secondary
Driving	63	15	6
Picnicking	55	13	9
Fishing	52	24	8
Photo/view nature	47	3	6
Swimming	44	3	6
Hiking	42	7	4
Camping	35	6	11
Canoeing	30	10	2
Hunting	20	7	3
Boating	20	3	1
Tubing	17	1	0
Other[a]	33	2	1
No Answer	--	4	43

[a]Off-road driving, bicycling, motorcycling, rafting

Preservation Attitudes

Motivation for river preservation was also measured by asking survey respondents why they believed river protection to be important. Respondents were asked to rate the relative importance of each of several reasons, Table 5. The most important reasons reported for preserving free-flowing rivers were protection of fish and wildlife habitat and protection of the quality of water, air, and scenery. These two reasons are comparable with existence value mentioned earlier. The third most important reason given for protecting rivers was for enjoyment by future generations (bequest value). Fourth was the satisfaction of knowing rivers exist and are protected (existence value), and fifth in importance was knowing access to rivers would be available in the future for possible recreational visits (option value). Again, the least important reason for river protection was to provide actual river recreational opportunities.

As seen by comparing Tables 3 and 5, the rank order of the motivations for protection correlated generally with the rank order of reported dollar amount of preservation values. Thus, there is a consistency between motivation for protection and willingness to pay for that protection.

Chi-square analysis revealed how the different attitudinal measures related to contingency bid values. A chi-square null hypothesis that contingent bid values and specific attitudes for the total sample are independent would be rejected for all attitudes measured except insuring resource quality and concern over options for future use, Table 6. This indicates a strong, although not overwhelming, association of bid values with attitudes on recreational options, access, habitats, and existence (p < .10).

Table 3.   Average Annual Preservation Values for Selected Free-Flowing Rivers.

Type value	Average river use and preservation value		
	River users[a]	Non-users[b]	All respondents[c]
Recreational use value	7.50	8.50	8.00
Option value/recreation	12.00	7.50	9.50
Existence value	29.00	16.00	22.50
Bequest value	23.00	11.50	17.00
Total value per year[d]	70.00	43.00	57.00

[a]River users are defined as those who had used a study river in the last three years.
[b]Non-users are defined as those who had not used a study river in the last three years.
[c]Weighted averages.
[d]Values will not add to total due to rounding and use of weighted averages.

Yet, a different relationship was observed when data were sorted by river use. Only the attitude that habitats should be protected was closely associated with bid values by river users, indicating that river users had strong opinions about river protection regardless of how they felt about paying for use or preservation.

The hypothesis that commitment to river use, measured in terms of number of river trips within three years, is independent of attitude was accepted (p < .10). Attitudes about recreational options did appear to influence the number of trips by active river users to some extent, but overall, attitudes toward river preservation also were independent of trip number.

Non-users, on the other hand, were inclined to assign values based on attitudes although the probability for independence between attitude and bid values was slightly higher regarding the issues of resource quality and future use and access options.

The relationship between bid values and attitude for both groups would seem to indicate that the guarantee for river use and quality options is more important to non-users than to active free-flowing river users. However, a significant finding was the fact that the general population, composed of 87 percent non-users, has strong preservation attitudes regarding free-flowing rivers and those attitudes tend to be expressed in contingent bid values. The fourteen percent of the population who reported active river use also had strong preservationists attitudes, but familiarity with the rivers seems to have tempered their reservation demand or bid value. Perhaps factors such as water quality, limited access, or other factors known only to those who use the particular rivers in question also influenced bid values. To make strong assertions otherwise would stretch data interpretation beyond reasonable levels.

Table 4.   Aggregate Statewide Preservation Values for Free-Flowing Rivers.

Preservation value	Value[a] in millions of dollars
Maintain current recreational use	11.2
Preservation values:	
Option value for recreation	10.5
Existence value of habitats	24.3
Bequest value for future generations	18.1
Total preservation and use value	64.1

[a]Values derived by expanding sample data to statewide levels.

DISCUSSION

The conclusion drawn from these results indicates there is a desire among respondents to protect free-flowing rivers. While study results did not provide sufficient material for estimating incremental consumer surplus, the aggregate and net benefits of a public good type of resource were in fact shown to be measurable and of significant magnitude to be considered in policy decisions and economic impact analysis.

The consistency of attitudes and willingness to pay among river users and non-users alike indicates significant strength in opinions expressed. The attitudes of river users do reflect their special interests. Yet, similar attitudes were expressed by the general population. Thus, the aggregate value of $64 million for all rivers represents a rather strong consumer surplus which should be reflected in policy decisions regarding river use and development.

Whereas the attitudes expressed did not associate directly with values bid for preservation, a strong general public preference for protection and preservation over recreation was still recorded. In light of the frequency with which rivers have been altered in Alabama and nationwide, these results indicate a concern over continued loss of these scarce resources.

Attitudes regarding river preservation proved once again that the hypothetical bidding game where no one is required to *put up* any money may easily be misinterpreted. Attitudes could be said to be a rather weak proxy for value in a policy context since there wasn't direct correlation with bid values. However, one must bear in mind that values derived in the contingent process are themselves merely expressions of attitude. That is,the $57 per household per year value in river protection indicates that the population (a) favors protection, and (b) expresses itself strongly in non-real

Table 5.   Motivations For Protecting Free-Flowing Rivers in Alabama.

	Percent Responding		
Reason	Slight to unimportant	Moderate importance	Very to extremely important
Protecting fish & wildlife habitat	3.0	4.5	92.5
Protection of water scenery, air quality	2.0	5.5	92.5
Knowing there is a future option for use	3.0	11.5	85.5
Knowing that future generations will have access to rivers for recreational use	2.5	5.0	92.5
Just knowing rivers exist and are protected	3.5	8.5	88.0
Actual river recreation provided	10.5	29.5	60.0

* Likert scale of 1 - 5 used for ranking.

Table 6. Chi-Square Analysis of Contingency Bid Values, Attitudes Regarding River Preservation and Trips Taken to Rivers.

	Independent Variables - Attitudes Toward					
Chi-Square Variable	Insuring Recreation Options	Insuring Resource Quality	Insuring Option of Future Use	Insuring Future Access	Protecting Rivers Habitats	Knowing Rivers Exist
	X^2	X^2	X^2	X^2	X^2	X^2
Contingent Bid Value-full sample	4.44**	1.33	0.85	2.86*	2.86*	2.65
Degrees Freedom	1	1	1	1	1	1
Contingent Bid Value-river users[a]	0.12	0.00	0.00	0.55	0.02	0.00
Contingent Bid Value-non users	1.93	1.50	0.95	1.50	5.48**	2.69
Total River Trips[b]	4.21	1.60	1.13	0.12	1.07	0.12
Degrees Freedom	2	2	2	2	2	2

*Significantly different at .10 level; Contingent bid value is independent of attitude.
**Significantly different at .05 level
[a]Continuity adjusted Chi-square (two x two table)
[b]River users only

money bids since no actual payment is made. However, when respondents were pushed to rank attitudes, the strength of the bids was reduced. Thus, the measurable attitudes are also useful in policy analysis and decisions. When used together, attitudes and bid-value assessments provide estimates of both the direction and strength of public opinion.

Strong emphasis on recreational market values in benefit cost analysis for resource development may tend to overstate the benefit and understate the cost of that development. This was borne out in the relatively strong relationship between contingent value and attitudes regarding recreational options, future access, and continued existence of the particular resource in question which are expression of reservation demand. Obviously, results of an attitude survey are not generally transferable across resources and regions, but they are applicable in specific situations such as represented here.

While this study did not attempt to determine an economic value for any specific river, aggregate consumer surplus was estimated. Furthermore, important information about the general population, as well as those committed to using free-flowing rivers, needed in making informed decisions concerning future development or management of free-flowing rivers was provided.

REFERENCES

Alexander, L. 1987. *The Report of the Presidents Commission Americans Outdoors: The Legacy, the Challenge.* Washington, D. C.: Island Press.

Arthur, L.M. 1981. *Measuring Public Attitudes Toward Natural Resource Issues.* USDA ERS Technical Bulletin. Washington, D.C.: 1657 U.S. Government Printing Office.

Ashworth, W. 1977. *Hell's Canyon, the Deepest Gorge on Earth.* New York: Hawthorn Books.

Bradford, D.F. 1970. Benefit-cost analysis and demand curves for public goods. *Kyklos* 23:775-791.

Clonts, H.A., L.S. Smutko and G.L. Brothers. 1986. *Trends Related to Recreational Development in Alabama.* Special Technical Report for the Alabama Department of Conservation and Natural Resources. Montgomery, AL: Alabama Agricultural Experiment Station, Auburn University.

Cummings, R.G., D.S. Brookshire and W.D. Schulze. 1986. *Valuing Environmental Goods: An Assessment of the Contingent Valuation Method.* Totowa, NJ: Rowman and Allanheld.

Davis, R.K. 1963. Recreation planning as an economic problem. *Natural Resources Journal* 3:239-249.

Diamant, R., J.G. Eugster and C.J. Duerksen. 1984. *A Citizen's Guide to River Conservation.* Washington, D.C.: The Conservation Foundation.

Ewert, A. 1985. Emerging trends in outdoor recreation. *Proceedings: Outdoor Recreation Trends Symposium*, Department of Parks, Recreation, and Tourism Management, Clemson University, Clemson, SC. Myrtle Beach, SC. February, pp. 155-165.

Krutilla, J. 1967. Conservation Reconsidered. *American Economic Review* 57:777-786.

McConnell, K.E. 1983. An approach to assessing the contingent or hypothetical valuation method. *Nonmarket Valuation: Current Status, Future Directions.* Southern Natural Resource Economics Committee Workshop Proceedings, Biloxi, MS. Pub. Southern Rural Development Center, Starkville, MS. May, pp. 38-55.

Milon, J.W. 1981. *Methodological Ethics in the Evaluation of Nonmarket Goods Allocation.* Presented at the American Economics Association Meeting, Clemson University, July.

Milon, J.W. 1983. Comment on: An overview of Current Issues in nonmarket valuation. *Nonmarket Valuation: Current Status, Future Directions.* Southern Natural Resource Economics Committee Workshop Proceedings, Biloxi, MS. Pub. Southern Rural Development Center, Starkville, MS. May, pp. 30-37.

Randall, A., B. Ives and C. Eastman. 1974. Bidding games for valuation of aesthetic environmental improvements. *Journal of Environmental Economics and Management* 1:132-149.

Shulstad, R.N. 1983. An overview of current issues in nonmarket valuation. *Nonmarket Valuation: Current Status, Future Directions.* Southern Natural Resource Economics Committee Workshop Proceedings, Biloxi, MS. Pub. Southern Rural Development Center, Starkville, MS. May pp. 1-29.

Strickland, J.C. and R.B. Roper. 1986. *Alabama Statewide Comprehensive Outdoor Recreation Plan, vol. 1: Assessment and Policy Plan.* Montgomery, AL: Alabama Department of Conservation and Natural Resources, p. 107.

Stoll, J.R. and L.A. Johnson. 1984. Concepts of value, nonmarket valuation and the whooping crane. *Transactions 49th North American Wildlife and Natural Resources Conference.* Washington, D.C.: Wildlife Management Institute, pp. 382-392.

Tietenberg, T. 1988. *Environmental and Natural Resource Economics.* Glenview, IL: 2nd. ed. Scott Foresman and Company.

U. S. Water Resources Council. 1983. *Economic and Environmental Principles and Guidelines for Water and Related Land Resource Implementation Studies.* Washington, D.C.: U.S. Government Printing Office.

Walsh, R.G., L.D. Sanders and J.B. Loomis. 1985. *Wild and Scenic River Economics: Recreation Use and Preservation Values.* Englewood, CO: American Wilderness Alliance.

Walsh, R.G. 1986. *Recreation Economic Decisions: Comparing Benefits and Costs.* State College, PA: Venture Publishing Inc.

Weisbrod, B. 1964. Collective-consumption services of individual-goods. *Quarterly Journal of Economics* 78:471-477.

PROFILES OF THE AUTHORS

Stanley K. Brickler is an Associate Professor with the School of Renewable Natural Resources at the University of Arizona. He holds bachelor's and master's degrees in zoology and natural resource management from Southern Illinois University. His doctorate is in natural resource manage-ment from Colorado State University. A member of the faculty since 1970, he has organized and directed research and teaching programs in water quality, wildland recreation management, and resource planning.

Thomas C. Brown is an Economist with the Rocky Mountain Forest and Range Experiment Station of the USDA Forest Service in Fort Collins, Colorado. He received his B.S. from American University and his M.S. and Ph.D. from University of Arizona. His primary research interests include water economics and management, scenic quality assessment, and the valuation of nonmarket goods and services.

Tommy L. Brown is Senior Research Associate in Cornell University's Department of Natural Resources. He heads the Human Dimensions in Wildlife Research Group.

Doug Chambers is a research officer with the Canadian Parks Service, in the Western Region office in Calgary, Alberta. He holds a B.A. in Psychology from the University of Alberta, and a M.B.A. from the University of Calgary.

Howard A. Clonts is a Professor of Resource Economics at Auburn University, Alabama. His career of 21 years at Auburn has been focused on the issues surrounding the use and development of natural resources, particularly those generally considered non-renewable. In recent years research on recreational impacts on the resource base has emphasized policy development with respect to longer term resource management.

H. Ken Cordell is the Project Leader of the Outdoor Recreation and Wilderness Assessment Group at the Southeastern Forest Experiment Station in Athens, Georgia. His doctorate is in Economics from North Carolina State University and he has conducted a wide variety of outdoor recreation-related research projects.

Terry C. Daniel is a Professor of Psychology with a joint appointment in the Department of Psychology and the School of Renewable Natural Resources at the University of Arizona in Tucson. His B.S., M.S., and Ph.D. are from the University of New Mexico. His research focuses on the processes of human perception and cognition of environmental stimuli. A major objective is to determine the relationship between measured physical characteristics of the natural environment and perception of environmental quality.

Steven E. Daniels is Assistant Professor of Forest Economics and Policy in the Department of Forest Resources at Oregon State University. His current research interest is in federal forest land policy, with particular interest in identifying policy barriers to innovative resource management. Much of his research has focused on recreation provision and policies designed to stabilize resource dependent communities. Results from this research have appeared in the *Journal of Forestry, Journal of Leisure Research, Environmental Law,* and the *Wildlife Society Bulletin.* He received his Ph.D. from Duke University in 1986.

Dennis M. Donnelly is a Research Forester with the Rocky Mountain Experiment Station of the USDA Forest Service in Fort Collins, Colorado. His primary research interest is in bioeconomics, especially the problems that emerge from mixing ecology and economics when implementing National Forest plans. He holds a Bachelors Degree in Electrical Engineering form Northwestern University, a Masters Degree in Forest Management and Biometry and a Doctoral Degree in Quantitative Forest Science, both from Colorado State University.

John F. Dwyer received his B.S., M.S., and Ph.D. from the SUNY College of Environmental Science and Forestry at Syracuse, specializing in forest land management and forestry economics. Since 1978 he has been Project Leader and Research Forester for the USDA Forest Service North Central Forest Experiment Station at Chicago. Much of his work over the past 10 years has focused on research to guide the management and use of urban and high-use forest environments.

Robert Flewelling, formerly of the Cooperative Parks Studies Unit at the University of Washington, is a doctoral candidate in public health at the University of North Carolina. He has applied his research and data analytic skills to a wide variety of topics, including natural resource sociology, social determinants of interpersonal violence, and adolescent substance use. Current research interests include socio-cultural determinants of preventive health behaviors, and the design and evaluation of community-based health status interventions.

Ronald J. Glass is a research economist with the Northeastern Forest Experiment Station, Burlington, Vermont. He also has worked with the Economic Research Service of the U.S. Department of Agriculture and the Alaska Department of Fish and Game. He received M.S. and Ph.D. degrees in economics from the University of Minnesota and the State University of New York at Syracuse.

Robert Graham is Assistant Professor in the Department of Recreation and Leisure Studies at the University of Waterloo, Waterloo, Ontario, Canada. His research interests broadly concern conservation and social implications of natural resource issues/resource policy, and the planning and management of parks and protected areas. Within this broad area there is continuing interest in marine conservation and recreation, visitor management, interpretation, public education and outdoor recreation.

Steve Hollenhorst is an assistant professor of Wildland Recreation Management in the Division of Forestry at West Virginia University. He also holds an appointment as assistant forest scientist in the West Virginia University Agricultural and Forestry Experiment Station. He received his Ph.D. in outdoor recreation from Ohio State University. Current research activities include commercial and organized recreational use of wilderness, modeling risk recreation participation, and recreation specialization.

Ray Hutchison received his Ph.D. in Sociology from the University of Chicago and has worked for the North Central Forest Experiment Station at Chicago and taught at Depaul University, UC-San Diego, and the University of Nevada-Las Vegas before coming to his present position of Assistant Professor of Sociology in the Urban and Public Affairs program at the University of Wisconsin-Green Bay. Over the past 10 years much of his research has focused on urban ethnic groups, particularly Hispanics.

David A. King is a Professor of Renewable Natural Resources in the School of Renewable Natural Resources at the University of Arizona, Tucson. He received his B.S., M.S., and Ph.D. from the University of Minnesota. His research has focused on the valuation of nonmarket goods and services of natural resource systems. Most recently he has been looking into the value of soil conservation and the impact of urban open-spaces on residential property values.

Richard S. Krannich is Associate Professor of Sociology and Director of the Institute for Social Science Research on Natural Resources at Utah State University. During the past decade much of his research has addressed the social consequences of natural resource development activities in non-metropolitan areas of the western United States. More recently, he has conducted several studies focusing on recreation issues, including projects examining the effects of petroleum exploration and development on public lands, and others examining public attitudes concerning the recreational uses of wildlife. He is currently involved in a large-scale research effort examining social and cultural responses to the proposed development of nuclear waste storage facilities in Nevada. He received his Ph.D. in Sociology from Pennsylvania State University in 1980.

Richard J. Lichtkoppler is Statistician and Coordinator for Survey Research, Denver Service Center, National Park Service, Denver, Colorado. His background includes service with the Bureau of Land Management, the General Services Administration, and Auburn University. He holds a BS degree in Marketing and a MS in Natural Resources from Ohio State, plus the Ph.D. in Resource Economics from Auburn University.

John B. Loomis is an Associate Professor with the Division of Environmental Studies, Agricultural Economics Department, University of California, Davis. His research interests include application of valuation methods and techniques to improve efficiency in public land management; also valuation of environmental amenities and recreation. He holds Bachelors and Masters Degrees in Economics from California State University, and a Doctoral Degree in Natural Resource Economics from Colorado State University.

Joy W. Malone is Recreation Specialist, Bankhead National Forest, USFS/USDA. Her background and training include multidisciplinary programs of recreational administration, resource economics, and forestry. Extensive work with models for valuation of natural resources has given her an appreciation of the complexities associated with management and policy formulation for long term resource use.

Scott M. Meis, as Chief, Socio-Economic Information Division, Canadian Parks Service, is responsible for the management of all social survey and park use statistical activities within the Service. His professional training was in the discipline of sociology, in which he completed undergraduate and graduate degrees at the University of Calgary and the University of British Columbia. Before joining the Service he also worked several years at a university research institute, and as a private industry research consultant.

Steven D. Moore is a Research Associate with the School of Renewable Natural Resources at the University of Arizona. He holds a Ph.D. in renewable natural resource studies with a minor in sociology from the University of Arizona; a master's in business administration from the University of Illinois; and a bachelor's in biology from Southern Illinois University. He currently focuses his research and teaching interests on sociological aspects of recreation in natural areas.

Robert Muth has worked for the U.S. Forest Service since 1970. He served with the Recreation Research Project in Seattle, WA through 1977. He then spent two years in Washington, D.C. Since 1979, he has worked as the Regional Social Scientist in Alaska, where he has conducted a program of subsistence research for the past five years. He earned his Ph.D. in forestry (natural resource sociology) from the University of Washington.

Louis J. Nelson is a Staff Biologist with the Idaho Department of Fish and Game in Boise, Idaho. His work includes surveying hunter opinion, and the design of projects for, and analysis of data from, wildlife research studies. He holds a Bachelors Degree in Wildlife Biology from Colorado State University, a Masters Degree in Ecology from University of California, Davis, and a Doctoral Degree in Wildlife Ecology from Utah State University.

Robert J. Payne is Associate Professor in the School of Outdoor Recreation at Lakehead University, Thunder Bay, Ontario, Canada. His research interests centre on parks and protected areas, wilderness, resource management and person-environment fit.

George L. Peterson is Project Leader in the USDA Forest Service, Rocky Mountain Forest and Range Experiment Station. Since 1982 he has directed a national research project focusing on the valuation of wildland amenity resource benefits. Among numerous contributions to the improvement of valuation methods are two books on amenity and wildland resource valuation. Before joining the Forest Service, George directed the Urban and Regional Planning Program in Civil Engineering at Northwestern University.

Martin F. Price obtained his Ph.D. in Geography at the University of Colorado at Boulder. His primary research interests are the sustainable future of mountain communities and societies in the face of changing conditions, and the communication of scientific information to improve decisionmaking. He has also worked on the societal implications of remote sensing imagery, and as a technical writer, environmental consultant, and park naturalist.

Merton T. Richards is Associate Professor in the School of Forestry at Northern Arizona University in Flagstaff. He received his B.S. from the University of Montana, and M.S. and Ph.D. from the University of Arizona. His experience includes research in the use of forest land for recreational purposes. Research emphasis has been on analysis of forest scenic beauty, economic valuation of recreational uses, and recreational demand projection.

Rick Rollins is a faculty member at Lakehead University in Thunder Bay, Ontario. He holds a Ph.D. from the School of Forestry at the University of Washington. His primary research is concerned with recreation resource management.

Richard Schreyer is Professor of Recreation Resources in the Department of Forest Resources, College of Natural Resources, at Utah State University. His principal professional interests are studying human perceptions of natural environments and seeking applications of social science knowledge in natural resource management. He received his Ph.D. from the University of Michigan in Resource Planning and Conservation. He also holds degrees in Natural Resource Administration and Forest Recreation Management.

Herbert W. Schroeder received his Bachelor of Science in mathematics from the University of Arizona in 1973. His Master's and Doctoral degrees in environmental psychology are also from the University of Arizona, in 1977 and 1980 respectively. His dissertation was on the perception of perceived conflict between natural resource management goals. Since 1980 he has been working for the North Central Forest Experiment Station doing research on users' perceptions and behavior in forested recreation sites.

James W. Shockey received a M.A. in Statistics and a Ph.D. in Sociology from the Pennsylvania State University. He is currently Assistant Professor of Sociology at the University of Arizona. His research interests focus on log-linear and latent class modeling techniques, on demographic aspects of the labor force, and on consequences of underemployment and over-education.

Cynthia Sorg-Swanson is a Wildlife Economist with the Northern Region (R-1) of the USDA Forest Service in Missoula, Montana. Her work includes an inventory of potential wildlife viewing areas and identifying opportunities for wildlife viewing. Her interests include deriving nonconsumptive value associated with wildlife recreation. She holds a Bachelors Degree in Wildlife Management and a Masters Degree in Resource Economics, both from the University of Wyoming, and is a Doctoral Candidate in Agricultural Economics at Ohio State University.

Daniel J. Stynes is Professor in the Department of Park and Recreation Resources. He teaches courses in research methods and comprehensive recreation planning. His research focus is quantitative methods and their applications in recreation research, planning, and marketing. Dan specializes in recreation and travel forecasting, choice, and demand modeling.

Erik Val is a graduate in geography from the Universities of Waterloo and McGill, with a specialization in resource management. He has undertaken socio-economic research related to native people and northern development, commercial fisheries and petroleum development, and national park planning and management. He is currently on secondment from the Canadian Parks Service to the Government of the Northwest Territories as a special advisor on parks development.

Joanne Vining is Assistant Professor of Environmental Psychology in the Institute for Environmental Studies, and jointly appointed in the Departments of Psychology and Landscape Architecture at the University of Illinois. She holds a Ph.D. in environmental psychology from the University of Arizona. In addition to her work on emotional processes in environmental preferences, judgments and decisions, she is presently studying amenity resource values.

Brett A. Wright is an Assistant Professor and Director of the Center for Recreation Resources Policy at George Mason University in Fairfax, Virginia. He holds a Ph.D. from Texas A&M University in Recreation and Natural Resources Development. His research interests involve natural resource recreation, policy and the human dimensions of natural resources management.

INDEX